MESSENGER ELIJAH MUHAMMAD'S:

THEOLOGY OF TIME

LECTURE SERIES

Transcribed from the audio cassettes of

MESSENGER ELIJAH MUHAMMAD

Dated June 4, 1972 through October 29, 1972

By:

PRINCETTA MUHAMMAD

Published by:

ROYAL WOMAN COMMUNICATIONS

Printed in the United States of America

royalwoman2004@yahoo.com

MESSENGER ELIJAH MUHAMMAD'S:

THEOLOGY OF TIME LECTURE SERIES

Copyright © 2011 By Royal Woman Communications

PRINTED IN THE UNITED STATES OF AMERICA

FIRST EDITION , FIRST PRINTING

Cover design by Princetta Muhammad

Library of Congress Control Number: 2011919565

PREFACE

Messenger Elijah Muhammad, once known as Elijah Poole, exposed the so-called American Negroes for the first time to a brutal appraisal of their actual standing in America, and what they could expect in the future from a system under various disguises, which still grips them in mental, physical, and moral slavery. In a straight-forward manner, Messenger Elijah Muhammad pulled the veil off of the falsehood and half truths that have dominated our planet for the past 6,000 years.

The so-called American Negroes have never had a Divine Messenger sent to them before the Honorable Elijah Muhammad. Therefore, there is much opposition to his teachings from his people who want to lead and not be followers of others. Especially the "middle class," the black preachers and the college and university students who feel so proud of their worldly education and positions.

This is the Time that the Bible and Holy Qur'an refer to as the "resurrection of the dead" (mentally dead or ignorant people) whom God wishes to make wise and set over the nations through His Guidance and Infinite Wisdom. After listening to what the Honorable Elijah Muhammad was Taught by Allah (God) in Person, there is nothing else left for another messenger or "preacher" to teach us of self, God, and the devil. Messenger Elijah Muhammad's message to us fulfills the Bible and Holy Qur'an, for the last Messenger's message is to bring us face to face with the knowledge of God and the devil, that we may make our choice as to whom we will serve.

The other Divine Teaching, the Messenger teaches us, is that which guides us into the Hereafter. He teaches us that Allah (God) warned us against taking up the enemy's arms against the enemy. He (Messenger Elijah Muhammad) put his trust in Allah (God), and he teaches us (the so-called American Negroes) to follow the way of Allah.

On numerous occasions, we have heard the term "New World Order" used by politicians and others. This term speaks to the ambitions of the "Western World" (White World), to continue and increase their dominance over the Black and darker peoples of the earth, through a method or science known to us as "Tricknology."

The Black Nation, the world over, has suffered a mental and spiritual death as a consequence of falling into the hands of such a clever and cunning enemy. We have been robbed of the knowledge of ourselves, our God, and our open enemies.

We, the lost-found members of the Tribe of Shabazz here in the Hells of North America are prey in the hands of our captors, and they refuse to let us go for ourselves. We are mocked and scorned, hated and abused, murdered and imprisoned, and held to disgrace before the civilized nations of the earth.

And yet, living under such incomprehensible conditions, the Blackman and Woman of North America has refused to accept their salvation that has come to them.

But instead, has chosen blind acceptance of the false and empty promises made by white politicians, and their black political and religious pawns.

Many times, these enemies and deceivers of Black people can accomplish their goals of exploiting the people by a simple pat on the back and a smile. And the people, lacking true self- identity and insight, see this wicked act as a form of validation for them as human beings. In the absence of dignity, pride and knowledge of self, they have been deceived into loving this degenerate world of sport and play of their open enemies, the white race.

Nevertheless, Blackman and Woman of North America, the time has come that you must Accept Your Own, And Be Yourself. You are the remnant of the Aboriginal Black Nation, the lost tribe from the Asiatic Black Nation, the Beloved People of the God Himself. We have been held captive here in the Hells of North America for over 400 years. The time has come that you must awaken to the knowledge of your true identity, and not the one given to you by the slave-masters and their children.

Allah (God) chose the Honorable Elijah Muhammad to be His Last Apostle, and there is not another so-called Negro "preacher" or "reverend" that can take his place till this very day!

The Theology (Secret) Of Time has been given to us from Allah (God) Who Came to us in the Person of Master Fard Muhammad. He (Allah), raised up one from among us (the so-called American Negroes) to lead, teach, and guide us back to the knowledge of our God, Ourselves, and Our open enemies.

I am grateful to the Honorable Elijah Muhammad for his love for us and his dedication and faithfulness to complete his mission of raising the dead (the mentally dead so-called Negroes of America).

All Praises Are Due To Allah (God) for the Honorable Elijah Muhammad!

DEDICATION

...To My People,

To the So-called American Negroes. Freedom, Justice, Equality; Happiness, Peace of Mind, Contentment, Money, Good Jobs, Decent Homes-all these can be yours if you accept your God, Allah, now and return to His (and your original) religion, Islam.

Elijah Muhammad,
Messenger of Allah

TABLE OF CONTENTS

TABLE OF CONTENTS

Messenger Elijah Muhammad

PART ONE:

THEOLOGY OF TIME

JUNE 04, 1972 – JUNE 25, 1972

A PLAIN WARNER WOULD BE SENT TO YOU

The man that is talking to you; next time don't have me to open my mouth until you have this thing opening its mouth. See I have spent many words that lot of people could not hear - good. I'm going to charge you all laborers with this, because what do they know I said before you opened it up? Now we can hear. [The Audience applauds].

The reason that you must know the Truth today, it is because the liar must be removed; and to keep you from getting confused over the truth and the lie. A plain Warner says the Holy Qur'an would be sent to you, whose words that will be easy for you to understand. He would speak your own language, and he will be chosen from among you. There will be no stranger coming out of the East to you. It will be one of your own selves. Like God has always done in the past. He raise up a Warner or a Prophet from among the people whom He will warn so they will not have no excuse to say that they don't understand that stranger.

There were no such plain Truth taught to us in the past. We've been shining our eyes looking for somebody to scale the Eastern horizon, and we'll look up and see them coming. But the Holy Qur'an, condemns such, because if that man comes from the East, he may speak a strange language and you won't be able to understand it. Then the Holy Qur'an says you will say "Oh, an Arab, an Arabic Holy Qur'an, can't understand either one." [The Audience applauds].

But, He goes into your family and searches for one of your own, takes him off aside and teach him what He want you to know. And then, when you hear the Word of Truth coming from the mouth of those among you or one from among you, you can't have an excuse and say you couldn't understand the language. He speaks the same language that you speak.

I want you to listen good today. You have something coming to some of you who have never heard it before. I am that little fellow that He taken off aside and Taught. [The Audience applauds]. Well I say that "little fellow," the Bible makes him little. He didn't make him a big sheep, He say "a little lamb." [The Audience applauds]. So I'm very little. I don't know how much is lamb about me, but I know I'm little.

It is up to you to listen, and as you listen, read and remember. If God says in the Bible, "Before that dreadful day shall come I will send you Elijah." I am Elijah! [The Audience applauds]. The Truth must be made very clear. If I had just jumped out of the College door or University of this people to you, I would speak their language. This

1

Theology, pardon me, the Theology as we call it Science, I would have been teaching you theirs, since they have never taught you theirs in many things.

As I was talking in Washington, D.C., back in the middle 30's to a couple of, of Theology Teachers of Christianity; and so we really had it for a while, until my fire out-burned his. [The Audience applauds]. So, at the end of our argument, we got up and shook hands, both of them and said, "I never heard that before." He say " because they just don't teach us negroes nothing over there like that." I say they don't have this over there to teach you. [The Audience applauds].

It is not that the white people of Christianity, the Theologians, that they have this really hid; they never heard it before. It is the first time they ever heard the Real Truth of themselves. As one priest told me one day, he says, "Elijah," he says, "We knew this was coming alright enough," he say, "But I never understood it from the Bible like you have it." I say your Bible teaches you that. I say it teaches you that the secret of it was never known, and would not be known until the end; and then God would send you that Preacher to preach to you the Truth of it.

As the Holy Qur'an warns you that Abraham and Ishmael, they prayed for such man that God would rise him up from among you, at that time; to teach you the knowledge of the Book, and to make known to you the Wisdom, which is hidden from you. This is the little fellow that God put it all in his ears. [The Audience applauds].

Why you must have it today? It is due to the removal of the old ruler; your old god that you've been worshipping. That you didn't know where he lived at or where he exist. Some of us said "he lives in my soul." Yes, that's the Truth that the Truth do live within Us. But, knowing where the Truth came from is the main thing. Who is the Truth giver? If you have patience with me for about a month, I will have you so smart! [The Audience applauds].Yes, I will have you so smart that you can tie him around your finger. [The Audience applauds].

I am Elijah of your Bible. I am the Muhammad of your Holy Qur'an. Not the Muhammad that was here near fourteen hundred years ago. I am the one that the Holy Qur'an is referring to. The Muhammad that was here fourteen hundred years ago was a white man; then they put up a sign of the real Muhammad. It's there in Mecca, Arabia; they call it the little Black stone. I looked at it; I made seven circles around it; I kissed the little Black stone, but I didn't like to kiss it because I knew what it meant.

It means that the people will bow to the Real Blackman that is coming up out of uneducated people, who have not the knowledge of the Bible and Holy Qur'an. And that's why they made that stone a un-hewed stone; he will be uneducated. So I was there kissing what the sign of myself, and I was afraid to tell them that this me you are talking about here. [The Audience applauds].

So, what you have been told, it was told to you to understand. This was not given to you to understand before the Time. This is the Time that you must know the Secret of all Truth that has been put in symbolic manner.

Now today, the veil must be lifted and you understand. If you believe that I'm he, then you are a very lucky man or woman. [The Audience applauds]. It is not that I want you to believe and worship me, but believe and worship Him, Whom I teach to you. [The Audience applauds].

Been a long time since I had a chance to get on the rostrum to teach. I don't come out very often, due to the fact that I'm forbidden to do so, until the proper hour.

We are going into the Theology Of Time and history of the people. We were not to do this until Time. This is the Time, and end, of what we call the white race. They are white, and the only people that was made white. You are to know, who they are. You are not no more to be blind, deaf, and dumb, to the knowledge of people, races; and why we have races.

Everything that we said to you today, it must be proven. God give me the proof. I'm the little fellow in your Bible that is written of, that they will "shut their mouths at him." If any man will be able to condemn what I'm teaching, you bring him to me.

We don't know more pay attention to a magician. They are considered liars, and they can be proven liars, if you understand the Truth.

Why you are so far behind, is due to the white man who knew the Truth of you. He taken and veiled it. Put it in books in symbolic language, so that you won't see and understand until the Time. And this is the Time that you must know the Truth. Regardless to how it hurts, you must know it. And regardless to what become of the speaker for teaching you, he must teach it as he know it.

So today, we're going at the Root the Creation of the white race. Show you how he came to be a white race on our planet.

As you used to think, and I used to think the same, that God made them all at once. No, and that the white man was the first. No, I was wrong. It is not possible for Black babies to be born out from white parents. No, that Black one got to come First, and let the white one come after. You can't bring them both here together. "Let Us make man," remember that word. "Let Us make man."

Well, if "We" have to make man, then what were "We?" Who was the "Us" that must make man? What man are you talking about? All this you will learn. You will learn the first step before you leave here. I won't be able to teach you all of it this afternoon, because I got to go step by step to the first step, to get you to see. But once you see, you will be like the donkey that Balaam was riding.

Remember the donkey had never met an Angel before; and he had never had no talk with an Angel. But he was confounded to see an Angel standing before him, teaching him the knowledge of what he was carrying on his back. He spoke with "man's voice," very good.

This is what We want you to do. We want you to speak the knowledge that he have; the made man not the Original Man, but the made man. You don't have to teach the knowledge to the Original Man because he was the First; He know it. But the made man, you must have the knowledge of him.

And that's my subject today. It is to start you off into the knowledge of the made man. You are the Original Man. There is no such thing as a birth record to you. You have always been.

The Adam in the Bible you never understood it who Adam was. You have been calling Adam your father. Adam is not your father! [The Audience applauds].

We are very happy to teach you if you would but listen. And I will assure you, if you listen to me teach you how all of this began, and how it will end, you will never be able to thank me for it. [The Audience applauds].

In the past we found where God in the history when He got tired of people being so wicked, and so far off from the love and worship of Him, He raised right up among that people a Prophet. And that Prophet began to warn the people of a terrible destruction coming upon you if you don't believe what I have received from God.

The same thing is here today. You hear and you see many changes coming to pass throughout the world of man. You never saw it nor have you ever heard any such things going on.

Today you can listen to your radio; look at your TV's and you see and you hear things that you never have seen and heard before. This is due to the removal of a world and setting up a New World on the old foundation of the other which has been removed.

We no more can accept the guidance of this world because it is turned down. The people have become so dissatisfied with the white man's world that they too being white would like to remove it. This is why they both are going to clash with each other. They are moving towards each other closer and closer every hour.

This teaching must come to you to save you from their doom. In the very beginning, there was no doom written for the Blackman unless that Blackman willfully and knowingly would follow the white man to his doom. The doom of the white man was written in the days that he was made.

There was never no doom written for you. The end of your world will never come to an end. We can change at Times We changes but we never end. No end written for Us. You can't find where the Blackman will end up one day and have no world. If he end up one day without a world, then there will be Nothing. It will be the same as it was in the First Life that was Created in Darkness for Itself. There is no God nowhere to take a hold to the Blackman's Wisdom and outstrip Him of his Own Wisdom.

Once upon a Time a Blackman tried to destroy the Blackman, so Allah taught me. But he failed. He couldn't destroy Himself because He was the Creator. So He left some of Us back here right on. That was a long, long time ago, so God Taught me. It was in the making of the Moon. His effort to destroy the Blackman caused a New World of Thought to come in.

He split this one in two, taken another one, another part of; put it out before our eyes to serve as signs for this part. He wanted to destroy Us but He couldn't. He wanted His Teachings to go like the one that went into Africa, and We came from Him.

Fifty-thousand years ago God taught me, a Blackman disagreed with the Eleven Scientists. And therefore the Eleven stuck together and let Him go and prove his New God Wisdom somewhere else.

So it was Africa he went to prove it in the jungles of Africa. He said He could make a people like Himself and would bring them to a naught because they would be strong, powerful, and nothing could defeat them.

So the Eleven said go and make your Man, but don't make him here. So He went into the jungles of Africa fifty-thousand years ago, so God Taught me. And He showed me the signs that I could recognize today.

He pointed out to me one night two little Stars in the Southeastern skies; a blue one and a red one. He said, "It's been fifty-thousand years since We have seen these two Stars." He said, "And when they go away out of the skies from our sight this Time, it will be fifty-thousand years before they reappear. Every time they reappear there will be a Universal change." [The Audience applauds].

The white man recognize these things; their Scholars and Scientists. But they don't dare talk to you on nothing of the kind.

See here showing a blue Star beside a red Star, that means removal of a world that don't correspond with the Original World. You say, "Well how many more times?" This is the end, it's up! The Wisdom that this One brought is to bring an end to these signs working forth to show something to come after this; this Man's Wisdom. There is no Wisdom to come after this that will be able to erase this Wisdom. Because this Wisdom is brought to you from the Root of Wisdom from the Originator of the Universe.

You notice (excuse me brother I will be right with you), you notice that the whole Universe is egged shape. The Planets in the Universe is also egg shape. They are not a perfect round sphere. Well then this is leaving a little work for some Wise Man. [The Audience applauds]. That I am not able to perfect, then someone must perfect that thing. This is the way We look at Wisdom.

When Scholars are arguing with each other, they take one word, most times. They don't take a whole book. One word is sufficient for them to argue on. If that is not perfect, then alright he challenges you to prove your work. These are Scientists. I don't say I'm one, but I can entertain them. [The Audience applauds].

I'm raised up in your midst; which Crowns you with Glory and Happiness that if you can think of anything in the "Basic Teaching of the Resurrection of the Dead" that I don't understand, I'll give you ten thousand dollars out of my brother's vest pocket.

We must have a man today to teach Us that know and not guess that he have. We no more going to rely on guesses and theories. Theory is not Truth until you prove it True. Many of us can have theories, but not all us can bring our theories Truth.

I hope you have patience with me a little. [The Audience applauds]. You did not see this board here last Sunday turned this way. This is the thing that I'm going after now. At the Root of the Signs and of the Make. We must go at the Root to prove today that the All Wise, the Best Knower is with Us, in the Person of Master Fard Muhammad.

Fard is the name used by the God of the last opening up the Kingdom of Heaven to you and me. The name Fard, is a name outside of the ninety, pardon me, outside of the one hundred Attributes of God. It's a extra name to itself. The Bible give it to you like this, "He had a name written up and down His Thigh that no man knew but He Himself."

Well, all of this is understood now. God have Taught me there is nothing of the Bible, nothing else of the Qur'an that is yet to be misunderstood; it's understood today. This is the little fellow that God have made all that secret known to, and I don't say I'm guessing at anything. It's all what God have given to me. And if you take it and tell it to the Scientists of this world; if you can find one that can dispute with me on one word I'm telling you, I will give you ten-thousand dollars out of my brother's pocket. [The Audience applauds].

You should be happy if you know that these are Truths that been buried from your ears all of your life, and all of your parents' lives. This is the First time that you ever heard this and they are Truth. I don't say that I tell you because I don't think you ever read nothing about it (excuse me). No, you read about it, but you was not unable, pardon me, you was unable to understand what you read.

I say to you, you should come out and listen to Truth, and stop listening to guesses. The Bible have been taught to you through people that guessed at it; not know the Truth but guessed at it. Well it's time to give that fellow the Truth and stop him from guessing at it.

The Bible teach you in the beginning God made Heaven and the Earth, Right? That is True in the beginning, but when was the beginning? You say in the beginning. When was that beginning? And how did He make Heaven and Earth? See we must know the Truth of these things, and if the Truth does not compare with what you see and what you hear; then you don't have the Truth.

So, I don't run from you when I teach. You can question me all you want to. No, because I have your answer. God have give it to me, not me myself. He give it to me to give to you, and if you use it, lucky are you.

We see here on this board before our eyes, two flags; and we see under one flag here a cross and a man hanging on a tree. All of this you know to be True. I thought I'd wait until you go over this cross, pardon me, over this drawing a little bit, as I'm coming in to it to teach you the understanding of it.

Here on this board you see the flag of America, and you see the flag of Islam. In the flag of America here, you see the sign that they use for their religion. You see red, white and blue as colors. Over here you see white and red only. These are very good teachings that you should know.

In between the two flags, you have these words written, "Which one will survive the war of Armageddon." "When will that be?" It's on now; Armageddon is on now. You would not be hearing the Truth of these things.

The Truth is only to come when the falsehood have failed. As long as falsehood can rule, it remains like night. As long as the night can rule, you won't see no day. So We use all these signs and Truth Teachings that we contend with each other daily.

Now, between here we have written, "Which one will survive the war of Armageddon." What is Armageddon war? It's a war that clashes with falsehood. Truth clashes falsehood; and falsehood clashes Truth. Falsehood will try to continue to rule, and Truth must overcome it and cast it out.

That flag to our right here contains only two colors, red and white. The meaning of these two colors is that red represents Truth. This is the First thing that We have in the Universe; it was a red ball of fire to lighten up the Universe, that's the Sun. The Sun is a red ball of fire.

JUNE 4, 1972 PART ONE / SIDE TWO

THE LIGHT OF TRUTH

The Sun is a red ball of fire, or something like about a hundred, pardon me, eight hundred, eight hundred thousand miles in diameter. That's a very big Sun, eight hundred miles in diameter right through it. Now that ball of fire which is nothing but fire. The Sun, don't get it mixed up with some old slavery teaching, it's no spook. We're sure it's fire. We have tested it and draw fire out of it. So it is a ball of fire that warms up a circle, which nine planets make. That Sun strikes all of these nine planets; and the farthest away of all the planets is the one you call Platoon. That planet is four billion six hundred million miles from the Sun. And yet that Sun strikes it just a, a few hours in our regular day which makes it revolve around them.

What sign is that? That wherever the Light of Truth touches human beings, it changes that person. [The Audience applauds]. Since that God teaches Us the Science that planet Pluto or Platoon is four billion six hundred million miles from us, He uses it for a sign of us. We being four thousand years off from him; four thousand years off from the history of the six thousand years that Moses taught Israel. Moses' teachings didn't touch Israel until it already had been two thousand years since he was cast out from Us in Arabia. That left Us four thousand years to work with him.

Now since we worked with him the four thousand years, he clipped Us for four hundred years of it. We have been blinded to the knowledge of ourselves for four hundred years. So we have this sign before you, for you to read and learn something from it. You see stripes of red, stripes of white; and then you see a blue square here full of stars.

"What does that mean Elijah?" [The Audience applauds]. It means Truth in the American people; this is their flag. It's the root meaning of themselves. It means that this white represents themselves, their color. That red represents the Sun; and the red representing the Sun along beside an equal stripe of white that, the red represents the Truth. And the white represents the white people. And that the blue represents untruth, like the sky. We say, "there's a blue sky." You can go up there a billion miles and you will never find no blue.

So today, God have given me the secret of all these things. And I'm here to teach you the secret. That blue represent untruth, just as the sky looks blue, but it's no blue sky. So you may chase it all day and night long in your planes, and you won't find no blue sky up there.

8

Let's don't get [The Audience applauds]. You may say, "Well Mister Muhammad, I see you have on a blue suit that means you untrue?" No, [The Audience applauds] this blue I'm wearing I live among untrue people; [The Audience applauds] and to get among them to get their attention you look like them, and you can creep up to them. He thinks that himself. [The Audience applauds].

The American flag and it's true meanings. When the Original Scientists designed this for white America, he told him, he said, "I put the blue in here for you because you will not be true. Blue represents untrue color."

See there is nothing by nature is actually true in blue. It always can be disappeared, because that's not the true color of nature or the Universe's Science. The true color in the Universe is the Sun. And the Sun is something that is fire, it's red and it produces color.

Wherever there is an artificial-like plant, it can change that artificial thing, plant into another color because it is the Master that does this. The Sun brings up the colors out of the Earth into plant life and into other life; creeping, crawling, walking life. The Sun can change it to whatever it want it to be or whatever is the Nature of the Sun, pardon my language, it will change it to something else.

Pardon me I'm going on a little, little slow with you. I'm not going too…[The Audience applauds].

You that have never studied the Universe and the planets in the circle of the Universe, as it's a circle itself; the whole Universe is a circle. You that have never studied this, though you have studied Astronomy yourself, some of you; but I said you have not gotten this deep in it because, the Teachers that taught you some knowledge of Astronomy didn't have it themselves. And if they had it and knew that the meaning of it, the end of it is you, he's not going to teach it no way.

This is why they don't attack me and put in their paper to make me prove what I teach. It makes him so little in it, until that you had to take something like a magnifying glass to try to find him. [The Audience applauds].

So therefore, he don't want to challenge me out here before you. I will love to have him to stand here and challenge me. I would give him twenty thousand dollars every hour if he would come here and try to contend with me. [The Audience applauds].

"Well Mr. Muhammad, I think you're talking too fast." No I am not. I have mine from God, and what he have came from God, but God give him the worst of that He had in His storehouse. And He made the worst man that ever lived in the Sun, as we have not gotten to that yet.

But you will agree with me when I have taught you how he was made; and give you the knowledge of how you can test the Truth, since you don't know how to test Real Truth because you have never heard Real Truth. I can teach you how to test it. I can teach you how to attack me; and show you how I can ward you off. [The Audience applauds].

We see these signs, and that Scientist that gives America her flag was a Blackman. He didn't know how to make one with Science like the Blackman, because the Blackman was the Maker of all this color and stripes. So He made America one with Truth and with Justice and with fire that will ultimately destroy the falsehood that will come in the Sun. He put it there before the white man's face in this color.

Don't call it "Old Glory," it's Old Hell to you, not "Old Glory." [The Audience applauds]. They are fighting the Truth, and putting other than the Truth with Truth. You can't call it a "Old Glory" for you because you are made of Truth.

But a deceiver of Truth deceived you of the knowledge of Truth. Therefore, you think that you the same fellow that he is. You are not because One like yourself made him. He didn't come with Us.

We made him just six thousand years ago. And he will tell you himself that Man has been on this Earth for hundreds of thousands of millions of years, billions. And the Man he refer to there means you. The man that didn't came with the Sun and the Moon, and Stars, he is not referred to as the Man.

The human made into man, he is called human man, and not to be called Man. Man here, is you and I. The white man is called mankind; and he knows himself to be that. And he refers to himself as mankind. Well that is in the Bible, He said He made him like a man, but yet he was not the Man. So that's pretty good, he admits these things.

When he say mankind, he's referring to white people; he's not referring to you. You are not to be called or represent yourselves as mankind. You are not a kind-of-like-man, you are the Real Man. [The Audience applauds]. And the Lord said, "Let Us make man," think over that. And you have believed and you thought that meant all of us.

There was no such thing that God said "Let Us make a Blackman," because no man knows when the First Blackman was Made. As there was no circumference or diameter, or I should have said first there was no diameter measured through the Darkness that We Created Ourselves out of, unable to measure it. We can measure it now, but not then. Ask me sometime after this evening, and I'll tell you what I meant by telling you that We couldn't measure it then.

Nothing I will say up here on this platform that God have not given to me is the Root of it. And, if you don't believe I'm telling you the Truth of it; just because you don't know it, then you get someone that you think know it. Ask him to challenge this Truth for you; and you won't find him.

The Scientists of the Bible and Prophets couldn't find him. They prophesied of me in these words there in Isaiah, I think you'll find it, "They will shut their mouths at him." They who? It means the science class of the white people. They will not try and dispute with me; and they don't do it.

And you should have remembered when I went to Washington in nineteen-fifty-nine they have great respect for me. The Government sent out its soldiers and welcomed me into Washington from the airport right up and down Pennsylvania Avenue. They respected my knowledge. I can hardly get respected in your back yard. Because you don't know, but they know. Twice they did that. They'll do that tomorrow if I go there.

Never have you had a Preacher to go to the Government's Capitol and they escort you from the airport up and down Pennsylvania Avenue. Because he don't have that kind of knowledge. They give him what he knows, but they didn't give me what I know. [The Audience applauds].

I'm like it's written in the Bible and they put it in the name of Jesus. But, this is the one, that is saying this to you. He says there when they challenged him for his knowledge of his education, he told them in answer, "Mine is from above and yours is from beneath."

They didn't question further because, what come up out of their civilization had no equal with that which comes from God, Who was before. It is the meanings of that "Mine from above and yours from beneath." See beneath means that what you know comes from a wicked man of whom We made. But, mine come from the Man above; that man's knowledge whom We have no birth record of. It takes time. [The Audience applauds].

We, we return now to our left here on the board. And, that on the left here under the American flag we find there is a cross; outside of his flag he has a cross. What does that mean? That he's at the cross-road of the Truth. He will lead you either way because he have no straight path to the Truth to lead you on, and he call it Christianity.

Christian, Christ means the Crusher. The plural part of the word it means all that follows such teachings. Christianity: Anything pertains to the preaching of the gospel of the Christian religion which refers to a Prophet that they killed when he came among them trying to teach them Islam, they killed that man. They killed and persecuted all the Prophets of Islam who was teaching them the Truth.

They being made just in opposite of the Truth, they could not have Truth to come up in among them, it would destroy the future of their civilization. And people was believing, and he could not get them to believe in his other than the Truth.

Christianity is other than the Truth. That's why white people who are made of other than the Truth want you to believe it. They don't tell you that it came from God when they made Adam. Adam was not taught Truth, he was taught evil so that he could trick the Truth Believers, and make it trick Believers, pardon me, the True Believers believe in their other than the Truth. This would get him off the path of Righteousness, and he would become an evil doer.

You notice all of your life you can get a good laugh out of white people as long as you act a fool. And as long as you want to jump up on the stage and dance and sing evil and filthy songs; and you pull off half your clothes up there, and show the filth of yourself, you alright with them. That's all they want the so-called Negro for, to show the world that he, the white man made a fool out of one of your members, and now you don't want him.

So, as long as your own people and my people of the good and of the good world refuses you; then he can laugh and say, "Oh I beat your God. I've taken him away from you, though he one of you. But I've robbed your God of him and he follows and obeys me."

So my friends and Brothers and Sisters of the Nation that have no birth record and have no end over yonder, there's no such thing as a beginning to Blackman, nor is there a such thing that you can prove Truthfully a end of him. You can't prove Truthfully his birth, though, we can get him after his birth. But we can't tell you the Atom of Life which started Him into Perfection of a statue and form of a Man. We can't tell you that today.

We can get back there. God have taught me so near to it, until I will not go in that kind of teaching with you. Because I don't believe you have enough knowledge to go halfway of the Man. But I have been taught so near to Him that you would have to put the counting of years on it yourself. I am not able because I would had to go to how long Darkness took to produce the Atom in which the Man was made from. [The Audience applauds].

For four hundred years, he made our Fathers and ourselves to bow to death. That sign there represents death, a cross. And, put the tree and corpse hanging off the tree to show you what he do for you in Christianity. He can't do that so easy when you come out of the Stars, and the Moon, and the Sun.

He will get overtaken one day and be slaughtered. He will not be able out of all the Muslims in the country; he will not be able to kill over three hundred before the end of himself would come. [The Audience applauds]. That three hundred is not from myself, but from the mouth of God. He won't be able to kill over three hundred Muslims before they kill all of him. He knows all of this. [The Audience applauds].

He's bound to attack us one day. But we have what they call in the Bible seven Angels here with us, and Allah told me he's not enough for one. That one, the seven of them, all

would like to get a hold to him. But he's like a mouse among seven hungry cats; and there is not a full meal of the mouse for one of these seven cats.

I'm not going to wear you, but I have not yet begun. As some of these Brothers and Sisters know that it takes me a long time to go through this history. I'm telling in the Root of what you've been listening to. And therefore, I cannot tell you the Root of the Creation of Man and His characteristics, and what He's to end up doing in no few minutes. I don't care how fast I talk, I couldn't do it.

The best I have made of in the time of teaching this History, is about five hours. I cut it down from six to about five. But it takes hard work to do it. As the world of the white man was given six thousand years to live and rule Us, and take Us to Hell with him if he can. It takes six hours to teach that History.

I have worked on this History for years, for forty years, forty years. I didn't say four years, forty years, I have been teaching this History. I have taught it at times when the Spirit of Allah would get on me until I could hardly lie down when I go home. My wife, if she was here, she would tell you so. But she is unable to be here with us today. She was here last Sunday. But she is in hospital now suffering with a very, very, very dangerous complaint; and she probably will be with us as soon as she is able to do so.

Looking at the old cross, "Christ my lord," they say, "My redeemer died for us." When would God be fool enough to come out and die for the devil? [The Audience applauds]. "Jesus died for us." Well if he died for you, how many more Jesus' does it take now to free you?

We have been mistreated by white people since the death of Jesus, more than before. We was not here in North America for the white man to mistreat Us in the Time of Jesus. We just came here or was brought here rather, three hundred years ago, four hundred years ago. If we had been here in the Time of Jesus when Muhammad was born, he would have come and gotten us, so says God.

When two of his Generals, when they got to the Ocean, the History teaches us that the horses' hoofs staved at the surf of the Sea and they lifted up soil shaking it at the Sea and said, "If it wasn't for this Sea, I would keep on to the ends of the Earth putting to death every infidel that I find." [The Audience applauds].

So God Taught me, He says, "Elijah," He says, "If you all had been over here at that Time," He said, He would have gotten over here and got you himself." He said, "They all love you," He say, "but the devil have spoiled you so, they don't want to take up the Time to put you back where you once came from." He said, "They don't want to teach you. You are so spoiled and ruined by the devil, that they can't stand your insults. So they left the work up to me and you to do." He says "We are not going to miss them."

"Marcus Garvey made an attempt," He said, "He love you all, but he didn't have the knowledge that he should have had to have brought you out of. Noble Drew Ali, He says, "He tried, but he was not able because he lacked the knowledge." He say, "Now They have all left them to Us, you and Me. There is no one to get them now but you and Me. The job is on Us." He said "But, when I have gotten through Teaching you, you will be able to get them all." [The Audience applauds].

Not that I would ever be able with whatever Teachings He would give to me, unless He was with it Himself. We can't give life to the dead without His help. Even though we may know the key to the knowledge of that which he should rise by; we still can't do it unless He is with us.

There is much that you shall know in this Day and Time. I'm so glad and thankful to God for giving to us this shelter to teach you the knowledge of yourself in. Because you are a proud people. You will go to church wherever you find the finest one, you will try to get in it. So now this is the finest one there is in the land. [The Audience applauds].

The devil will bear me witness. He have already bore witness. He called it the ten most finest churches in the country. Now, we went to an extremely task to try to buy it. If we had been white, we probably would have gotten the church for two million dollars. But since we are Black and haters of white, they doubled it. They charged us four million dollars for this church.

We have not paid the four million dollars. But, having True Friendship and Brotherhood with our people in Africa, they loaned us the four million dollars to pay. We have Friendship all over the Earth. Throughout the Islands of the Sea we have Friends.

This was done to let you know that we have Friends. For these people of ours in Africa to loan us the money to buy this church with; they didn't give it to us, they loaned it to us. They may give us some part of it later on when they learn of our great work that they too must come by it before they can be saved. [The Audience applauds].

The old Christianity, the old doom of Blackman; this is the thing that doom you. And that the knowledge of it today will save you. That cross is enough to put a cross there representing their thirsty for death for human beings of Righteous.

All throughout your Bible they were after Prophets who would come among them preaching the Truth. And some they beat up, jailed up, and some they killed. And I'm the last of those Righteous Reformers. I'm the Last One. Your Bible will teach you that; and I will prove it to you if you come and listen. There is no need for a Prophet to come after me. Why? Because I bring you face to face with God and man. [The Audience applauds].

...hanging over there with a man swinging from a limb. As he swung that Righteous from the cross, he made following him was his people going ascending the limbs of trees for his body to be riddled with bullets from the Christian guns. That's right! So we are here sent from God, Himself, having the Power from God to put an end to it. My work is to put an end to it, and by Allah, We will do it.

SIGN OF THE CROSS

Christianity, what is Christ? What does Christ means? What is the Real Truth of the meanings of Christ? It means One coming in the Last Day to Crush the world of evil. Christ is the Crusher. You don't get that name in the Bible until his Time. Then you read of Christ coming. He's the Crusher of this religion; a lying religion; a religion teaches you, you must die before ever that you can see the Hereafter or Heaven. This is True, if you understood what the liar was saying. Sure you have to die mentally out of the evil death that he put you in. [The Audience applauds]. He teaches you that there is a Hereafter, after you die. That's right, after you die the mental death that he put you in from slavery up until now until the Judgment…Then, you got to be resurrected from the mental death that you died in, not physical.

There is nothing after this flesh and bone go back to the Earth. I got it from the Earth to build me a body for breath to enter; and when breath entered into the body, it made a sound. And from the sound I could walk and I could guide myself. Breath, the breath of life. Every human being that is born from a parent, if it does not breathe the breath that carrying the Earth and that we all are breathing it won't live, we say it's a stillborn. Right?

But he made you to look at it different. He made you to look at breath as something of a spirit of a body that we can't see, that's right too. We can't see the air that we are breathing unless we get a microscope, and then we could see the very Atom of life in the air. And those Atoms of Life in the air is the thing that gives us life. And whenever the body gets to the place that it can't draw them it in, then we say he's dead. That is right.

The biggest soul we have is air. Deprive the man of air and he's dead. You could come up here now and start doing this on me, on my neck, and soon you will have me so I can't breathe; and I won't be talking. Well, that's the soul that they preach to you about. That's the Real Soul; It is your Breath. There's no such thing as a little man going out of your mouth, going to an unknown place. No, No, when you get so you can't breathe the little man in, you … be a little man yourself. [The Audience applauds].

So take this home with you and study it, and you will come to the knowledge of Truth. You seen people probably drowning, and you see him standing up the man on his head to run water out of his lungs. If too much water is in the lungs which brings in the breath of life, then the man will expire like that; he have too much of it that will kill him.

16

But, I say to you in what I am saying, there is no such thing as a spirit jumping out of your body going someplace. It's the spirit that can't come that keeps the man alive. No, we don't have a soul going out, it's the one that we can't keep in.

Oh Christians[The Audience applauds], he show you the sign of his great religion that has doomed millions and billions of people to their graves, and never knowing the Truth of him. Now, he says, "believe in the cross, that sign."

I've got to take this along with you. I can't get over there where I want to get you at until I get you the knowledge of where you are. He says, "believe in Jesus," and you don't have sense enough to chase him. You don't have sense enough to make him to give you the knowledge of what he's teaching. You take it for granted everything he says is the Truth.

The cross, "believe in the cross, my brother" he says, "I will cling to that old cross." Yeah? "Over yonder," he says, "On yonder hills stands an old cross." Yeah? "It's a sign of shame; it's a sign of my guilt of murdering the Prophets of God because I was at cross roads with them in the Science of Truth."

So, here it is blind deaf and dumb Blackman, follow this and you will go to Heaven and meet Jesus." Yeah? How many have been there and come back and told you that? [The Audience applauds].

There is no man that dies and go back to the Earth returns again. That is the thing that just don't happen. You say, "Well Jesus rose again." Yea, he's rising now! [The Audience applauds]. The resurrection of Jesus means the resurrection of Justice among you and me. That's what it means. It don't mean that, that man will come back alive like he once was. [The Audience applauds]. And, he puts that sign and makes you believe it whom he have made blind, deaf, and dumb to the knowledge of Truth.

You believe just as he say. Jesus will come back and he will take us all home. Yes, that's right, if you understand it. Justice will come and condemn the liar of his lie, and take you back home again. What home? It is Justice that take you back into the knowledge of yourself, and you can live in any part of the Earth: Africa or Australia, or of the Islands of the Pacific which actually is ruled out there now today. I say Australia is ours too, and we are bound to have it pretty soon; all of it! [The Audience applauds].

If I were among the Australian whites today, on this continent, I would tell them the same: pretty soon we will own it again like we once owned it. New Zealand and all of those other islands and inlands out there in the Pacific and continents, they all belong to us, but, we were not to take them before the Time of the present rulers, the white people.

Now, their end has come and you will see these islands falling into the hands of the Black people very, very, very soon. [The Audience applauds].

We the little people in North America called every name but the True names of ourselves, God will soon give you this whole entire Earth; and He will begin here in North America. This is the country that He will take and send to the doom, the once honor of it pretty soon. This the first one because he acted so brave and mockery of God and His work.

So, He will make him His example for Europe. And Europe settled far away off as Revelation teaches you there of John, "And the people looked at the smoke of her ascending up forever and they cried and cast dust on the heads for the loss of her trade they have once had with her."

The Bible says, "They use to have ships going by sea with ship loads of great valuable merchandise, even to men. They sold slaves of us. Went to our home and taken us, brought them over here and sold them between each other. This is the way our Fathers was handled.

Now, God wants to deliver you and me and destroy them. First, He breaks their power to rule. He brings to a naught their trade between each other. That's going on now. Never have you since you've been born seen a President of this country going over the Earth to the nations of the Earth begging them to agree with him to live longer.

He have everything the other nations have. But he knows the other nations have their weapons trained on him, and that he would not last long if he would train his mighty weapons upon the people that is now against him. As they will tell you, "We have it, but we're scared to use it because others have the same."

And so he's pleading with the nations not to use these dreadful destructions of nations on each other. "Do, we will destroy ourselves if we destroy them. And which we can't, because they have their Champion of War with them, the Mahdi; and He won't allow us to take no fight upon the Blackman in such way that they can annihilate them from the Earth.

He told me and Taught me about what they would do; our people, those seven Angels that you read of in Revelations. What they will do when he starts. They are capable of cutting a corridor in the air between this country and another country, and confining all of his destruction in this sphere. Think over that.

The Holy Qur'an teaches you and me that We made the white man. This Book challenges the white man to prove that we didn't make him. "Who created you?" "Whom made you?" "Did you make yourself?" "Is the way it reads" or did We not make you?"

The white man know he came from Blackman, but he have killed you of that knowledge since he had the use of you for four hundred years. He killed you of that knowledge. He had to translate the Bible and he covered it up so cleverly there in his make that, you who he had in chains would never be able to understand it unless God Himself come, or sent one from Himself.

So the Holy Qur'an teaches you here a prayer that Abraham and his son Ishmael give to God for Our learning. He says, "Abraham, raise up from among them one from among themselves and teach him the Knowledge of the Book and the Wisdom that he may teach others, his other people the Knowledge of the Book."

The Book is the Bible. "And bring them into the Knowledge, the True Knowledge of it because they only use guesses." Well, that's true. The Preacher will tell you sometime in his sermon "I fancy." That I fancy is the same as saying I guess that it means thus and thus.

My Brothers and Sisters, you are lucky and myself to be living in this day. Seeing the old world go out and the new world come in. God is so Powerful, Mighty, that He don't want to accept living in a house where His enemy have lived. So, He threatens a total destruction, so that He can build a new one.

The Bible say "Behold, I make all things new, old will pass away." He don't want to use a lame sheep to eat. Israel was told to not to use a lame or afflicted sheep or a calf. "You must get a healthy one, one that is not afflicted."

Picture to you of the period of the Kingdom of the Blackman. He says over there in another place, "I don't care nothing about your offering to me; your burnt offerings of lambs and calves, because all that is upon a thousand hills is Mine. You don't have to give them to me, I give them to you. And, in my Day and Time, if you cut off the neck of a calf to sacrifice him to Me, be just the same as cutting off a dog's head. I don't need none of your calves." Think over that!

Gradually, He want to turn us into forsaking the flesh of any animal and give us a better one. He give Israel better meat didn't He? It was such meat that they didn't know what it was, but yet it killed the interest and desire for meat. But they say, "I don't know what it is," so they named it that, manna. Don't know what it is.

If He could bring down meat in a desert to save the hungry and draw out a rock, water to quench their thirst. What can He do more for us? I tell you my friend, getting acquainted with God is not like getting acquainted with a common fool.

Now, you see how much time I have spent trying to lead you up to the subject I intend to take you? For this that I have led you up now, near to the steps in which I want to put you in, and see you walking. It's near five o'clock...Three hours, I have been here three hours. Think over that.

I know one thing, you can't go in the common church today and listen to the Preacher three hours. If he takes a step, God told Jonah to go to Nineveh and preach, yet forty days, I will destroy her.

Getting there, what does forty days mean since the city was not destroyed, and He told Jonah to preach the preaching that he bid him? What he meant by that: Don't deny one Truth regardless to how foreign or how strange it look, or may be the end of your life to tell the people that, go tell them that.

And, if I give them an extension of Time, don't grieve over that extension of Time. You have some people way in the distant future that need an extension of Time. But you don't know them, Jonah.

So today, the Time of our enemy was up in nineteen-fourteen, but God would not kill him less he kill us. Because we have never as yet not come into the knowledge of Truth. They must know the Truth, and if they know the Truth, the Truth will free them. I don't have to kill them. Think over that.

So now, this Truth is to make you have knowledge of yourself and knowledge of the enemy, devil, the blue-eyed Caucasian. My young Brothers, do not grab these blue-eyed girls of his. They are doing this today to get you away from the God of your salvation.

The girl has been taught a long time, so when this Day come, that she will sweetheart with you; and she will blind you to the knowledge of Time, so that you won't recognize what she's doing.

She will make you think that we just now realized that we have to live as one people, and you yet blind, you will say, "yes, yes, that's right." But no, understand what she means. That the time has arrived now that I will make you to think that I'm in love with you. I will marry you, you will marry me, but you are headed for Hell. I will try to enticing you, work on the very nature of you. I will go nude in front of you. Think over that. He gives them the woman corrupting themselves. That's here in your Bible.

My beloved Brothers I say flee from her. She is a Universal Delilah. That's what that was put there in your Bible for. See how Delilah deceived Samson, the strongest man. You are yet the Strongest Man. You are yet the Wisest Man, but no one has brought you back to the wise Wisdom of yourself, and the Strength that it will do and produce others to succumb at your feet.

This little Atom, God raised up from you, to teach you these things. There is nothing secret now about them. God has revealed the secret of them, and that secret is in the head of the man that you are looking at now.

UNALIKE ATTRACTS

They are made unalike to attract you. Their father, Yakub, who made them, he was the founder of unalike attract and alike repel. And now, the only way that he can get his people to attract you, is to get them before you who is made unalike. And this unlikeness will attract you. And so, they're using this boldly today to get you to go to Hell with them. They know they can't overcome the Black God. They know that because He made them. So, he tells his women, "Go now and attract them. Tempt them so that they will believe with us and become deserving of Hellfire like we are." This is what he's done.

Well my beloved Brothers and Sisters, the time, I don't want you to get restless. [The Audience applauds]. I want you to return and let me give you the History of the makings of this white people, and what they were made out of. You could never be one of them. You could only believe them and follow them. But you could not never be one of them unless you was grafted out of your present self into what they are in. But by your marrying intermixing with them, that never yet will drive you out. You will become white speckled up, but actually the blood that have the origin of what you are, it can't be destroyed so easy like that.

Next time we meet, we'll tell you why we will tell you. We have the Roots of everything. We have the Root of the Universe. This, I don't want you to get excited and throw stones at me because I speak that which you never dreamed of hearing, but it is the Truth. [The Audience applauds].

So, I want to say to you at this hour, and this these minutes, that we will discontinue our subject, it's five o'clock....I was looking at your clock on the wall...is it... I'm wrong ? Well that's the time we supposed to dismiss our people, at four o'clock. Because, that we don't want to bore them. We want them to return, and two hours of this kind of work is hard enough on any human being. [The Audience applauds]. I have taught six hours, six hours, but since the time is helping me making manifest so much of what I'm teaching and would teach, until I want to wear myself that long. I want to learn to give it to you in two hours or an hour and a half. But I can't do that until I get you on the first step.

So, I am going to dismiss you and let you return again. You can sit a long time if someone will do the hard work of talking. It's a hard job to stand up here and talk two or three hours. [The Audience applauds].

So, we don't want to bore you today, because, Allah is making manifest the Truth all out in the streets; all around you and above you. So we don't have to go after it like we did forty years ago. I used to stand six hours and teach you what I am trying to teach you up to now, to teach you. This, what I've been saying here today is only trying to shape you for listening to the real thing I want to give to you.

So, I say I will be back…, if it pleases Allah, next Sunday. [The Audience applauds]. Thank you. Bring your friends with you. Five, ten, fifteen, twenty, a hundred, bring them with you because I have just now got up to the steps of what I intend to teach you today. And seeing that you do not know these steps that I am taking, I build them all up one by one to you, and then when I get you up to the floor, you can take a seat and sit down. [The Audience applauds].

I want that good Brothers and that good Sisters who come here last week and donated to the cost of this mighty Temple, which was built by the hand of white people. I thank you Brother and Sister and I thank you to continue, because Brother and Sister, we borrowed the money. We have not been given the money, we borrowed it. And we pay fifty thousand dollars a month on borrowed money that we have to keep you in to the best.

We now look down on the worst. We look forward for the best. We thank you for every dime that you could give us, or able to give us. And, we know and believe that Allah will restore it all back to you seven fold and more, because He did us like this. That's why we're up here today. [The Audience applauds].

I see a card here of Brother James 8x from Mosque No. 25, donated to us today one thousand dollars. [The Audience applauds]. The Minister of our Mosque No. 25, Allah blessed me to convert him when we both was in prison. And when he came out of prison, he started teaching our people. And the devil got a hold to him and pulled him back into prison; and he came out again preaching to our people. [The Audience applauds]. I thank you Minister James for your donation from your followers of No. 25 Newark, New Jersey. I thank you. I know you as I myself.

Think over those days when I was teaching you in the District of Columbus prison house. That is you in jail now? That you listened to what I had to say. Everywhere I would go there in the prison house, you were coming up beside me to learn more of what Allah had revealed to me and Taught me. Therefore, you held fast to it.

Now you have a wonderful Temple in New Jersey, great one; and the people are flowing to it by the hundreds there. So I thank Allah for you, Brother Minister James.

My beloved Brothers and Sisters, I thank each and every one of you that offers so much as a penny for the help of this great work. To get a nation out of a nation, and reform them in such way that they won't return to that which they are reformed out of. I thank you.

I Pray Allah that Heaven and Earth both come to you, because both belongs to you, so God have Taught me. And, I thank you for respecting me enough to come out and sit
before me and listen to what I have to say. [The Audience applauds]. I thank you and I pray to our God, Allah.

Allah means the First and Last. In this name is meant what you have in the Bible. He is the First and He is the Last in Arabic, Allah.

Now, I'm going to ask you, if before I dismiss you, I'm going to ask you, any of you have any doubt in anything that I have said, stand up and question me on it. Show me that which you doubt. No one, thank you. [The Audience applauds].

What I have as yet to teach you or what I have started stepping you towards, come here at two o'clock next Sunday. And we're going to add a few more steps towards the Apex of what God have given to me. Then, if you can find that you can walk out of it, then you will have to build more steps. And I don't think you will be able to do so. So I'm going to expect every one of you with five new ones with yourself next Sunday afternoon at two o'clock.

So since you have nothing to say... you want to be here so the Minister invites you next week or this week at eight o'clock Wednesday night and eight Friday night. And, I will come and see what you look like two o'clock Sunday evening. [The Audience applauds].

Excuse me for saying Sunday evening, Sunday afternoon two o'clock. I will be here, if it pleases Allah, right here where you found me today at two o'clock ready to give to you some untold Truth. Ready to give you that which has been hidden from you all your life, to bring you forth and put you as Gods over your people as you once was. Not as God, but be the God that you once was. Let us stand.

The Sun is going down in the West. This teaching as I hinted to you last Sunday, will rise a powerful Sun of Truth and, the Spirit of Truth from this part of our planet by us, whom God has raised up among us. No more will you look toward the East after this for a Light of Truth to come.

So, the Light of Truth which the Scientists of the East were not able to give you, will come from the West. That will change the disposition of worship. You won't look to the West, nor to the East, nor North and South for wisdom. Everywhere you go you will find it. [The Audience applauds].

So the Bible says the prophesies of the Truth, in that Day, it says "You shall no more go up to Jerusalem to the Temple or there at Jerusalem seeking God, but wherever you may be, you will be a Temple yourself." And therefore, it won't be necessary to go to no certain place, pointing out a house with Truth in it; you will be the Truth.

Let us turn towards the East. As we stretch forth our hand for the Light of Truth coming from the East. Oh Allah, make Muhammad successful in the wilderness of North America, and the followers of Muhammad successful, as Thou didst make Abraham successful and the followers of Abraham successful. For surely, Thou art Praised and Magnified in our midst.

Oh Allah, bless Muhammad in the wilderness of North America, as Thou didst Bless Abraham and the followers of Abraham Blessed. For surely, Thou art Praised and Magnified in our midst. Amen.

Brothers and Sisters, may the Peace of Allah and His Mercy go with you as He did when He brought you from home, may He return with you home. As I say unto you, As-Salaam-Alaikum.

JUNE 11, 1972 PART ONE / SIDE ONE

A TIME OF TROUBLE

In the name of Allah, the Most Merciful. All Holy Praises is due Thee, Oh Allah, the Lord of the Worlds, The Most Merciful Master of the Day of Judgment in which we now live. Thee do we serve. Thee do we beseech for Thine help. Oh Allah, Guide us on the right path, the path of those upon whom Thou has Bestowed Thy Favors, not of those upon whom Thy wrath is brought down, nor of those who go astray after they have heard Thine Teachings. Amen.

Brothers and Sisters, I'm very happy to see your smiling faces here this afternoon. We have a great time of trouble going on, and it's getting worse and worse every hour. Therefore, we should be here to decide on what way we shall take. We have no Time to think about trying to correspond with the people of this world. Don't be trying to imitate them. This is the "Time of Separation" and the destruction of one and the safety of another. I don't want you to think that I am here before you for no fun and foolishness. I'm here like the traffic officer trying to direct you into the right path or lane, or road. No more time for foolishness.

The Theology of Time that I am teaching you, it is mostly the secret that has been held back on religion. We cannot depend on the road which we have been put on by our enemies. We have to forsake his guide, his leadership, if we want to see the Hereafter. We are not any kin to them at all, and they are no kin to us. This is the way you can easily get deceived today being ignorant to the knowledge of self. You want to be friendly with the same enemy that has brought you to nothing. That you "love everybody". Just wait a few days coming round talking about you love everybody. They have a place to put people that love everybody. [The Audience applauds]. You must remember that if you love everybody, you love first your enemies, theirs included and that our enemies included. So we can't tolerate with you if you love everybody, cause you're loving your enemies and ours too.

We must understand the Truth. The Bible doesn't teach you to love your enemies, do, you throw that Bible in the waste basket. The enemy put that in there to help himself. You'll be loving the enemy of God, and yet, you claim you love God. You can't love God and love His enemy and your enemies included. What do you look like loving the devil? Let the devil love devil, and not you loving the devil thinking that you are getting friendship with God. You're getting to be an enemy of God. How foolish he have deceived you in believing in loving everybody. Everybody's not to be loved. We have various kinds of people.

25

You love your Brother as you love yourself. But let that Brother be one that God loves, and one of your blood and flesh. You can't love every kind of flesh. You don't have that understood. The enemy made you to think so. But you can't love him. No, this is why he declares to God that he would take them all, in the Holy Qur'an. Deceive you, and take you to Hell with him by making you to love him.

You cannot intermarry with them unless that you want to go to Hell with them. [The Audience applauds]. I know this don't sound so good to you who has been deceived. Well, I'm telling you before it's too late. There is people that have a nice clean home and if you love your dog they advise you don't bring him in here.

Some of us love dogs and wants everybody else to love that dog. You find these people who love dogs, they are classified with the enemy, the devil who used to use dogs when he lived in the caves. And he made friends with the dog to help protect himself and his family.

Brothers and Sisters, Truth is Truth. I have been given the knowledge of the devil. This is why they hate me. They don't want me to tell you what God has Taught of the Truth of them. The Theology of time. You must know the Truth that has been hidden from you.

"Oh them old folks they hates white folks." Yeah, we're the people that "hate" them. We don't love them [The Audience applauds]; and they don't love you, only to get you in trouble or bring you to your end. He was made to destroy us. He was not made to save us, but to destroy us so that his people could rule you and me forever.

I want you to listen good, and I'm not afraid if you're trembling, I'm not trembling. [The Audience applauds]. For forty years I have been teaching what you hear me teaching, only a little addition and into the Science of it now.

But, for forty years I have been going over this country preaching to you my kind, that the blue-eyed Caucasian people are devils, and that they were made that way. And you can't change them unless you take and re-graft them back into us where they came from.

You say, "Oh, well then, we're all devils." Oh no! You got it wrong. Because that you made a car it still don't mean that you a car yourself. [The Audience applauds]. We are going into that extensively after a while how We made devil. We are the God that made him, but, We didn't intend for him to touch us. No.

Well you know that I'm not no young man, and I'm not flying off at the handle. [The Audience applauds].

You see these Brethren sitting in front of me with…these Brothers what they wear on their head represents the Universe. And why they are wearing it is because now God is turning over to the slave, Blackman, the Universe. And they are within their rights to put it on their heads, because it's theirs.

Well, I guess I'd better just bring it on out. [The Audience applauds]. If you don't see the white Mason wearing it but once a year, you wonder then why we don't wear it along with them once a year? No, we the Father of it! [The Audience applauds].

So, if the Father is going to lay his emblem aside to go along with the non-owner, then the Father is doing this either for Time to make acquaintance with him in his own country, or the Father is just laying his down for a certain Time.

Today, we are suppose to wear our Fez, which represents the Universe. But white people don't do this, they wear them once a year in some kind of turn-out because this is not his. That's why he don't wear it. He's a man put in the Universe for a Time; and at the end of that Time, he gets out of our house. If he don't get out, we throw him out.

The world, not really this world, but the Heavens and the Earth belong to Black people. And this is why this Teaching has come to you. It is to acquaint you into the knowledge of your own.

Last Sunday, I think we left off talking about stripes. There is so much to tell you, that I could put it into books after books. There is plenty books wrote on it now, but, some of them I don't go for. These books are books that are piled up into libraries throughout the world. Books after books, mostly to commercialize on. You don't need all of these books.

As the Bible teaches you back there in the last part of it, that he saw God give a man with a symbolic name a little book, and that little book was enough to take care of all the big books. [The Audience applauds]. That is true, Allah gave me a little book and He's preparing another little book. Well, He got it prepared, but He waiting for a certain Time to give it to me. [The Audience applauds].

If we are to know the right way, the right way cannot be taught by the wrong-way-Teacher. You've got to have the right Teacher to teach the right way. Believe it or not.

These stripes here that we spoke on, I think it was last Sunday…They are to acquaint you with the knowledge of signs. The signs here, as I told to you last Sunday over to your right of this stand, on this board, is the American flag and his religion. So, with it to the left, with an awful sign of your Brother swinging on a tree, and the sign of his religion beside him.

Don't fear, they will not try stopping me from putting this up here, because they can't condemn it. Their religion they call Christianity. Christ- ianity , to me that ianity there is the plural of the Christ...isn't it? The righteous people of Christianity will swing his own brother up on limbs like that.

Every since we have been in this country, we have been in his religion. Now, you are Black and believe in Christianity, but he will take you and swing you on the tree. This just proves that you are not a brother of his.

And the reading in between this flag here and our flag it says, "Which one will survive the War of Armageddon?" I don't have to ask you. You know that the stars and stripes are not going to survive the Star and the Moon. You know that! [The Audience applauds].

So it's a big question mark there. Again, if I asked you when was Christianity inserted in the religion of man? If it didn't came with the Earth, with the Star and the Moon, you don't have God's religion.

You must have the religion of God, Who Created the Heavens and the Earth, and Taught Man the right way. You cannot boast of a religion that did not come with the Heavens and the Earth; that is right. No theologian will condemn you; take you down to the road a piece and get you guessing and wondering when it come about.

God never changed His religion. If He would change it, it shows that He didn't fore-know things. He's suppose to know the future and the end of all things. So He chooses Him one religion. That religion must be capable of defining the Truth of what He has made. If God made the Universe and did not define it in telling you and I what He made it for, then the God is not accurate on His Truth of His Creation.

Let's listen good and try and learn something. I don't argue with you because I know what you know [The Audience applauds], and I'm not boasting in what I know. I put it out here to you, you are welcomed to take it or leave it. It is yours as well as mine.

There is a lot of boasting and proud-acting among us, but I say put it down because the Bible teaches you that God will destroy the proud. He don't like proud people, and I don't either. We like humble people who can recognize the humble humility of us all. And that, if we can recognize our own humility, then I think we got just about the whole.

Not a one of us is not up from slavery. Not a one of us is the president of the United States. So I say, let us be careful what we boast of. If you have quite a bit of money, that's alright, it's here in the Earth maybe we could get some one day; you didn't get it all. [The Audience applauds].

This teaching that God have brought to me is to level us off. That's right, some of us are up too high as the Holy Qur'an speaks to a proud man in this way trying to be up over everybody. It says, "You cannot reach the top of mountains in your height, nor can you go and step through the earth." So, since you can't step through the Earth, its too deep; and you're not able to reach the top of mountains and hills on the Earth, then even the Earth is taller than you and deeper than you. So let us take our place where we was Created, and try to man it. [The Audience applauds.]

The secret of the Time has been held back from you by your enemy, because they have the worse feeling of Time. Time is that which have a motion, or start and an end. When it comes to this world, they had a beginning and they have an end. This is why they talk most of Time, because they were put on Time to go so far, and then leave.

This "forever" this bowing out is forever. This is well known to them, but it's not well known to you. You read in the Bible, you find in the Revelations that his Time is that figured of the man is six. But I'm afraid that you don't know how to understand the Time. "Let him that reads understand the number of the beast."

Just to be named a beast is sufficient for you and me to stay away from that man. A man now the Prophet calls a beast. He is called a beast because his characteristics is that of a beast. You never seen people kill and delight in killing like these. Beast doesn't take sorrow for the beast they kill, if they want to kill him. This is the same kind of nature he has. He don't care nothing about killing, because that is put in his nature. If you think that he has some kind of mercy or a heart, you are headed for his net. He don't have no heart like you and me.

You have heard and you probably have seen how the Black Brothers pleads to them to not to hurt them and he pay no attention to that, he laughs, because he don't have no mercy in him by nature. The devil gives one of his Black servants just a buttered biscuit and he'll go fight you for that because he was born with the devil, and he's not in the knowledge of the devil....

I have long time to speak, and you don't have to hurry me. [The Audience applauds]. I have two Books up here. One the Qur'an and one the Bible, both books ours. The white man has never produced a Righteous Scripture for you. He tampered with that which he got his hands on to make it correspond with what he have in mind.

Now, the Bible says, " In the beginning," but it doesn't teach us when the beginning was. [The Audience applauds]. It also states that when God Created the Heaven and Earth and created Adam, okay. Who is Adam? And when was it that God Created the Heavens and the Earth? They don't exhaust themselves trying to teach you that Wisdom. But you're sitting before a little man who has been Taught in Person by God; and I think I can come just as close as that Man can come to it from what He Taught me.

There's no man that knows exactly when the beginning of the Heavens and the Earth took place, because there was no one to record the Time. There was only one Man there, and He didn't have the Knowledge of keeping Time like we have. He was Laying the Foundation for you and me to learn how to calculate Time.

Mathematics is True if you know how to use it. The religion of Islam is equally as true as Mathematics, and Mathematics is equally True as Islam if you know how to use both of them in the proper place.

We only want you to understand that We are here to bring you the Truth. And that We defy you or any other Mathematician to disprove Us. So I must get along with our Christianity, Islam.

If Islam stands out before your eyes as a sign of the Universe; if the Universe was made wrong and that it's Truths cannot be found in it, then we live in an awful Universe. If the religion of Islam takes for its Base the Root meaning of the Universe for its Religion, then I say you have an awful job trying to tangle with that type of people. They'll have you running around looking for something to prove what you say.

A religion, if its Roots is not base upon the Universal order of things, you have no religion. [The Audience applauds]. Christianity, as you see, is based upon the murder of a man two thousand years ago. And such sign is not in accord with the Universal order of things. It's only in order of a murderer.

He stands over here, his sign by a tree out in which he got his cross out of. Then he place our Brothers on it. Then, our poor Brothers having not the understanding of what he's taught to believe in, falls down and worships it. He says he loves Jesus. Well why? How can you love the Jesus and love the murderers of Jesus and his sign. [The Audience applauds]. You just can't do it!

So you are blindly wondering in among a people who's your deadly enemy and mine. And they take and make mock of the Righteous by making signs that they murdered them on, and hand them over to you for worshipping. This is evil, and evil to the eye. We don't want no such religion.

What you think I ought to do for you? In the South I met a devil who had a piece of a Blackman's ear in his pocket. Showing it to me to make me fear him because " I am a murderer and a killer of your people." That's what he wanted to let me know. But, we are so blindly and ignorantly in love with the enemy, until we forgive him for killing all of our people except ourselves.

I say Brothers and Sisters wake up! This is the height of ignorance. A Black woman wanting to marry a white man, her murderer. A Blackman wanting to marry a white woman, his murderer. You must remember the parable of Delilah was for her people and not for Samson. Because Samson was a strong man that her people didn't like; and she only wanted to find out his wisdom of strength. So, it shows how he tried to shun her, but later he give in because she was unalike and that she was much smarter than Samson in wisdom. Therefore, she could force Samson…

CHRIST MEANS "THE CRUSHER"

Therefore, she could force Samson to give up himself to her. Remember, that was put there for us. We are the Samson of the Time, but we can destroy our self, pardon me, ourselves by giving over to the enemy all our secrets. Some of the Brothers call them Uncle Toms. I don't think he should put the "Uncle" there. [The Audience applauds].

If we look into the face of Christianity as it stands in it's teach and practice, I think you ought to put it down because you don't understand it. The first part of it here spells Christ. Christ actually means The Crusher that's coming in the Last Day to Crush the wicked. And it don't mean what you think, No. That's the man to rid us of that "anity" out there at the end of it. We have been deceived so long and with so little, that it shames us to know just how we have been deceived.

Over to your right there, a blazing red Sun with a Star and a Moon in it, which on analyzation of it is right. The Star and the Moon is in the Sun, and the Sun is the Big Master. And down at the bottom of that red and white flag representing Sun, Moon, and Star, it reads, "Islam." Islam in the first sense means that which is of Peace. I don't care how long you look at the Universe out there you don't hear any noise. [The Audience applauds].

Here on my left is a flag with stars, blue stripes of white and red. It seems to be confused on which colors it want to take. [The Audience applauds]. That's exactly what I want to do, not say preach, but teach. [The Audience applauds]. This flag to the right, it have nothing but a background of red and a Star and a Moon going in it.

The lower Heavens that the Scientists refer to as our Heavens, the Sun family they call it, contains about nine planets. And that it have this for herself, that red Sun rules the nine planets. And the nine planets is the Kingdom of God which also represents His Godlike Wisdom and Power; just those nine planets.

Then He makes a woman to imitate that nine planets. So Brother don't take her for nothing, she's something too. [The Audience applauds]. You know, we always have, since the devil white man made... us do it, looked upon our woman as nothing. And yet, so many of them can guide some of us men folk. They not all fools. They wise too, because you made them wise. [The Audience applauds].

And the most beauty of them, God made them to comfort us; and that's the best that man wants for. He wishes for comfort, and that's in the woman. Without our woman Brothers, we would be pretty lonesome creatures. [The Audience applauds]. In fact about it, we would not have nothing to produce ourselves.

You've got to have the woman to keep the production of the human nation going. To put her out, kick her around in the street, disgrace yourself and her too, you've doing a very wrongful thing. If she produces us the likeness of ourselves, and you can't get that production without her, then treat her like you treat yourself. [The Audience applauds].

Notice the enemy, the devil himself. He have had all the while we've been among him, respect for his woman. He have had it regardless of his evil, he takes time to force you and me to respect her. But he disrespects our Black woman, and we in turn, disrespects her too. [The Audience applauds]. I'm trying to force you to see her in the light of respect and honor.

This morning we heard in the room a baby crying; she brought it forth. Okay, treat her good if she's producing men and women for you and I. She should be honored and respected to have this kind of power. I studied our women, their actions, and the creation of them, in regard to the Knowledge of the Man, what he had in mind. I say Brother, I'm with the Holy Qur'an.

The Holy Qur'an teaches us that she is to be respected as we. The only thing that's different, we are a little greater than her in the power of our creation. We have more powerful brains than she because we was made to Rule. [The Audience applauds]. She's a helpmate. She helps him wherever she can.

It's wonderful to know thyself. That's the greatest thing you lack. You don't know yourself. We must get away from mistreating our woman folk. We must treat them right and honor, and they will learn to honor you. And they will produce you a little baby that will honor you. [The Audience applauds].Even animals is grateful to the mother of their baby. They try to help build homes for them so that they can produce babies of their kind.

I say we just have act a fool. A white man out there beating and kicking your mother up and down the streets, and you stand there. We should commit suicide before we take such steps. Let the white man come over in our yard and beat up our woman, our mother? No Brother, we both go down together. [The Audience applauds]. He love our woman to destroy her; that's all he knows.

He go into foreign lands of our people, and the first thing he go looking around for with his green-blue eyes, is to get up to the woman so that he can leave, the seed of the devil with her.

I say to you my beloved Brothers and Sisters, turn around and take a new thought for your people. Let the world know that you love self and those that look like yourself. Don't let people see you hating self. Who are you going to love after you hate yourself? Nothing but your enemy.

I see some, pardon me, I saw some chickens one day. These chickens was standing around in the yard acting proud, the rooster was; and he was scanning the skies for his enemies. Anything like a hawk he warns his family to go, but he don't run. He stay out there to battle the hawk when he hit the ground. [The Audience applauds].

.... you learn to stand up to the enemy, die or live, live or die, we will be respected by all the people of the Earth. We must learn to do this. The Muslims is trying to learn to respect their Black Sisters. The Black Brother Muslim is trying to show you how to do the same.

A coward Muslim is not a Muslim. [The Audience applauds]. If we claim that we are backed by God, and that we are with God to back Him among enemies of His, I say Brothers and Sisters, let us prove these things. Don't talk it, but prove it.

In the oath of Islam, it goes like this: "My prayer, my life, and my death, is all for Allah." [The Audience applauds]. This is an oath, that we take in our Prayer. If we don't do what we say in the prayer, we are telling other than the Truth to God.

In Christianity, it was a religion that we do as we please, not so in Islam. You can't do as you please in Islam, because some of your "pleases" may not please Allah. So, we do as Allah will be pleased with us. [The Audience applauds].

If we are asked to pray five times a day in Islam to show a good Muslim. Well, if we want Allah to take care of us every five minutes, every five seconds, every fractions of a second, then I don't think we're praying too regular to him just putting up five prayers. That's not so much for the much that we're getting from Him; and the mercy we hope from Him.

Over here to the left, the first, [The Audience applauds] "Which one will survive the War of Armageddon," which is now taking place. We're going into that war, and we're in it now, this very minute. If you believe Christianity which has mistreated and hang you on trees, then I think you should look at this and think well. If a murderer will survive peace, which have we experienced all of our lives?

The Heavens does not give us no trouble, but we disobey the laws, rules of the Heaven which are obeying the Creator. The Star and the Moon and the Sun obeys the laws of its Creator. But, this stuff over here to our left, is the make-up of an enemy against that to our right looking from down...

He is opposed to the laws that governs that which he cannot do without himself. He cannot find no place to live but in the peaceful Kingdom of the Universe. And regardless to how he boast, he can't build one outside. Let him try and build him a Universe; then he can be independent of ours. But since he was not able to build him a Universe, then obey the laws of ours.

But that he can't do because one of our Black Scientists a little over six thousand-six hundred years ago made him according to His wish. He didn't make him according to our wishes. He made him according to his wish.

This troublemaker was made of the nature of making trouble. When his God made him, he made him and he said to him after he had made him, "Go to now, and make all the mischief that you can before the coming of the Mahdi."

Who is the Mahdi? He is the God we call Allah. We call Him other names, but He is the One also that is referred to in our Bible that will come. Mahdi means a name of self independence. The Man don't rely on others; He's self independent, and He's one that is coming in the Last Days to bring about the Judgment of the made-man. And He's referred to by many as being the Son of Man.

I don't know whether I should tell you all of this or not? [The Audience applauds]. The Son of Man is that Man that is given Authorities and Power by God to carry out His Judgment upon the people. That's what Son of Man is. And then, it goes also for the Mahdi being born out of His nation by a woman that was not of his nation.

But the Man that produced the child that she gave birth to, was of us, the Black Nation. And that he married her to get an unalike child so that he could send that child among our people and his people to produce a Ruler of us who was lost among the unalike people. And that Man He made from among his people and the enemy was and is the God of the Judgment of the Destruction of the unalike who has attracted us for these last six thousand years to....

The unalike is the white people. They are unalike of us, and we are not like them and they're not like us, only in the nature of a man that's why they call him mankind because he's just kind-of- like the Real Man, but he's not the Real Man. [The Audience applauds].

A God who is able to fulfill His promise to us come and offering you that flag on the right, means that it is Time now that you ... rule your own. That's your own and He have offered it to us. We have a song we sing of that beauty like this, "Allah has give to us our own, the Sun, Moon and Star for a flag."I don't think you will find the white people running all over the Earth with that on their head. They know better. They don't have part in it. They have Time in it, but not part in the Creation.

When you ask the white man about his secret order called Masonry or Masonic, he wants you to answer that you was not made that, but you were born that. That's true, We are born Muslim and cannot be accepted by saying I was made a Muslim. We were Created Muslim. Some of you may be Masons in here, and I want to come over in that corner with you to teach you how. [The Audience applauds].

In reading a book in the Washington Congressional Library on Ancient Masonry, I had to laugh sometimes to see how we have been fooled. And now you are getting the highest degree in that order that no white man would ever teach you. But however, we won't stop here to deal with some kind of society. We will move on with Truth.

If we bring to you, I'm talking about the disbelievers and hypocrites, if we bring to you that flag and tell you that's our sign or emblem, you that have studied degrees in Masonry should not hesitate to come over because we give you more than what the devil has given you. [The Audience applauds]. These brothers sitting here before our eyes and patrolling the floor space, they are men that have learned more about Masonry than you.

Your Masonry have included the history of your slavery. And that it also teaches you that, but you don't know it. Your first three degrees takes you into your slavery. Those three degrees there, they are the answer to your slavery, if you understand. But not understanding them as the white man would not teach you the Theology side of it, it makes you dumb to even that which you actually own. I don't like to call you such names, but it's a easy answer to the Truth of it.

You look ignorant among, look at that and laugh at it because he's ignorant of the Truth of it, and he don't know what he's doing. But, he'll smile at his old stars and stripes he calls it "Old Glory." I was you, I'd change the name and say it's "Old Hell." [The Audience applauds]. I know it's hard to take, but if you would let me teach you, you'd go sticking out your little chest. It'll make you feel like sticking your chest out, but I say, don't act proud, be humble and yet commanding.

If we bring to you the Sun, Moon and Star, and you laugh at it and criticize it and say you don't want it, that you would rather have a made square of the devil. And that, that's enough for you to get by with because you're only wishing to be recognized by the devil, not by your people. That's why you go and join up with them in every society that you think he will let you in.

You want to be his equal, be recognized and respected by him. He didn't make his society or societies to make you his equal. He robbed you of money alright enough to be called one of them. He don't like to call you no brother in no society. Not before ever that we will tell him that we will accept him calling us brothers, he try to call us brothers. Many white people out there call us brother or refer to us as " the brothers," because we have the Truth and the Light and in our right position of the square. We don't do this for forms and fashions. No, it is the Truth. If we say that we are on the square with you, it don't mean that we're just saying that, or because of the sign of the square. No, we say that because we are the Square ourselves. Not that we makes a sign to go by. We're the Square; and we are the Star and we are the Moon.

While you do these things according to his teaching just for the respect of the white people who are one. They'll get recognition of it in America, Australia, and in Europe. This is just the act that they have for you to buy to get among them, and Freemasonry in and of itself does not take you any further than Australia, and into Europe. But this on the right here takes you all over the Earth. [The Audience applauds]. I want you to wake up and know yourself to be people of the First Order, not of the last order, but of the First Order. We are to respect each other as Brothers and not as enemies. We are to respect our woman as our mother. I say my friend, this mean that we have to love each other. We can't do these things if we hate each other. That's why we are very careful with you. We know the poison in which the devil have put you. Poisoned your mind against self and love of yourself for him, and want you to be like him. Hope that you don't be like him.

These people were made for hell fire. They was not made to live, only until a certain time. He tells us himself some places he goes, now that the children of the natives see him and say, " there goes a foreign devil." They know him better then you. A real devil is one that is made by nature of evil. His very nature and material which he is made. I don't say the word created, because he is not from the Creation. He's a made man that our Scientist Yakub made here six thousand years ago. But we have been on this Earth every since it was Created. And if it's the home of the…that you can classify me of talking that which I do not know, the History of you have been Taught to me as far back as the Atom that First burst forth to give away sound. And that was beyond seventy-six trillion years ago. One trillion years is a long time, cause when you put seven-tens of them together, it runs you out of reading.

I want to talk with you on the Time. If I don't do it, God will hold me responsible for Him giving me the knowledge that you never have dreamed of getting out of the head of God, The Knower of all things. I will be held responsible. I go slow with you at times because I know your disbelief. You are a people who were raised by the devil who hates the Truth and loves lies. But I defy him to disprove me of any word that I teach to you. If you could go outside and bring me a white man that says he can prove that I'm lying to you, I will give you ten thousand dollars for every word that I have said that was a lie. I defy them every time they're among us and they don't do it. If that door was slung back on its hinges to let them in, you wouldn't have sitting room. They want to be here listening to that which they never knew because a baby cannot tell mother and father what he's done when he comes forth. He's got to live long enough for the action of matured brains. So, that he's only a baby to us, and a very young baby at that. He has our number because he could not have another since we are his Father.

JUNE 11, 1972 PART TWO / SIDE ONE

THE TRUTH WILL MAKE YOU FREE!

So he was not made of, of himself. We made him, so say the Bible and Qur'an. He was made by the Blackman, the Original Man, and he's not hard to make. We could produce many... I'm quite sure you're asking yourself, "When is he going to teach what he said?" I am doing it. I'm teaching what I said I would teach you, but I'm coming in such a way up to it that you will be able to master it if you accept it. It's useless to have something of wisdom that you cannot master; give that wisdom to another one. But, the way I'm teaching you, you can learn to master what I'm teaching and you'll be just as big a boy as I am, of which I don't call myself no big boy, but I hate, pardon me, I hope to make you the big boy, then I get behind the door and peep at how you will react. [The Audience applauds].

The Truth, the Bible says, will make you free; that is Truth. If you know the Truth, you will be free. Having the knowledge of yourself and others, and of God and the devil and both of their worlds, it will make you free. That's right, rightly...

We must take you out of this flag here, so that we can get going with the Creator and the one that did not create it. The main thing to know who the right one that made the Creation, and the one that didn't make it. This flag over here to our right, was not made for white people. They can't produce a flag like this. This flag over here he had to use some of the material of ours to make it.

Don't mind Brother and Sister, my son is either getting hungry or he feel for his father. [The Audience applauds]. He think his father should stop and go home. But my son don't know that I have thirty millions to teach. [The Audience applauds]. And, if I can get thirty million people to believe in America, I could take that thirty million people and rule the whole Earth. [The Audience applauds]. I don't think anybody here is so hungry. At least he can't be any hungrier than I. I haven't ate nothing today, and I'm teaching and you sitting. You shouldn't send for me if you didn't want to be patient with me. [The Audience applauds].

Theology is not so easy taught, especially to people who do not know Theology. Theology of Religion, you got a very hard job with people who don't know it, and who are wrapped up in the belief of religion which that True, True Theology opposes. But this what We had to do, is to bring you out of that which you do not know, into that which you and me can make others to believe is Truth.

38

I love to stand before you and teach you the Science of Religion and others. If I didn't know and understand the Science of other religions other than Islam, I could not prove to you that Islam is Superior. But I know other religions who boast that they have a place in the Sun to rule the people with; and these religions is not worth their name, no not even worth the name.

As the Holy Qur'an teaches you and me, that if you come up on the Day of Resurrection before God with a religion other than Islam, it won't be accepted. Because the Religion of Islam is over all religions and it's work. It's Science proves itself. Not that you have to get somebody to come and prove it, it proves itself because it is Truth without help to make you believe it is the Truth.

So, Brothers and Sisters, I see somebody getting white-mouthed around here looking for other food, and I better let you go so [The Audience applauds].

We must know Truth to join and become a member in a fully-recognized society. We can't become a member of recognized societies without having the knowledge of Truth. And this is what the American Blackman needs most of all. He needs to be shaped so that he can be accepted in the best moral and educated societies of the people of the Earth.

We thank Allah for blessing us with this house here. We thank Mister.... for letting us in here. We shall not forget Mister..... He give us a nice place, one of the ten most nicest places in the country for spiritual service. And that, we like the place. Hope you ... visit it, like the place [The Audience applauds], ... will learn how to be as clean as the building. It's walls are clean.

We hope that we can be accepted in the clean societies of the people of Earth. Like all people of the Earth will come in here. They all will come here if we permit them. You will see every member of every nationality or race nation is on the Earth, if we would let them in.

Now, I will ask you to think, think this over. If you are to rule after other rulers has ruled since they have experience ruling and you have not, you probably could be easily cheated in your freedom to rule by other rulers. So we don't allow them here until We know that you are able to master what you are being taught.

Well, it's not open for foreigners, it's open for the new baby being born, the little black baby. [The Audience applauds].

So now I'm going to dismiss you. It's been near two hours or more since we begin. And that's long enough for people to listen to the Theology Of the Times and get in the full and clear knowledge of what we have been deprived of by an enemy. And I thank you for being so nice and quiet to sit here and listen to me for these two hours. And, I believe that you will be happy over what has been said [The Audience applauds].

Now, I bring to you that which you don't love to well. To stay in this place we got to keep money going by the tens of thousands. So when you go out there, don't forget your place. This is your place. Do something to stay here. [The Audience applauds].

As I have just begin to teach you the history and the secret of the world that you're in, I can't say when we going to finish, but I'm inviting you to come back next Sunday. [The Audience applauds].

As you know, we carry on our own school independent of others. We will never get our own by mixing up with others and letting our children be brought up in their school. That has been the wrong thing to do. Teach your own children the knowledge of their education yourself.

I have long since been seeking teachers. We have some mighty learned teachers out here, and what we want you to do is come over and put your wisdom here. Let us raise up our nation from your knowledge. Love to teach and train your children in the knowledge of the Black Nation, who had no beginning nor will we have an ending. [The Audience applauds].

They are chasing the white man all over the Earth to push him off the Earth. And you that like to go long with him, they'll push you off too. This is the end of the time of white people ruling Black people. Believe it or not.

Mighty curious and strange things is…. happening now, even into nature. It is changing up against our enemy. Look what you hear happening up in the North part of this country. It's happening every hour, but they don't tell you every hour what is going on. They think you already know and you do know some.

I say my beloved, I thank you for your presence here this afternoon. In the basement we're trying to set up a school down there and up here on the surface. And we're going to try and create a better classroom up and down Stony Island on this side, running all the way back down far as we have land.

We have so many applications in for Teachers to teach in our school, that we can go home and almost cry that we don't have the space for you, but just keep putting your applications in. Time is here that we must do something for self. I thank you. If there is any questions, anyone have any questions to ask me about what I … been teaching you.

Yes brother…Brother I can't hardly hear you back there. Will you come up here? Brother I could tell you a little something. Don't be ashamed, time for us to get away from being ashamed.

Messenger: Wa Alaikum Salaam

Brother: Question Unheard

Messenger: What did you say? Oh, Brother Jesus. I want to give you his whole history as God give it to me, but I don't have time now . But I can say this according to that which you can read. The Holy Qur'an does not call him a God. He was not a God, and he admits in the Bible that he came before Time to do his type of teaching; and he also admits it in the Holy Qur'an.

It was not Time of the Jews. Their Time was not up to have Judgment teachings taught among them, because they had yet this Time to live. And, therefore, they cut him off like they did many Righteous Prophets that he couldn't set the world in righteousness; and they live unrighteous when they was made to live under wickedness and deceive us, and make us do the same. That Time wasn't up.

And he was not sent to us at all. Jesus was sent to the Jews, or rather taken himself to the Jews. There is no prophecy in the Bible that Jesus was to come to preach to the Jews salvation, because he was two thousand years ahead of their Time. And so, there's much more we can say, but I think we'd be losing time.

He admits, himself, that he was ahead of Time, and he prophesied of another one "When He come, He will teach you and lead you into all Truths." I can't do it. I'm here for a special thing, but that one will tell you all." Like the one that Moses prophesied of, I bear witness with Moses in his words and his teaching, that, "that one will lead you into all truths. I can't do it."

So, I think it is very good that we are living in this Time, in a time that we learn the Truth of that which Prophets before us couldn't look into. But, now the Book tells you, "When He comes" whom the God will send, that is you, and you will hear from him that which you…. been longing for. This is him, Brother. I object to you and no man from questioning, I don't care who it is. Whatever question you want to question that's your privilege. And, if a teacher who claims to know the Truth objects to you asking him questions, he's not the one.

We cannot learn if the Teacher won't let us ask questions, because that what he teaches I didn't know it, so I may want to ask you questions. And so, if you block me from asking questions, then I'm afraid that you're blocking me from learning what you teach. But this little fellow don't object to no one. I put myself before the world. I don't put myself before just a certain organization.

I defy the white Theologians and Philosophers to ask me anything they want, anything. I don't care what they want to ask me. Go ahead and ask. I, I am not boasting. I'm just as humble as you. Wisdom don' t make me proud, it make me humble. And if a man get proud of his wisdom, he can't teach us. But, if he get down here with us, and humble himself as nature has created everything in the stage of humbleness. And, if you're too proud to go along with the law of nature, then maybe you won't be able to teach me much.

So, if I teach you and you don't understand, it's your freedom to ask me of that which you don't understand, to make it clear to you. And, if I can't make it clear, I am not the Last Teacher, and I believe I am the Last Teacher that ever…What we want above all is Unity and Brotherhood. That's what we want. That's what Islam is here for, to unite us into a circle of Brotherhood; everyone of us believing that we are the same. Islam is not made up of no big "I's" and little "you's." We all…alike before Allah.

As the Holy Qur'an teaches us, "The most best among you is the one who is most careful of his duty to Allah." So, if we have a Religion of Equality, Islam is Equality. That's what that Moon stand for in our Flag, Equality, Equal. It's equal with the Earth and the Earth equal with the Moon, and all is equal in the Sun. See? All the planets is equal in the Sun… because…

THE MOON: A SIGN OF THE BLACKMAN

Because it being the greater attraction, it don't make it be greater in the eye sight of God. You see how this Scientist of ours ripped up the Moon sixty-six trillion years ago. And we now going back there through the white man looking at it; the destruction of that piece of our planet to let man know that you don't worship that either. That's just the same as that you own it. But, it has been deprived of its life, like you hold the Blackman deprived of his life. This is a sign of us.

So, I hope that I could slip out here some night through the week, and help you out in this. This is no say silly question that you are talking on, this is wisdom that you're talking on. And I love that my people come and ask me such questions so I can tangle with them whether that they are proud; or if we don't make everything clear to our people what God has Revealed, then the revealing of it was unnecessary. I like for you to ask questions. Don't be afraid that we are going to look at you as somebody want to dispute. Asking questions are educational in nature. The man is not disputing and trying to bring up a argument. This bring up something that we all want to understand. Well, I thank you Brother for your question.

I'm now going to turn you back into the hands of our Assistant Minster to dismiss you. We have a wonderful Minister. Is there anything anybody else wanted to ask me? Yes Sir, come up here Brother closer where I can hear you. Thank you.

Brother: Question Unheard

Messenger: Because there was no one there to record it. He is the God. There is no God in the Sun before you. The Blackman has no beginning. There was no God before Him, do, we would be following another people. But, we are here on the Earth and We made the white race ourselves, just a little while ago.

The Holy Qur'an teaches us that God didn't make us to live forever. Only the Nation, always the Nation is here. The Blackman is always here, but not no single Blackman living forever. We have of them living near a thousand years, but they not to live forever. You know why? After the Scientists live here and learn all about his Earth, and know what is come to His Earth tomorrow, tomorrow could mean a thousand years or twenty thousand years. Since he know all of this, he not particular about staying around to see it come in because He already knows it. And so, he gets tired and start to living a life which he know will have an end to it.

43

The Saviour said some of these Great Scientist just start eating three times a day, and He soon die because the food is the thing that sustains life, keeps us here, and the same food will take us away. Because, the poison that's in the food will eventually destroy our physical form, if we continue to put it in. So, this is the way that highly learned Scientists among the Blackman gets away out of our family; they just start eating against the way that he should eat. Because as I just said, the food is the thing that keeps us here, and it's the food that takes us away. Anything else Brother?

Brother: Is one God greater than the other one?

Messenger: Yes. We are now living in the last, well, some people call it different things that was here now fifteen thousand years ago. And each Time Wisdom was suppose to go twenty-five thousand years. Since the Mahdi has come in against all the previous Gods, because He is God of Us all. His Wisdom is not matched by no God in the past nor, in the future to come. Therefore, the Scientist say that He live forever, because nobody can remove His Knowledge.

All of these questions that you asked me, I intend to teach you that anyway when I get further over into this subject, that will come in. I have to bring it to you, to prove that you are the First and the Last, if there ever be a Last. And, you have gotten so wise now nobody can't cut Us off and make Us a Last. Every time One come in after a certain Time, He's Wiser than the Other One. That keep Us... Was there something else?

Brother: No Sir.

Messenger: Come back and bring five with you. [The Audience applauds].

I want all of you to go away from this Temple, with your minds set on bringing to me next time you come five more besides yourself... I will turn you back into the hands of our Minister, and he will do the dismissing. And, I have had a very, very good time here with you. But I will be looking for you with five more with each and every one of you, next Sunday afternoon. We haven't forgotten our subject, it's just so long. But if you keep coming, you will keep learning.

I'm the little boy that challenged the world of Science to disprove just one word I said. If you are able to condemn me as false on one word that I teach here, I'll give you ten thousand dollars out of my Brother's vest pocket, and then I'll pay with my life for lying to you. We must not lie in this Day; it's the end of this world...Not to become no minor liars...

May Allah's Peace and His blessing go with each and everyone one of you, as you return to your home. Bless you...I want you to pray that Allah take us home without a broken limb... and without our property being marred...I thank you, Salaam Alaikum.

WHAT IS TIME?

Well, we don't want to be like the preacher. We know the preacher had been coming… to get his audience to listen to him so he could teach them. But every time he would get there, they would start talking about the party they had on Saturday night. So, the old preacher got tired of that. So, he studied up a way to get their attention. So, he put his forty-five in his pocket, and he taken his Bible, and he put a bottle of whiskey in his Bible case. He got up before the people, he put the Bible down to his left, and he put the forty-five over to the right. Then, he looked over the people and said, "Brothers and Sisters, my text is today, "some of these things will move you." I don't have any of those kind of tools to use. I have to make out with one Book up here.

We're going back to our subject. What I'm leading you up to is the Theology of the Time, and as it was written in which we didn't understand. Now, if I happen to get a little weak you know I just… I didn't eat no breakfast this morning. You know, the preacher, most of these, eat a little piece of fried chicken when they go out to work. Well, that will strengthen you up a little, but we Ministers of Islam does not do that. We don't take on physical food first. It hinders us from getting the spiritual food.

So, what we're teaching here to bring your mind and attention to the Time. What must be done in such Time? This is what we're trying to get your attention on, it is the Time. And, if it is the Time, what is Time? Time is motion. We can't make Time without a motion. Whenever we make a motion it is registering Time. This is the way the Universe is made. There was no such thing as Time before the Creation of God.

The whole Universe, as we call it now, was not a Universe. It was just a Darkened, unlimited amount of Space. Darkness is still the limit of Space. If we could get out of the light of Stars, we will find ourselves again into total Darkness. But, I don't think you'll be smart enough to do that. You're just not going to get out of the light of the Sun and Stars. To get out of the sunlight into starlight, you will have to go a long way. It takes care of what Astronomers call a family, the Sun does.

The sunlight does not go all over the Universe, that's why you have Stars. Stars picks up and keeps the Darkness lighted up throughout the Universe. They are like Suns like our Sun; nothing but balls of fire. Don't look and wonder what kind of life live on a Star, none at all. It's a ball of fire. There is no life in all of this great Space extending beyond four billion, six hundred million miles.

We have the last planet in the sunlight, some people call it Pluto and that's pretty good according to those people who found it. They give its name after themselves. A lot of planets is sometimes called by the name of someone else; the astronomer who discovered. But, I'm going to talk on you, of that First Man who discovered these things, Who made them.

There was no such work as going into some great shop carving out a planet, to see what it look like on paper. The Gods didn't do that. They just willed the planet and there it is. That's pretty smart isn't it? It is your own Brother doing that.

We are practically bringing you up to the Time in what God has Revealed to me. If you would like to ask questions, think well of how you perform your questions. You're not asking Elijah Muhammad. Just remember, you want to question what God has Taught Elijah. And, if you are the winner and find that Elijah lying, you're saying God has lied, and I will give you ten thousand dollars, well, out of the Captain's vest pocket.

The mainly thing about this meeting and teachings is unity. We have been so divided against each other for the last four hundred years that we want to unite. We look alike. You don't look like you're more whiter than I, and I know we can unite if you're Black.

You know, I was sitting down this morning reading about the Indians talk over Oklahoma. They claim that's the first state, indirectly, in this little book that I was reading, that they are going to take over.

You know, the Red Indians have been mad ever since that the white man came across the Atlantic and taken over his country. So, he has been crazily angry ever since. We have been here, have been made so blind, deaf and dumb, that we not angry. We satisfied; we don't want no other place.

Suppose Allah give you this place, and He will see how you will act? You rule over a country, that's nothing hard for you to do. Your Fathers once Ruled the Whole Earth. And so, for you to get back ruling, you just getting back in the chair that you belong.

I know one thing, the officers has did a very good job of seating you. I know now I am talking to those that I been talking to last week, last year. I'm talking to you people. I call or we call them new, because they never heard what we have heard. This is a very small group of people, that have never heard the Truth. You never have heard the Truth as long as you was by that cross, or under the cross glorifying it to be the way toward God. You glorify it to be the actually, "the right way to Jesus" you say and "God."

I want you to know this, and I guess I'm bringing up a fight now. You don't have Jesus to guide you today. I want you to know that. You can tangle with me, and all the men I will give to you. There's no such thing as the Jesus that they crucified two thousand years ago, is on the scene. There is no such thing.

He says in the Bible, "I go away," Right? "But, nevertheless, the Father will send you one." Huh? He did go, but you say, "he's still in the way." Brother you are blind, deaf, and dumb! The Bible tell you he said he is going away. Going away means that he is going to die. Not going to some Heaven and listen to you for two thousand years. Aaaah!

Yeah, sometimes I'm very fiery to fight. So, if you happen to find me like that today, I'm ready to fight. It makes me and you, that is awake to the knowledge of what's going on, so angry with this blue-eyed devil who is blinding you; making you to hate me, when I'm loving you. He makes you to hate because you love what he gives, and not what God and myself giving you.

God and myself today, as I made the joke in front, we have something that is going to move you. If we come before you with the Universe on our head or coat lapel, this means that we come to Rule. That's what it means and nothing else. You can't produce a argument against us that you could win with. It is not for you to know as yet, but, to argue on that could condemn what I am teaching you. You can't think it. You can't think the question to ask me that I cannot answer.

I sure want you to hear me all right, and I don't want to lose a word. I want you to hear me, because you don't have next year and year after next to come out here and hear this. You better make up your mind today. The change of the world is going on now. It is not to come, it's in the workings now. On the radio, I'm sure you have one, TV's, they're teaching you that this world's Time is now going out. They tell you that.

The fight over in Vietnam is not a fight of yours. It is not a fight of mine. It is not the people that my God sent after to try to save, Vietnam people, nor the white American's who are fighting them. We have nothing to do with that. And I will tell anyone, regardless to who he is, and regardless to how wise he is I will tell him, "You're not wise enough, yet, to tell me to go to Vietnam to fight." You know I'm trying to go after you today. I'm ready for you.

The last couple of Sundays ago, I was a little of weak. I'm struck with some of these devil complaints and diseases. Well, I don't know if I should use the word disease, but, however, I must fulfill that which is written of me, "In all their afflictions he was afflicted, but the pleasure of the Lord will prosper with him." And if it's not prospering with me to get to you to save you from the destruction of the world of the devil, then maybe God don't want you. But, if you are listening and you believe what is said, and want to follow in what is said; the teachings of yourself making you to know yourself; and to know the devil and God. I bring these two great Gods before you, and make you acquainted with both of them. It is up to you to choose whom you will serve. Elijah's not here to force you to accept what he's teaching. It's just his duty that God has sent him with, so he must tell you.

Now remember that's all, and I'm not going to try and force you. I'm not going to spend time arguing with you. I was not raised up among you to argue with you, just to tell you. Then, you believe it, or let it alone.

I would like to say to you, that I thank Mister….,who was the president of this church. It was called church when it was under their authorities. That is their religion. That…meeting is called a church.

I may make you hungry today. I'll keep you here for a long time. We know there is Truth today, like the Jesus prophecy that the Truth will make you free. You ought not have to look up nothing else to free you but Truth.

Why would the Jesus prophecy that? Because the Truth is on your side. You are the Truth man! I'm here to contend with the world, not you all. Not you alone, but the world. I am not boasting. I'm just trying to get acquainted with you, that's all. That the Scripture is fulfilled…It teaches you and I that, He would raise up one from among the dead, and teach that one to teach the other dead what He really thought we should know.

Well this is him standing up here. I'm not boasting. I'm not trying to be independent… I'm only trying to make myself acquainted with you. But, I'm your Brother and your best friend you'll ever have.

Because this is why I'm up here before your eyes. I told God when He was looking for one of us to do this job, I said to Him, back me up and I will do it. He looked at me and smiled and said, " Brother, are you with Me to put our people on top of Civilization?"   I said, Yes Sir, if you back me up. He says, "I will back you up Brother. You go," He says, "I will back you up."

So, He has been doing that for forty years. I have been in many, what you call close calls; somebody after your life. I have been there many times. I'm still in it.

We have a class here called, two classes called F.O I. and M.G.T. & G.C.C. The F. O. I. is Brothers that you see wearing the initials on their head pieces, which also represents the Circle like this, only does not give to you little signs of the Theology side of the head piece. This here give you the sign of the Universe; the Sun, Moon and Stars.

Well the Sun is not up here, but the Star and Moon is here. The closest thing that represents us as who we are. You can't get away from round being what you are, if you represent the Sun, Moon and Star.

We are the First people in the Sun. In fact about it, the Sun did not make us, We made the Sun. And, the Stars that lights up the once Darkened Globe, our God made them. Not the same One, the One that Created Himself and brought forth life from Himself. Other Gods behind Him dashed these balls out there in the Darkness, and made light so far into Darkness that you can't find the end of it.

Light out there is so far, that we can't take and make a telescope... to pierce the distance to get to the outer edge. So, it must be a long ways. It goes into trillions and into sex-trillions; and into all the trillions that you can mention of. You just can't find the outer edge.

Well, let us get away over here on this board again. Would you say getting away with the board. Would you follow a religion that will hang you to the tree like that you deal with? Would you believe in a religion that teaches you that, that cross is the sign of what the murderers of Jesus did? Would you then now, follow that same people? I would ask you, would you say the Christian or Christianity is right if they teach you that they killed the Jesus, their last Prophet? Would you now follow them? You follow because you don't know, you don't understand.

You are so Righteous by absolutely nature, that when they had you tied up under slavery, they could tell you anything in the world they could get you. They know you would follow because you were created religious, and you want something to...teach you religion of some kind, whether it is the right one or not. That's right.

You were born a Righteous person. And, the devil taken you away from Righteousness and enslaved you. You in log houses and what-not, and taught you different from what you was Created and made of. And, put into you his way, and, his way is opposed to the right way. This is what I am here with from God to challenge the world that they are un-righteous and we are Righteous.

Look in your papers and in your magazines. Listen over the radios of the land and the TVs of the land, and you will never see him on there trying to condemn me. If he says anything in condemnation to what I'm teaching, he'll hide away. He won't come out in the front and do it. I would like to pull him out, stand him over there before you like I am, and question him. He's not going to do it because he knows it's the Truth!

Islam have produced him, not for Righteousness. Their theologians and scientists are making new additions to the Bible, of the Bible. And, that he is doing it for two things. This is his purpose and aim: It is to keep you blind to the Truth in it; and one to keep the Book away from your knowledge, and keep it to himself...others that have not yet caught up with his lies. "Is the Bible a lie Elijah?" No, it's not a lie if you understand it. But, if you don't understand it, it make you see wrong. And, we see that that wrong way was put there purpose by the liars to keep you away from the Truth.

Well, I say to you, you are a great blessed people to have God to raise up from among you, your own Brother; and teach him the knowledge of the Book. I have been given the knowledge of the Bible. This is why I tell you that I will give you ten thousand dollars if you can find me lying, because God Taught me the knowledge of the Bible wasn't born like that. He said that I was pretty good material that was born. That's why He taken me over, that I already....born with the right material that He wanted. But, everybody's not born like that. You find that in the Bible, that the Master went out...

We have so much to say that we may bore you a little, but anyway it show that we are not wise if a man offered us a cross and then tell us that they killed a Great Man once upon a time by hanging him on that cross. We should have done this, "Away with you. We don't want you teaching us nothing about a religion." But, you wasn't able, you didn't know what a religion was; and you didn't know what to tell him your religion was.

If you tell him that you don't want this, he will ask you, he know he have dumbed you. He'll say, "Well, what kind of religion do you have?" And, you couldn't tell him because you didn't have one. He had not taught you one but his own. The white man was created, or rather made to take all Black people out of their Real Religion. Not just one, but all. He's been gone all over the Earth taking Black people out of their Original way of life.

Now these two signs up here we have gone over them. And, we're going...to line up the new man to where we are going. This flag over on this side, we put it over here. It don't represent what you think it does. And that you always worship it, "Old Glory." I want to know, where in the world have you found "Old Glory" for yourself? You have not found no glory in that flag for yourself.

You say, "Oh he teaching us against the flag of the country? Then he must be a Communist. He must be." No Brother, this is not the Communist flag that's over to the right. That's the flag I'm trying to teach you that is your own flag, and no other people is to offer it to you.

Go and look over the flags that the nations have in your encyclopedias, and also, in the regular common books. They teach you over here to that one to the right, all the nations of your kind and my kind have a little piece of it in their flag; that one to the right. Some of them have just a Star of it. Some of them have a Moon. But, he did not say...those that have their flag, pardon me, their flag made after the design of America's flag. America or Europe's have something to do with it. What I mean that, Europe and America rules that people.

Even your good little brother over here in Africa you call Nigeria, not Nigeria, Liberia. Excuse my blunder, but, that's America's flag; and that's the Blackman over there that he owns over there in the midst of others. That he can take that one there and try and sway the others to go along with him. That he is backed by America.

So you say, " Liberia is my country, my state." No, it's the white man's state; he rules that. When he gets out of the state or country, then it's that native people. Their own rule, or can rule themselves.

Let's go from here now. I think I have been talking long enough. Brother Minister James Shabazz, turn the flag over please, and let's get to work. We fool around here, you know, we can talk a long time of just this and that because we know this and that.

Now as I teach, I will ask the Minister to do certain drawings and figures over there on the board of what I am saying. Now the first thing Brother, I want you to draw me a long hyphen. No don't get dragged back there…I may have something else for you…don't go to the…go to this side with your line. Cut it off about six inches of it on each side. Now, put a "Zero" on this end. Yes, now this "Zero" he puts here represents nothing. [The Audience laughs]. Well it is not say really funny things that we fixing to do for you. Now we going really into teaching you. Now, he could change and put another "Zero" on the other end. Yes that's right, everything I say Brother…do it.

JUNE 18, 1972 PART ONE / SIDE TWO

ALLAH MADE SOMETHING OUT OF "NOTHING"

Pardon me, now, "Zero," "Zero," Right? Now you have nothing to go from, or nothing to start with, right? Because the beginning of "Zero" is nothing, and the end is nothing. Listen good, now if we have "Zero," erase this other "Zero." If we have Zero here and we go from "Zero," and out here at the other end we'll find "One." And, then from Nothing create a, what we call in arithmetic, number "One," we go from that to study the others.

How many more do we have to study? It's "Nine" isn't it? Well put it down everything I say you put it down Brother. No, No, not like that. You put "One" and you come. No, you don't put it, yes you can. You could put "Nine" beside that, but you have it long after all. Keep the "Nine" away and keep that "One" away from there if you're going to write.

Brother you have forgotten some of our way. You use to know this very well. Wait a minute, take that "One" now, take that "One" away from the "Zero" here you, you, what your fraction say now? Have a "One" sitting in front of a "Zero," that's fraction. And so, from this "Zero" we go out at the end of that long hyphen you have up there, and we find "One." What produced "One?" It was Nothing wasn't it? If he bring that "One" back here where he started to make it, it makes a fraction right out of "One." But, if you put it in front, it makes a whole number, Right? Now, take the "One" and put it in the rear of your "Zero." That is not in the rear.

I'm going call my Mathematician out here after while. You're…we use to do this so fast Brothers and Sisters that you…he, he had forgotten, because he tied his one here with the long hyphen line here. He should not have let it touch because that look like somebody fixing to draw some kind of frame or something. But, if we take the "Zero" here, and put it on the inside, it's a fraction, Right? But, if you put it over in front of the "One," we are making a full number of that "One." We are taking and multiplying that "One," by putting just that "Zero" in front of ten-fold, that's right? Alright then.

That…represents you and me. You were nothing Brother until the coming of Allah. We were like that "Zero" there, nothing! Now He came and put Himself with us. When He puts Himself with us, He increased us ten-fold. Since now God has increased us ten-fold by adding His Number-One-Self… He's the Great Number One God, putting himself beside nothing ten-fold, Right?

52

He made something out of nothing by coming standing beside nothing, which was no more than a "Zero." But, He made the "Zero" something we could count from. So this is you and me. [The Audience applauds].

We're getting up in the world now, capable of being looked upon and respected because the One God is beside us nothingness. I only want to bring you into the knowledge of yourself. Why are you nothing? Are you any ways tallied with the Universe? Yes. "Elijah why did you make the "Zero" round?" Because, that's the way the Universe was before the Creation of Man. And, since out of it which we came by One Who was Self-Created. He didn't come from the creation of another.

He's the Creator Himself, the First. Remember that. And, He made Himself in a Circle so that the Wisdom of His Self-Creation could keep going to give Knowledge, Wisdom, and Understanding to you and me.

I want us to remember that. Don't tie your "One" Brother no time with that long hyphen, you don't know what figure you'll make. Don't never tie it. And, today I want to say to you, out of this Darkness came One, and then He taken the Unknown, and put it in front of, for what? To produce the Known. That's why the "Zero" go in front.
Now, the more "Zeros" He put up there beside "Zero," it keeps producing or making this "One" tenfold more Powerful than it is. Just add "Zero's."

"What are you trying to drive us to Muhammad?" I'm saying the more of you who knew nothing, and was like that "Zero," the more you add to the One God, you become something.

I'm only, now, making figures of us. And, from the figures we teaching, you can understand. Let's take another look. Since we started from nothing; and since God Himself started from Nothing; and we're going to something because the Creator found something more in the Darkened Circle than He had thought that He would find.

He's not here today, that same Man but He laid a Base for a Wise God to come and get a platform out of His work of Self-Creating.

Once every twenty-five thousand years, write everything I said…Once every twenty-five thousand years, there's a New God that's been coming up in the past, so God Taught me. Their Wisdom would always run through to about twenty-five thousand years. And, then they would change and bring in another One.

So, all the Gods that Ruled as you didn't know that Gods Ruled by Ones, and not by just the same One. This is why you are taught God is One. That's right, but it's not the same God. With us. They All are dealt with Righteousness until about six thousand years ago or better. They produced a contrary that wanted to make his name known in Power and Wisdom in the Universe. This was only six thousand years ago. And, this was taken up by One God to Rule the people for six thousand years.

So, six thousand years we had a Black God. His name was Yakub. And that, Yacub was playing with two pieces of steel one day, and that's where He learned his Own work, by playing with two pieces of steel watching their reaction, one attracting the other that this steel would attract each other and come together. And, He looked at that reaction. He looked up to His uncle and say, "Uncle when I get an old man, that was now when He   was six years old.

He was a man born a Black Scientist with a big head. He had a great big head, and they use to call him, so God told me, "The big head Yakub" because his big head contained so much Wisdom or Brains of Wisdom that He was called "The big head Yakub," meaning that He had a lot of Wisdom.

So, He told His uncle, He say, "When I get to be an old man, I'm going make a man that will rule you." So, His uncle looked at his nephew and said to Yakub, "What will you make other than something that will cause bloodshed and mischief in the land, making mischief in the land and bloodshed." He says, He didn't tell his uncle that, No, No. He know his uncle was telling the Truth. He say, "That's all right." He say, " I know what you do not know." He did not tell him that he was wrong. That was just the thing he was going to do. So, he told Him, I know what you do not know, and he did.

You would say "Muhammad, who is this questioning, Muhammad ?" It's Gods! He was in the Circle of Gods, and that was God speaking to Him, questioning Him on his make of a man.

Now, when He got six years old, this Yakub begin telling the people that was what He told them, pardon me, when He got to be a grown-up Man. Then He went out to start grafting that man that He decided that He would make the ruler from us. Think over that. He didn't go out to make him otherwise, but to get him out of us because we had the Right Material in Us for the making of such man.

You would say to me, "Well Muhammad, what kind of material?" He, in His college school in His Day and Time, in the laboratory of his Day and Time, He taken the germ of the Blackman to experiment on it to see what was in it.

And, He saw in the Blackman's germ had two people, and one was a weaker one than the other and that germ was brown. So, He kept experimenting with it, He say, "Yes, I can separate this brown germ which is weaker than the other one, the Black one. And, I can make a man out of that germ and then I will teach him My Wisdom, and he will rule the Black one until the Black one produces a God greater than I."

So, He discovered that Black germ that He would use to make an inferior man to rule a Superior Man, or to rule a Superior Man, it would take ten thousand years, pardon me, six thousand years for the Black germ now to produce a white man that would have more Wisdom than He. "Then He could erase My Civilization and set His into orbit."

Listen at what I say to you carefully. Maybe someday or another you'll, or this evening, you'll think that you'll argue with me. But, I say, in ten thousand years you not gone ever be able to condemn me. You can't, because I give to you that of God, and you can't condemn God.

You know, we up from slavery with the white man's teaching and education. We think he have the know-how of everything. He got the know-how in his world, but he don't have the know-how in our world. And our world was First and it'll be the Last if there be any Last. We can take his wisdom today and wrap it around our little finger and ask our little finger, "What's that round you?"

I am risen up among you to condemn the white man's teaching and to condemn him for death. This is what I am here for. I don't want you to think you're playing with no light boy, at all. My size is very small, that's why they symbolically prophesied of me being a little lamb, instead of a grown up Lamb.

No, Christian believer, that don't mean that was Jesus, and I'm trying to steal him. Jesus was a well learned man. The Lamb there give to you a man that is not only little in stature, but is little in education. But, Jesus was a highly educated man. He was not any dumb-bell. He graduated at Al-Azhar, and he was no dumb-bell. Then, he walked…six hundred miles from Cairo University, Al-Azhar, into the land of Israel to start teaching Israel, two thousand years ahead of Israel's Time to live.

But this one is on Time. I'm not only on Time, a little ahead of it, but I'm a little behind the Time.

The Time of Israel was out in 1914. Now, count the years since 1914, as the FBI told me when I was arrested by them in 1930, 1930, no that's not right, no 42, 1942, excuse me, in Washington D.C. Not for what I was teaching. He say, "But, if you had come with this teaching twenty years ago, you would have been shot outright, but it's Time that your people should know this."

"So, we are not trying to stop you from teaching, but the President Roosevelt don't want you out here in the public with that kind of teaching while America is trying to prosecute the war between her, Germany, and Japan . So, that's all they're putting you up for, is to keep you out of public while that they are trying to prosecute the war between Japan and Germany." Well, I say "This a terrible thing to set a man up in jail to wait till a war ends, to free him." No he say, "just that one."

Well, I was freed by them in 19 and 46. They told me down here in the loop, the U.S . parole officer, they say now, "Elijah, you can go ahead and teach what you always has been teaching, nobody will bother you anymore. You teach whatever you has been teaching. We didn't put you up for that what you was teaching, but just to keep you from teaching others while we're at war. So that they will say, we don't go to no war with you like you were doing."

Now, there is two wars since then that you have fallen in with them wholeheartedly because you don't know yourself. You're blind, deaf, and dumb to the knowledge of self, so therefore, you say, "Come on, come on, let's go to Vietnam and kill them so America can rule without her." You didn't know what you were saying because you didn't know yourself.

What is the root of Vietnam war with America? It is to let these two fight. They both is enemies of God. Let them fight, let them kill off as many as they will of themselves, the Christian and the Hindus. Vietnam people is Hindus and you have no right, whatsoever, to try to make yourself a Hindu by trying to defend them. But you didn't know that.

Now, I'm telling you they're no kin to us. They're no brothers of ours. They hate you if you let them go free and let their Hinduism, which is their religion rule longer. If you don't believe like they believe, in Hinduism, then, they would want to kill you.

So, in the first place, you were the dumb-bell. You had no rights over there. But you went because he called you and told you to come and go with me and fight my enemy. "Yes sir." "But if I don't go he will put me in jail." How bout that one that he put in the grave? We have been made just like our enemy the devil. And, we have the desire to defend him even at the price of killing each other.

The Hindu people is not no brothers of ours just because they have black eyes or something like that, or you see some nature part of the man looking like you. No sir! They're not for us at all. That old Hinduism has been taught by them, so God Taught me, for thirty-five thousand years. Not just three thousand, two-thousand from Jesus, thirty-five thousand years. That's the age of the Hinduism.

Now you can't change them hardly. As the Muslims tell me over there that if they make one a convert to Islam a year, they think they're doing fine. He's a old enemy of God. But, this is to run him and his Hinduism off the planet. That's why God let him and the Christian fight each other, because He intend to get both of them.

And why that He is here after us, because we was born under the enemy, and the enemy has taught us from the cradle to do as he do, which is against us and our people. His teaching is so strong that we start cutting each other throats or shooting each other down. Two brothers shooting each other to death, cutting each other to death. Think over that. It's strange to see two Black men, by nature, out there fighting and killing each other. For what? That's your Brother. You don't kill your Brother. You kill other than your Brother, if other than your Brother attacks you, but not another Brother. No, No.

He put fear in our parents when they were little babies, and they came up nursing that fear from the breast of their mothers. She sits and nurses her poor little baby boy child with fear of the white man. It went right into the baby, and then the child come up trembling. He's scared of white folks. I'm saying to you Brother, take it or leave it; it's the Truth!

So Yacub; Who is Yakub? He was the Brother of our people, and the Maker of him sent among us to rule us for six thousand years. There was no man come up that had the Wisdom of Yakub to take away His Rule until the birth of the Mahdi, Whom I represent to you in the name of Master Fard Muhammad.

That is your and my God, Master Fard Muhammad in Person. As the Bible teaches you, "You will see God as He is in Person in the Judgment." If you will deny it and say that you will not believe in no man for no God, I will tell you to produce me then, a God other than man.

Everything that man desire, man prepares it and gives it to us. This microphone here was not prepared by no spook. It was prepared by a man. And just show me anything that was not prepared by man.

As I am coming from this sky, I'm telling you what the Stars are, how they was made, and what they was made from. And, I come to the Sun and I tell you what the Sun is, what it is and what it was made for. And, I come to the Moon and tell you what the Moon is made out of, and why it's called a Moon, and why it has not been replaced since it was taken away from a certain place. It has to serve its purpose to raise you and I up Brothers and Sisters to Rule the Whole Universe in the Hereafter.

And our word will become "Be" over the Creation of the First God who said "Be" and there it Is. Our word must be that now. It must come to pass that one of you tomorrow, Oh tomorrow, we'll say the same; and we'll have something different, though it may be a hundred, it may be a thousand, or it may be a million years, it will come to pass. Remember that. I don't have time for us to go in argument over these things, as I got to get you up to the position where you can argue if you want to.

Twenty-five thousand years this Man that made the white man was here six thousand years ago, breaking the twenty-five thousand years into the six thousand years of his Rule. Now, he don't go to the end of no six thousand years where we at in the calendar of our Rule of once every twenty-five thousand years We change Gods. His Wisdom is limited to only twenty-five thousand years. Here, this Man come in a vacuum like of that twenty-five thousand years.

From the year nine thousand to the year of fifteen thousand. Nine thousand years of Our Calendar History of twenty-five thousand years, this Man Yakub was born and his civilization was to rule us for six thousand years until the year fifteen thousand of Our Calendar…That year six thousand, the wise theologians of the white man, they know all what I'm talking about. They know their Time is out. It went out in 1914. "Then why are we not ruling?" Because, you are yet still sleep; and this my work, to wake you up completely and make you command your way now; and that you will lay hold to the Rule, and Rule the people of the Earth, Blackman of the Earth.

I'm sorry Black Brother that's from abroad. We are raised up to Rule the next world which is only Black. That a Class of Rulers must be prepared to Rule that people. We are the Ones!

The times that you hear us say, "Accept your own," this includes that you accept the Rule. That's what you are, once upon a Time, before the making of the white man; the devil of the Earth. And, that you are suppose to run for it now; not to say be taught to run for it, because, there is no man in the Sun that can condemn what Elijah teaches. Nope, you, you may feel that you can do it, but that's just your feel!

When I get through with you, you can rule with what I teach you, and get respect and honor throughout the world of Man. If you leave America, go in any parts of the Earth among any people- you tell them that you a follower of mine, they will respect you immediately.

It was six thousand years ago this Man, the God of the white man, saw His way in making this people by playing with those two pieces of steel. That one is attracting the other one; and he's still playing with steel, right? This is the base of his knowledge to rule. It was to turn steel into weapons, and use the weapons that he turned and made out of steel to kill you and me. This is just what he's doing.

We did not make a great navy to put on the high Seas. We don't need them, as long as we have Power over the water that the other one is on. We, the Nation of Islam, Our Scientists, Our Gods, they don't need a navy. They're capable of sinking yours that you have made without a navy.

Did not you read in the Bible where that the Bible teaches you that one Angel they saw, he was on the Sea and he caused the Sea to become a corrupted power for anyone to use. He turned it all into poison by dropping something out of the Heavens. The Bible teaches he dropped a Star in the water from Heaven, and made it unfit for the people to stay on the water. It says, "When they dropped that Star, all the people that was in the sea died."

YOU ARE THE SONS AND DAUGHTERS OF GODS OF YOUR KIND!

I want you to know that this is not white people that will drop that Star; they Black people. You are the Sons and Daughters of Gods, of your kind which Rules the Whole Earth. They can take the Earth and move it off from its regular rotation and turn it backward if they want; and you won't ever know the difference.

To prove it, whatever goes on in the way of terrific explosions in China or in Vietnam, you don't feel it here do you? No, it's because the Earth is so large that you could cut away half of it on the other side, and you'd never feel it.

The Earth is eight thousand miles, eight thousand miles approximately through in diameter. So, since she's so near to that figure, most Scientists just say eight thousand miles. She so near to being twenty thousand miles in circumference, so the Scientists say twenty five miles approximately in circumference. Okay, let me get back over here and give this man a little more work.

If now that a God was made nine thousand years of our Calendar History; and from that nine years they count their Time; He was a made man according to the very Nature of us. We can produce a man in nine months. So, he's not away from us yet. If we can find one thing that he has done without Us, We wishes to show it by taking and combing the History, and piecing it and looking for any wisdom that he had of himself that We didn't give him…in the slang, big shots.

That this Holy Qur'an here asks the white race to produced what he has created; that which We didn't give him, and he can't do it. All that you have, We give it to you. The white man have nothing that he created. He fashions something after our Creation. We Created everything that he got the piece from to make what he wants to make.

The iron, the steel was already here in the Earth, and he made his rule or kingdom from that which he found in the Earth. That which he found in the Earth was Ours. That is why you find in the Bible here in Isaiah, he cracks down on him to prove to him that He is God, and that he has nothing to fight God with. He tells him that, "I Created the fire that you blow. I Created the gold. I Created the instrument that you made for a weapon. I Created the iron and steel." Show me Mr. devil man, what do you have to fight me with? I have Power over My Creation. Do you have power over your creation? No! Because your creation is from Mine.

Nine thousand years ago, remember this, that an enemy was produced to cause all of this trouble that has been coming to the Blackman for the last six thousand years, whom we call white man instead of just saying devil. That's his real name devil. You go by his color, because that you didn't know who was under the color.

When Yakub was making him, he taken the brown germ away from the Blackman. And he taken that brown germ which was weaker than the Black germ and looked into the possibility of making a weak rule the stronger. This is not out of the order of Science Brother, don't, don't think, don't even attack the man that say these things, because you may fail to win.

This weak germ in us the Blackman, give a color that was brown. So Yakub said, "I will take the brown germ away from the Black one, and make a man of the brown germ and then teach him my Wisdom." He say, "Give him my Wisdom, my Knowledge, and he can rule the Blackman from whom I taken him from until the Blackman produces a man that is Wiser than I. Then, He will take Me and My made-man away off the scene, to never rise anymore."

He told his people, the white people, "When you live on this Earth six thousand years, then you don't try to rule on the seventh because the seventh thousand year your Brother coming from the East and is going to eat you up." This the white man or devil knows.

This is why he goes over in the East and stocks his artillery over there to try to keep the Man from coming out. He starts working on him before he leaves. But, they know that he is going to do that. As this Holy Qur'an teach you, "We made you and We know what your mind suggests."

Whenever he thinks up anything, this already has been known and he can't pull off nothing on Us like a surprise. He got no surprise to make on Us. Listen at him while he's thinking of it. Think over that Brother.

This is what Jesus was equipped with, the "Knowledge of Thought." That's why he could always get out of the way of his enemy before they get there. He has already tuned up on them. And, when he know they coming from this way, he'd go that way, and they couldn't over take him because they, their ears was not equipped with the instrument of thoughts of other people. So, he could always evade them.

So my dear beloved Brothers and Sisters, this man Yakub, He was not that type of Man either. He could not tune up on the people and tell them what they thinking about. But, this One that I preach you of, He tune up on you and tell you what you thinking about. And, then if He want to stop you from making any progress with that thought, or make you make progress, it depends on how it affect others and yourself.

I would or not saying this making no prophesy of it for you to carry out, but I do believe that within about, well I would say in about twenty or thirty years, you will be

able to do just that same thing. The cleaner you keep yourself and your heart, the more easily you can hear. If you keep your heart clean with God, you could go over there across the street; you could go over there in Oklahoma; you could go in California; you could listen at what I'm saying without the aid of anything like this.

The devil dumbed us, and now Allah intends to unstop our ears so we can hear spiritually as David teach you in his Psalms, "He have unstopped my ears that I may hear. He has cut a loose my stammering that I may speak plainly." That's there in your Bible.

This coming true right along now, at this Time. You don't have to live in that Time, it's now. I will tell you as God have Taught me, how this is done. It comes to your ears just like the bell in your telephone. It start ringing in your ears. But now you can't pick up who's on the line. But, you do have that ear ringing. Well that's me or somebody trying to get in touch with you.

I'm not trying to make you think that I'm no great Scientist that I can pick up and tune in on you at will, No, No, No! God didn't raise me up to do that. I go so far as He let me go. Regardless to the nature; the organs of nature is there to use for such purpose. But, I can say to you about David, he says in his Psalms, He, God had opened his ear that He may hear Him. You have it there in your Psalms. And I think maybe God will bless me with the same someday when He Pleases because I don't think David was anything better than I.

So, now we move on a little further into Yacub. Let's. As a God, He was the God of this people and he made gods out of them. As the Jesus teach you or tell you that they are the god of this world; they are. Anything they want, they don't get on their knees to pray for it, they make it. They make it for you and me. Anything that the civilization needs, he produces it. This is what you call god-like power. He is god of this world. He can produce for the people their desire and material.

You remember when you was a little boy, fifty and seventy-five year old Brothers, that you didn't see all of the scientific achievement for the advance of the civilization as you see now, right? Indeed I'm right, because I was back along there myself and I didn't see it. All praise is due to Allah!

I was so dead to you. I am honored to be living today, by God. So many of my Brothers have fallen since I was born, and I can't find them. Don't be shame to tell people that you a hundred and fifty years old, if you are that, because God have blessed you.

What if you would live as long as Moses? What if you would live as long as Methuselah? He lived nearly a thousand years. Now, what are you talking about being under a hundred years? You're nothing but a baby! I know some of you may think that you should tell me that "you're too old". I want you young Brother to come up and tell me whether you can master the mission that I am giving to you from Allah. And, I suppose if you had lived in the days of Moses and the other long-life Prophets, you would have killed them to get them out of the way, by what you was thinking, they're too old.

The Bible teach at the age of a hundred and twenty years, Moses he walked upright. He didn't walk stooped. And that when he died, he was like that, and these others. So, Brother, I think you need to study history. You think I'm too old and you're yet not able to take my place. You would leave the world in a bad condition, because you wouldn't be able to carry on.

So, kind of stick around until God take me away, because I will go away. Don't think I'm here forever. Of course, there is no death mentioned in the life of Elijah in the Bible. He comes up from the Kings and runs out here in the New Testament in the Revelation. So he comes all the way through the Bible; and if he died, we don't know where he died at.

I'm not saying now that I will live no great long time. I don't know how long Allah will let me live. He may not let me live another year far as that's concerned. I don't know, but while I'm here, I must work, and do that work which He brought me up from among you to do, for you. It's a powerful job, as He told me out of His own mouth, He said, "Brother, you have the worst job of any man ever lived." So, when you start contending with me, you're making the burden heavy, because you can't win; and you're wasting my time and yours too.

This man being six years old when that He started his works. Now, if he was six years old, He was on Time, because He was going to make a people to live six thousand years old, six thousand years. And, He did do just that as we see them and they call their number six. And, in the Bible, they say their number is equal with the man. Well that's right, because we was also our self Created on the number six, but it was not just a little six years.

Ours went into billions and trillions, while their stop here in just a few years carrying twelve months, three hundred sixty-five and one fourth days. This is his type or his kind of years that he has lived this six thousand. There is no more for him regardless to your love for him to continue to stay here and let you enjoy his civilization. That don't make any difference, his Time is up.

And, you should be happy that his Time is up, as much hell as he gives you in this Time. He didn't give us nothing but hell. Now, why should we want him to live? It's because we are so lazy, we don't want to go for self; and we rather, that's right, we'll rather be a slave to a smart man, than be a smart man our self.

So, remember that Brothers. I may not please you so well in speaking about the white man, because you love his way of life. That's why you don't like to hear me say too much against him. But I'm at the Time when it is your Time and my Time, that I don't need to worship him. They just staying around giving you hell while they are here; and as long as you don't remove him.

It is our people to remove them, but they can't remove them as long as you are here worshipping. They got to put a stop to your worship. So, the thing they going to do is break his power on land, sea, and air. This is what they are fixing to do now. Believe it or let it alone. And then, if you want to go long with them, they give you a fair chance. On every other corner of the street here, the Messengers of God separating the people for Final Destruction.

He'll ask you, "What side are you on?" If you tell him that, "I'm on America's side," then another one will tell you where to stand, where to take your stand. So, that they will not...They come to another, "What side are you on?" "I'm on Allah's side, the Black people, the Muslims." "Okay come go with me." This is the way it will be done and it won't be long, and you will tell me, "You certainly taught us the Truth."

This is what the Bible calls the "Great Separation," putting the sheep to one side and the goats to another, that's people. The goats represent the white man and those who follow him. The sheep represent you that believe in the Truth, and believe that you was born of the Truth; and that you belong to Allah by Nature. Then you will easily take your place.

Be aware, that these Days and Times and the words that is dropping into your ears is nothing for you to ignore. Do you ignore your own life? It is not twenty years to come. It is not the lifetime, unless you get killed accidentally. It's right at your door now.

I'm satisfied to teach you the Truth of this; how it began and how it will end. This is what I'm doing now, teaching you the beginning of this world, and how this world will end. I have everything of that knowledge in my head from God Himself. You may say, "When will this be?" I'm not to tell you the Day, if I knew it. But, God didn't tell me to do so; nor anyone else, until that Day come.

THE WHITE MAN'S TIME IS UP!

There is no man knows that Day, that hour. Some of them think they know the year or something. I have read them, that knowledge they have; and what they calculate from. I don't say that they are millions of years away from it, according to what I have been Taught, but he's not going to tell you. The wise one, if he knows that, he won't tell you; and nor will I tell you that closeness that God give to me of it.

But, I say to you, the Time that you live in, we'll soon know no more. It won't go out this calendar history that we're in now, which reach up according to the equalization of Muhammad Calendar, the Arab Calendar I mean. It won't go ten more years, because they just don't lie. When they told you anything, why it's, it's just that. What you read in the Holy Qur'an, it's just that; you don't read no "guess and lie Book." It tells you the Truth. And, according to the Holy Qur'an, we are not very far from the Gabriel sounding his trumpet.

We're at the end of the white man's world. This is it's beginning of that end that I talked on. Showing you up to this Time, that it is Time, from the Time that he begin. If he was to live according to our Calendar History and the Scientists, which is right, six thousand years from nine thousand years of the Arab or Islamic Calendar History, his Time is up; and a long ways up. God give him an extension of Time around sixty or more years, due to us. If he had been destroyed right on the date of his Time, he would have, or rather his Time would have destroyed us, because we wasn't ready; and you are not yet ready. This is why I'm hastening on to you this Truth, that you didn't know I know what's fixing to happen. Allah has told me and I can read it to you or send it to your address.

The Time is now, and according to the very pre-fixed word of the Time by God and His Prophets, we're overdue; they're over due. They know that, but, as I just said, it was due to us being blind, deaf, and dumb to the knowledge of ourselves, and all wrapped up in the belief of white people and their way of life. You love their way of life, because they made you to love it by not teaching you the way of your life.

We are Real Righteous People, but we don't know it since the devil robbed us of it. The more you practice the faith of Islam, the more you want to practice it. And, the reason that we teach you is because that you are Muslim yourself; you wasn't made one, or we are not making you one now. We are making you to act on the Principles of what by Nature you are.

You was not what you are practicing now, you never was that. The devil got you doing that; and that's the way of his life. And, you have not, within a hundred years up from slavery been able to practice his life as perfect as he does, because by nature he's that; by Nature, you are not.

When you get back to yourself, into Righteousness, you will love it. You was not to do the white man's wickedness. And, that makes you then, for the First Time love yourself. You must learn to love yourself.

It is true that these names that you hear us going in, is not names that you should be laughing at; making mock of them. You should make mock and laugh at the names that you go in of the devil. He don't have no name, as the Bible teaches you. He don't have no worthwhile name; and his name will be destroyed from the face of the Earth.

Brothers and Sisters, I know it was something or other; every day I tries to eat long when this hour comes in; and so, the bell of that time is ringing.

We must learn to create, make a New World, over the old world of Satan. We must do this. We must have our own. Our own must come to us. We must seek our own, as even the Indians out in Oklahoma is trying to seek Oklahoma for their first state. They want their own.

Here you and I, millions of us, while there's only a few of the Indians. But, millions of us don't know how God's Wisdom, and the Tact of Wisdom to get our own. You don't need guns; guns you don't need.

You see the Muslims and myself walking and riding around through this civilization without arms. We handle sometimes ten thousand people at a gathering. Strip them of their arms, and let them go into our place, our meeting. And, you never come around saying that we had to go kill some of the Muslims, because they was being other than them self; and, they had killed some people. We don't carry weapons. We don't need weapons if we have God on our side.

What do we need with weapons? If He Created the Heavens and the Earth and the iron and steel that you're using for weapons, don't He have Power over it? Certainly He has Power over it. So, this is why we pay no attention to his weapons building and arms building, which he going to try to stop himself from doing.

He see we an example of people who believe in love and unity of Civilized Man, instead of forcing them by force of arms to do so, because that don't last no longer than the arms is capable of empowering us through the force of it.

So, He came without arms, and I don't carry weapons myself. And, I go everywhere He asks me to come for a big crowd with no weapons whatsoever but His.

So, He puts His Own Power around me, and under me, and over me, and I come to you and I speak out boldly.

The first thought comes into you when you have a weapon is killing a nigger, or a Blackman, because that's what was in him. He made the weapons; and his desire that the weapons help him to kill you, and his own kind. So, let's don't carry weapons for our God; but the Truth. And, the Power of the Truth will protect us, because it is, pardon me, it's Author is God.

Brothers and Sisters, I think I'm just about said enough; and I think you have gotten to the birth of your worst enemy ever was on the Earth, that's Yakub. Yakub the name don't mean an enemy to us, but the Man that had that name, He made an enemy for us. But, you can be called Yakub and I can be called Yakub, but that don't mean that we are devils, or no friend to the make of that Father of the devil, Yakub.

So, Brothers and Sisters, I say to you, I think you're getting hungry maybe like myself; and I don't want to over tax you here, because I will be back next Sunday.

There is many Muslims in here, who use to hear what I'm teaching you on. Use to hear it six hours sometimes a little less. But, I was not taking it up with them at that time, piecing it apart, showing you the in and out of it, like I am today. So, that is why I take about two hours each time to pull you up gradually, so when you get up on top, you will know how far you came to reach the top. And that you could master your seat up there on top. See, God said to me, teach you, He will set you in Heaven. He didn't say run you in Heaven. He will set you in Heaven.

This is similar to what Yakub taught his people. This mean that you will not be no slave to nobody; not white nor Black. That's just it, set you in Heaven with plenty money. There's plenty of money here, and plenty money all over the Earth. He took it out of the pockets of nations and blessed you and me with it.

So, I'm going to say to you that if there's any one of you that have a question that you want to ask me, you may ask. Anyone? There is no questions, then we're going to dismiss....

Messenger: Wa Alaikum Salaam Brother...Yes Sir...

Brother: Was Sarah a white woman?

Messenger: Really Brother, I don't know whether she is white or black, but I believe Abraham had a very great love for Black. And, maybe he had a Black wife. If Sarah was white or Black, her husband was a great Prophet; and the Time that we are now in was revealed to him. His prophecy, mostly, was on the base of us, and our return to our own.

I don't say that she was white and I don't say she was Black, because the Arabs, for a long time, that has been ruling they was white. After the taking away of the History of us, that was in Abraham, which is true, that we are following and fulfilling that which was prophesied by him.

Whether Sarah was white or Black, it have never been much of a concern to me, because I wasn't following up Sarah for no particular prophetic sayings in order to bring out some Truth. Only, our woman here who are sitting under the guidance into Righteousness. We use Sarah as a very good woman that they could take pattern after. This is only reason we bring her history.

Brother: Question Unheard

Messenger: You follow it, believe it, practice it, and if by believing the Truth and practicing the Truth cause your life to be taken from you, then you were willing to die for that which you believe in. If we believed in Christianity and the white man as a leader for us, we go wherever he tell us to go to offer our lives for him and what he teaches. Ok, now, your own has come to you; now if you do just what you say that you intend to do…

Yes…pardon me sir, pardon me…Yes sir, I never could have striped these men of that which they was in when they come to me, unless it had not been for God's Power working with me in the way of teaching that I teach them. They would of have still remained in that which they was in.

So, this is the proof. So, I thank you Brother for coming up, giving that respect and honor to what I am teaching. And I pray to Allah that one day that you will see alright, and that you will be with the others in the faith, or in the nature of which we were Created. That is Islam. That is not…Wa Alaikum Salaam…Islam is not a religion.

We call it a religion, but it's not a religion because it is the Nature of Us. Therefore, the nature of us can't be called a religion. That's why the 30 and 30 of the Holy Qur'an teaches you that, Islam is not in the words, is not a religion, but it's in the Nature in which we were born.

If you go to higher Masonry, they'll ask you where were you made a Mason? You'd better not tell them you were made one. You've got to tell them that you have always been that. You are…You…go back with you before the fellow that disagrees of that particular order; and he's not going to disagree with me.

And so, you can go home now and study over what has been said here to you; and if you see good in it, then bring me back five people each one of you next Sunday. But, remember when you goes out of here, that you do no more to no one than you would have done unto yourself. Treat everybody right if you are Righteous. Don't go out mistreating people just because you are righteous; enemy that does that.

But, you go out treating the people right. And remember that Black People all over the Earth is your Brothers and Sisters. Whether you like them or no, that's alright, they're your people. And don't run to Africa claiming you the Brother with the African there, before you recognize Brotherhood here.

Be sure you're the Brother of your Brother here. See they not looking for no such faith, they are looking for Unity. And, that you carry out what I teach you, they will love you; they will fight for you, as they are talking now to do anything for you that is following me. They wants to do that for the whole of American Black. And, that's what I'm trying to get you in order, so that they will do just that.

And now I thank you, and I have enjoyed this very happy, lovely afternoon with you. And, I pray Allah that I will be with you next Sunday afternoon. And, to continue this world's history with you- the secret part of that you never knew. This is what I'm trying do to give to you, that which they never taught you, which is the Truth of themselves and you too.

But, I don't want you to go out of here socking them in the eyes and mouth just because you have learned that you are the Greater person of the Earth. Don't do that. Go out and show the world that you are the Greatest, Righteous, and Justified person is on the Earth. That will kill Yacub's civilization just by you doing right.

I thank you, and I will turn you back into the hands of our Assistant Minister to dismiss you. As I say unto you in the name of Allah, As -Salaam Alaikum.

THE EARTH BELONGS TO THE LORD

As-Salaam Alaikum, In the name of Allah the Most Merciful, all Holy Praises is Due to Allah the Lord of the Worlds, the Most Merciful. You may be seated.

Well, I'm kind of, sort of, like letting you look at me. Kind of, sort of like an old story the Saviour told me about when the trains first started running in Egypt. When it came through everybody was out looking for the train, to see the train come through. And, after it passed, one of the Muslims say, "Oh, it's a good thing it stayed on that track." He say, "if it had come sideways, it a wiped us all off the Earth." [The Messenger and the Audience laughs]

Thanks be to Allah. I'm glad to see your smiling faces here again. But, I'm so sorry that you are only just a little family out of the Southside of Chicago, and out of the cities outside of Chicago. I don't understand why that you don't want to get yourself saved before ever that you be caught up in the net of the devil.

This is the end of the devils. They're only going to kill him off of the face of the Earth, to keep him from ever filling up the Earth again. This is actually the Earth of the Blackman and not of the white man. He said that he have a place wherever you have one. He talks as though he have as much rights as you. But, the Bible teaches you and me that the Earth belongs to the Lord, but, it never explained a hundred percent who the Lord is. We are the Lords. And, since we are the Lords, which mean Masters, we let them use our Earth, control the people on it and what they worship, evil.

The Time has been up every since 1914. This shows how Merciful God is. He won't kill you, even when the Day comes. He give you a little more extension of Time. Well, I don't have much time to talk on those old Scriptures of the Bible, because I think you know them. You have read them, and you can continue to read them as long as you understand them. But, the Bible is a kind of a Book, that if you don't understand what you read, you are headed directly to the fisher's net.

You will find the fisher's net don't mean that one out there in Lake Michigan. It mean that the fisher is the devil, and the net is his tricknology. When he get you tricked in his net, then away to the Lake of Fire your going.

We want to tell you what is Islam. This is what you came for. To know what is Islam. You have never known what is Christianity, though you glorify that that's your religion, and that's Jesus Christ's religion. Jesus Christ never taught no Christianity and you can't prove it to me.

The "Christ," on the front end there means the Crusher. The plural part of it means that which the people believe in. But, actually, you are in a religion, probably believing in a religion which is not yours. And it means, a Crusher coming at the end of their Time, to crush the people who believe in that kind of religion, because Christ it definitely means a Crusher. So, today we have a lot of work to do, a lot of work. And the Brothers have beautified my board.

As I said, again and again I will say, the Earth belongs to the Blackman. The white man's history is in the Bible, but it is cloaked over with symbolic language and teaching, and therefore you cannot understand it. The beginning of the white man was the beginning of a murderer. And the Bible teach you that. Cain slew Abel. Two brothers, and the two brothers been killing each other every since they been on the planet, right?

Every few minutes somebody is killed, and if you take the war with its death of people, maybe you'll find it much shorter, much shorter then few minutes. Every minute, almost, someone is slaughtered by the devil, or by his tricknology rule that is set up.

He was given authorities, knowledge, wisdom to rule all life on the Earth, in the sea and in the air, for six thousand years. As the Jesus said, and I agree with it, "He is the god of this world." But, it is only limit to the Time he is to rule. And the Time have arrived and passed by. Giving him a chance, if he wanted to repent for those beings he have deceived…

So, you were reared and I by the devil in his Hell. So, since we was reared by the devil, it takes an awful Powerful Teacher to get you out Hell. He claims that his number is the same as ours. It's got to be the same as ours since We made him. He didn't make himself; We made him.

The Holy Qur'an teaches us that God of Islam, called Allah, which is His Most Proper Name, because Allah covers it all. But, He being the Supreme One, they distinguish Him by calling Him the Mahdi; a Independent God; He's Self Sufficient.

I want you to know this God, that the Holy Qur'an teaches us, coming at the Last Day, in the 22nd Surah of the Qur'an, with the name "Mahdi," it means He's Self-independent. Well, I'm not in such hurry. I want to look at you and you want to look at me. We must strive hard to set up self.

Satan, the devil, is not going to take you and set you down in his seat, and he get up and walk away from it. You've got to take him out of his seat. They don't tell you, but they know it. That they were made, not created; when they was made,-m-a-d-e, made. And, the Bible teaches you they was made. "Let Us Make Man."

But, in the Holy Qur'an and Bible, the 'make' was condemned by the Black Scientist in those days. In the Qur'an, it's got it very good there. He questioned the Scientist; questioned the Maker of the white man, in these words, " What will you make other than something to cause or rather to make mischief and cause bloodshed?" This he has done and still doing.

In the Bible, the first from Adam, killed one of them before he was able to exercise any rule; Jealous. And, did you know that comes all down through us today? If we would not
envy and be jealous of each other's progress, we would have been a long ways from where we are.

Yea, Satan boasted that he have the number of a man. He's referring to Us. He do have our number, because, as I repeat, We made him and not he made himself. He can't make a man. He been working on us every since he had the privilege; but he just keep coloring them up. And, that's working with another man's material. So, I guess I'd better work with another man's material too.

You see this word, Armageddon. And your question is: "Which will survive the war of Armageddon?" " What is Armageddon?" Now, you have been listening to this all your life, that the Armageddon war will be fought at the Judgment. Let's look and see what the first three letters pronounce, "Arm," A-r-m. "A-r-m-a-near-doom-geddon," Armies that has been trying to get to each other for ages, working towards the doom of each other.

It is this fellow with this man here hanging on that tree. There is no shadow of a doubt what you have read how Christians, under this flag, especially, these certainly under this flag, that they have murdered and hanged our Brothers on the tree; this is good. I want you to remember that the good is you see how you has been mistreated.

Now, if the people have treated you with such evils, and they're still doing it, what right you have to defend them, to live that same life under their flag? I'm only asking you for
Truth. So many of us are so lazy, we don't want to leave the white man, because we want him to take care of us.

I say my Brothers, if you are that lazy, who do you think wants you? No one likes a lazy fellow who wants someone else to take care of him. They don't like it. And, it's getting more apparent today that every eye can see this in the working.

But, we want care from someone else, we can't get it a lot of time we put our gun in our pocket and go out and take it. The devil have seen us go round for many years without weapons. And, he see that we don't go around fighting each other carrying guns for each other. And, he comes here and finds that we searches everybody that come in for weapons, take it off them.

You gets along when you're unarmed. When you're armed, you're always strutting about what you got in your pocket. And, the worst part of it, you buy arms to kill each other. You don't buy arms to kill your enemy, who is the devil, but you buy them to kill yourselves. I'm saying to you, we have acted very crazy. Then the devil come in, kills both of you. He knows he's well protected. Not a one of us is going to fight back; this is terrible.

Which one will survive the War of Armageddon? This is Islam's flag over here to our right, and this is the Christian flag over here to our left. Now, you would not dare tell me that this flag will survive that flag. This flag was made, while this flag was created.

Oh, you love that old cross, but yet, they swung you up on a limb. You fight for that old cross, but, they tell you themselves, "Over yonder stands an old rugged cross...." Think over that. They made it up. Over yonder where? Over in Christianity from killing a man that was a Prophet. They killed him. "Over yonder stands an old rugged cross, a emblem of suffering and shame." He make you to worship that kind of suffering, and shame, and finally death. You put it on your coat lapel. You put it round your neck thinking that you on the way to Heaven, and on the way to Hell!

It make sense for you to worship that flag rather than this, because this is copied from that and decreased or destroyed the value of that. He have several stars here representing that one. He have the sky over here, and he will tell you follow it. Blue, which the blue can't represent something that is pure and something that is eternal. But, he tell you this blue here and the stars here, the blue represents True. How can blue color represent Truth, when it passes away. You can start upward and you will never get to this. You'll go through and pass on out. Keep going to other planets, but, you'll never find this.

A blue gas that we call Ether sent up from the Earth towards the Sun, and, they'll make a ceiling out of it, at a distance. But, you go and try to catch hold of it, you don't find it. So it is with falsehood you chase falsehood with Truth, it disappears and you just don't find it. Oh, Brothers that's alright, you getting restless. We won't hold you, we'll let you go.

If we take this flag and wrap it around our head, then that represents what? The high Mason. They take their flag, take this flag, put it on their coat lapel and on their head and walk out celebrate one day a year. Why don't he wear it every day? Because it don't belong to him. So therefore, Muhammad, when he permitted the devil to wear the flag of Islam on his head once a [year], he's got to be one that had been studying the Principals to act on the Principles for thirty-five, forty, or fifty years.

THE MEANING OF THE NUMBER SIX

You don't see young men in the devil's high Masonry, or Masonic. They all is elder men, because he's not suppose to come out with this on his head, that red fez until he's so old, and so old in the study of it.

Now, let us take a turn of this board. Last Sunday. I think we left saying something about the devil and his made world. If we have here "Six," which he claims is equal to our "Six," he's right. We have a "Six" over here is ours. This is what we was made on. He says the number "Six" is his too. That is True, because We made him and he had to go under our number. He had no other numbers to go under. This is why he don't attack or dispute with me. He know I will tell him that.

This is the Original Man's "Six!" How did the Original Man himself become being a "Six" instead of being a "One?" Since you the First, then your number should be "One." But, since you are not saying in numbers that your or his number or his number is one, he uses a "Six."

Now, I'm going to tell you where that "Six" came from in him. It was six trillion years, so God Taught me, before He put into use the Sun. But, after the Sun, then other Gods were born and they thought up the same idea; make something out of fire. Never have you known what and how fire came into Space. And, that Stars of fire and a big Star, We call Sun, nothing but a ball of fire. I want you to remember these things, so that you don't make a mistake.

If the God Created Himself out of matter in which still existed here, then He taken it out of the Darkness of the Space. How then can We declare that the fiery Stars, along with our Sun, were Created out of Space? Where did the fire come from? So today, everything is full of fire. I'm full of fire; you're full of fire.

This is our figure here. No, I'm not gone tell you today, but you keep on coming back, I will tell you. But, if I tell you everything, you'll forget most all of it. Then you will start adding in your god-Science; and I won't remember what I said after you get through with it. For this is our number "Six" from that which We begin to make to revolve as We was, as He was, pardon me. He made Himself to revolve, and then He caused whatever come in the Darkness; it will revolve like Himself; and that He's done.

We can't help from revolving. We are not a perfect human being, because, actually, our form is not perfect. So, since this is our number here, what were We before that number? It was like this: We left out of Nothing and We made ourselves "One" over there. I'm taking my time; don't worry.

Now, if We made Our self in the beginning "One." Okay, here comes this Nothing again, and it goes over here a piece, and here stands "One" over at this end. Well now, if we say, I think if you had four hundred years to wait, I think you still have a little time to get this.

If we were in America for four hundred years before ever the coming of Allah to us. If from Nothing here now this "One" comes back and gets behind nothing, that makes that nothing there increase its power ten-fold, right? And, with four hundred years nothing. Well that's right. You were just everything what the white man made you of, or taught you of.

These four hundred years now have received again is nothing here "Zero," "One" behind it, and that "One" is Almighty God, Allah. And then it made us ten-fold the Power and value that we were before He come, right? This is cause Power from this "One" is generated into nothing, and made nothing become Something.

If I had moved this over here in front of that nothing, it still will keep this as a fraction of nothing to build. But, it didn't do that. The "One" came not, here in front, it got behind us, backed us up to make us to be recognized from the Power of "One" generated into the "Zero," right?

Anything that I say that you think that you don't understand, when I'm through working on this board, ask me. I'm not the Teacher that teaches something I don't know. That we are really catching up to get going with the God of this world.

Then we say the Time of the making of this world was nine thousand year of our Calendar History. Back into the year nine thousand of our Calendar History, we has been, for many millions of years using a God Wisdom for only twenty-five thousand years. One Man's Wisdom Rules for twenty-five thousand years, after that, We take Him down, put up another One to Rule for twenty-five thousand years. And, this is in accord with the circumference of our planet.

Our planet Earth is approximately twenty-five thousand miles in circumference. Not quite, but it's like just a little being twenty-five thousand, and We use the word twenty-five thousand. Why do We not have it twenty-five thousand? Because, up here at the top of our planet's rotation, We call it the Axis of the Earth. We have here working at the end of the Axis of the Earth, twenty-three and one half degree here to the Circle of the Earth at the Axis point. We have twenty-three and one half degree here.

Now, We have also twenty-three Gods, here, and Justify History once every twenty-five thousand years. They equal the pole degree here, either end, they both measure the same twenty-three and a half degree. I think it is twenty-three and a half or

twenty-three and a third, twenty-three and a half. And that, it's equal, almost, with the Gods that Rule. They are really twenty-four. But, this number is used whenever They make up History. Twenty-three Gods work, and One does the calculating on what They find.

As Salaam Alaikum. Can you hear me? My mic [microphone] fell off my neck just while ago, and Brother had to put it back on so you can here out there, or up close, it don't make a difference I'll make you hear…I have some voice. You just not hearing me. I use to speak sometime to near as many as you with only my voice, and they all heard. Yea it don't take all the whole sky full of clouds to thunder.

We have the god of this world taught for us by the God of our world. He said in the year of our Calendar Time, that year was the year "One." And, in the year "One" of our Calendar Time of twenty-five thousand years before that We make another or allow another God to Rule, so God Taught me, that in the year "One" the Scientists said in that year, that in the year nine thousand, in the year nine thousand, this is year "One," there will be born in that year a man, his name will be Yacub. (I don't want to get tangled up in this wire.) His name will be Yacub. And, in that year He will make a people who will live for six thousand years.

This nine thousand year is the beginning of the birth of the man you call white folks. They were made by this man, not created now, they were made by a man called Yakub. In the Bible you call him Jacob. That's the same man. Jacob, he made there the Bible say he had twelve sons. Actually, Jacob could not produce the twelve Scientists. The twelve Scientists were already here.

Yakub did not come out making Scientist. He was not that wise, but though He was a wise man. He was a wise God. They called him the big head Yakub- meaning He had a lots of brain.

For in this year of nine thousand, this Man comes out with a new civilization to take over us. He did not make no mistake; he took over us, and it's hard for us to get away from them today.

The Bible is right, "Have dominion," He says to Adam, "over all creatures, all life." And he have had power over all the life, regardless to what kind of life it is. He have had power over it, and to use it as he pleases. Even to the Original Man; the God, the Original Creator.

We, the Original Creator just was allowed to keep just a little, just a spark, to keep from going out of the Time. The Holy City Mecca had this little spark in it. This

Holy City Mecca of Arabia, the Original Scientist didn't rule there; nor does they rule there today; but they gradually easing in. These are white Scientists that is ruling there. This is why Muhammad must destroy the old. You'll find in the History of Muhammad, he declared war on Mecca, and he overcome it.

So today, I'm telling you that we are not going to fight to become the Ruler under the same thing that the old world have ruled under. We're going to make our own Holy City. You'll read in the Bible where it says that, "I saw a New Jerusalem coming down from out of the throne of God," the New God. He have a New City. He don't let His New Wisdom and His New Kingdom be built upon old foundation.

So, this Man or God, Yakub, when He was six years old, He was sitting down playing with two pieces of steel, watching the reaction of these two pieces of steel attracting each other. He looked up at his uncle, He say, "Uncle, when I get to be an old man, I'm going to make a man who shall rule you."

Unalike in the steel was attraction, making the steel to come together from the unalike; the attraction, the magnetic power, drawing the two together. So, he saw His future right from steel reacting.

So today, for six thousand years, he has been playing with steel. And, he saw that that steel was a good piece metal to murder with. He fashioned all kinds of weapons out of steel. They're using it today. They're clashing in war with steel.

The first time they went to war with steel, it was with bow and arrow shooting arrows. They began from stone to that. They learned to put a little piece of steel on the end of the stone. So, today he learned to make a gun that could shoot steel into our bodies. He's been a murderer ever since he sat on the face of the Earth; let's not forget.

I think I have my figure setting on ought. I can preach if I wanted to, but, this is teaching, and I think you need teaching.

Now, if I add six thousand on to nine thousand, we come to the year fifteen thousand. This man's number is "Six," because he rules from nine thousand years to the year fifteen thousand. And, this is the fifteen thousand we're living in of our Calendar History. And that, no, don't forget now, I'm not talking about Christian's history, but here is Christian's Time. They've been here for six thousand years. And, we take their six thousand years that they've lived making trouble on our planet, brings us into the year fifteen thousand. So we are living in the fifteen thousand year. There's a many little things in the Bible, and in History and Science of Us, that I could take up with you, but I don't think it's necessary till I lay the base. Then, when I lay the base, I will come right back and answer your questions that you fail to pick up on in the base.

THE MEANING OF JACOB'S LADDER

Fifteen thousand years ago now, and a little fractions over, this Yakub made his people and put them on Time to rule for six thousand years. He says to his people, "After you have lived six thousand years," He says, "your brother coming in the seventh, will eat you up." This is well known by the Theologians of white people, among white people. They know all of this.

The fifteen rungs that you talk about that Jacob, you know, had a ladder that had fifteen, you know, rungs on it. And, he saw Angels coming up and down, ascending and descending. So, this bird over here knew all of that, that, in this Time they will take him off and his people. And, the people will be going to Heaven and coming down to Heaven. "Because of what, Muhammad?" It will be because, that those that are down on the first rung of the ladder will be freed to come up and meet the Angels of Heaven; and the Angels of Heaven will be coming down meeting those who have never come up the ladder. This is what that means.

The old saying that Jacob, the devil of our people who made a devil, he dreamed of seeing a ladder reaching from heaven to the earth; and that he saw Angels ascending and descending up and down. He saw the end of his civilization; and He saw the beginning of our Time. This beginning of our Time here-I'm not through with that; I'll take care of it next time-I'm not through with it, No, by a long way! I did not tell you how he got here. This man got his people here by killing the Black baby, and saving the brown, so that He could grafted the brown into its last color, which is white.

I will say to you right here, so that you will always know how the races become races. We had here, our figure out of Creation, but here, I want to say that the first race that was made from Black man, the first race, was brown. Don't look at my writing so much, because you have heard of my mind's doing. So don't look at that so well. When I got to schoolhouse, the bell was ringing to dismiss.

This race you call the Japanese people, that's the brown race. Okay, the next is a yellow race, right? I read this, right? Brown, yellow. Now, from yellow…this other race that you see here-let me get back out of the way of you, is white. This number "One" here, I shouldn't balled it up there so close to that what I was saying. The brown race was the first one come out from grafting

The First Man here is Black. Then, when He started grafting out of him to get to white, He was grafting for two, two hundred years. And, for two hundred years it taken him that length of Time to get the brown baby out of Black. Yakub found that brown germ in Us while studying at college. He discovered in the germ of the Blackman, that he had a brown germ in him.

He had two, we will say two babies, one brown one and one Black, or one Black and one brown. And He kept looking at that germ, brown; and He discovered that He could graft it out of the Blackman. And, He could take that brown germ, keep it to itself and keep grafting until He take that brown germ out, and replace it with a more different color. If He just keep taking the more lighter brown that come, keeps it to itself, and then kill off the brown. And, He did that for six hundred years.

He taken this brown baby, set it over here aside, and kept every brown baby that was produced over there with a lighter brown color to itself; and He killed off the other brown. And, He made this lighter brown kept going to itself, until it produced a lighter and lighter baby.

There was not but actually, two races, from the Real Blackman. When he got to the third, it was a white man. All through grafting this was done. And, every time he graft one it was weaker than the other. So the brown baby was weaker than his Father, Blackman. And, the brown baby was stronger than the yellow baby. And the yellow baby, who produced the white baby, was a little stronger than the white.

So, the more near like to the Father of the races, Blackman, this little yellow baby become kind of evil and wicked like the next brother, the white. This is the Chinese that I'm talking about. The Chinaman is near equal with white folks. He loves to fight. But he's braver than white because he back more closer to the Father, than the white; the Father of races, the Blackman.

And, these people goes and mix with many. And, by mixing with many, they produced many different colors. And, that makes many different races. So I want you my beloved, to remember that the white man didn't come from the same God that you came from.

My son think I have taught you enough. He saw me all his life teaching this stuff. And , he think now that I'm to old to go through all this stuff. But, I got to get back use to it for a while. So, I'm going to stop right here, and that I'm going to get you ready to go home before you sue me for over time. But, I do want you to remember (I'm scared I'm gone get trapped in that line…okay I'll go up here where I won't get trapped).

The reason that we don't, and can't be a equal man with the white man, because we don't know what he knows. But, God have now have mercy on us, and He has raised up out of nothing, something!

I don't count the white man's wisdom. God have made me like that. They even scorn his wisdom. And, when you get from Allah and from His servant what he's teaching, you will not think the white man knows anything.

So, I want you to read our paper because I'm going to write in it ...now on this same subject, because that we're not able to stay out here all the afternoon to listen. We get tired and bored, and our seat is not the, you know, the rocky-bye-sleeps, and we get tired of sitting on them. One of these days we gone have some real beautiful seats, comfortable like anything. And, then they'll be walking around you always telling you to wake up.

We need a lot, some money. If we would give to...one dollar a piece, we'll put it over. What if I give one dollar, and then another Brother give fifteen or twenty or a hundred; and then I have to skip a hundred to get another hundred or two. This makes it slow. If one million people in Chicago would just give one dollar a week, which he would never know he's given anything, he'll never miss it. We would be able to build the Southside up so beautiful for self, that the North side would move further North.

I'm going to say to you that I have enjoyed a very lovely afternoon, and I hope to return next Sunday. It takes a long time to get the Wisdom of six thousand years unfolded to you, so you can understand it. But, I do think that I can have you in about a month walking around and talking back to me.

This thing came about; He told Adam to give them their name. Make them known, their names. So, Adam named them. This work, all Divine work, mostly done by a servant of His. So, I want to say to you that I'm this humble servant; and I don't want to take over that which He has not given to me. But, let us prepare ourselves by coming out here learning the way of God. As the old Book say, "Come and learn of His way." So, I say, I'm here to make you known to His way. And, I don't think that no one will come up and tell you that "he's teaching you wrong." I am for you, and you're for me.

So, I'm going to turn you back into the hands of the Minister and the Secretary and Captain. And, I hope that they will not let you go out of the door, until they did like Jacob with the Angel. Jacob told the Angel he say, "I'm not going to let you go until you bless my soul." The Angel started having an excuse, he say, "It's day now." He say that's alright " I'm going to hold you, I'm going to hold you."

I heard a preacher in Macon, Georgia preach that once. My Brother next to me, who is now dead, he and I got so happy over the preacher's subject; and the way he preached it kept us laughing all the way through the meeting.

His name was Hennison, and Hennison took that text that Sunday night; and he was a tall big fellow, and his voice roared loud. He would say, "Jacob said I'm going to hold you, I'm going to hold you, I'm going to hold you." And, actually, he was holding us. He was not the dumbest preacher you ever heard. Yes, he was a very good preacher of that which he preached.

So, I'm going to say to you may the peace and blessings of Allah be with every one of you on your return home.

As-Salaam Alaikum

PART TWO:

THEOLOGY OF TIME

JULY 02, 1972 – JULY 30, 1972

ROBBED OF THE KNOWLEDGE OF SELF

As Salaam Alaikum!

I won't ask you how you feel. I'm afraid you may say to me, "how do you feel," and I'm afraid to tell you how I feel. You may be seated. You know I have to take my time. Thank you. You know Jesus, according to the Bible, he never did have many people. And, the Saviour told me that he never had over thirty at one time. So, all of those thousands of people that you read of that he was feeding and all lack of that, I didn't get that from our Saviour's mouth. So, I think it must be me. I am blessed with more people to listen to me than the devil himself.

You know, the devil always tries the people, but, if I keep on being increased by Allah, you'll see us in the soldiers field pretty soon. Thank you.

Well, we went visiting New York once here, not so long ago. And so, there we got into about the biggest area they would let us have at that time. But, however, we intend to visit New York again. So, we had like the Jesus, that little small Calvary Hill while we would have to send over to somewhere else to another hill.

Well it's near Fourth of July and people is getting off from work to have a big day; and I say it's alright with us to have that big day. They been having a big day. But, we would like to have is a little big day for ourselves.

Very beautiful when you look from here. Look like to me I heard one of my hard working Brothers, and if he's here, I should give him something to do because he would feel lonesome without doing anything. As the Lord said to Abraham, "take a look Abraham. You see whether or not you can count the sand down there on the seashores. Look up Abraham, and see if you can count the Stars above your head." He couldn't count either the number nor place. He say, "Abraham, that's the way thy seed shall be, you can't count." So, you know you were looking like I had to stand here a long time to try to count you; wonderful.

Oh yes I must say this, that my wife, I checked up with her before I left home, and she's doing much better. And the doctor got me her X-Rays, we went over them, not this morning, but last evening. And, according to the way the first looked to me, I think she's doing fine. So, we talked with each other this morning, and I know her voice was sounding good, and I told her that Allah, is a mighty fine God.

82

I'm not in no big hurry today, because you can't tell me, I know you not going to work much more. I know you going to be home soon sitting down. So, why not sit down here and let's talk today.

You know one thing that I think about every time I come out here, how we was laughed at holding meetings at some of the worse places in the city. And I don't care how much we would…our Brothers in the….Just think over that! They would look at us and laugh scornful at us as we deserve "what I look like helping you. Don't want to help you, or want to help this…that you are teaching."

So today, all of us suffered, all our Christians, whatever. Now we have the finest Temple, Church, whatever they want to call it, of any Black group in the country. There is no Black group have a finer Temple or Church as we have. These are the things of the devil. That's right, I said it right, I'm putting it on this board over here. All white people is devils. You may think some is good. Some is better than others, but that don't remove the very nature of them; he's still a devil.

There is no small snake that is very dangerous. There is no small snake that is not dangerous. That is not his fault. Nature just didn't make him that dangerous. But you can see in his little eyes, and his actions, that he wished he was a bad snake. Oh yes…that's right. I'm trying to teach you the knowledge of that snake. Don't you trust none of them, all is bad.

They robbed us of our wealth; rob us of our Freedom; rob us of our Justice. So, after all of that robbery look like should be enough. No, that isn't enough for him. He robbed you of the knowledge of yourself. Any man that is robbed or that a robber rob him of the knowledge of self, is the worse robbery that you could have.

Oh I'm going to take my time today, because I may not have nothing to do tomorrow. But, so if you get too tired, well, walk around and come back because I want to talk with you. I want to teach you that which you never dreamed that you would hear. And since you don't have so much work to do tomorrow, let's stay round and talk to each other a little while. From the looks of this place, we have near two thousand people in it. And I don't want them to go way; not empty handed, but if…

Where is that apron I told you to put around over there? You should have a skirt like over there, running cross in front of you.

What are you typing sister? You typing something or you taking down what I say? You taking down what I say? Well be careful now, won't I'll be saying something about you, and well, you take that down.

Know the Bible; this is not…Well, the Bible says that Delilah was a terrible tricky woman. She tricked Samson going and coming. And Samson was so foolish to let h trick him. She says to Samson, "Oh Samson, where lies your strength?" That was enough for Samson, Samson to not to be foolish. If she was so anxious to find out where his great strength lie at, he should of have been so greatly smart to never tell her, especially when she was not one of his people. Then he would try to see was not she putting one over, and found out she was. Then he went right back and let her trick him again...

This means a modern Samson and a modern Delilah. She's out there just looking at you winking her blue eyes at you, only for fire to wink you into hell. She don't love you today anymore than they loved you yesterday. Yet they want to get you to go to Hell with them. Believe it or not.

Well, I guess we better get back to the board again. Looking over my board wants some company so bad, it have move up here near me.

Somebody got to take down what I say and leave off saying, so I'll know what I said. I start playing it back on the tape recording machine before I left home, but still I didn't get everything in order.

We have, I think recited quite a bit of the front of this board; and I think you just about know what we have been teaching on this board here. You have been told the meanings of the American flag, her stripes, stars, and blue. Background under her stars, which you think represents the sky. Oh No! And the flag over to the right with her red background and her Star and Moon.

"What do that mean Muhammad?" They up over your head day and night, you should know what they mean. And, with that F.J.E. on it, I don't have no letters over here on the left of the American flag. But, we know what these stripes and stars represent. But, over here to my right, that's so beautiful over there.

Think about it, that if I would tell you I don't want that flag, I'll rather have this one, I would be making a fool of myself because you could easily tell me whether you like it or not, you're under it, and that you worship. There's no fool even as much about worship the Sun, Moon, and Stars. And, if he tone it down...

AMERICA'S PLAN TO DESTROY THE BLACKMAN

And he's telling other than the Truth, he do love that flag. He look for the Sun to rise every morning. And, if a night passes him by he can't see a Star nor Moon, he will go crazy. But, they can take and shoot up, tower up the stars and stripes representing America's life anytime, because he's going to live under that Stars, and that sign, and that Moon. No one can tell there that the Gods…that six trillion years from the beginning.

We have in time now, such figures as six, seven, eight, nine, and the zero counts for nothing until something is put there with it, to make it something. Add zero, look, we got six over here and we got a zero here. Now that zero counts for nothing, unless you put something beside that zero to make something out of it. Unless you mean that in all of your figuring here up to nine, there is nothing…to that unless you take one of these figures between nine and zero and put it beside zero. If you put a figure on either side, then you make something out of this, right? You can put it on this side and it counts for ten, and you put it on that side it counts for one tenth, right?

So, it's not very much, I'm not making fun. I'm only trying to bring you in reality. There's a, I'm not making fun of you. If I was a man to make mock of you, God would not have chose me.

So, we got here "One" besides nothing, and made this nothing become ten-fold. If we put it on this side, we still don't have much, right? It's a fraction on that side, and on this side it's a whole number. Okay.

So Allah came, and He came on this side. They was in here, nothing. So, He came and got behind us, understand? And, by His number One Self getting behind nothing, it made nothing ten-fold more valuable. And if we say that we are in this figure here, nine, we got in up to nine going forward, right? Not backing up, we got it forward. And, then if we reach up here and grab this old big old nothing, look what it made.

I know you know Mathematics, I'm only just trying to show you where we were. If our Father was made on the number "One," how did He get that big a "One" that had not been anymore on the Earth or in the Universe before His Creation? How did He became "One…?" We just on "One" to build up ourselves, so, that we may know who you are; how we got to be who we are. If Atom was one, could it have been "One?" We are taught that an Atom is one ten thousand of one, right? If it's one ten thousand of "One," certain parts of it, elements of it, then, how did our Father get up all those other parts to become "One" Father? I'm only driving at points. I'm not saying to you, that I'm trying to be no god over you, I'm just trying to be just what you need me…

But, if the Universe or the Darkness of the Space before life was Created in it, what was in that particular Space that could produce life? We, Scholars and Scientist, attack each other. That's what makes us know more. We attack each other; and then if you can't answer for what you are attack with, proof, okay then, something is wrong. We go back again, after you and ask you then, "What did we mean when we say Space?"

My subject is Theology Of Time. So many people think were fools because they don't believe in Islam. And that is due to them not having the knowledge of what Islam is. Islam is not only your religion and my religion, but Islam is, and should be respected as the religion of everybody because of what it mean. When you laugh at Islam, you're laughing at the Creation of the Wisdom of God. So, from this on, please do not laugh at God's Wisdom when you are trying to survive by it; don't do that!

He's ready to strike out of His Universe everyone that now don't like it. As long as Satan world ruled, he yet to pass up. As the Bible teach you that, "He winked at Israel once upon a Time." But now He call us Actual Facts now. We must give account of that that we know, and that we don't know. That we don't know, we got to give account of our actions against that.

Well Brothers, I told you I wasn't in a hurry. Now, if we see "One" emerge out of all of this Darkness, what Awesome Power in the Darkness brought it out? "One" could not have come out of Darkness, unless Force was in the Darkness to bring it out. In the Universe now, there is a Force in the Universe that move…unmovable Star. After so long and so long, the Star, which we saw here at this point, has moved over here to another point. And, if that Star moved over here to another point within ten, twenty, thirty, forty, or fifty or a hundred years or a thousand years, Force made it to move. It could not move alone.

So, this teaches us Brother, and you go back and get your Scientist and I will contend with him and he will contend with me. That's the Force of the actually Space seemingly looking as though it's Nothing, is moving to bring us objects that is hidden in it to our view. We don't wind up the Universe like that, and tell it to bring Jupiter over to us. No, Jupiter is moving by force that's already out there. And then, we don't say to a Star that is a hundred trillion years…to come out and show us itself. There already is Force out there that's going to bring it to our view. Yes, so we have these things in Space just by view.

Now Brothers, I don't want you to pass so many baskets around. The Brothers is getting broke. Fourth of July is coming up, and I want them to have some money next Sunday too.

This "One" here was already here in this Darkness. But, Nothing did not give it to Us, until the Time brought it about. Then, when the Time brought it about, it merged out here in our view…to a Revolving Life. Life revolved, that was hidden here in the Dark. We don't know how many trillion of years it was there, but, it was there.

Now, with a fine Atom of water out there…or made Itself out of an Atom of water that is found in the Darkness of the Universe. We could not realize emerging out of this Space without water, because we can't produce life without water. So, therefore, there was some water out there in that Darkened World, Space. And so now, this Space have produced Us Life, but how long was that Life out there before it produced Us a form?

To calculate on how long Life takes to make "One" Atom, this is way to understood. But, you and I being dead over here in North America for so many years; and North America been dead so many thousands; and this Space over North America so many thousands that we can't calculate the actually Time on by the instruments that we have now, that we can calculate Time from. Then we say, we estimating so long and so long.

Are you understanding? If you want to ask questions, I'm fixing it up so you can ask questions. But, remembering before asking questions, they must be intelligent questions, not foolish questions. We don't have that kind of time to waste.

If "One" emerge from this Darkness and put the Black Darkness moving with instruments that the Black Darkness can count Itself in the clear of calculating on Time, this is a Wise God. Don't play with Him.

So, just imagine that this Darkness here we are looking at it in Space and here "One" came out of Space. Out of that Black Darkness. How did He produce Himself to talk, walk…? What is Earth made out of?…Wait a minute Brothers, I don't want you to think I'm crazy. The Earth is a ball look like of finely ground stone, right? And it have great stone supporting that little fine stone. What did God mean other than His people, when He said, "Can you count the grains of sand on the seashores, Abraham?

Now, the number of His people could not be counted, but why did He point out this sand on the seashores? It was not just because that Abraham could not count the sand. But, Abraham must learn who identity lived round those sands. Somebody put them round there. They beautiful and someone made them. He could have asked Abraham that after Abraham had known the grains of sand down there. He could have ask him then, "Who made them like that?" But, Abraham was far off from being that type of Mathematics, Mathematician, pardon me, to be able to calculate on how many grains of sand that had been made down there on the seashores.

But, let us go back to what we got. Here we have, we're dealing with a bigger figure, which will lead us into unimaginable figures, "One," and a "Six." These two figures here is the outstanding figures that we have. One of them represent the God, that Created the Heavens and the Earth, and the other one represent the same.

The "Six," "how is that done now, Mister smarty," maybe you would say. He didn't start knowing till He growed into the Scientific knowledge of Six. And when He got into number "Six," He still had Us puzzled. We didn't know how to over take Him then, because this was sixty-six trillion years after this. And we can't hardly count in to six thousand years.

So now, we say we have six trillion years from the year One…You know my followers Brothers, when I say a thing, they go do this. They heard me talking about a skirt brought in front of the Sisters, so now they got it over there.

Now, you have this "One" and this "Six" here dealing with the beginning of Creation. And that, since we are working in the Judgment Time, we want to carry along much to get you into the knowledge of the Time.

We can draw this Mother Plane. You have forgotten how, the Mother Plane? Okay if you have forgotten I'm going to run you out of here when we're through. I will get back up here…

I want to…if you will have patience, not like Moses was by the man he went in search of knowledge with. So, the wise man told him he would not be able to go long with him. That he would not be able to do it. So, they went travel down over the junction of the Nile. And Moses could not go long with him on nothing without asking him "Why you do that?" Until finally, they got to the junction, and then he explained to Moses why he did that. And so, Moses learned from this guide that he was the best guide if he had just kept his mouth in trying to teach the guide, instead of the guide teaching him.

So, since that we are traveling on Yacub's history, we think it's good to take along a little something every now and then to show you the destruction of this history, this people. It's pretty sad that a father, after producing his son, then look at his son and tell him the end of him. Tell him the end of himself. It's pretty sad to do that.

Since America have invented many dangerous and destructive weapons to destroy the Original Blackman from the face of the Earth…God have already prepared a destructive weapon for him. This is something that you have read of, but you didn't know what it was. The Bible is a very good Book to study, if you understand. But, when you don't understand, Allah don't let you stay into the darkness of the Truth that is in it. He raise up a man in that people, and give him the knowledge of that which they don't have the knowledge of.

So you're lucky, this is the Man that love you so well, that He raised up one of you in myself to teach you that which have been prophesied by Prophets, the understanding. While you may be disgusted with him…

Pick up on your outer line. Make your outer line heavier Brother, it's too…your outer line. Then your large Earth picture there should be cut down into just about half. You got it up there even where your Great Earth should be. Make this half, just a small corner down there…yeah because you got it to close…

So we want to carry long a little something with…right in there. I know that this could have been move way out higher. You could erased my, my letter. See you could have erased my figure, being that we…but since that we didn't, so we don't have time now to wait. Yeah make your borderline, make your borderline Brother…get your borderline of the wheel a little larger so we can be through. I wished I could hold a steady hand…Brother. I can't draw a circle so good because I can't hold my hand that steady. We want you to know what's going on and will come on.

I'm far from being that man, that just want to teach something to be seen and heard. The work is too hard to show off with.

Take your opening over here to your left, and not over there…you should had that…over there on this side in this corner and very small, must be very small.

For forty years, Brothers and Sisters, I have been doing this; not above it brother, brother, brother, brother, brother, brother, you…drawing this Earth; come here Brother Minister. Don't bring that…out clear just have it in the corner…Brother, years ago I use to have him up to date with this.

So, since Moses went off, you know for awhile. No, No, No, No, No you got it wrong. down here Brother you come down here in the corner that's your Earth. I was with you when you wrote it. That's not the Earth, the Earth is in the corner. Yeah that's right…Yeah, to the Earth. You don't write Big Earth up here. Come out of that…cut the Earth out all together. No, your words there; yeah cut that word out.

Now, I make you go head in that corner. That's too high Brother. Make it square like that, yeah. Now, now you don't write no Earth up there now. No, you write, you draw the small plane coming down from the …field up there…Yeah out of that gap it's coming down; you don't cut it, yeah, you just put the Earth, you just put where it spins and take the corner here and cut it out for Earth, you know; and then you have a plane falling out of that gap there.

But your gap is not made on the angled with the Earth. No, right, it's that mark there would have been; well don't do that now, go ahead and make the plane out there in open space there, right there where you put your…right where you put your Earth right there. Well, you didn't need to do nothing but make a mark and cross it, that's all you needed to do, just made a mark. Don't cross it, that can represent a, a flying plane coming to Earth.

So Brothers and Sisters, I, that's the mark. My Brother have forgotten the work I use to carry him over, so this makes me to believe now he been off somewhere else, teaching it other than the way I do it for him. Got to be twice that long Brother, and then you write this like a plane Brother. I don't see how in the world you could forget! Don't make an errand out of it, just, just. These people know that we…got no planes that we can…bring it directly to you towards your Earth; and that you now need to bring the Earth up to, Brother…We'll let you go home after while.

THE MOTHER PLANE:
REVELATION OF THE END

That's alright, that's alright. Well you have a pretty sturdy hand, that's why I don't want to take it away from you. Brother you got it to far up, Brother...if I was you now I would not put anything of the kind in it. I'd just put the, the one circle mark there just what you got there...No, you, you make it go all the way back in; you don't close up out on the ends. You don't, you don't, you don't put nothing there Brother...you don't make no close up on the end, you make it all the way through; don't cut it off there...Now check the center with, Brother...

Now Brothers and Sisters I reckon I...start my mouth again. In the Bible there you have a prophesy of a Wheel in a Wheel in the Book Ezekiel; come on, come on... keep making those that's wrong. You keep making it...No, there, don't represent, you know...

I have to take Brother home with...teach him there...He use to could do this before ever we could get through talking about it, but he went off, I guess and got mixed up with some bad company have taken all of those thoughts away from him. The things that is wavering around now.

This represent the Ezekiel Wheel you read of in the Bible. We actually have it up there, it's up there now. The devil know it is up there. This is why he is continue, I want to be sure you hear me, to go up and make planes that can fly so swift, that if he could discover in the skies, he would be able to get back so he could through a rocket at it before ever that he could...He's making planes to search the space with the highly speed known to the Scientist.

And this Wheel in a Wheel here that Ezekiel prophesy of, that it got so high up in the air that it look dreadful. This Wheel is up in the air now, which is what they are trying to locate from the Moon. If they could get a good station there at least on the Moon and watch for this thing.

He'll drop that bomb on the Earth and that His height would be something about twenty miles above the Earth when He drop it not getting to far from atmosphere, because He want to use the atmosphere to help guide His bombs. So, it's that this bomb, when it strike the Earth, it will start right into the Earth...You find that it's timed and that it have a motor to the bomb that when it strikes the Earth, that motor automatically goes on and takes that bomb one mile into the Earth before it explodes. When it explode bring up a mountain one mile high. That's a powerful bomb. Allah Taught me that, that's the same type of bomb that God used to make mountains on the Earth; it's the same thing. It goes into the Earth with a very….touching it…like a air hammer…I think it just suck, just suck right into the Earth like a air hammer sinking it down into the Earth.

And when it get, it's time to drop this bomb into the Earth, they'll have in this bomb the type of hyper-dynamite that they used to bring up the mountains of Ararat mountain range. Hyper-dynamite, it's more powerful than America is using. America uses thirty percent dynamite. These people have their bombs equipped with a hundred percent dynamite today, to blast just a few mountains cross the Continent of North America up.

And that, these mountains bring up out of the Earth dust and debris. Now, it will kill people for fifty miles around that crater it makes, pushing up a mountain on each side. And, this will go into action when America start using her high explosives dropping it from the air. This thing will come out and get her.

So, there is fifteen hundred, or rather…fifteen hundred of these small bomb planes. Each one of those bomb planes carry three bombs, and these three bombs will take these bombs over a area of just what…circling around dropping a bomb at the…and to destroy for a hundred and fifty miles that it was dropped.

Excuse me now, this is time and I want you to try and understand this. And, I want you be looking out for it. I have seen that plane. This is no perfect drawings of it, but the Brother did the best he could. That's a powerful plane that can dot in the skies just like you see what they call those…those that, the flying saucers. Right through the plane measures one mile. I like those…planes.

As I tell you, if you find me lying…I tell you I'll give you ten thousand dollars out of my Brother vest pocket. And, if he don't happen to have it, I will ask you to loan it to me and then I will pay you back.

I've seen this, I saw this plane. This plane can move about into Space so wildly, until their way of trying to shoot them out of the sky…it was a Scientist, no other than a Scientist. I think the first five hours explain: it's a half a mile by a half mile. And, this plane when it be, look like up here, it can get out of your eyesight so fast until you look like, nothing to say.

You will see this plane one day, because this plane have associates. They stay up there a year and sometime a year and a half in that plane. It's a wonderful plane…I'm not trying to deceive you, I'm trying to show you what you going to see pretty soon. I stop drawing this plane for years, but now I think I should go back to it, because they seem to be up there fixing it up to come near to the Earth.

When America think that she is going after this plane, she admit she saw it…Someone is on that plane go to rush and change America, so that she can't come far to the plane. She can't see it. Write in your paper if you want, and tell them what I am telling you. See if he'll try and deny it.

They know it's up there. I sit down and I talk to them years ago about it. They asked me questions. They have the drawing, they have a whole blackboard up there that they taken from us when they arrested us. And I had drawn the planes and words, and they taken it to the F.B.I. office and there they have it there today. Because they know this to be True, and they are willing to admit that it's True.

I say to you Brothers, in the Day when that thing is seen in the sky of America, make haste and run to some post. They'll be two Scientist on America's streets every two blocks. They'll be guiding you to tell you where to go. Everything has been prepared while we were sleeping to save us. That's a terrible thing though, those little dots there that you see that he made in that circle in the green, represents murderers, great giant murderers…

Well, telling it like Jesus was. Jesus was a Scientist, and he could tune in on you and what we thinking on. And when the Jew would be planning to come to him, he tuned up on him, he listened to him. If the Jew say they'd go this way, he went this way. That's why they could never catch him. He knew what the Jew was thinking about, and knew what they was planning.

Now they have one out of every hundred over there, that can tune up on us over here; tell what we thinking about. Think over that. We're pretty smart people. You can do it yourself, if you will take time, clear your mind and then go get into some place where no one will annoy you and concentrate on nothing but that… and that Brother. And after while you hear what the Brother is saying to himself. And maybe you'll hear the words coming out of one of your ears.

It is not that we are such people that we have to wait and see everything happen before we know what's going to happen. We would not be gods if we did not know what was going on around us, among other than gods, No. It is nothing strange that I have seen Scientists and ones who may be in with a little …on it, get down to business quickly. Yes, that this is true.

Ezekiel looked up at it then he said, "Oh Wheel," "Wheel." The Wheel was so mighty to the man's imagination, he cried out, "Oh Wheel!" Seeing that dreadful thing up there in the sky and so far off then he stopped, he said it looked dreadful!

These things are now going into action pretty soon. The Time is up for them to go into action. You and I being Brothers, and with me walking around you day and night with the knowledge of these things and don't tell you, you would hold me responsible, say, "why didn't you tell us?" I'll say, well you wouldn't believe it no way, "why didn't you tell us anyway, let us just...that wouldn't have been your fault." And that would be right. So, I'm not going to let you come calling be back. I'm going to judge these things now.

There is two certain places...on our Earth that I'm bound to tell you about. Better I told it to you cause since the Time is here, just about right to drop that bomb from that plane to destroy our enemies. I'm going to soon tell you, but there are two places on our planet, have been made for the purpose of hiding people. And, they can stay there a long, long old time and you will never know we are there. It is not so secret that I shouldn't tell you, but I'm not going to say so this evening, tell you this evening. Because, I go home, and I will think over it; and I will ask Allah should I share this with you. Should I reveal to them what you has revealed to me. Revelation of the end of the world and what will carry on the destruction of the people that is here now. And they...and search with a surprise, as the Holy Qur'an refers to it, it's moving the Earth to act like a revelation has been received by her.

So, all these things is to make known to this world that they are not forgotten over the other world. This is what these things is coming into being. Now, in my conclusion, I ask you to do this, try and get out of the name of the white man as fast as you can. That is True...that the devil's name will be destroyed with it and that God will give to you and me a name that will live forever. Muhammad, that name Muhammad will be here a billion years to come. We had better names...some of them are great long names, three or four inches long. But they didn't need all of that name. So, the names that you get, make shorter than them old names that our people use to go in. This is, I think what is used by some of us long names. They also have some long names in your Bible.

So, I say to you in my- just leave that like it is Brother don't erase it. I say just leave it as is, but don't erase it, leave it like that. Maybe one of Yacub boys will come in and they'll look up and fall dead!

So my beloved Brothers and Sisters, how to live intelligent acting that I can say that I had in the past known to take...So, God and I love you so well, that He sent me to tell you these things make gods out of you. This, that is...make gods out of you. You say, "Oh, I know I will never be a god," yes you already is a god.

So, I thank you, thank you, thank you. I know you don't have much money, none of us has much money. We were robbed of that by our enemies, the devil. But, whenever you being asked to keep building a safe and honorable place for you, please do so.

We have in mind now, of two fast jets. We want those two jets...with our other Brother Manager in the hospital. I just almost tremble when I see you out there fighting the devil, then go tell the devil that he...And, if you would just follow me and give whatever you can, we would soon have these things. Think about it, if you have a million people here in Chicago, if they would only just give us a dollar a piece, we'd have a million dollars every week. And that we could build what we want without begging people bout it. Then if we just get half that much, we seeing that half the Southside owned by Black people. Elijah don't want to own nothing personally; he want something that he can divide with you. The only thing I want personal is my wife.

So, I'm going to dismiss myself, so that the Brother Minister can take over. I think he's getting hungry, and he wants me to hurry and get out of the way so he can get out of the way too. So I have enjoyed a Brother time with a Brother with you here this afternoon. A Brother and a Sister, I have enjoyed being in your presence...

TROUBLE ON THE WAY TO AMERICA!

In your presence Sisters… pray Allah that you will be back here two o'clock next Sunday. And if you can't find five to bring back, each of you just put two figures back of the card, and bring five-hundred.

Now Brothers it is a lot of trouble headed to America, and I don't want you to be the loser. America, her friends is gone from her and has become enemies. And they all is looking towards America with murder. "Let's go and take her," just like the Bible teaches there in Ezekiel, "Let us go up and rise up take her…take her at noon day, anytime that she is not expecting us." This is what they talking about.

They thought Pearl Harbor was terrible, but Pearl Harbor will look like a gang of girls playing, for what they fix up with to come up with against America. It's…to talk about, especially when you know…I know what they got planned to do to America. I know that but I can't tell you all of these things less you'll go and talk too much.

So in the name of Allah I pray that each and every one of you will go out of here happy and return home, find your family happy to see you on return as they saw you left. I thank you and hope to see you next Sunday evening, as I say unto you,

As Salaam Alaikum!

JULY 9, 1972 PART ONE / SIDE ONE

ALL BLACK PEOPLE ARE
BROTHERS OF EACH OTHER

A Salaam Alaikum!

My dear beloved Brothers and Sisters, I feel like I'm a big man. You may be seated. Who is that say go head? Come up here, I think I know your voice, oh you alright! No, right here Brother in this, in this seat Brother take that seat. You know Brothers, as I bring you up our helper, you don't want him to get out of your sight. [The Messenger laughs] Old folks use to tell me son don't talk back to me [The Messenger laughs].

My beloved Brothers and Sisters we are so happy to see your smiling faces here today, until we could almost cry with a smiling face for joy. We're happy to see this day, but we still think we're short changed yet. We still think we go outside some place that have been more than this.

I looked at a little church once, and the little church from the outside looked like to me ought to have been talking to somewhat about, at least three or four hundred. So, I say let me go in this little church. That was in Harrisburg, Pennsylvania. So, I got in there and I looked around, I didn't see but about a dozen people or less. I say what are they making all this noise out here for?

So I went in, and it was a sanctified church. And so, the pastor, as you may realize was a woman. I sit down and she start patting her feet and a tambourine and whatnot, looking right straight at me…After while she come back when she had them all in a high tune, she say, "Are you saved?" I say, I don't know that's a mighty big question. I say, if, I'm not saved, I'm in a terrible condition. She didn't know I was talking bout her church.

So, she said to me, well, you stay right there. After while she got to preaching; she had a stick in her hand, and she started pruning it right at me, you know. And she came back later, she says, "How do you feel now, do you feel like you saved now?" I say I'm not too sure. [The Messenger laughs] So, she told me, she say you keep coming here, and you will be saved. I say thank you.

And, I looked at the poor woman, and I say what a pitiful thing now. Our people have been robbed so by the devil, that they go round and insult the God of Truth and Justice; The God of Wisdom; The God of Understanding; The God…Our Saviour, Our God. So, this lady…after she got through, she ask me, "Well, except Jesus." I say, may I have to say something ? So, she was so, you know alert to tell me come on up. I say to myself going up, I say you think I'm coming up to join your church, but you're mistaken!

"So, go tell them,whether you are saved or not. Tell them whether you will join up with us or not." She start to patting her hands, and, when they got started I say, that was great thing to say that you are saved. As long as we are Black people, I told her, I say we are saved. But, as long as we believe in white people's religion, we're not saved.

So, she told me she wasn't teaching white people's religion. That she was teaching Jesus religion. I say oh thank you, I say that's the teachings that I'm teaching. So she started to patting and beating on pans again and she ask me, how long had I been saved. I say since I was born.

We can find lots of things that our people who have not the knowledge of …and others. It make you feel like crying, not to laugh at them. But, to cry over them because they don't know.

I'm little late today but, I don't think that I have fed you with a late meal yet. I convene in a way, even though it seem like I'm late; and I can't eat…and we're all here late anyway. Since we're talking bout eating, I'm hungry now [The Messenger laughs]. And I think you who made us late, they should pay for us a good meal. I was constantly told at home, just a little while longer they'll be there. We waiting for such and such buses. So, the dinner was smelling so good I wanted to tell the Brother…

We have been working on there the teaching on the Time, the Theology Of Time. But, this afternoon I'm pretty late and I ought to just get me a text kind of sought of like that old preacher taken one day. He had not had no converts to join up in a long time. They all would come in and start playing, ignoring him. So he says I'm going to get these fools one of these days anyway.

So next time he came back to his people, he went in his pocket, pulled out a quart of whiskey, he set it down. Went in the other pocket laid down a forty-five. Then he set his Bible right in between the two. And he says, "Brothers and Sisters my text today is that some of these things will move you." So, I'm about to take that kind of text too. [The Messenger laughs]

We had few Sisters and Brothers that we wanted to bring them before you. I don't know whether the Minister have or not. Have you Brother Minister? Pardon? The Minister love to preach so long himself, so he didn't want you to break up his text [The Messenger laughs]. Well I love Ministers that love to preach like that. But, I do like to learn who you are, and you learn us.

We have a very smart little sister here. She has been with us every since she was born. And she has learned so much that the Messenger said, until every time she come round me now she wants the Messenger said something; know how smart she is. She'll come to me and she'll hug and kiss me, wanting to show me how smart she is.

So, today I'm going to surprise her. I want to know how smart she is, our little sister. This little sister is...little daughter. Come on up here baby...Put her down over there in front of that stand, because she can't get up here, they won't see her. Stand right in the center baby. Greet the people baby. Greet the [The Messenger laughs]. [The little sister says, As Salaam Alaikum] [The Messenger reply Wa Alaikum Salaam]. [Then he began to ask the little sister Student Enrollment questions]. Who is the Original Man? Who is the colored man?

Very good, very good for her to know the difference in the two people; to know the difference in the two gods. You have anything else to say to us baby? Tell her what... [The Messenger asked the little sister's mother to ask her a question. She was asked three questions, in which, she answered all correctly].

You can go to the High School and Colleges, and if you are able to bring out a star out of either one of these cases where the parents have gotten their efforts...degrees and whatnot, I will give you a nickel.

We have some very loyal children round here. They visit my home sometime to let me know how much they have learned. And, they just make me feel so happy to see a child using the educational language of College students. They are very smart. This is not the only one now. This is just happen to be the first one I look over here and saw. But there are lots of them here.

We have been teaching here on the Time, the Theology Of Time. But, today we a little late, and we feel like that we want to just teach you this and that, which is what the old folks use to say. My grandmother use to tell my brother and I when we go to see her, she say, "Sit down there boy and tell me that which you know and that you don't know." [The Messenger laughs].

So my brother and I when we returned home say, " I simply tell her that which we didn't know." When we don't know a thing, she'd tell us then we were telling a story, and she would beat us on top of it. So I came up under such parents they loved our backs [The Messenger laughs].

Pardon me Brother. Well, Brothers and Sisters, I don't want to prolong the time with ourselves. I know what you came for. You heard what I was offering ten thousand dollars for anything like a word, or a mistake that you could find that I'm...I still have that up for you, that prize. That's a good amount of money for you to win. Some of us have never owned ten thousand dollars. You do have the chance of winning it here, if you can find me telling you other than the Truth. Not in the whole lecture, but just in one word will get you ten thousand dollars to carry home, if I can get my Brother back here sleep, so I can take it out of his pocket. I didn't say I had ten thousand dollars [The Messenger laughs].

We see quite a few of our beloved people here with us, and that...Brother come giving me some little papers here and I told him when I get here to let me know whether or not that there was lots of dignitary people here so that I could tell them that I'm just a little skinny fellow and I'm not able maybe, educational...to compete with them. And that, after I'm through, I will give the speaker stand over to them, they can talk. I believe in giving everybody a chance.

So I see some great professors listed here by Brother. There is a Real Estate man, and we certainly need some houses. We need a lot of them. So I'm very happy that you are here. We will be contacting you soon. But...you may have to help us-you with the down payment.

All of these Real Estate men Brother? Yea, all of these Real Estate men? From the Police Department? Brother I don't want to meet no Police! What that is you have planned? [The Messenger laughs]. You got to get this straight or I'll be going home. The Brother done got me scared now, so I'm going to make him call those names off, cause I don't know who you got out there to catch me Brother. You know I, you know I talks pretty open, and I talk about white folks.

Excuse me Brother, my little humor, I don't mean anything. But, you know when you go to talking about Policemen, somebody may start shaking, "we don't know whether he there for me or you."

Brothers and Sister, and Mister Policeman feel at home, we're your Brothers regardless to what you are. You can be the High Sheriff of Cook County, or whatever office you hold, you still is our Brother and we come here to make that known.

We are face to face with Judgment, and if we don't understand that we are face to face with Judgment, we may be the loser. America, stands before death; America, is doomed to death; America, is bound to go to her doom because of the way that she have treated us. America have mistreated the Blackman in America so wrongly, that God cannot hardly wait for us to choose our way. You can say yes or no I don't care. I'm certainly independent of what you choose.

God came to me in 1931 in Detroit, Michigan. He Taught me for three years and four months, in Person. I was not dreaming. I was looking at Him in Person for three years and four months. He Taught me night and day. I use to be glad to get a little sleep. When He would tell me, I will be back I would say, I hope He be there long enough for me to get a little sleep. And He Taught me what you here me teach you three years, night and day.

I don't think I would be wise to say that I taught myself, and I taught you thus and thus. No, He Taught me thus and thus. I didn't know nothing. I didn't know my name. What I was calling myself, it was the white man's name. So, whatever you hear me say here this afternoon, it came from His mouth in the way of Divine.

Whenever you hear me talk other than that, well that's me, that was me. But, Divine, it came from Him. Though He Taught me bout non-Divine and who non-Divine was; and I have been teaching it for forty years. Think over that. That I'm no boy if I been teaching Divine Wisdom in America for forty years. I didn't start when I was a baby. I'm a old man, and I'm ready for you.

So today, we are here, and we thank you for coming out to listen to what I have to say, or rather I should make it more…what God has Taught me.

I see here Mister and Mrs. C. W. Williams. I don't know whether this is my Doctor or not. This is from Detroit…Brother give me all of these names of people and I want him to call them out to me because we want to thank them for being present [One of the Brothers called out the names of the people on the list of dignitaries that were visiting the Temple].

We thank you for your presence. And we pray Allah that you will return again. We are afraid that you won't eat enough this afternoon, but we pray that you will return. One thing we want to say to you regardless to your profession, we still teaches that you our Brother. Whether you want to say yes or not, you are Our Brother. All black people are the Brother of each other. You have been told that all people are brothers. In the way of being people we are brothers, but we are not all brothers by races and nations.

We have a stranger in our midst, and that is the white man. We are not brothers to the white man. He is a total stranger. He didn't come from the God that we came from. He come from a made god. Not a Created God. Our God is a Created God, and we are a Created people. But the white man is a made man. Yes, he didn't came here with us. We been here ever since that the Earth was made. We was right there beside our Father that made it.

And that, we, the Black people didn't come from white people, but white people came from us. We made the white man, and can do it at no limited of time. But, when it come to us, we were Created. If this was heard and believed among you alone, would set you free.

When the white man hear you say that your Father, a Blackman created him, or made him, pardon me, and that you a Created man from a Created Man, but the white man is a made- man; when he represent himself to you, he puts it in such way that you don't make a mistake that he is not the created man, but he is the made- man. He puts himself in his place. But you put yourself out of place when you go and follow him and call yourself the same thing that he calling himself.

No equal! We been here on the planet Earth according to the Teachings of God to me, in the Person of Master Fard Muhammad to Whom Praise is Due, every since life have been into the total Darkness of our Created Man. We are not people came here just six thousand years ago. We are people that came here trillions of years ago.

The white man is a made- man from one of our Scientist six thousand years ago. That's no time with us. We been here for trillions of years, and if you try, put his time in our Time to calculate it down to the Number One Man that Self-Created, you wouldn't hardly find a second to give him in Time; hardly would run into a second.

Take a trillion years and divide it by six thousand; see what a little time you will have there. Then take six thousand years and divide it into sixty- six trillion years. That's nothing on the Time we been here. Take that same six thousand years, push it through sixty-six trillion years and move it over to seventy-six trillion years, and you will hardly be able to find him.

You may think that Elijah Muhammad don't know what he's talking about. Never heard nothing like that. How could you heard anything like that following a baby only six thousand years! Now how could you know anything about billions and trillions of years with man's voice ranging throughout that Time. How could you hear it in just six thousand years ago?

We don't care nothing about the little white man. We don't care anything about his big talk. We know it's like a little puppy running long beside a great big hound.

I'm going to move over to our work, but you, but you should know this. Know how old the man is that's walking around with a cane cracking you cross the head with it. How long this big shot been here? He just been here just six days to our Time. He's not been here but a few days. Six thousand years aint nothing to trillions of years.

Blackman remember that you are the Father of Creation. Blackman remember that no white man can dispute with the One that said it, Elijah. He can't dispute with me. I am a God Taught man. I am a God raised man. I wear this on my head, but We dare the white man to wear it publicly but once a year. You know why he can't wear it but once a year? Because he had nothing to do with the making of this. The Blackman made this Sphere.

What I mean the Sun, Moon, and Stars; the white man know nothing about the Creation of such things. This is why I want to teach you the Theology of it. Anything in the Universe; anything on Earth of human beings, of life of any kind. I'm here to tell you what Allah have Taught me of that. Not what I know, it is Allah the One Who have Taught me. And, I don't think you will be able to make Him out other than the Truth.

We was teaching last Sunday on this board where's my son-in-law? My son-in-law? Come on up here Brother Wali! Where in the world you been? Is that your...? Is that your...? Brother...is standing here with your...You know in these people we have a, very, very, powerful prophesy; and one that is kind of frightening. Don't you come here with no little something cause I'm hard to take. Make it good, and time don't, I'm going to run you way from over there.

You know I'm a pretty tough fellow, especially with these Brothers that I been knowing ever since near forty years. I know they don't want to be called forty years old, but I been knowing them for that length of time. And that, this man is my son-in-law, Wali Muhammad, he have my name.

You know when I found him, he had the devil's name. And that, when he start following me, he married my daughter and I thought I would make her call him after her name. Because I didn't want a son-in-law in my house called by the devil's name.

I gets away from the phone sometime, and the Brothers try to line me up with a mic [microphone], and the thing slips away from me every now and then. I have to get back to this one.

And that, in this world we love to worship; and we love trying to be called by the white man name; love to look like him. And, but I'm going to see whether you love to look like him. The white man has been here on our planet for six thousand years, and he has ruled.

Now Brother I certainly like your job, yes sir! And you have that basket; and I could get a little stronger if I hear something in it. I went in a Church once; they passed the basket so fast, I kept hearing something rattling in it, you know; thought that sound... So I didn't have much money, but I did put in a dime. I didn't have...

WHAT WAS THE RELIGION OF THE PROPHETS?

I didn't have no more because I know they was asking for charity, and I love to give charity. So, I give them a dime and they looked at me; I shook my head. I didn't have no more. But I don't want you to do that. See we may follow you and prove that you do have more.

And, we going to spend most of our time on…the East Coast, bout, nine hundred miles, and some from the West Coast, I suppose; I think they are. People coming from these long distance don't mean to make them for nothing. They want you to tell them something. And if you not going to tell them something, get off the stand and let them tell you something [The Messenger laughs].

You know my Brother, I have learned to be humor with people to get friendship. You going to be stern and tell them bout the pitchfork, the thing they going through in the fire with, you only get frighten. But tomorrow, pardon me, tomorrow morning you wake up, "Ahhhhhh I don't believe that." No we don't want to fool with you. We going to talk about some fire, but it's not the kind of fire that disappear overnight. It's the kind of fire that lingers round with you; you'll feel it.

My beloved Brothers and Sisters, you take for an instance that I have the Holy Qur'an here lying beside me. I don't have the Bible here with me. I can soon get it. We was never taught to read the Holy Qur'an by the white man. We never was taught that there was a Universal Religion besides his that was called Islam. He never talk about no religion but Christianity.

And I want to say Brothers and Sisters, that if God made Adam and He weighed Adam's children at about two thousand years old, and then, He send to teach them the right religion, I say God put Himself in a very ugly thing. Why, the people could force Him, say, "Why did you leave us without a religion all that time?"

Two thousand years after Adam, before ever that He sent Jesus with the Right Religion. Just think over that. What kind of God was He. Now He say that this is the best one; and that if you believe in Jesus and Christianity, then you will go to Heaven. Well what about all those people before Jesus was born? Where did they go? Just think over these things.

What kind of God was that that Created the Heavens and the Earth, and then would not Create for man a good religion until He give birth to Jesus? Just think over these things. I don't ask you to do much but just think and reason over this. Would God be so evil, that He would let us live here all that Time before ever that He would make us, a good religion, and a good man.

You say Enoch was a good man. What religion did Jesus have? Just think over that. You say Moses was…good. What kind of religion did Moses have? Just think it over for yourself. He said Moses was good, that He sent him into Egypt to bring out Israel from bondage of the House of Pharaoh. Well then, what religion did he preach to? Huh?

Now, he didn't…no religion. The Prophets say he brought Israel out of Egypt by the hands of a Prophet. But what kind of religion did he carry in? They said, Pharaoh didn't have no religion he worshipped of, whatnot. What did Moses worship? And what kind of religion did Moses offer Israel? Have you ever thought of this?

We still had to wait two thousand more years for Jesus to be born, to have a religion. Answer to yourself, a religion, what was it? He said that he didn't come to change the law of the Prophets, but to fulfill them. What was the law of the Prophets? We want to know where we going to; where we headed to.

Since the white man have…among us and kind that he have the right religion. I want to know Mister devil, who you think that you could fool in the way of religion while you blinding the people's eyes to the knowledge of the religion of the Prophets. Oh I love to get after this devil!

Deceitfully tell us to believe and follow Jesus. How bout Moses? He don't teach you to follow Moses, he say Jesus. Well, what did God give the book of Moses? Was Moses religion different from Jesus? No, you say no. Well what was it? Tell us the name of these two great Prophets religion? And, he will tell you Jesus. Well, what about Moses people, did they go to Hell?

Talk back to him, and you will find he will run from you. Face him with Truth. God has Taught me He calls him the skunk of the planet Earth. Don't get scared Brother I'm going to hold you. Oh you start running out of here I going to hold you, so don't get afraid. I been here forty years teaching this same thing.

He is so wicked, and so filthy that God call him the skunk of the planet Earth. Look at what he is doing. Look at him now going nude. This just fits him, a skunk. Taking your wives and daughters stripping them off. Parading them up and down the street. All of your knowledge spent trying to make and model a nice, respectful daughter; he go out there and make her disrespectful. Pulling off her clothes, showing her shame up and down to the public.

The Holy Qur'an says, "He pulled off their clothes and showed the nations their shame." Believe it or not, but you can walk out the door and see. They out there doing that; or maybe she may come in your own house. You don't have to walk nowhere, just look what he did for your daughters, your wives. Made them pull off their clothes, and made them to like it. I'm only telling you the Truth, I'm not...

What a preacher, Baptist or Methodist, Catholic, look like preaching to you decency, and there sit his daughter with nearly all of her clothes off her? Just think over that. Any new preacher, if you are in here, follow the white man to pulling your wife and your daughters clothes off to the public, you need to go back and ask God I think you made a mistake if you sent me. You say God sent you, but I say, go back and tell Him that He made a mistake.

One Minister of any religion will allow another people to pull his wife and daughter's clothes off; and make them walk in the public nude almost; you would never be able to convert me. No, because you should first do like the preacher in the jungle of Africa, Australia, and other far off Pacific Islands; preach to the savage to hide his nakedness. This is the first preaching we give to a savage, to cover your nakedness.

You here in what is called civilization. Think over that, Civilization! You say you a civilized man and got your wife and your daughter walking out there in the street half nude. This what we see in Africa in certain spots. Yea, I been there. I have traveled little in Africa myself, and also in Asia.

I'm not telling you something wrong. I'm telling you what I know, and if you been there you will bare me witness that you saw the same; it's ugly looking. Wives sitting down under a shade tree with her body near nude with her baby nursing from it, as though this is the right civilization.

We got to civilize people. We got to go to Africa. We don't consider the jungles of Africa's people anything for us to follow to be taught. To be taught what kind a way? If you're not civilized, you can't lead a civilized person. Talk back if you are able!

I been around a little myself, and I know what you have. Not guessing, but I know from actual things. If you tell me to go to Africa, I will go there, but don't tell me to go there to be civilized. I'm already civilized, and I'm ready to civilize Africa. But some of us rise up boasting of Africa. I say first get civilized, and go there and civilize Africa. Then I say, we all is together in civilization. As you see the drawings at the head of our paper, Muhammad Speaks; He speaks too.

We love Africa people like we love you in a way, not quite as much because they been free and then let England, Germany, and other European people go over there and rob them. Pushed them back in the jungle, and taken over their country. I dare us to get a country. They certainly won't push us over out of it!

I'm only perking you up on this simple things. We love Africa, that's why we have our hands joined on the top of our paper. This is just what we want to do with Africa. We want to make Africa our brother, but Africa cannot lead us until they themselves have become perfect civilized.

What God have Taught me is a Perfect Civilizing Teaching. It is not something you can add to, to make it civilizing. Perfect Civilize Teaching to civilize any savage regardless to where he come from.

I have been visited by many Africans, many of them right here in Chicago at my home, 4847 Woodlawn. They come to me, they're happy to meet me and I am happy to meet them. They are many find Scholars and Scientists in Africa. But, in all of their knowledge that they have, it is not from the right source. White man have taught them.

They have some of their ancient teachings. But now, it must be replaced for the new wisdom, knowledge, and understanding that is brought forth to liberate the Blackman all over the Earth. And that knowledge is here with me.

This I don't say criticizing no one. I want to join hands with you, and be your Brother. But, not with that which England, Belgium, and these other slave-making rascals. They give you their knowledge to enslave you. Like they did us here in America, Africa.

Anyone come from out of the country of America see you acting a little foolish, ignorant, they jump on you and rob you. And yet, they give you nothing to relieve you of the robber that you was born under; brought up in his...

But I'm here to fight any robber, as the Bible teach of me; and you thought it was the Jesus back there two thousand years ago, but it's Elijah. All before me was thieves and robbers. This mean leadership. The Jesus could not say all before him was thieves and robbers. Then he would have been classifying his Prophets before him to be thieves and robbers. He could not have mentioned anything like that.

But it's me; I'm the one that said that in the Spiritual and Knowledge of the Prophets that wrote it; not before Jesus. Those was Prophets before him and not thieves and robbers. But, thieves and robbers was before me. Robbing you of all they could...Black leaders, come before you without robbing you. Was all of them; they always look to see how heavy your pockets is, and they set out to rob you. I see how empty your pocket is, I set out to put something in it.

The Time that we are living in now is the Judgment of the white folks, and America is Number One First. God have made the whole world turn against America in order to destroy her.

As Daniel says in the Bible prophesy of America, of the four beasts; think over four beasts is the name given to the four greatest governments of the white man by the Prophets. He didn't call them nothing but beasts. And now you want to call them angels, while the Prophets call them beasts. And that's bout what they is. They got a human look, but their characteristics is a beast.

You may not believe me, but, the Time will prove that I am teaching you the Truth. This, particular drawing here, that my son-in-law just did for you is found in the first and tenth chapter of Ezekiel. He say he saw in a vision a Wheel in a Wheel. It didn't come down to the Earth, he say he saw it come up, rose up from the Earth.

I want you to listen at me good. As I thought that it would have been best that I talk about this Wheel; no you keep that. I don't want the stick, I want the Wheel. My son-in-law saw me make the Wheel in Washington years ago, so he can draw it now better than I can. He don't add anything to it, but more perfection. He can draw better than I can.

So Ezekiel, I'm bout to lose my…here. So Ezekiel says that he saw in a vision a wheel in a wheel. Now you see only the outer of the Great Wheel that he say he saw. But he said he saw a Wheel in a Wheel. Where is the other Wheel Ezekiel?

Now, if Ezekiel saw in a vision; Prophets don't see visions of lies. Whenever they have a vision it's the Truth. He said it's a Wheel in a Wheel, and that this Wheel rose up from the Earth. He didn't say nothing bout where it was made at on the Earth. But he said a Wheel rose up from the Earth. And that it got so high it look so dreadful, that he said when he looked at it, he said, "Oh Wheel! Oh Wheel! Wheel! Wheel!"

So it must have been a great thing for Ezekiel to behold. A Wheel he say got so high that it looked dreadful. And, out of that Wheel he say he saw something come down from it. Then he called it, what is that thing? He give it a name. Some kind of Cherubim, yea Cherubim. And that, we thought that he was talking bout Angels, but that is not Angels. No, that was another plane coming out of this Plane.

This is a Plane here that measures, Almighty God Taught me, a one half a mile by half a mile. That's a Mighty Wheel! And that, when it flies over the place where it's going to drop bombs out of it, He sends one of the planes like this one coming out of, then he drops that bomb out of the plane on the Earth. And that, that bomb that He drop out, have a bomb inside of the bomb.

Then it have on, in that bomb, a thing made kind a like a Earth drill that you see people drilling out here in the streets. We have that type, but it's so much more powerful. It comes down from this plane, drops it on the Earth, and when it strikes the Earth a motor goes off in it. And it takes this bomb here into the Earth, something like a mile before ever she explodes.

That bomb have a steel drill that it can't batter, and it can't be stopped until it get a mile. At that depth, in the explosion goes on and we have a hundred percent dynamite, while we're using fifty percent on Earth...

But God taught me that they have a hundred percent type of bomb that they drop on the Earth from a terrific height of what height the mountain is to be. If it's to be two miles high, He drop a bomb down into the Earth that go down two miles into the depth of the Earth. Then...blew up a mountain two miles high.

This bomb don't have that dreadful, pardon me, this Wheel does not have that dreadful bomb. These bombs will only go into the Earth for one mile. They will blow up a one mile high mountain.

This Wheel here have fifteen- hundred those planes you see the brother have drew on; the fifteen-hundred of them on it to drop off on America. They will take a height over North America, and they will drop off these bombs. They will save three of these bombs to drop on England. They will drop the other three on England, which it will only take just three of them to rip England apart.

I'm not trying to frighten you to believe; that's immaterial with me. I'm only telling you what was told to me by God to tell you before these things take place.

This plane here will make one trip across America and drop a bomb. And that, when she drop one, she know the distance which the explosion will take effect. Then, just three of these planes will be sent to the British Island to take care of England. Believe what I'm saying, or wait around a few days.

This plane goes above the Earth forty miles to unload those bombs on America. She gets up forty miles. "Oh we have jets fly that." Right! But brother when this plane unloads her daily destruction, you won't have no planes up there. No, they won't fly up there with your jets. They going to get rid of your jets on the ground First.

How they going to do that Mister Muhammad? They'll do it like this: First thing they will do, they will go and destroy all America's airplane bases. And, they will also destroy her planes what you see running up there in the air now past the speed of sound, at a terrific speed of a gun...and more faster than that. They get rid of them First.

How they going to get rid of them? Oh yea, they going to make her enemies get rid of them. She has some enemies has the same thing that America have. Put them to fighting First, and, make them to get rid of each other, just about it. They will almost kill each other. This is what they driving them to now. To do away, as one Scientist said, "America, the white man were not worth using no such high explosion on him."

Do him like the Muslims did the people use to live over here next to Turkey. What's the name that Turkey almost annihilated? When they thought the last war was…No…people there, they all but annihilated them…some of them still around. Albanians, Albanians…they were victims, that lived there next to Turkey. Armenians, that's who they are, Armenians.

So they first thought that it was Time to get rid of the Christians. So, the brother went out and just, just slaughtered Armenians like it was nothing, till they were told that it was not Time to kill all white people.

So that's just what you going to do. Get rid of all white people that is the devil to Black people. You will see! They will bear me witness if they was in here; I could make them bear me witness that the war that is breaking out now, the war of Armageddon, it has already begin. This is to get through to white folks.

You don't need to go over to Vietnam to fight. No, you, what you going to fight for? If America win you still will be her slave…and she will have Vietnam to divide…But, she won't win. Those old ancient Hindus that they fighting over there against America, against Christianity. He put them to fighting because He don't want either one.

So He let, America the Christians kill Hindus all they want. And then the Hindus will be killing her too. But, they probably will not win, but let them kill each other cause He don't want either one.

You notice how smart the Muslims act in this war? You never hear tell of no Muslim going to war to defend either side. No, because they don't want either one of them, Christian, nor Hindu.

A Hindu is one of the oldest enemies of God, of Man. You running over there talking bout our people; killing our people. Just because they look like you a little, they not yours. They been on this planet for thirty-five thousand years trying to destroy God Own religion, Islam.

You don't see no Muslim… I wish to my God that I could get one of these bombs and one of these planes and fly over there…I would show you how long they would be here.

There may be some Hindu believers in here, but I don't care brother. Yes I would fly over your territory and kill everyone of you. If you are here, I don't love you myself. I don't care if America kill all of you, and you kill them too. I don't love either one of you.

Oh Wheel, Wheel, Wheel. Think over the prophesy. Looking at it. Oh Wheel, Wheel, Wheel. You look dreadful. Loaded up with bombs to rain on America. God told me, that He make one trip across America, and America will be all but finished off. And, just three of these bombing planes go to England, that be the end of England.

Just one of these bombs will…go in the Earth one mile. This will bring up here a mountain, a mile high and kill the civilization around it for fifty square miles…Don't come trying to make war with God. It's a dangerous thing to do.

Today…deadly weapons is being manufactured to destroy man from the face of the Earth. All is angry with each other, as the Bible prophesied. "And the nations was angry. God Himself was angry for it had come the Time of the dead, that they should be risen up and be Judged according to"…

That's there in your Bible in the Revelations. God was angry; the Lamb was angry; everybody is angry because the world of the devil was against God and His Messenger. So God and His Messenger both was angry. I'm angry now; I'm ready to fight.

This is why that I'm here today. I come out alone. I don't have no armies with me. My few followers is very weak. They have no arms, but if they follow me to my God they have perfect arms; arms that don't…

I guess someone is hungry like myself. I too is hungry.

Save yourselves from this war. This is a terrible war. Everyone throwing at the other one all he have, and deadly bombs, guns, and everything. They're doing it. They're prepared to do it.

If you don't have a Saviour in this Day and Time, make haste and get one. Over in Europe it's a boiling point. In America it is the point of death. Everything pointing at her. "Oh, save America you will say." Yes, with America…

ANGELS: THEY ARE MEN, NOT SPIRITS OR SPOOKS

If America had not destroyed you she could be saved, but she have destroyed you. Night and day she killing Blackman. Someone must stand up for Blackman. So I have God on my side to defend me.

Storms, rain, hail, earthquakes, droughts, plaques of all sorts going on. I won't tell you that I'm doing that; this is what they want to charge me with. But I just charge it to the Right One, the Powerful One, that's God Himself, not me. Certainly I'm with Him. Certainly I hope that He will...just of our enemies.

So my dear beloved Brothers and Sisters, I have given you a description of what's in...There's a Scientist...that tells every spot where America, her bombs and where she got her dreadful. She have something dreadful. Dreadful planes scouting around with bombs that is capable of ripping this apart; but they face up to her.

That Scientist on there, if America bomb the Coast of California, they take this and just sneak away into another place. He have seen, he admitted to me seeing the airplane, but they can't get to her.

We are like the Jesus was when he was here. He had the knowledge of hearing you and hearing what you think about. If the Jew started at him on this side of town, he'd go on the other side because he heard them when they were planning to come...

One out of every hundred-eighty of the Righteous can hear you thinking over here. Tell you what you thinking about. There was two of that type of people visit my home here not so many weeks ago. They both look like Brothers.

Wherever there is a God raised man, or a Prophet to do a big job, these type of Scientists visit him to assure him of their friendship, that whenever the Right Time come we'll be with you; we will take care...

These the type of Scientists that you read of in the Bible that one or two go forth and do this and another one do that. These are the ones that I'm telling you bout visit me here not so many days ago.

They have orders by Allah, to do a certain job; each one is to do a certain job. Like you read of in the Bible, that one Scientist, he went out and his job was t

112

send a plaque of wind; send a plaque of storms, or to send a plaque of fire, or something like that.

These are the type of men, I know them and they know me. And that, everyone have a job to do. It's seven of them; Allah says that the job is not enough for one, but seven of them will be ordered to do it. And think over it, not spooks, they're men.

And last of all it's that dreadful Angel, which places one foot on land and one on sea. That's that dreadful one, that's the seventh one. And, the Book says and Allah affirms it, "He lifted up his right hand and his left hand to Heaven." This is the way Muslims pray. They lift up their hands and they pray like that, both hands. Then he said in his words, "Time, Time, know it now, we'll soon know no more." And then, he cut a shortage into gravity, and set the nation on fire.

This cutting a shortage means cutting a shortage into the atom of the gravity of the Earth, and make the atom over the Earth explode. When they explode, they set all the atmosphere into a flame of fire. And, there is no people can live on the Earth, because it will all be in a flame of fire.

This is the way the Heavens and the Earth will display the Judgment, as the Bible teaches you. But, the flame will only go up twelve miles high. But, it will most certainly get you that is on the Earth, if you don't get with Allah.

Our people have never been taught of Allah; they been taught of God. Well, in fact about it that's one of the Attributes of Allah, that's God. And, Allah is God, and He have ninety-nine of such names. Each one meaning something of Himself and of His Power and Wisdom.

So, I'm going to hurry now to dismiss you, as you have been just so faithful and patient. And especially my Brothers and Sisters who have drove along way trying to get here to see me and hear me. I'm so sorry that we was a little late today and I couldn't carry out what I wanted to. But, my people know me. Some of them came here; they have known me to teach this for years and they came out because they just love to hear it again and again.

Don't sleep, which is what the Book say happened with the five wise and the five foolish. The foolish went to sleep and Judgment was called before they could wake up. So don't sleep.

I want everyone of you who are visiting us to go to our restaurant and eat your fill for have price. I won't let you give me charity, and then not feed you, but, you have quite a few and I'm afraid that I may hurt myself if I give all of you a meal. I can give two, three thousand people a meal myself. I have feed ten thousand myself. I'm not your, hungry Preachers, of the Baptist Church, that is too stingy to give you a meal. I can give all of you a meal free, but, some of my Brothers may think that I'm over stepping the limits. But I don't mind. I know you'll give it back to me one day. I'm not preaching for you to give it back to me, nor am I cutting the price for you to give it back to me. No, I don't care nothing bout you giving it back to me. I love you and I want to give you something.

Certainly go to our eating places this afternoon; help yourself for half price. I wished I could give you a meal after you go home. That meal you eat then, I wished I could give it to you. I love you, and I hate to see the devil triumph over you and take you to Hell with him. So, I'm willing to do everything, even to my life…

I'm the little boy that challenged the world of Science to disprove one word I say. If you are able to condemn me false on one word I teach here, I'll give you ten thousand dollars out of my Brother's vest pocket, and then I'll pay with my life for lying to you. We must not lie in this day; it's the end of this world…we must not become no master liars; we must not become no minor liars either. Thank You.

May Allah's Peace and His Blessings go with each and every one of you as you return to your homes. Bless you with safety…But I pray and I want you to pray that Allah take us home without a broken limb or a scratched flesh, and without our property being marred and scratched. I thank you,

Salaam Alaikum.

THE ACTION OF TIME

Yes I, well I was told I was almost ready to stay home, and there you done made me now kind of sort of independent. If I don't see a lots of you out here, I won't come. So, now I see you do have the house full here before my face. Well guess I had to do something about it, if I just had to come up here and tell you how you acted in 1901, when you wasn't here in 1901.

Our subject has been for the last few weeks, The Theology Of Time. And that, I have Ministers behind me saying go ahead. So you must know the Time [The Messenger laughs]. To my Ministers As Salaam Alaikum to you. Certainly glad to see you here.

Know the way to get Ministers to go to work? You come out and work yourself, and then ball them out. See you can't do until you do your work yourself. You got to let them see you work. So they been thinking that I been sitting around taking it easy, lounge back in the shade. But now, I fooled them. I come on out and go to work. They have to watch me now.

Well, I got to look at you a little bit. I love to look at my pretty people so very; Minister Farrakhan is calling you beautiful, so I got to look at you and see whether you're beauty or not. You're not beautiful, I'm going tell you made a mistake. You know...

You know Brother Farrakhan is a very good Minister. He has been with us for a long time. And, he is a Minister to follow, to follow the Holy Spirit of Allah. Wonderful Minister, wonderful.

Let us go back over here, take a look at this, Theology Of Time. What is time? That's the main thing that we should know, what we mean when we say time. We mean from the distance of something else that has taken so long, and so long to get to the other point; and if the two points here to meet together becomes the time that we going to try and meet between the two objects.

So, it means that then, we have motion and motion makes time. We cannot have any meetings of time until we set up motion, then we reach how long it will take between this motion and that motion to reach each other.

Well, we can say like this and get you further understanding. Maybe I'm getting myself all tied up. If motion is made, we calculate around that motion takes to meet with another motion, or an object, right? Well, if I'm not right you ought to take me to school, and I better get away from there…

The motion radio, talk, and these, these pictures on some of these things that I say, you find a answer right there. I don't know whether you hearing me or not. Okay, you hear? Then I make some noise to see if you hear [The Messenger laughs].

You know, I'm very happy that we have here, as I was told, some visiting physicians whom I know, and they are visiting us. These people can cure everything that you can't cure. That's the kind of people they are. But, I don't want to make you sick. They don't have time to cure you in here, while that we are trying to cure you of a very bad spirit that an enemy put in you, four hundred years ago. And we don't want to get these two spirits still mixed up. We want to divide them, send one back where it came from, and keep the other one.

I'm quite sure that we have went over this board here so many times that you almost know what we have here. For the last five weeks, we have been talking on what's on this board, and on what we put on the board.

If we're going to acquaint you with the Time, when did Time start? We cannot talk on Time, unless we know when Time begin.

Well, we don't want you coming out here saying that we talking on something that we don't know nothing about. We know you, and if we know you, we know we talking about something. Yes.

Time, when it started. It started way back then, long way back. It started when the first motion of an Atom moved in, out of Darkness. When that Atom moved, It tell Time. That was according to the Teachings of Allah to me, was something around about seventy-six trillion years ago.

Now if you a Mathematician you will tell me what a trillion years is. I'm not trying to fool around there thinking you're a Mathematician. I might get tangled up.

Seventy-six trillion years ago, when that these things took place; that thing, the motion of time. If I do this, you can stare at me like, making, some kind of time, right? Because I'm doing this, making motion. So if you read the motion, then that is what I want you to do. And if you read, you can tell how long it took this hand to get over there, or go back here, that's time. But if I hold my hand up like that, it's making no time. Nothing is going on. It's just a hand being held up.

But, we as Original Black people here in North America, we had not been making time ourselves. And if you keep up, not knowing how to make time, time that is made if we left it, but it know I'm lost. You don't want that kind of time. You want time that will produce something.

When you're making, time, and there is production made by the actions of time, then you say we're doing pretty well. As long as we have no production from the time that we are making, we had best to sit down and let somebody else come in and make time.

We has been sitting down here in North America every since the slave-master said you a free nigger, so sit down and ask them for something to do. When a man has become so dead to the knowledge of the things in which he should be doing; and the knowledge of himself, he is wasting the time that man is in bad condition.

After a hundred years up from slavery, we have not made any effort in trying to produce something out of the Time, that the Divine has given to us.

We want to remember these things, and put them in your mind to continue to keep calculating on. If we calculate from the number One, Who is God Himself, then I think that we could get a starting point; and a starting point is what you need.

In the Day and Time that we are living in now, all round over the world and especially the country of America, I say it's Time for the dead to wake up. If the dead is to wake up, how are they to wake up?

If, we have nothing to wake them up with, or by, then we should produce someone to wake them up. But, if you have not one to teach, to align a kind of instrument to make the dead wake up; I say get after them yourself, yes get out there. And that, all the talk that we hear night and day on each one is full of war. All the talk you hear now got some war in it.

The Theology Of Time, it took place as we have been teaching, there, back seventy-six trillion years ago. We should feel good to know that we were the First people. We should feel good to know that we are the Righteous. If we were not the Righteous, there would not be a Judgment because, if you going to judge one wicked fellow, and you have another one to judge, it shouldn't be a Judgment at all. Just take these two wicked fellows and make them to agree they're wicked, and go head on with your work.

But, there are Righteous in the midst of wicked people who must be herd out and give them a chance to live with themselves; and, while they live themselves, you could take care the wicked. It is True about the sheep on one side and the goat on the other. That is True. And, symbolic sheep represents the Righteous.

Why did they choose this animal or this herd, to represent the Righteous people?

Because the characteristics is similar. That's why they choose the sheep. Sheep is a very humble animal, and a good and a very tough fellow. So therefore, I mentioned the symbol between the two, the two animals that really represents the people. A animal means right; a animal means wrong.

You know what somebody told me, when I was at home? That they didn't have hardly any people down here. I can't hardly tell the difference myself. I see every where is fill with people. I think the people trying to get me to stay in.

You know, I don't feel like David said he wanted to be; he wanted to be like a, some young, jumping...goat. He wanted to be like that. So, I don't see why you should say that I can't be like that too.

You know, I got some Brothers, well I had some Brothers that think that I'm always [The Messenger made a whining and crying sound], I'm not like that. They getting one over on you. They sending me home; need to stay home and rest. They tell me rest, rest. I don't want to lose you. I stay home and rest, the devil will come get you. They keep on fooling me, I'm going to come down here every Sunday.

You know I have Ministers; they out everywhere. I have Ministers everywhere. I can't exhaust myself...some Brother who wants to teach, and I like that.

No, don't get in a hurry trying to tell me why don't you go head and preach...No, No, No, that's wrong. We help the poor little Minister; he been talking all the while, while you was sleeping and eating.

Yacub, the father of the white race; that's the name of the God, Who made the white man. I don't want to bite off this, much. You know we use to think that the white man and the Blackman was made at the same Time. Now God came and told us the Time, and give us the knowledge of what was made in the Time.

I was so surprised until I actually wanted to go back and beat up all the preachers. I'm not talking bout you brother, we're not that type of people now. I'm not going to get after you. So, just take it easy. I will take our conversation personal; not out in the public, because my father was a preacher, and I'm afraid you will make fun of him. He was one until Allah made me one.

"What will Thy make," says his Uncle, "but something that will make mischief in the land and cause bloodshed." Today you have mischief going in all parts of the Earth, and bloodshed is following. This is the white race made to start us killing each other, while he himself kills.

Today, it is the idea of the white race, the devil, to kill all Black people. That is what they want to do. If they can't kill you like that, they will go to work and deceive you. Make you go long with them, whom your God will kill. They like all of this.

I was listening at one last night, talking about Black people, what they should do. I say, mister white people, what are you going to do? They talking over wholesale killing Black people. But I say, you can't put that small time stuff over on Allah. Allah will not be a Saviour if He could not save you and I, the Righteous.

All Black people are the Righteous. We was Created Righteous. Never was the unrighteous. Your make is that Absolutely Right. But the devil made you and our parents to follow him; that put unrighteousness acts in us. But by Nature, we are the Righteous.

This what the Bible mean when it say He will separate the goat from the sheep. Kill the goat, save the sheep. We are talking about us and the white man. The white man is the goat, and you and I are the sheep.

So, I want you to remember at all time, that you are not the goat, it is the white man that is the goat. Remember at all time, that you are not no brother with them; remember that.

When Yacub made them, He made them out the essence of evil, and not out of the essence of good.

So, this what we have been talking on all the while, we have been talking about the evil race and the good Nation. And, they are the evil race. Stay away from them. Don't be trying to marry them. It's just like going out there marrying fire, because they created, rather made from fire.

The Bible teaches you that and the Qur'an too. Made for fire; and we was Created good, and we are now removing from us that which is no good. And, I want you and me to unite together and be good. You remember this: we look alike, act alike, and yet cannot agree that you are one; you are one.

I want you Brothers, when I turn the mic [microphone] over to my Brother Minister, to unite with us. You say, " Uh, I don't know nothing about no Islam." What do you know about Christianity?

This is the thing that we must answer to. If we are not dead, what are we? If we are not deaf, what are we? You can't answer to your own self, because you don't know self. But I say today, I'm raised up among you to teach you who you are. And, to teach you who the white people are, who you been bowing down worshipping. And seeing them as gods. They are the god of this world.

But, you must get away from this. The Blackman is the God of the Earth. He is the Creator. I don't care how you been mistreated, still your Father was a Blackman, and He was the One Who Created this Earth; and now taking it over. This is our Earth! [The Audience applauds]. Thank You.

When did you ever see people like us come out with Moon and Stars on our heads? You aint never see that before. You didn't never dreamed that you could ever accept yourself, the Blackman, and the white man will respect you. You didn't never dreamed that it would ever come in your lifetime, but it's here today; and I mean it's here to stay.

Well we been trying to get you into the knowledge of what you own, and what your God and my God made for us. What on this Earth our Father made it for us. He didn't make it for no goat. Yes. And I say, let's act to go that this is ours, and leave what belong to the devil, to the devil. Yes.

We have some very find intellectual people in here, and we want them to say whatever they want to say about us and we'll be like Lot. No, not like Lot. Be like the Muslims when the City of Mecca was invaded…They never had saw a big army like that in all their lives. So, here come this great big army. So the Muslims say, yea, we can't save the City. We can't beat this Great Army. So we escape with our lives and leave the city to you [The Messenger laughs].

So, we know people confronted with such army, they just look at the thing. They know they couldn't whip him; and they didn't want to try to take a chance on driving them out. So, they give them back their land.

I have enjoyed looking at you. As you are the finest people on Earth. Easy, easy to get along with. You 're a fine people, Yes. I want again, to thank you for coming out to visit our Temple. Thanking you for thinking enough to come out, allow me to come in among you. I thank you. I'm so honored, until I go back and look in the mirror to see what you come out here to look at.

You know, I was going long the street one day a few years ago, and I heard a fellow say, "There go one of those people that don't believe in God. Man they talk about Jesus Christ like he something like yourself. I walked along. And so, I waited till he caught up with me again. I say, did you ever see Jesus? "No, facts about it, I been trying to find out what you talking about." [The Messenger laughs].

So, I'm going to let you; don't; I see a lady over here looking at me pretty…sour. "Next time I'm going to go somewhere else to try to find Jesus!" [The Messenger laughs].

You know I went out one day, and this old sister was doing her laundry, and she was really happy and singing, " Oh I'm going home to my Jesus one of these days." [The Messenger laughs]. I say sister they killed Jesus, stabbed a hole through his heart, killed him. I say, would you like to die like that? "For my Jesus I would!" I say, suppose Sister I would take my knife now and start at your heart, would you stand out here and let me kill you? "I didn't say I'd stand!" [The Messenger laughs].

Brother I tell you, we have some good people. They really will talk about dying myself with Jesus. But, you never see one get up there. The only time they get up there is when the devil put them there.

Now, I want to tell you, we desire for you to help us to make this place what it should be. And what you want is all the way down, way on down, way on down. Wait a minute now, I'm no preaching like I preach so hard to keep, you know, stepping back. I'm not going to fall off....We want to own quite a bit of property on the Southside for you, not for me, but for you. We want to rule the Southside of Chicago. This is where you live; Yes we can...

JULY 16, 1972 PART ONE / SIDE TWO

WE ARE GOING TO OWN SOME OF THIS EARTH!

Yes we can. We'll own it one way or the other. We must have a place on this good old Earth that we can call our own. Fine looking Black people, walking and riding the streets, and don't own it. No, No, we going to own some of this Earth.

Just a few years ago a gentleman was telling me, I was in Detroit, he say, "You talking about the Earth belong to the Black people," he say, "what about the white people?" I say I have to see your father Yacub about that. [The Audience applauds].

I see a man round here, you know, he comes around my house sometime; he is a Doctor. He tell me, he say I watch you, you should not talk so long; you should have stopped within a hour. See I'm scared tomorrow he may tell me that. So, I'm going to stop so that he don't have to tell me that. [The Messenger laughs].

So my dear beloved Brothers and Sisters, I'm going to turn you back over in hands of my dear beloved Minister and Secretary. And they are very nice Brothers. Oh yes they is. [The Audience laughs]. They don't ask you for but a little money, you know but they want, want you to fill up all the pales. [The Messenger laughs].

And I thank Allah the Most Merciful God, for Whom Praises is due forever, for sparing me to come out here, to just look at your smiling faces if I couldn't see nothing else. You so beautiful. Don't think I'm making mock, just come up here look at you. Come up here stand up here you look back over here, and there you will see a room covered with nothing but beautiful Black people. I'm telling you!

So I'm going out, and imagine you all the time before me a great, loving, beautiful people. No one is like you. So I'm going to turn you back over to the Minister and Secretary; they not going to increase your…I just was talking; they're nice Brothers. If you don't have nothing to give, well just come back next Sunday. Then if you don't have nothing to give, I will tell the Brothers take in all the monies that you find on them. And, I say you hold the bucket. I will say of this one, oh yea I know you rich because the Earth belongs to you. So why you not rich? It's because that you didn't give me no money, that's why. Well you give me some money, you stay wake.

Well, yes I'm not joking Brother. No, No, they will stay wake. Yea, and I will stay wake too. Any time one go to sleep, I…[The Messenger laughs].

Well I really have enjoyed myself. I see that Sister now smiling. She wants to hurry and

122

get out of here. So I 'm going on out of here before she get to looking at me tough. Well, that's...I'm not saying to you that I have a Sister here really don't like me. She would not have come out if she didn't like me [The Messenger laughs]. Well she don't like me I like her, and I want her to return next Sunday, and bring me a little change [The Messenger laughs].

Oh Brother, God told me Himself, he say we have the most beautiful people on Earth, and if you come up here where I am you'll say God told the Truth, you are beautiful. When you think you're ugly, you just making a mistake; you're not ugly, you're beautiful.

Well, this time Brothers and Sisters again I thank you for coming out to listen to Elijah Muhammad, who love to be a little humor sometime when he think he not going to get nothing much [The Messenger laughs]. So, so, he turn immediately into humor. When he say he going to get something, then he, he dig up all the Science he can find [The Messenger laughs].

And I don't want you to forget our visitors, our great, wonderful Doctors and Scientist, that have visit us here today. I want you to show them the greatest respect. Let them preach their sermon if they like to. And, we will listen at it. We'll ring his telephone in his office tomorrow morning, tell him says if you preached to us yesterday, I thought I heard a little and I didn't know it. [The Messenger laughs].

Well we heard Doctors don't come around looking up little folks; they looking up big folks. As the Jesus said, making a Spiritual and a Truthful, you know, answer..."The well do not need a physician, but it's the sick. He was referring Spiritually to Israel, that she was the sick.

So I say, Doctor we are sick. We are really sick. When you give us a dose of medicine, leave us a little money [The Audience applauds].

So may the Peace and Blessings of Allah be upon each and every one of you as you go out of here this afternoon. May you find your family all happy to receive mother and father, sister and brother again as they left, as I say unto you,

As Salaam Alaikum.

THE TIME OF JUDGMENT

As Salaam Alaikum,

I know that you didn't came out here with all these beautiful clothes on just to set to look at me [The Audience applaud].

You know my father was a preacher himself. When I was born I use to sit up, when I got old enough, pardon me, I use to sit on the speaker stand with him. And, everybody would try to hurry to get me on the speaker stand. And those days, much different from these days. My father was poor and he never could buy me a good suit of clothes. And that, I would sit up there, I was about two or three years old with a little dress on [The Messenger laughs]. That's right! They put us on little dresses. The boys is really growing some now.

I'm certainly happy to see all of you smiling faces here today. This really beautiful city. If you was here where I am, you would agree with me.

Well, I'm not going to take that preacher's text that I told you bout. But I'm going to have something similar, but I'm not going to have all of his works on the book stand. See, he had quart of whiskey up there and a forty-four lying between the Bible and the quart of whiskey. And he told his people he says, " My text today is that some of these things is going to move you." So I have a Holy Qur'an lying here in front of me, but I do say, some of these things is going to move you.

You may be seated. I had forgotten you were standing. You look so even looking cross your heads there; it look like you was sitting down. But anyway, looking over your head, I see something about your heads that I would like to get a hold to.

As I use to hear my father preach in the South. He was a preacher of the Baptist Church. And, he use to preach about that fire, Hellfire. He would teach it so frightening, but then even I myself being his son would be trembling sometime. Thinking, wonder will I live to get to Heaven before ever that come. And that, I was lucky, I didn't had to go to Heaven, Heaven came to me. [The Audience applauds].

We been preaching here, for the last five or six weeks on what you see on the board. We, had for our subject up until today, the Theology Of Time. And we are still working on Time. And since we have arrived here, and it's little cooler than it was earlier this morning. We want to take a hold to some of this, Time, subject. We want to take a hold, to, the real Root of Time as you, really, takes it for yourself all the time to talk about the Time is coming. This has been our subject for many years; and Time is what we been looking for. But Time, what you been looking for is the Time of Judgment. So, if you been looking for the Time of Judgment, this is just what we're preaching on today, the Time.

I'm very happy to have with us today, some of these people who preaches like myself. We have from Wisconsin, Reverend John Jr., Wis, Reverend Morris Neal, Wis. Then we have, Mister Richard Stocks Teacher, Wis. We have some Wis in here. Oh, here the Brother say these are abbreviation for Wisconsin. I know one thing, I was looking at how it spelled here like; and I was getting mixed up.

So, I go back over it. We have Reverend Morris Neal. We have Reverend John Jr. We have, Mister Richard Stocks, a Teacher. All from Wisconsin. Wisconsin is a smart state. I went out there and made a Temple in it, years ago. We have a Sister by the name of Miss Doris Watts. She's a Teacher from Wisconsin.

Now, all of you wise people coming here from Wisconsin here to hear us today, I may have you to say something… after…hear you see whether that I leading off for myself or not. I'm going to always try and protect myself.

So, I'm happy that you are visiting us this afternoon, and we pray Allah that you will be happy to continue. I'm not, say, really a rabbit, but I don't like for people to through bricks at me. I got to look around.

So, to have these professional class people with us this afternoon, we hope that they will leave feeling like that we're their Brothers and not their enemies. We're not here to teach against each other. We're here to teach the togetherness of us; and not to teach against each other.

Whatever you know; whatever you believe in, that's you. Whatever I know; whatever I believe in, that's me. If we like one or the other belief, we will let each other know. But, first I would like to say to you, beautifuls sitting here before my eyes, that's something that we don't have very often.

In the world today, we find their congregation very small in places. They're braking up and their running here and there seeking something more than what they have had. I see here before me, an estimate, somewhat little over a thousand people. I estimate them to be that. You come up here maybe you and I will get together on that. I think you look like you will number into a thousand or a little over. In fact about it, this is a small group to, when I go out in the public to teach the numbers up to ten thousand and more.

This don't make me feel like that I'm bigger than you. No. It make me feel that we are getting together. Not that I'm bigger than you. We're all the same. We must remember, as the Holy Qur'an teach us, we just cannot be so proud that we can reach the height of a mountain, or hill. Since we cannot even reach the height of trees and hills and mountains, why should we be so proud, when these things is higher than we are.

So, if we cannot reach the height of mountains, hills, and even some of our animals is walking round by us much taller than we are. So, why should we feel proud. I think that we should relax. Take a seat and sit down and look and see around us what all is really higher than we are.

We cannot step through the Earth, not by no means. The Earth is approximately eight thousand miles in diameter through it. Our legs don't measure that. I'm only wanting to ask you not to be proud. We can't reach the top of the mountains. And we can't step through the Earth. So, why shouldn't we be on the level on the Earth? Right?

This is what have ruined the Blackman in North America. He's taking steps after his slave masters. Want to be proud and big boys. You cannot be big boy even with him. He have the world, and you have nothing.

Well, I just want to talk with you a little. Little to hot for anything else we just want to talk to each other. We have, with us, men of all type. And, these men want to know whether or not that we have something above what they have or something equal, that we listen to each other on.

We don't believe in criticism, because we all came from slave parents. And that, if we want to criticize each other, we have to go back and get a hold to the devil slave-master, and see how many of us did he raise higher than the other.

I love...I love to be equal with you. I don't like raising myself up above you just because I believe I know more than you. No. We don't do that. I may have insulted you when I said that. But, a man Taught by God; lived with God for three years and a half, and He Taught him His Wisdom; I know you didn't hear all of this. I know you did not see all of this that was taking place forty years ago, that I'm teaching you about today.

But, I want to let you know that I'm not proud over you, in the way that we say it in proudness, comes to us. I'm not that kind of man. I'm a little old man that just love to talk with you. Love to see you in a better condition than you are in. Love to make acquainted my God and your God to you. This the kind of little fellow you see standing here.

We don't like showing off, by no means. If I have to hurt your feelings, I will try and rub the sore down somewhere in what I say. But, if I hurt your feelings, I'm hurting it for the better. Sometimes the Doctor have to hurt before he can heal. So, this may come to us in our talk or discussion.

Since we have preachers here, who do we say sent preachers out to preach? According to the reading of the Book, God…never sent no army of preachers out. The English language uses the word preacher. This is alright for us we understands it. We don't intend to make fun. But preachers of the right source, sent to people to teach them of something that is about to come to pass, they are sent from God and they don't never, and He never have a whole group of them. He place the responsibility of life on one man.

He sent Jonah to Nineveh according to the history of Jonah in the Bible, to call the Ninevehites to warn them that yet forty days and forty nights Nineveh will be overthrown. Why do He specify the forty days and forty nights? We want to find out why did He give him that length of time. Because forty days is used; forty nights is used in the end of the world. And to compare his preaching with the end of the world; man's Time death. Okay then, if it's right, he should have that number to give us a picture of what the end of the world figure will look like.

Jesus fasted forty days, you say, in the wilderness. What wilderness did Jesus fast in? We must clean up as we go. This is the way Scholars and Scientists get together after you. Everything you say, they chase you on it. I been chased by Scientist and Scholars; serious chase! Not much now, and, because they see me and they know me. But, I just want to teach you Science. I'm just grieved over that. I want to teach you the Science that you should know.

I want you to learn about the Person of God, and the person of His Messenger. I want you to learn Them. Then, you can battle if you want to. There is no Messenger of God comes in to bully the people that he's sent to teach. He let them do that; but he's not to mock and bully them. No!

We have thousands of preachers of Christianity in the country of America. You can't find in the Bible where God ever sent a thousand people. The preacher may have to go there and get a thousand, but he never sends a thousand to them. So, I'm not making fun, but I'm only wanting you to understand.

If there had been sent with me a thousand more Elijah Muhammad's, you would have seen me bowing out that group. Because, I didn't think God was so weak that He would had to send in a thousand. No fun, just want to tell you the Truth. Giving you the Theology side of the Truth. This is what I'm here for.

I know where we came from. We came from an enemy. Think over in the time of slavery. The enemy made his own preachers, and they had better preach what he tell them to preach. He still likes that. Remember reverend, I'm not after you; I'm just only trying to teach you the Theology Of Time.

At the present time, you see he will back up any reverend, if that reverend continue to believe what he tell him to teach. He will give him money to teach his Christianity.

I say reverend, lets us look at Christianity; when it begin? Did not God Created the Bible say Adam. And then, if God did not give Adam the True Religion, what does He look like then saying to you and I that here is now since Adam died I raised up Jesus.

Brothers, I say we have to remember: if Jesus had brought to us the True Religion, and yet Adam didn't have it, what are we going to say to Jesus? If Muhammad in the seventh century after Jesus brought out another religion, which is sweeping the Earth have more followers than Jesus, then what shall we say?

And, if God needed a prophet in the Day and Time of Jesus to tell the world that they didn't have the Right Religion; and Judges to give to you the right Religion, what did he say? Did he say he came to give the Right Religion, or to preach the old religion of…?

TEN THOUSAND ANGELS ARE IN AMERICA!

The God of Moses, Abraham. He say I came not to destroy the law of the Prophets, but to fulfill. But where I got my…from God. The God that was to come and is come. I don't say, that you believe in a man being God. Maybe you don't…If you don't believe man is God, I don't want to argue with you. Just show me that which you believe in.

So is there any one of you visiting preachers or teachers that is visiting us here this afternoon. I want you to know that our Temple, you welcome, to say whatever you want. I know you not going to say anything ugly, but, I'm just saying I take you to be intelligent people. Whatever you would like to come out here and say, or get up here on this stand you're welcome.

Come up here, help yourself. Anyone of you would like to have something to say that is visiting us and that is already with us? Anyone that have anything to say against or for what I am teaching our people, there's the stand. Or you may stand where you are, but I'm not the best of hearer.

Messenger: That's why, yes sir. Come up here Brother. Yes sir. Have a stand. Wa Alaikum Salaam Brother. [The Brother thanked the Messenger on the teachings. He stated that he love the Messenger, and that he wanted to take back home what he has learned and spread it to the people].

Messenger: Is there another one? Is there another one? Yes sir Brother, come right on out. You can come up here…

Brother Kenneth Williams: …My question…is about the reading that I been doing; and you mentioned that ten thousand Angels were here in this country. And I wanted to ask, would, would they be from among the dead?

Messenger: We can't hear him up here.

Brother Kenneth Williams: I wanted to ask if the Angels, the ten thousand angels that are in this country to help you, are from among the dead, so-called Negro?

Messenger: Well yes Brother. Yes they are here. They are not to be pointed out to people who will point them out. Like, in the day of Sodom and Gomorrah destruction, there was the Angels there with Lot that was going to do the job. But they couldn't tell the people before the Day that they was going to do it, then the people would have tried to kill them before.

The same way it is today, you can't point out the Destroyer of the world to no one, do you are pointing them out to the enemy to take attack on them at once because they're human beings like you and I. And we can be killed. And, if you have power to keep you from killing us, well then, we may bring about the whole thing before Time that the others get right and get ready to go out.

These things is used by very wise people and not by people just would like to tempt God and like to tempt His Messengers. You're not to tempt God nor to tempt His Messengers for just yourself. You got millions of people in America and they may all not be ready, and God wants to save us All! Not to do something just to please someone who would like to tempt God. You can't tempt God Brother, this is dangerous to try. And, to satisfy one person and his desire, you can't do that. We have billions here to please, or rather to try to save, and we hope that they will be pleased with our Saviour.

Brother Kenneth Williams: Thank you…

Messenger: You welcome.

Brother Kenneth Williams: As Salaam Alaikum

Messenger: Wa Alaikum Salaam

Messenger: Is there another one? So Sister Director; this is the Director of our schools throughout America.

School Director: As Salaam Alaikum Dear Sir, I would like to say on behalf of…

Messenger: Wa Alaikum Salaam Sister.

School Director: I would like to say on behalf of the staff members and the students at Muhammad Universities Of Islam, we thank Allah for you for allowing us to teach Muhammad's children the Truth of self; the Truth of the living God; and the Truth of the devil. I too would like to bear witness and say that I knew nothing before you took me in your hands. I, with all of my degrees and everything behind me, it was there to do nothing but to perpetuate the devil's civilization. I thank you Sir for teaching me the right way and enabling me to help you throughout the United States. Thank you Sir, As Salaam Alaikum.

Messenger: Wa Alaikum Salaam. [The Audience applauds].

This our Director of our schools throughout North America. She's head of our schools. What college and University did you graduate from Sister? This is what you should have told them when you begin. Go head tell them where you was graduated....

School Director: I got my Bachelor of Education Degree. I received my Bachelor of Science in Education from Chicago State University. I received my Masters Degree from Chicago State University. I have had graduate courses in Engineering Design from the University of California, the University of Wisconsin. I have an Associate of Science Degree in Electrical Engineering; an Associate of Science Degree in Arts with Photography as a Major. And, well a few others that I can't think of at this moment Sir.

Messenger: Thank you. [The Audience applauds].

Messenger: Why I ask her to come and tell her schooling to you and me, is due to the fact that we hear lots of people criticizing us out there in the streets, that, the School Of Islam, you can't learn nothing there when the head of it is no graduate of no school. And that, they do that to keep you from coming here.

Messenger: I want you to remember that there is not a Prophet in the Bible nor Holy Qur'an was a graduate from the people that he was warning. Not one! If you can find me a Prophet in the Bible was a graduated man from some University of the land, I, will pay you ten thousand dollars for lying.

Messenger: The Bible say Moses was highly educated; the daughter in the house of Pharaoh. That Moses we don't find in the Bible where he was educated under Pharaoh... in the school with a degree. And we find this man Moses whom they say was well educated out, away from Pharaoh. When Allah called him to go to Pharaoh, he was not in Egypt. He was out of Egypt where he was called.

Messenger: Now, we, I think, talks a little too much on that which we know little about. Moses was educated alright enough, but Moses did not boast of his education to Pharaoh. If he had, he would have been talking to Pharaoh in his own language. But, he didn't do that, because it meant that they had between each other about his non-expert language; he didn't argue; Pharaoh didn't argue with him that he had taught him an education. But he condemned Moses for not having an education capable to talk with him.

Messenger: So, we want to be right in these things. Some of these places where you find where Pharaoh and Moses exchanging arguments, is due to this time and not in that time. So, I won't go to far with it because we don't have much more time. And I don't want you to go back with your money wearing out your pocket because here is a rest place for it.

Messenger: So, if there is someone else would like to have a word to say for or against…Yes sir Brother?

Brother: As Salaam Alaikum Dear Holy Apostle.

Messenger: Wa Alaikum Salaam Brother McGee.

Brother: As Salaam Alaikum Brothers and Sisters. My name is Arthur McGee, and I'm a Mathematician. I have two degrees in Mathematics, a Bachelor Degree and a Masters Degree. And I have done most of the work with a PhD. in Mathematics. I'm not saying that to boast. I am saying that, to say this:

As long as I studied Mathematics and I worked in Mathematics, which was a period of fifteen years for the devil, I always wondered why it was, that I could never find the Original Creations that had been done in Mathematics by the Blackman. I always wondered why there always seem to be something missing. And I always wondered why I even though, I had made certain contributions always seem to be on the verge of arising, but I never really arise. But it was plain to me that I was doing the same thing that they were doing in some cases more.

So when I came into the Nation, I found the one man who could teach any professor that I have ever been taught under. He could teach in Mathematics. I have studied under some of the best professors in the world, at the University of California at Berkley. But the Honorable Elijah Muhammad, I'm here to tell you can teach them. He can teach them Chemistry. He can teach Biology. He can teach them Mathematics. He can teach them the Root of Creation.

So, I want to say to you my Brothers and Sisters who have degrees, in whatever field you have, come to the Honorable Elijah Muhammad. He will not take anything from you. He will look at you, and see what, your capabilities are. He will develop those capabilities. Whatever your strong points are he will develop them. He will find whatever points you are liking in, and he will develop that too, so that when he finishes with you, you will be well rounded. You will be twice, three times, or four times, whatever you are imagining you would have been before. As Salaam Alaikum!

Messenger: Is there any visitors here reverend or teachers…have something you would like to say? Is there any preachers or teachers that is visiting us would like to have something to say? If so, you will have to get over here to this mic [microphone] because we can't hear you where you sitting. You have to have a mic [microphone].

Brother: First I would like to give thanks to the Honorable Elijah Muhammad, the Nation of Allah. My name is Lloyd B. James. I live in Grenada, Mississippi. I have corresponded with you before Honorable Messenger, and I received a letter from you.

The reason that I am out of Grenada, Mississippi at this present time is because the police authority in Grenada Mississippi, they always harass me.

Not too long ago when I got a application from you to fill out, I was taken by the Sheriff department in Grenada County to Whitfield, Mississippi. I was given eleven electrical shock treatment to my brain. But I know what I am qualified to do because I know what I did in the Air Force. I don't have my high school diploma because I failed in English and history. But I do know how to build. I can build homes. I know how to set up sawmills. But, I have nothing to go on, I'm not strong enough to go by myself. I have written letters to you and the Temple is one hundred miles from my home in Grenada, Mississippi.

So I taken the letter to them and they told me that I should be able to move closer to a Temple, or I would have to visit at certain times. I have a family, a wife and two children. But, I would like to be able to prove to you what I can do, if there is any way possible. I would like to prove to you what I am able to build. I would like to show you the blueprints that I have drawn, but, I have them in my car. I never been taught to draw blueprints, but I know it, it just come natural to me. And these are some of the things that I would like to show you.

Messenger: Pardon me, I'm just standing here with another talker on my mind, and I did not see the Brother until he had walked away. Thank you Brother, thank you, we can use all the skill that our people have within them regardless to whom that they may be; man or woman we can use all of their skill. We want our people knowledge taken and put together and go to work for the good and the future of we, their people.

I thank you Brothers and Sisters. I think I have now to dismiss myself, and I will expect you back here next Sunday. I'm going to turn you back over into the hands of our Assistant Minister, and then he may have something to say to you.

Thank you for responding. But don't beg nobody Brother Minister. Don't beg no one to give us. Don't beg them, ask them, but don't beg them. Thank you, I have enjoyed this afternoon...

JULY 30, 1972 PART ONE / SIDE ONE

THE FIRST TRUMPETS THAT SOUND

As Salaam Alaikum!

In the name of Allah the Most Merciful to all Praise is due. The Lord of the Worlds; The Most Merciful.

My dear beloved Brothers and Sisters, I am happy to see your beautiful smiling faces. Makes me smile when I don't smile very often. You know why? I don't see you smiling towards Islam very often. When I see you smiling towards Islam very often, then you will see me laughing all the time.

You know, in the South, once there was a Judge and every time he would be late he would pay a dollar for every minute that he was late. Of course you know he didn't pay that dollar fast. And so, I'm late this evening, according to you and your count. But I'm not late as long as you see my followers here I'm, not late.

We have been teaching here with you for the last six or seven or eight weeks on the subject, the Theology Of Time. The Secret of Time. Let's just take it like that. You may be seated.

We have a very much work to do this evening, this afternoon, pardon me. And, the Secretary here, I would like for him to tell us, or rather announce to us which is the same, who we have here of the people from up state. And, pardon me we have new languages around here sometimes that maybe you don't understand. But, we going to make you to understand it, if there is a language for you.

Brother Secretary wants to announce to me who is here of the intelligent class of people of this world. And we are the intelligent class of people of the other world, to come.

First I want to say, I'm thankful to Allah for the presence of my Ministers back here. They don't carry a gun, visible gun. They have hidden guns in their hearts. Once they shoot, they silence all of the little guns. So let us hear from our Secretary....

Secretary: As Salaam Alaikum. In the name of Allah Who came in the Person of Master Fard Muhammad, and in the name of His True Servant, the Last Apostle, The Honorable Elijah Muhammad, Salaam Alaikum.

Secretary: [He announced the visitors list].

We want to thank you whom the Secretary have called off for visiting us here this afternoon. We hope that you will enjoy yourself. And that, we're going to do all we possibly can to get over to you all that we can. So that when you leave here, you will have some knowledge of us and our presence in the world.

In fact about it, this is what we are here for, to get over to you and acquaint with you of that which God have said to you through me. We want to get acquainted so fast, until we're nervous. Our acquaintance means much.

For long time, forty years, I have been among you sounding this kind of a trumpet. So, there was a end to Noah sounding his trumpet in his day and time. There was a end to Abraham and Lot sounding their trumpets in Sodom and Gomorrah people at their time. And, also came an end to Moses and Aaron sounding their trumpets to Pharaoh and his people.

These kind of trumpets is the mouth of men and the words proceeding from their mouth. These are the first trumpets that sound, call a easy sound because they coming from man's mouth. The other trumpets is not heard directly from the mouth; it passes through some mechanical instrument. That's the kind of trumpet I'm warning you to be aware of. They are lining it up now.

Don't forget that you're in the Time that has been kept hidden from everybody in here of the Time. Why do they keep this Time in secret from you? Because, they don't want you to know the end of their Time. They know that you will be happy to meet your God, and serve Him because they are not the God that love you; want to serve you with Freedom, Justice, and Equality. So therefore, they keep it hidden that Allah has raised me up from among you to open my mouth and tell you these things about them.

The Bible, a book of books. And, it have the one in Genesis, if understood, you also would know the Time. It's in there in the Bible, but the enemy knowing that it is referring to him and his Time, that he made translate in such way that you would never know. You would be just like the people of Noah and Lot and, Pharaoh. That is why that he had to take one of the dead and give him life First so that he can go down to the door of the other sleeping dead, and ring on it and tell them to come on!!!

In this knocking on the door to arouse the mental sleeper that he may wake up, join on to his own, kind and go...This is due to the fact that an enemy is shaking them to sleep as fast as the waker try to rouse them. The enemy, the blue-eyed Caucasian race have had the right to keep us asleep for six thousand years.

Now, he admits to me that he knows that this Time is meant for us to rise. But, he said to me in Washington, 19 and 42, he say, " Elijah we know this was coming, for a long time.

But if you had start preaching it twenty years ago you would have been shot outright." Think over, yea, think over that!

Me, little old boy standing before us and getting such action against you, and to qualify, the Bible teaches and Holy Qur'an that they killed all of the Prophets. A Prophet of Righteousness. A Prophet of Justice has your place upon the white race, before today.

They have tried to kill me as you know…many times. Many of you know this. They still trying to do so through you. He's afraid himself, but he thinks you're foolish and that if he tell you, "Go down there and kill Elijah," you'll certainly will make an attempt. You just that silly. You don't love yourself and therefore you would not expect to be loving me, to not try an attempt to take my life because the devil told you so!

But here's a boy standing on this platform that you, nor he can put that small time stuff over on us! We don't search you at the door thinking that your gun will go off and kill me. We just want to let you know the Science of the Time that the weapons at the door will not be used. No more using the devil's weapons to kill the Righteous of God. No! This is your last Brother, your last…before our…I'm not here to show off. I'm here to show you something, not to show off!

Their secrets of the Time been kept from the Blackman of America so long, that he himself don't believe in Time. We the First to rise from among the sleeping dead to instruct you, teach you the knowledge of the Day and Time you're living in. This is your Day and my Day. The white man don't have nothing in this day but death!

We can be proud if we want to, just because we wish they have a few dollars that is dying all the way round because… everywhere you find a currency, it's all cursed; it's dying a natural death. The stock market tells you…what your money is doing, it's dying.

I begged you last year, year before last, to loan me your money, pay you ten cent on the dollar. But you, think your great god, the devil have plenty money. "No, I will give it to him let him pay me interest on it." Really soon he won't be getting any himself, nor you!

But, there will come a time, I want you to remember, I'm not dumb of this, he will come out making you to believe that he have a great future. God will fool him like that to get you, like He did all the other great, strong people that He destroyed. He give them a little break before their actual death. Made them to think that they were going to live a long Time. But after that little, deceiving break of joy, happiness and their way of life, death came to them right in the midst of it while they played; while they married; while they were, hating the Messenger that was among them. All of that, the call came. We have it written in the Book, that as it were in the day of Noah, so shall it be in the Day of Son of Man.

"Who is the Son of Man, Mister Muhammad?" We're all sons of men, Brother. But, this Son of Man is different from a lot of the other sons. The thought that I call your attention to today, is a Son, of a Man. You use to hear this from the Christians pulpit, and you had plenty of imagination about that Son of Man. What this actually means, that God, Who have the Power to bring in the Judgment over the made-man; He also is a made- man, and is a Son of the Real Man.

I, know I, I don't…In the church they'd through me out [The Messenger laughs], because they don't understand. The Son of Man to usher in the Judgment, Judge-man, is a made - man too. The Original Man went and made Him out of the made- man, and out of the Real Original Man. For what? He wanted to get part of each, so that He could come and get you and me. And to…from the made-man put us back where we belong. And the Original Man Who was actually not made but Self Created. We are from a Self Created God, not a made God.

I hope you understand. You are a Great people! A Great people! Just think over, you are not a made person but a Created person! We can make something from us, or that which is Created, we can make all we want…But now let us Create something. You can't do that. This Temple here is from the material that was Created in the Earth, when the Earth was Created. So, the material is old and old, and old, because it is made out of the material that was Created.

The devil have not created nothing. If there be one of you before you leave here can prove to me that the devil have created something, I will give you ten thousand dollars out of my Brothers vest pocket for lying. The white man have not created nothing. Everything he want to build his world with, he found it here that our Father had Created.

"Who is your Father, Mister Muhammad that is not the father of the white man?" My Father is not a made father! My Father is a Created Father after His Self Creation. He began Creating Us. He is able to produce out of Nothing something.

I want to say to you, Theology Of Time, the Time that we are living in. The Secret of the Time of the Time was made so that you would not be able to know exactly when the Time- man is going off; for he will have you so fully fired against him; if you knew you probably would take him off before ever the Time expire.

Who would not be angry with a person that was not satisfied in taking away our… but took away from us the knowledge of self. That is the worst robbery you can do. To go and deprive a man of the knowledge of himself. You can't be robbed any worse.

I'm not so powerfully late. We have been teaching on many things. We have also, in here, today, teaching you how to eat, what to eat; how to eat to live. Why? Because it take eating to live; you can't live without eating. But, you must know what to eat and when to eat.

Oh, no sir I'm not after you. I know you still want to make a few more nickels.[The Messenger laughs]. But let us all move more toward a healthy corner. All our food been prepared by Satan is the death of us.

How To Eat To Live:

Number one: We must learn the right kind of food to eat.

Second: We must know what time to partake of that food.
And then, after we correct these errors that we has been making in food, then we will start living. God cannot prolong our lives unless we obey Him in what to put in our mouth because what we put in our mouth keeps us here, and the same takes us away.

You say, "Well Mister Muhammad you get sick." Yes I get sick. Maybe sick now. But it's not because of Muhammad ignorance that he's sick. No! He's well aware of the cause. How can I fulfill the Scripture if I don't suffer like you?

We, today must learn the mistakes that our Fathers made for following this devil out of Africa to come to the West. But, it was for a good purpose. We learned something for following a enemy to his kingdom. A enemy was made to rule for a limited Time; not forever but for a limited Time.

That God wanted us to get a thorough knowledge of the enemy, and then make us the most wisest and the best people to use to build the Kingdom of Heaven, as they call it, on Earth.

The Prodigal Son. He had went off and went astray in a far off country where he found the enemy of himself and his people. The poor man, he had no friends among them. And the Bible says that, "No one give unto him." But, after God went out at the Time when He know that he would be seeking a friend, met and escorted him back home to his family of kin people.

He knew that this man was without the knowledge of self, and the knowledge of the people that he had been serving; and the knowledge of his people back home. He had lost knowledge of all. But God fore-knew this, so He came out and met his son. Just the Time that his son had decided in his heart that he will go home, He went out and met him. Beautiful parable!

At last, there arose a famine in that land to make that Prodigal son come to himself; a famine rose up. The famine became so...that it taken the place away from the Prodigal son and all the money he had; he became in want.

Yeah, we like to talk on this, to show you where you are. He became in want and the want fell upon him so hard, that he begin to think over his own home. Looking around at himself seeing hogs eating getting fat off of corn and he getting lean off of nothing. He begin to think over his Father, wondering could he return to him after being such devil of a boy. He says, "In my father's house." Think over those words. "He had bread to spare. Though this…of mine don't have food for himself, nor me. I will arise. Begin to fix-up his story what he will tell his Father. He says, "And say unto him, I'm not worthy."

He begin to think over the things he went through with taking a enemy for my friend, and now he himself have nothing. I don't have no job. I can't get a decent job. He want to give me a job feeding hogs. I'm not suppose to be around hogs, and my Father…and the idea I got to get around a forbidden animal that I should not touch. But yet, that is the only job…I got to get out of here!

Father I don't want you to recognize me as a son, you're too Great for that! I will insult your whole house, for I have lived among strangers. "Where have you been?" I better pray. "What did you find there?" Animals, they don't have nothing to eat Father, but you have bread to spare. And I'm here and I ask the stranger for a job. I didn't ask to be a guest of his, I just asked him to let me have a job, and he soon had no job for me.

America will soon not be able to give you a job. You are the non-American. You are not the white man kin, nor are you his friend. Regardless to how you claim that you're his friend, and will do good by him, you can't do it by nature. You both are different people all together.

He can't be your friend, nor can you be his friend. By nature you are different. As the Holy Qur'an says in the…that "you are created by the nature, that nature which calls you to Righteousness, and the devil is created by nature which calls him to oppose," and he is doing it!

And you want to have your parties, your conferences to get together to seek a way; some kind a way of telling the white man that he's mistreating you. He know that! He wasn't made to treat you right, and he will tell you that. And he listen to me every minute of the hour. He have his mechanical instrument set up on me all the time. He hear every word I'm saying now. But he cannot condemn the words that I am saying. He can't find that they are other than the Truth.

You will never see him out trying to face me to condemn what I say. Never! You can go get him tell him come on down here Elijah talking about you, he'll say "I don't want to see Elijah." No, he don't want to come down here to try to tangle with me and the Truth.

It's just like the Bible teach you, "They will shut their mouths at him." This is the him the Book is talking about. They will hear me raising at them; sometime they will ask some of my boys that stay round near his house, "Was he mad with us?" If I am angry with you, what are you going to do about it?

Now remember, that I'm the only man in America of your kind can talk like this; and don't you get out there to try to do what I'm doing. You can talk like me if you stick to what I teach you. But don't go out like Peter, just because he saw Jesus walking on water, he thought he could do it himself. He had gotten so powerful, now he could jump out. And from his own self, walk the water. And the foolish man start sinking. Then got frightened to death, calling on Jesus to help him. The world...

THE DAY OF SEPARATING
THE SHEEP FROM THE GOATS

The world represents people. You notice that brave Peter was scared of the Judge who was trying to judge the Jesus in the court, and he refused to bear witness that he was one of his disciples because he was afraid of the consequences of the Judge. But Jesus told his enemy, when he was threatening to death, he told him that he could not judge him. So if, I'm wrong, let me go before my own Judge, and not you. You're not the one to judge me. So here he stand, this is he. [The Audience applauds].

The Theology Of Time…let me stop wallowing over this stand. Make you think that I'm a very sloppy fellow…not recognizing his stand that he's speaking from as a sloppy fellow. No I'm not, but I'm taking my time because, I have been coming out here speaking to you on this subject for a long time. And, I mean to bring this close to the end. Really the end is execution.

I use to preach in Detroit and many other cities. You never see me take a drink of water. But now, since my voice is getting, little kind of old, and, it's got to have a little rest every now and then, I take a drink of water every now and then. I have a very good grandson. That's my grandson that you see pouring the water in me; he can't pour the word in me; he can pour the water in me.[The Audience laughs].

The Time. What Time? The Time of a race of people that was made on Time to serve Time. A certain limits of Time. What is Time? We have Time as a motion and we calculate from motion to motion, or from movable to movable things.

The Caucasian race, the white man was made by one of our Gods who looked into the germ of the Man, of Man, the Original Man. And He found in the Original Man in His laboratory, that the Blackman germ had two men in it, or two people. And He learned from that knowledge how to separate the two germs.

Our brown germ associate with our Black germ that that brown germ could be separated from the Black. This is what He learned. And He could deprive one of his life, and make that… He say, rule that which He deprived of life.

That's what happened six thousand years ago, where you find it written in the Bible, "Let Us, make man." And, the Holy Qur'an, "We made man." Let Us make man. Who was the Us? The Us was Black people. That was the Us. Let Us make man and give him dominion over all life. And then at end of six thousand years, we will remove him with death, and sit the Original Man back as Ruler.

"Well, now Mister Muhammad, come on we have something we could ask you." Yes! I'm producing a argument! Yes. Although I am producing the material to refute the argument. What that that fellow said in the Book? He said this Mister Muhammad, he said, that, "In the volumes of the Book, he comes." You can't single out a single book for him. [The Messenger laughs].

If he comes in the volumes of the Book, why? He answers himself, because they are written of me. Then, he challenges the reader, He say, "You read the Scriptures and in them you think you have life," Rather, "you think that there is your salvation, but they only speak of me."

I don't want you to think that I am boasting, but look what is written! He said, "this one is his First born." First born from what? "There's plenty men on this earth mister. Who are you to say you First born?" He's my First Spiritual born from the Spiritual dead.

I don't want to get rational at you, because you don't have the argument to come back and challenge me with. But I want you to get away from that Bible whom Satan poisoned by the touch of his hand, taking out Truth adding in lies.

Well, he took the Truth and made un-understandable for you by putting Truth into...types, of poems, making poems for you to understand. And in so doing, he cost you understanding using symbols. And you never was able to read the symbols and understand the Truth of it.

So, God love you so well, He taken one of you off aside, open the Book say, "Son, read, I will analyze it." For three years...and a half, I would just sit beside His side. Three years and a half, Teaching me night and day that which has been hidden from us for six thousand years.

And that which was so poisoned that it just absolutely put us to sleep for the last four hundred years. But I thank Allah, and I have been sent by Him and He's backing me up to bring the enemy to his well bought doom, hell.

You're looking for God because that God, you don't know. You never was taught to know. You're taught he, he, he. Where is he? And you look up in the sky, where is "he" up there? And he can't single out "he" up there.

Do the Bible teach you, and me to wait for a "he" to come from out of the sky? He said the Son Of Man. Man is on Earth and his son. You can't look in the sky for God and His son to come jumping out the sky; that's what the devil is up there looking for now. And he will never find him.

The parable is given; here is the parable of the water that was gushing up out of the Earth at the heel of his heel, while his mother running all over the hill looking for water. There was a ever flowing spring at the heel of her son. [The Messenger laughs].

Yes, I, I, I, feel like going ahead! I don't feel like staying behind at no juncture. I want to make you acquainted with the Almighty God, so that you will know Him as I know Him, and whom He have visit in your midst out of Nothing to bring you into something.

Well I reckon it's a good thing for me to be held down as the Holy Qur'an teaches you, that suppose Allah shut the Messenger's mouth; and he don't warn them [The Messenger laughs].Well that's right, because He know I'm so over anxious to tell you what He have told me. And if He didn't shut my mouth every now and then, I certainly would keep it open. [The Audience applauds].

Speaking to you, numbers here of around about two thousand people. I want to tell you what God have told me. The secret is for me to tell after God tell me in my ear, I jump upon the housetop and tell it to you. [The Messenger laughs]. He told me He say, "Brother, when I tell you, you can get up on top of the house and yell out your wisdom." But I'm so anxious to tell you, He have to pull my coat.

The Time, the Book say that Time He says, "tell them that, that Time is up, and Time shall be no more given to the Time of the expired." He will have no more Time, though God give him extra Time. But nevertheless, Time that was set for the white race, now is up.

They're constantly telling you about their disagreements that they are having with each nation. I'm not going in to the politics of the nation because I have declared to Him I would take nothing to do with the politic; and I was not raised for no political man, and to do that kind of service. Because, to even know it…not going to take no part in it long as he live. He got a corrupted political world. Let us stand and look at his die, then when we build one, it will be one to live forever. Let him die the natural death of an enemy!

As you may hear daily, like I, we, that's our people in studying the white people, we must do this and we must have that. We must serve this man, and we want this and that. He's wasting time. Get out, get out and do something for self! Stop wasting time sitting round. Stop knocking up and down the street begging the white people to give the old once slave something with him.

As you know these preachers, begging preachers, they don't beg for a chance to go for self. They beg for a chance to live with the enemy. He wants to go right back into the slave house, sit down beside his slave-master, tell his slave-master recognize me as one of you. You would think he would want to get as far from his slave-master that is the East and the West.

He see his slave-master killing his Black Brother all up and down the streets, all up and down the highway, and he still begging, let me live with you; accept me like you would accept yourself. All the history of slavery he reads, he should be begging the white man, loan me one of them cannons you have.

This is awful to see a people treated like that by another people, then go back to that same people begging them to make us their friends and their brothers. I get so vexed when I hear our people begging for a place with the devil, that I can hardly sleep anymore that night. That's the Truth!

Begging his enemy now, to take his own life. "I don't want to live, I want to die with you." That's what he's telling him. "I don't want none of Elijah's teaching. I want to be your friend, not Elijah's friend hating white folks." Poor foolish man. I don't want to go with him, I'm not going nowhere with no god from you Mister white man!

Oh my Brother, if you could only see where I'm looking at, you'll wish that you had not been born on the same Earth that they're born on. Oh my beautiful Sisters, running around laughing in his face every time he look at you, you want to show him, "yes sir, I love him."

Why do you love the white man? Because he's unalike this is why. You not looking at the principle of the nature that he's made out of. And then, all you are looking at is the surface of un-alikeness; and you're ready to cast your little black baby into fire to go along later with him later in fire. It's awful!

But this is the Great Day Of Separation Time. We heard of this Time coming every since we were born, right? Time, what Time? Time for the Great Separation of Black and white.

The Bible teaches you there will come a Great Separation. And that the sheep and the goat will be divided. The sheep to the right. Why to the right? Because, in the Creation they were Created right, and they should stand to my right, representing the members of the Creation as being Righteous. You don't want to stand there.

To my left, stand the goat. Why do I call him a goat? Because the mischief-making goat, this man is like. A goat will go out, climb the clothes line, eat up your clothes. They will walk on your nice clean rugs, then turn around and chew it up. The God give him the right name when that He said he was like a goat. Poor little sheep stands over here making trouble with no one. Oh Brother it's something to think on!

"And I saw a Lamb." Not a kid, goat, but I saw a Lamb. Think over how that he style… races out. "Out of the Lamb's mouth proceeded great words," that the enemy couldn't stand the words. Their all the people rose up blind, deaf, and dumb to the understanding of the symbolic Lamb. They call it Jesus back there two thousand years ago. Poor things, they had not studied the nature of the animal of why a person is called a sheep.

How could he be called a sheep? How could he be called a Lamb? He was not First of his people for you to call him a Lamb newly born. Do, the world would have been changed in his Day and Time.

Why he's called a Lamb here further in the Revelations? Because he's the First that is born to bring about a New Civilization, and he's the First of that New Civilization. This Brother is something.

Now, if we say the Time is come all of our life we have been blowing off our mouth over the Time will come; when the Time come and when the Time come this and that. Now I want to talk with you, and in talking with you, how much knowledge do you know of the Time?

Why do they know and refer to the Judgment as the Time? Their talking about the Judgment of the devil Caucasian. Why is there referring to it, the Time will end, and they mean Judgment, the understanding of it?

If the white man was made, and that the God liked the man and he give the man dominion over all things that was created by Him; Okay then, why did He make this man for destruction knowing when He made him that he intend to destroy him? Why did He make devil? He made the devil Brother, to show you and me how much Wisdom was locked up in the Blackman that never had been made clear to the Blackman, the Wisdom that was in Him.

So, if God made a man to kill, why did He make this man, since he's born like He made Himself, in the same form that He made this man? That's why He say he's made like unto his God.

I guess you would like that I hush. But this mankind, not the Man, but mankind, must be destroyed because mankind effects the Man. Therefore, we must remove from Man that which affects Man; for it is the mankind that affects the Original Man.

Read the devil blue-eyed Caucasian's history. From start to finish he has been a enemy to Blackman all over the world. He's poisoned everything that comes to us; he lay his hand to it to poison it.

Now you getting books to read how that he has destroyed and continue seek to destroy you. You have lots of books teaching you today; he spreading out himself. How that he's poisoned the Blackman in his food and in his water, in his medicine he's poisoned him. He don't want especially to leave his Black slave here whom he taught from the cradle. Now for God to take that same Man which has arisen that He has taught; He will teach him the Wisdom how to rid the Earth of him.

You must remember…that Jehovah did not drown Pharaoh; He made Moses to do the job. And run over here to the last of the books [within the Bible]. He did not sound the trumpet Himself, but He made an Angel; told the Angel where to go and how to stand. You must remember how to understand the Theology Of God Teachings. You must understand.

I'll teach it to you; How To Eat To Live. Now, after you eat, I can tell you about how long you will live if you even eat like that, but I can't tell you if you're going after eating your good meal, go then and spoil it with a poison meal. God cannot lengthen our lives unless we take control over what we eat, because, what we eat keeps us here and what we eat takes us away. You eat the right food, and at the right time.

You say, "Well Mister Muhammad, is you doing all that?" No! I have to live a period among you like yourself. Then after living the same life that you are living, and then God bring me out of that life that you are living, then still give me life to live the life that He want me to live.

He fixed up Job and He turned him over to the devil. Told the devil there he is, do all you want, but save his life. I didn't give you his life, but I give his life for you to do as you please with him. But yet after you do with him as you please, he'll be back to me.

You speak, probably as…"you must have done something Elijah that God afflict you like that." Yea I did something; I did the same thing you did; that's why you are sick. But don't think I don't know how to be wise and healthy; I already have that long with me. But I want to show you that I can live your life for a certain time, and then come out of it.

As you know, the next or the past six or seven weeks I was up here, "yes Brother, that's right Brother." But today you hear me speaking. As the Bible says, "…the secret of the mule and Baal. Baal told him when he asked him, " Why did you beat me these three times?" Baal says, "Because you mock me." He never said why, and what was the mocking that the donkey was mocking him with. He never did say that the mocking was due to the nature in which he was made.

And the donkey had learned that by the nature in which his master was made in, that he shouldn't be carrying him on his back. So he looked around and he stop and he said, "get down man." And what he said it was meaning get off of my back you are not such that should ride me; I should be riding you. [The Messenger laughs]. You must, from this day on remember, that you has been the donkey for the white man; remember that. Yes I feel pretty well.

...Eating the hog. Doctors won't tell you to stop eating the hog because they wants a job. But not that they don't know that the hog is a poison animal which should not be touched by man's flesh. Well, when a man want a job you can't fault him for trying to find him one. But I say to you, tell your Doctor don't eat hog; he'll be a doctor for you a long time.

Those little pork worms that you call...that weave through our flesh and they keep weaving, keep weaving till they get into the spinal cord and they keep weaving, building up a family into millions every where he go. They are not the kind of worms that will prolong the life; they will shorten your life.

Don't eat hog; don't eat no kind of meat if you can help it, but if you will eat meat, eat the best of the meat. The sheep's meat, it is not say no glorified meat, but it's better meat than the rest of the meat. Don't eat either kind if you can help it. There is no meat that is good to eat, so God Taught me. If you just must have a piece of meat, go take that little young pigeon that never flown away from its nest, eat him; but after he leave his nest, don't eat him.

When I went to Egypt for the first time, I saw so many pigeons one morning...coming in early to Cairo. They look like little cages of birds that we cage up here when I looked out and saw them. So, I went down to the market to look at them there. And when I noticed at the market there, saw all these little birds [The Messenger was making bird sounds], I say those are the birds we need in America. The whole truck load of them, coming in like the chicken raisers here come in with their...birds.

I want to say again...I want to say again, you don't go among Muslims asking for no hog, or he'll show you the way out. This dirty no good animal live off of filth. You can't offer hog anything that is too filthy for him to eat; he eat anything. He is a dirty rascal. And he so dumb, if you feed him he'll never look up to see where it's coming from until you stop dropping it down to him. Then, he'll run all over the...looking for another mouthful of that food with his nose in the ground.

When he get through he, go driving his nose up in the ground looking to see if anything went down in the Earth. He'll turn up the Earth for you. He is a no good animal; he got a ugly eye. Don't eat the hog. When you eat him your children born from you, they will have some of his characteristics: going along with their head hung down, having muddy reddish looking eyes. Don't eat that animal please! You'll never see the Hereafter if you keep salting your hands and your mouth with that flesh.

They won't let you live near to them. Nope, they're wise. God said to Moses, "Don't eat that animal. Don't touch that animal." Think over that. Don't touch its carcass. He's a forbidden animal to you to eat.

Here the devil come along, "What's wrong with this. I don't see nothing wrong with that hog; his meat is good to me." Tell him, say you devil, you go ahead that's what he was made for. "Well God mad…for us all except what He make is good and very good." Brother, you haven't learned the Truth. He made the hog, to cure, the white man's disease. This not, the hog is a medicine animal.

I use to in the South, if I got a boil on me I'd go cut off a piece of that salt pork, apply it to that coming boil to help bring, you know, to an end by bringing up all of that poison to the surface; then I burst it. And there go the poison that was making me sick running out. And then I'd go now and eat that thing…

HOW WILL YOU ESCAPE THE DESTRUCTION?

And then I go now and eat that thing! Ah Brother this terrible! Let us never eat another piece of hog as long as we live if we live twenty thousand years...you won't be classified as good member of first class society; and you won't see the Kingdom of God. Not one hog eater will enter the Kingdom of Heaven, unless you stop eating the hog. This is one Teaching God give me specially; don't you eat no hog.

Over there in the dominant society of Islam, if you mention the name of it, they don't want you in their society. Don't even talk about a hog in their presence. I had experience, I been over there and I visit both Holy Cities, Mecca and Medina. And all the others here in what they call, the Near East, Holy Land. So, you're not listening to a man don't have some knowledge of what he's talking about; and the people and where they came from and been observing it all of their lives.

I'm a man that have visit the people of Mecca and Medina. And what you call the Near East here round in Egypt and the Northern part of Africa. So, I'm not saying things that I don't know what I'm talking about.

I have a Captain here that have been all of these places herself, and that's why I choose her for our Captain. Because she had experience of the people of Islam. And...in Islam; and she can help me with my women folk, in teaching them the knowledge and characteristics of the Muslim woman. And then if she don't carry it into practice herself, I got a big Lake over there. [The Audience laughs]

How To Eat To Live. I'm bringing out to you a very beautiful book on that. It will be a hard back; and you going to like it. And I'm not going to try to get rich off of it in price. I don't want that because I want to give you the Truth; but what it cost me to get the book in shape to be publish, I have to pay the man. He won't give it to me. So, then I have to charge you a little something.

But it will be out probably before the year is out. Then you'll have that nice little hard back book with golden letters on it. How To Eat To Live, which means how to live and have life that you are satisfied and you love to live that life, because you get something from that life.

I reckon ya'll say, "He certainly does teach a long time."

You can make life faster than you can remake it. I hope you understand. How To

Eat To Live. Did not you know Man has been studying this all Man's history, throughout his history; how to live longer. His life become so short after the devil was made, and make the Blackman, the Original Man follow after him to shorten his life, that he has been praying to God all the while asking Him night and day how to live.

How to prolong his life; this has been the study of the Scientists all these many years of Ours; how to lengthen man's life; and it's simple, but the enemy makes it a very...study, but it's simple.

In the Hereafter there will be no doctors; only for certain things as bruises and broken limbs, but not for the present care of the physical body. There are people over there right now, I ran into them, that they ashamed to tell you if they feel sick because they know they should stay well. Go there and meet them for yourself. If they are sick, they shame to tell you, because they made themselves sick. In fact, sickness comes from your own self and from another man.

It is not that God created sickness for you; He didn't create death for you. We kill ourselves by not knowing how to live. You can, and I can live as long as I want to, and you can live as long as you want to, if you know how to eat to live.

And the water of our Earth being poisoned by this blue-eyed devil. Cutting your lives short by drinking even the water; he have learned how to poison. And, that he is the one who furnish us in our drinks for our lives; and he fixing us up too.

Yes sir, he know that he's going! He know that the Blackman is going to put that going to him. He know that, therefore, he's angry with the Blackman. He seek to destroy every Blackman on the face of the Earth; believe me or let it alone. I don't care how good you think your beautiful snake eyed, blue-eyed devil look to you, he want to destroy you; and doing everything to destroy you and me today, not tomorrow, but today.

Oh, would that you understood. "Well how you going to escape?" I'm going to follow my God and do everything He tell me to do. Don't think that they mean any good to you and me. No! No! He come to me laughing "How you do Mister Muhammad?" How you do Mister Jones, shaking his hand. Both of us have death in our hearts for each other. Yes Brother, because, the Time have arrived. I want to eat; for what, Mister Muhammad?

So, my beloved Brothers and beautiful Sisters; you are beautiful. Soon after this war... the going out of the war, you...as the Bible says, that it's not yet or we don't know yet what we will be like, but we know that we will be like Him.

Why? Because, He must make us like Him in order to prove His Civilization-He's Making. If we don't look like Him, then He could deny making us; as we could deny being made by Him.

But we will be made like Him. He told me all about that; that's a great long lecture within itself, of what you will look like in the Hereafter. He have given me that knowledge of how you will be changed into that way. So I have all of that in my, little old big head here. But, you as a child, you might know your alphabets first.

I'm looking for help. I'm looking for the Black Scientist that know something about how to build and how to tear down. I want both a wrecker and a builder. So if you will, write me, tell me what you can do; and what you're willing to do for me and my work that you are learning now, very fast. Do something for yourself; buildup for the Blackman, wherever you can.

We have adopted here on the Southside, that I'm determined to bring it through; make the Blackman rule himself and others in the, Southside. You be your own Ruler! I will teach you how, as you see I'm my own Ruler. Those that follow me, they are coming along fine. They soon can go for them self. Some of them already going for them self.

This is what I want to do. I want you to be yourself and Rule yourself. Don't jump out before now you get your diploma; lest you come running back to me. Wait till I tell you that you can go for self. Don't try it before you get the diploma, or your degree as you have already gotten a diploma from some part of this work; or over some part of this work. Get now, your degree.

I thank you, and all of these visiting people that is visiting us this afternoon; and these scholars and scientists that we have among us here. I hope that you will remember to write me and visit me again. This is my house here; you'll find me here.

I'm grateful and thankful to Allah for you. I want you to follow me to save your life. Go home tonight and listen to what the radio is telling you; and if you give it your attention, you will say, "Muhammad is telling me the Truth, I better run for my life."

There is much more that I would like to say to you that you probably wouldn't have the patience to listen, because I could stand here the way I feel right now [The Audience applauds].

I want you to remember, today I have one of my greatest teachers here...what are you hiding behind...come up here where they can see you. [The Messenger laughs]. We have with us today, our great national preacher. The preacher who don't mind going into Harlem, New York; one of the most worse towns in our nation, or city. It is our Brother in Detroit and Chicago, and Harlem, New York.

But, I want you to remember, every week he's on the air helping me to reach those people that I can't get out of my house and go reach like he. I want you to pay good attention to his preaching. His preaching is a bearing of witness to me, and what God have given to me.

This is one of the strongest national preachers that I have in the bounds of North America. Everywhere you hear him, listen to him. Everywhere you see him, look at him. Every where he advise you to go, go. Every where he advise you to stay from, stay from.

So we are thankful to Allah, for this great helper of mine, Minister Farrakhan. He's not a proud man, he's a very humble man. If he can carry you cross the lake without dropping you in, he don't say when he get on the other side, " you see what I have done," he tell you to see what Allah has done. He don't take it upon himself. He's a mighty fine preacher. We hear him every week; and I say continue to hear our Minister Farrakhan…

We want to unite together, but it takes a God Who wants to save us. We can't be saved from the destruction of a enemy by making friends with the enemy; and believing in him more than we believe in God. "Come out of her," your Bible say, "Come out of her, and be not partakers with her and her destruction." "Come out of her." I tell…what I'm going to do, if you don't come out her, Brother, I'm already out of her and I'm going to keep running to keep from getting back in her.

Let us go home and eat to live. We get hungry; all the Scientists that ever lived …..fasted and prayed…was eating people. Some of you hear and read of…eat nothing but vegetables, but they was eating. So let us eat to live. God have Taught me to teach you How To Eat To Live.

I thank you for your patience… Let us go and Eat To Live. Thanking you all with I, I pray that God able you to live the years of Noah; of Methuselah. I pray that you live a thousand years too.

So, I thank you again for your nice, beautiful, respect, of my presence among you. I thank you. May Allah respect you in the Kingdom of Heaven.

As I say unto you, in turning you back in the hand of our Assistant Minister to take care of your dismissal. I don't want him to beg you to death because I will be back next Sunday asking you for a little.

So may, may the Peace and the Blessings of Allah go with you wherever you may go, and find your family with the Greetings of Allah on your return, to you rejoicing that you went out, mother and father to hear the word of Allah, and I say unto you,

As Salaam Alaikum.

PART THREE:

THEOLOGY OF TIME

AUGUST 06, 1972 – AUGUST 27, 1972

THE PRAYER OF THE PROPHET ABRAHAM

As Salaam Alaikum. You may be seated. Again I say As Salaam Alaikum.

Brothers and Sisters I'm very happy to see your smiling faces. That makes me feel good to see no vacancy, but a little and I think before we are finish, it will be filled.

We continue our subject, the Theology Of Time, as this is the thing that you should know; what has been hidden from you, and what is being kept hidden from you. I'm the fellow that is raised up here to open my mouth and tell you what Allah has revealed to me that was hidden. And that the prayer of the Prophet Abraham and Others, should be fulfilled.

That is, that God will raise up a Teacher from among ourselves and teach us the Truth of this world, and the Truth of ourselves which this world have deprived us of. And so, this is the little boy that you read of there in the Bible.

If you take note of the name Elijah in the Bible, it comes in the Old Testament and leaves out in the New Testament. He's followed by many witnesses of the Prophets, and the local Prophets. Some of the local Prophets don't have too much to say, but he goes directly at the point. We call them Minor Prophets. He don't miss nothing of what has been revealed to him. He tells it right out.

I hope you are hearing me. The mic [microphone] up here you will have to tell me yourself whether you are hearing well, because you are listening and I'm speaking and you can tell me whether my speaking is getting over to you clear enough for you to understand. We don't want you coming up telling Allah I didn't understand him. I didn't hear him so well; something was wrong with that mic [microphone] and they should have fixed it so I should of have heard it, and I would not have been out here with the disbelievers. So, we don't want you to have no excuse.

In the past, we find that the Messengers of God had people claiming an excuse. But this Messenger is to make it so plain, that you can't claim an excuse; and I watches you to see if you misunderstand. And you welcome after I say all I intend to say this afternoon…

154

THE MEANING OF "LAZARUS BEING RAISED FROM THE GRAVE"

This afternoon to ask me questions if you didn't understand. But I don't invite you to ask me something just to be talking. Yes sir, I will try and keep you from that, in what I say. But, if you think that you have found something that I failed to say, in what I say, I want say No, because, you want have time to stay here to hear all that I have to say; and I won't have time to stay here and tell you. [The Messenger laughs and the Audience applauds].

But, if you had said in the beginning, which was about so long and so long, or it was so long and so long, don't say about because it had a beginning. There is nothing before Us, nor behind Us, what didn't have a beginning.

We use to say nobody knows; that was right but there was a beginning… you see, if God was not before the beginning of what counts….then who was it before Him?…He was the beginning Himself.

Listen at it good! The beginning of Time was made by the beginning of God. We had no beginning before He made Himself. We could not calculate on Time because there was no motion making Time. But after H e made Himself, He made a motion and we been reading Time every since. Understand me good, let me go back over it.

In the beginning, that was when God was making Himself from a Atom of life. And, the motion of the Atom was counting Time, but, we didn't know how to count it and He didn't Who was being made. So, we had to wait until His complete Make, and set up a Time clock for Us. His motion in coming out of the Atom was making Time, but there was no one to calculate. He couldn't calculate it Himself because He had not yet been matured enough in His Brains to calculate His Own movements.

So, we have here today, sitting in the arena of Time, Me and Myself. God have Taught me in the Person of Master Fard, Muhammad, how these things begin working. And I'm teaching you so that no man can deceive you, as the Bible say; and that no man can argue with you and win his side of the argument, unless he's on your side.

We really happy that the coming of God, Whom the Christians call- which is one of His Attributes to be living in such Glorious Time. It's a Glorious Time because you are being accepted for something that you thought you were not as a Righteous person and not as a wicked person. Think over all the sin that Satan caused us to commit; we're not guilty of it. Allah declares that He will not charge us up with the sin of Satan before He arrived. So, some of us have quite a bit of sin and we are certainly happy too, that book won't be shown to us. [The Messenger laughs and the Audience applauds].

And that, the world that the devil have poisoned, I don't mean no spirit now I mean that blue-eyed Caucasian walking out there where you can see him. You never will meet anything like shunning the devil after you're dead. You won't need it. No, because death takes away everything; there is no coming back.

I don't know, I don't know whether you Christian believers is ready to believe it right now or not; but anyway go home and think it over and you will come back and tell me if there is any coming back, that Muhammad done told other than the Truth. You see I'm here, and I will say, Great day in the morning! [The Messenger laughs and the Audience applauds].

There is so many people that, don't like to come and listen to Muhammad because he says there is no Heaven or Hell for us after we die. That when we die that's the end of us. I say brother, if there was a end coming back to us; there was another chance, I would be a greater believer in that than you, because that would convince me that I'm preaching wrong, I will come back. And I would like to have a chance if there is anything like coming back to come back.

But, if you put the cold chilly hands of death on me now, and then wake me up and warm them up again, I would say that I would not feel like getting up. I would be afraid something else is going to happen. [The Messenger laughs]. So I say, once death put me to sleep, let me remain sleep. That I'm not conscious that I'm sleep; and I don't want to get conscious that I'm sleep if I got to come back again to that same grave.

Like the Bible teaches you, and there's a lot of Christian ministers take it just for that, that God raised Lazarus up out of the grave, give him life again. Well then, why did Lazarus had to die then? God is more intelligent than that. He would not have raised Lazarus up, and then let him die again the physical death. He would have been mistreating Lazarus.

But, that's the misunderstanding of the preaching. The death there don't mean a physical death. He declared that himself when he was told to come to the grave and that Lazarus was dead he say, "he's not dead, he's just asleep," meaning that he's not physically dead.

Show me where you have read and he went and looked at Lazarus still declaring he's not dead. And then he called on his Lord not to try the God. He was well aware that God know what he was wanting. He says, in words "I'm not trying to tempt you, but for the sake of these that stand by, the disbelievers, that you answer my prayer for what I am asking for because I'm not trying; I know you can raise him, but for the sake of these disbelievers." You, I say I could say that today for the sake of these disbelieving Black people, let him lie.

The white people, the devil, have so thoroughly killed us of the knowledge of self, that they don't think that no man could take you out of what he has put us in.

The F.B.I. told me, an Agent, one day he was asking me about some of my followers, he says, "Elijah you have a hard job." I say you made it hard. He looked at me and smiled, he say, " Elijah I was not here three or four hundred years ago." I say, but you are from those that was here three or four hundred years ago with the same mind. He laughed again. He say, "You want to just accuse us anyway like, and we wasn't here, that was our fathers." I say, show me whether that you have changed your fathers teachings to our people…are not only in a more…way of putting a man physically, pardon me, mentally dead. I say you know more how now to put your fathers work to such high degree that the man don't know he's dead.

So, my beloved listeners we are here with the Truth. Whether you believe it or not, you're here to hear it and believe or let lone. I'm not here to force you to believe, but I am here to condemn that which you believe in, that you won't be able to condemn me in what I believe, because we make it so plain.

Even in the Book that we read, Bible and Holy Qur'an, you want to make the Holy Qur'an something that is not worthy to be respected as the Bible. We make the Holy Qur'an more respected because that the people that translated the Holy Qur'an was not liars. But the people who translated the Bible, they added in to the Truth, not that the Bible don't contain Truth; plenty of it if you understand. But they made it hard for you to understand by making the Truth in symbolic language and you cannot understand that which they has made symbolic.

So Allah has risen up for you an interpreter of the Bible. And the interpreter of the Qur'an which He have given to me to rely on to teach you the Truth of Islam. The religion of Christianity does not make it clear enough for you to know the Truth. You will say, "Ahhhh man go on." Yeah I'm going on, but I'm going on with the Truth to you. [The Audience applauds].

In the Bible, as I said the Truth is covered up by symbolism and you don't know what the symbolism is. Look at those horses in the Bible, they tell you they're speaking. The Holy Qur'an does not use no such…But the Bible uses all of this to blind you to the knowledge of Truth. And I saw another horse come out and on him was such and such type of rider. These are governments that he is referring to of his own civilization. But he don't want you to know the Truth that it's referring to him, because, the picture of it looks ugly.

And I saw another horse, a Black horse and his rider has a pair of scales in his hand. This is you and me in our Time of the control of the world. That we have been robbed of the Truth by them. And that this rider is your people on that Black horse.

This is one thing that they don't deny, that the Blackman will be Last. Even in his teaching he still is declaring that the Blackman will be the Last.

My friends, to get born and nursed into the knowledge, not the knowledge into the civilization of the devil, the white race, you cannot realize it until you have been made right in the understanding of the Truth. Then you understand then, that you was asleep to the knowledge of it.

Well let us move along. I'm not going to run, hurry you didn't run to get here when I called you forty years ago. [The Messenger laughs and the Audience applauds].

So this time, I'm going to take my time because I know what is going to take place. Allah has Taught me what's going to take place in this Time. Some of it I don't like to tell you, not, it won't make you feel so good. And so, I want you to feel good while I'm teaching you.

Let us get back again at the Time. If, the Bible teaches you that the devil that have the power over the people to live until God come and destroy him, this is True. And that God prepared Hell for him in the day that he was made. Think over that. Before ever the man was made Hell was prepared for him.

Now, if the Bible teaches you that Christian believers, why you want to go along with him since his destination is hell? But you say, "I don't know when that will be, neither do you." No one is given that hour, but God Himself and then He passes it over, to that Angel that you read of in the Revelations, that places one foot on water and one on land.

The preachers use to fancy in that. Of course, they didn't get to far from the Truth. They, use to say that the Angel would ask God how loud with a sound; he'd make a little fancy there. I use to hear my father preaching, and he'd put fancy to it because he didn't know.

But, today all fancy or fantasy is removed. And the Light of the Truth must Shine so clear that you cannot claim there was a cloud between you and it. This is the little boy that is talking to you now. There is nobody coming behind me but God. I better tell you that. [The Audience applauds].

I'm like it's written there where it says in the Bible that before that Dreadful Day arrive, I will send you Elijah, and he shall…He must have enough converts to lay claim to the devil's world that God have some people in it. And we can't extricate Judgment on the enemy until we separate them; separate the enemy from the Righteous.

So the first thing that He did was He called all of Us Righteous. How could He do that? Because you followed Satan in all that you do of evil, you gotten it from Satan. So now, Satan is to be destroyed, and God have come to take that which is not his, and give them His Own.

Now, how we going to escape? It's plain what you were doing; you was following after him, the devil. Now God comes and declares you to be not one of the devils, that you are Right or Righteous. You say, "I haven't been right." No you haven't; that which you was unrighteous in was not you, that was the devil; his work and you had no people to argue with the devil that his works that he has caused us to do was not our work by nature, because we not a devil by nature.

So being deceived by the devil, and we didn't know who he was, we didn't have no Teacher of our own to tell us to come back don't follow that man. He kept everyone away from us. When they come in the country, he kept him among himself. And, we never knew any of them were here because we didn't know our self. We use to wonder why these Black Africans coming here and he show more respect to them than he do us. We all look alike. He was trying to keep your Black brother from Africa from mixing with you, to teach you some Truth of that which he has lied.

That you are learning today, because, as it is written in the vision of the name of Jacob, that he saw a latter reaching from Heaven to the Earth and Angels, ascending and descending. Well you didn't never understood what it was because he had put your mind so far in spooks; something that is not a person; it's something like air out here; a form is out there of air in air.

Well, you just didn't never understand. If he saw a latter reaching from Earth to Heaven, and Angels ascending and descending, this was people and this is the connection lane. This is what Prophets teaches of God; it's going to be done; that the people in the devils civilization come out, go up to Allah, the latter of Time and Teachings.

So, why Jacob saw this latter which means the connection of you and I with the God Righteous people called Angels. If it's true that he was looking at the end of his Time, that the people he had deceived would one day be connected with the people of Righteous; and that they would be going from Heaven, and, from the Earth where they lived.

Today, you'll find this in the Muhammad Speaks Newspaper on the front page over the head of Blackman locking hands with Blackman. This have that interpretation that we who has been lost from the way to get to God in the Heavens that He prepared for us, is now coming to past that you can shake hand with your Brother all the way round the Earth.

He will respect you highly, respect you if you say that I'm a follower of Elijah or a believer. [The Audience applauds]. He recognize the fact that this man is the man we been looking for to join us together again.

The Scientist comes to me sometime almost weekly because they recognize what I mean. This is the Day of Uniting. Africa is uniting with us because as the Holy Qur'an teaches, they heard a calling, calling to the Right Way. Therefore, they are here among you today plentiful; Scientist walking around with…mouth shut waiting for a certain Time to open it.

So, the Time given to the white man is up and he don't deny it. He don't deny his Time is not up; he preaches it himself. As in the Holy Qur'an, it is said there that where he tries to clear himself of mistreating you, he says, " I did not call them to go astray I just call them and they come." He say, "I'm not responsible." They are responsible!

He goes to try to show some things he have did to open your eyes, but he know you was not gone open up. And, he couldn't tell it strong like a God sent Messenger, because, by nature he was made to hide the Truth.

When you go to the white man to set down for him to teach you the Truth, he mislead you because the Truth is against him, and the Truth is his doom. So never go to him looking for no Truth from him. He's not made of the material. When he was made he was made a liar and made to oppose Truth; and to oppose you that believe in it. Oh yes I'm taking my time this afternoon! [The Audience applauds].

I was looking at the lip profession how it is taught in the Holy Qur'an. But I don't think, that, you should be worried about that, neither should I. We go a little closer to the Teachings of Truth and how to end the white man…

The greatness of Man is this subject here in Chapter Two of the Qur'an under the name The Cow. This the name of the Chapter because it's teaching about the devils worshipping a cow. So they took cow for their subject. Here we're reading Chapter 2: 34-35 reads like this: "And when We said to the Angels be submissive to Adam, they submitted, but Iblis did not. He refused and was proud…" This is the devil white man. "And he was one of the disbelievers."

Now what it says here he was one of the disbelievers. It means that there was just a stronger opposition and opposing of us at this Time, as was in the Days of Adam. "And when We said "Oh Adam" dwell there and thy wife in the garden and eat from it a plenty of food." Now listen what it says here now, "And approach not this tree," this tree is the devil, "lest you be of the unjust." We have already experienced this.

Now, we have for many years followed the devil, and what he said was the Truth. And now, for taking his advice we are here now being brought up to the knowledge of the Truth of this man.

And that next verse says, reads like this, " And as to those who disbelieve in and reject Our messages, they are the companions of the Fire; in it they will abide." What fire can they abide in? You can't abide in a literal fire. That the fire He's referring to, is the punishment of what you will get in this life for not accepting the Truth. You'll be unsuccessful in carrying out that which you think you have of the Truth. If it is not of Allah and the Message that He give His servants, you cannot be successful.

And the Holy Qur'an teaches us, "you want to know the successful one" this is the way It teaches, "Those that believe in Allah and His Messenger, they are the successful ones."

Over here in the 45th verse it reads of the same Chapter 2, it reads like this, "Seek assistance through prayer." Think over that. Some of us don't never pray at all. Only when we do get in trouble. Then we are like a man sinking at sea. He never believed that Allah will help him until he's going down in the water of Allah; that water Allah made and it can sink us as good as it can make us feel joyful by riding on its back.

Seek assistance through patience and prayer. And this is hard, except for the humble ones. Because they don't pray, and when they need to pray in their most troublesome time of life disaster, they don't know hardly how to pray. They didn't believe in Allah in the beginning, but he will call on Allah, any God that is powerful enough to hold back the power of the water to keep you from drowning.

This, the Holy Qur'an teaches that Pharaoh did not never pray and recognize God that He was the All Wise and the Most Powerful One, until he start sinking in the Red Sea; lungs getting full of water. He know that was the end of him, so the Holy Qur'an teaches. Then he said, to Allah, recognizing His Greatness and Power over him; he called on Him in Arabic, " Allah U Akbar."

So, by admitting that Allah was the Greatest after death had taken hold of his body to take him in; Allah, at that moment recognizes Him to be the greatest whom had opposed all his life. That he now given him a over drink of water in which he was suppose to live by. His lungs all filled up now with water; "Allah U Akbar, Allah U Akbar." Allah heard him.

Think over that. He heard him, and He taken those two words. Think over that. To make him live in order to convince other disbelievers that if you call upon Him and recognize Him to be the Greatest, He'll pardon you of your sins.

So, He pardoned Pharaoh and caused Pharaoh to be talked about and be honored. And those who had, or would have the knowledge of Truth that this king opposed Adam, or pardon me opposed Moses until he had no air in his lungs to continue to oppose Him. But, by recognizing Allah as being the Greatest, that was recognizing Allah to be better than he was. So, Allah forgives him, though he was dying. But He made his name to be remembered.

This Time is referring only to the white man and those who willfully after knowing will continue to fight, though they had a chance. God forgive them if they would leave the devil and come to Him; and go back to their people because they are not guilty of the devil's sin. And, He have declared them to be free of the devil's sin.

So the Angel is a very beautiful sight here. He put one foot on water and one on land, so the Book say, the Bible. If this is true universal, out of both Books here is the secret of it: The man was raised off of the food and water out of the earth. And out of the water he ate food to survive.

So the Angel is cutting him off from both; and he put...foot on land and on water too, because without either one of these you can't exist. So his left foot, the Book teaches us, and his left hand and his right and his right foot. The right hand and the right foot hanging on water, and the left foot hanging on both water and land.

So there must be a division made now. Think you gotten your life out of both. I have to declare that the Time that you was to feed from both is up. "Time know now will soon know no more." The Time given to the enemy is up; and it won't be known any more. God is declaring that he won't exist in no form; nor will his way of teaching the people will exist. So he got to go, he and all his work. [The Audience applauds].

The 45th verse say, "Seek assistance through patience and prayer. You need to have both. You need to say your prayers. And you need to be patient, to wait on the Lord, and don't try to run ahead. [The Audience applauds] because you can't be the head runner; you'll run into something that you cannot put out of your way; very beautiful. So if you get in a hurry, ask Allah to assist you to be patient. [The Audience applauds].

In the 46th verse of the 2nd Surah, here in Arabic they call it, call a Chapter, Surah in the Qur'an. We call them Chapters in the English language. He says, "Who know that they will meet their Lord, and that to Him they will return.

THE MEANING OF "THE ONLY BEGOTTEN SON"

And that to Him they will return. This is the believer, the Muslim. They know that they again will meet with their Lord like the Bible teaches you because, He came to them they recognized Him to be God, and He put the faith into their hearts to continue to believe like oil they put in a burning vessel to keep light.

So, therefore your five wise and five foolish…Those who know that the Bridegroom was coming they kept their lamps burning; and those who didn't believe it, they let the oil burn out. And that when the Bridegroom came the noise was made, "Here is the Bridegroom, go out to meet Him."

These was surprised because their belief had gone out, and they had no belief that He was coming back. Just like oil burn out of a lamp; and that the oil have no more power to give light. So that's the way it was with half of these who started out; all had oil; all had the faith but it went away from them.

As the Holy Qur'an refers to this kind of Time of those who turn hypocrite, "Time came prolonged and hearts hardened." That show how the people love this world. They can't have patience to wait too long for an execution of it by Divine.

So they get unhappy and restless, and they say something similar to what you find over here in the Bible involving gifts, it says they would say, "Why have we walked mournful and the wicked being those that is not doing this, they 're happy. Here we going around mournful looking."

But, the Lord heard this sayings; and the Bible say when He write up those people; those that was afraid to turn back into the world, He say those will be His, "These will be mine."

When a man is afraid to break the law of God, which is good, then he's defying God to bring about his execution to him for breaking the law because he disregarding he don't like it; and he goes back to the end of God to join up with him again. Then when he see the approaching doom, he will want to go back in and join up with God. But Allah is not cheap, He is Self- Independent. [The Audience applauds].

"He so loves the world that He gave His only begotten son to save the world." Wrong!

163

God never was so foolish to give the best Angel to save the wicked. His only begotten son means he is the only one that was raised from the mental dead, and was prepared by God by Teaching him how to teach the people to bring them back to…life. [The Audience applauds].

So, I'm here calling you to return to your own. What's wrong with your own that you don't like it? When you are the beginning and the end of this world. You begin this world from making it from you and me.

Yacub, the father of the Caucasian race; He made the Caucasian from out of the weak germ of us .He didn't go out and get something that was not already in existence, to make Him a man. He come right back to Himself and looked into the germ of the Blackman and found a man. That, or it is True that you are the First, and will be the last. No man can produce another man equal to the Blackman without going to the Blackman. [The Audience applauds].

As we go along, you will notice that we leaving nothing to be explained. [The Audience applauds]. If you would, ask me questions after I'm ready to dismiss myself. Remember now, that you don't ask a question that I have already answered. I'm not going to leave no question for you. [The Audience applauds].

Allah warns us here in the 44th verse of the 2 Surah, or Chapter, He says, "Do you enjoin men to be good?" Do you enjoin men to do good? Or in words He's saying, do you teach other men to do good and neglect your own life? Do you enjoin men to be good and neglect your own souls while you read the Book? You read the Book, it teaches you to be good; Bible and Holy Qur'an.

And then if you don't be good while teaching others to be good, you will be the loser and they will be the winner because they did good; they believed in it, but you being the preacher of good and then neglect to be good yourself.

Did you, I'm saying this, did you think just the name was going to save you? No, you have to be saved by works. Your work will save you, but not telling others and you not doing your own teaching yourself.

Very good! He draws our attention to some acts of Israel: "Oh children of Israel, call to mind My Favor which I bestowed on you, and be faithful to your Covenant with Me." A Covenant is a agreement, "I shall fulfill My Covenant with you and Me, and Me alone should you fear."

There is no god to fear beyond God. He is the Chief of all gods. "I am the Lord thy God," He says to Israel, "And Me and Me alone should you fear. And do not set another god besides Me." [The Audience applauds]. Don't try keeping another god to try and make him My equal. Yea, the devil is powerful alright enough, but he's no equal to Me. [The Audience applauds].

This is why Allah makes a Messenger or Apostle to contend with an opponent of His. He's not enough for God himself to attack. So, Allah makes an Apostle to attack him, and show His Apostle how to win because He know both .He know the devil and He know His Apostle. His Apostle is from God, Himself, the beginning of Man. [The Audience applauds].

From this He makes the Apostle aware of all the arts and all the attacks of Satan; all of his arguments. And give him the knowledge to refute the enemy's arguments. Give him the knowledge how to make the enemy to bow to him. This is true; as I'm here, the enemy do bow to me. [The Audience applauds]. I'm going to tell you this as the Time is up. I'm put here, and, to what you read in the Bible that Jesus said of himself. That he would get done whatever he will; whatever Allah willed they both was together in the will. For little you think of it, I'm just like that. Whatever I will, Allah will make it to come to past. [The Audience applauds].

This Jesus recognized the fact that he was not that man, that Prophet; that one that will come in the Last Days. He was not that one. He had to die for his mistake. What was the mistake? The mistake was that he thought he was on Time, but he learned that he was not on the Time to usher in the Judgment of this world. So then he prophesied and admitted that he was ahead of Time; he was not on Time for it. So then he prophesied in his acknowledgement of this failure to come on the due Time of the end of the world; that he couldn't do it, because it was before the Time of the world.

So then he prophesied, but, words he said, " When he come..." What he is that? He said of one that Moses prophesied of. And now I see through the Moses prophesy that that man is yet to come. He will give life to the dead; and he will destroy the enemy that I read and hoped to destroy; that I'm ahead of the Time.

So, in words he was saying, keep waiting he will be along whom the Father will send from Himself. I guess you saying you preaching to long now. [The Audience respond in applauds]. But, when you go to analyze what is written, that take you longer to do than the writer. The writer can soon write it out, but he don't know what he had wrote. [The Messenger laughs]. So, I say, my beloved listeners, that it takes more time to untangle the entanglement, than it did to tangle it up. [The Audience applauds].

Now, if this, and it is, the end of the world, you should know what the world is and what it has done contrary to the world that is coming in. So that you won't later say I didn't see nothing wrong with the people. And that, if they was wrong, why didn't they prove this; why didn't they prove that. Well, we're here to prove it. [The Audience applauds].

Let us take for an instance, you see, pardon me, I'm all place getting short somewhere. You see that the white man's world is now dying a natural death. Everything he lay his hand to is a failure. If he were living in righteousness according to the teachings of the Prophets of Old, he would be prospering instead of being unsuccessful even in that which he has prospered. He has prospered and been successful in his wicked way.

So now a Righteous One comes which is an enemy to the enemies of .... He sets up His Kingdom on the very base of Righteousness. He gets a servant to champion His world; and makes him so firm that he is declared to be like a rock; a stone that is capable of braking up stone. That if a stone falls on that stone, it will break to pieces. And if this stone falls on that stone, grind it to powder. He's a tuff stone. [The Audience applauds].

So if you have a stone that you want to build on, get one that won't crack if you put other stones on it. [The Audience applauds].

So the Bible say, summarizing the man and a stone, he said, " he's is a stone that is a tried stone. We don't make no mistake that stone won't stand up and hold the weight. We have already tried it; and since we have tried the stone that we want to build on, we want this building to stand.

So we build it on a stone that will stand. I'm not here just to preach to you Jonah went to Nineveh, but I'm here to preach to you why the trip was made for Jonah. [The Audience applauds]. I don't want you to think that I'm up here trying to show off. I'm up here doing my work that God sent me to do. [The Audience applauds].

You notice that here in the…as Moses gives us some history of his travels with Israel in the desert; which also must be interpret because it all reaches back at us. And if we don't know why he was out there in the desert doing what he did; that it is a History made to reach us. Here today, we must prove it.

So, what I'm getting you is what he prophesied, he say, "The Lord thy God will rise up from among your brethren a Prophet like me." How is he like Moses? He's qualified; Moses seen that God will send us a Prophet like Moses.

Well, number one: Moses went after a people that had been deceived by a people. He got hold to Pharaoh, who was an enemy to Moses and his people. And so, in this History, it gives us more rights on the last Messenger and his work.

I'm not going to preach that sermon. I'm just catching up as I go long. What you really need, it is knowledge of understanding. For misunderstanding is the Hell to Man. So, I'm here to give to you understanding of this of Divine, which you have failed to get from the enemy of Divine. Let you see what he look like from the inside out, then if you want to after he have deceived you to continue to live, in his deceiving, that's up to you.

No place in the History and in the Scriptures that you will find where the last Messenger would like to argue with you after he give the Truth to you. He leave you to later ponder over it, or you can go on disbelieving it till the Truth having witness to the Truth of the Messenger, coming from God in His actions against you.

There is many things in the Scripture which some of you think that you still have the freedom to do as you please. You can't continue to do as you please in this world, because of our relation to this world. So you won't have no place to carry on your evil.

The other people they all Righteous, and they won't allow you to live in their Righteous world with your evil from the devil of this world of whom they are destroying. You can't hold on to this. This is what I'm telling you. You're not free to hold on to it. You're not free to act; I reckon I'll…after while I keep on. [The Audience applauds].

This is a free world granting you the freedom of doing like this world do. Now the next world coming in, you won't be free to do anything you want to. You will have to do just one thing that that world rules, laws, and regulations bring to us.

You take for an instance that this devil having the freedom to do evil and to teach us evil; he did not allow his appearance by prophesy. They worked against them, so says the Bible; deceived and he enslaved them, imprisoned them, and then killed them, because they was not wanted in his world; he wanted to rule the people by wickedness and not by righteousness.

So, I being as the Book teaches you the last of the Prophets, he won't put that small time stuff over on me. [The Audience applauds] because Allah have caged me in His Mercy and Protection. Therefore, you can't get to me no more than you can get to God, in the way of doing harm. [The Audience applauds].

Now, this I shall tell you; He have made me like Himself. [The Audience applauds]. Whatever I do and whatever I want done or will… like He Himself, it will come to past; don't worry. [The Audience applauds]. This is just as much important as I'm teaching you the knowledge of him, the devil that you should know the Teacher.

You not going to see God coming down from Heaven and stand here beside me and verify. Here's where the verification come from Him: If I see you continue to be contrary to what I am teaching you of yourself and the word of God, that will within me, too, you see. And that, if you fail, Allah will let my will be done on you. [The Audience applauds].

My wife is at home, gradually dying. But I didn't want her to die in a hospital, lest Satan would boast that the wife of the Messenger, his God couldn't save her… So, okay…I knew he would have something to say. That thing that he say would weaken your faith in me and God, Whom you have never known. And you never did know the god that he preached to you because it never exist, only himself. There is no such thing as a God living upstairs.

As one preacher I know in the South, I use to go to his church just to hear him get on this part; that God or that the Earth is God footstool; and the Heaven is His Throne. So I kept listening at that preacher kept listening at him. I say he got something like right there. And he did have something right; The Earth is His footstool.

This planet we on is the First planet that was made with life on it from the Sun. Regardless to the astronomers saying Mercury is the first planet, Mercury was not the first planet that was made. Mercury is a sign; it's a sign of Allah's Messenger.

Oh that if you had time. [The Audience applauds]. The planet Mercury so close to the Sun, that the Scientist think that no life could exist there, it's too hot.

Suppose now, that we would be drawn through the atmosphere of the Earth to the Sun; through cold that is so terrific, that we couldn't live in that cold. The cold is always near and surrounded by a planet of life.

You get where there is no such thing as a planet to mar the atmosphere with its water. You are getting into a altogether different universe around your earth saturated with water. When you get into a dry space where there is no water to kill the space, you can't tell nobody what that space fill like to you, since you are made of water. So you got to put on something to shied yourself from being destroyed by dry space.

Let me keep on I'm not going to teach astronomy on that to you as God have Taught me most everything I see, most everything I hear, He have Taught me that.

Did you not remember reading in the Bible in Psalms where David says that God have opened his ears and that to make him to hear, and his eyes to make him to see. These two factors of Man David picked up on it; God Taught him that, even to the knowledge of birds and their language.

He told me that He went in Africa in the jungles and learned the language of the birds. So, I thought over David and I smiled I said to myself, wonder is you going to teach me the language of birds! [The Audience applauds].

Why did not He say the beast? Because, that is the more finer characteristics bout a bird than that...bout a beast. The Revelations, He refers to this devil as a beast, due to his characteristics is similar to a wild beast.

Well I guess you think you getting away from your subject. Nope, I'm teaching my subject. [The Audience applauds]. If you don't know the Messenger who brought the message from God, how can you learn the Sender? You got to learn the Messenger and his message; which he have brought to you all but forcing you to listen to learn the Sender, God Himself.

You think that I'm stepping out the way, when I say that I am sent from God. The people of Earth been hearing that every since that they made an enemy for Man for six thousand years. And that I'm only verifying what the Others said. I verify them and they have verified me before I was born.

And after they prophesied that Elijah will come and must come; he must come, why? He must come to make a new path for his people. They're in the wrong path; that path they're in is a crooked path. The people don't live upright in that path because it's so crooked.

Like the snake, serpent; the snake is so crooked that you got to follow his trail around to find out where he went. You couldn't stand at the end of the line and look straight down the trail or the track that he made while he was crawling. You had to follow him because that curb there is subject to turn anyway, right? [The Audience applauds]. And that, if you don't follow the curb that he's making, you won't over take him. So Allah have made me to follow the trail and catch him. [The Audience applauds].

The Theology Of Time. What Time? The devil's Time, not our Time. They didn't build no clock for us. The Time piece that was given to Us, it don't ever run [The Audience applauds].

We all want to live, says the Bible and Qur'an. We have history of Prophets, and non- Prophets living a long time. The Bible says by David, "that the wicked doesn't live out half their Time." Well that's right. But, every Man history that we read in the Bible and in other books and in the Scriptures of the Holy Qur'an. All these long livers was Prophets or something of the kind; some Righteous person, not a wicked person but Righteous, because the wickedness of the wicked destroys the wicked man. Because, by Nature, Man was not made to destroy Himself, unless he be guided by a destroyer.

We die quick under the guidance of the white man, because, that he comes here to live for just a few days and go.

Oh yes Brothers, I'm going to let you go after while. [The Audience applauds]...I guess it's ten minutes after four. [The Audience applauds]. That I been going for a hour and a half. Well, look like to me we getting a new time fixer. I thought I was the boss of my time here...that I have a boss too. I feel pretty good Brother and I, I don't feel like I been teaching but thirty minutes. [The Audience applauds].

I set up and laid around my poor wife suffering with pains and whatnot, and I prayed over her. And so, I don't care anything about to much sleep no way. God didn't make me to sleep very long. He told me, told the Brothers that was there listening at Him, He say, "He will be like Myself." He say, "About a couple hours would be sufficient for him to sleep." [The Audience applauds].

So, I sit up, lay round on the side of the bed honoring her in her helpless state, her sickness. So she, I notice would sleep sound as long as I was laying around on the bed, or sitting there where she open her eyes and see me. So I hated to leave out for the sake of wanting…to sleep and rest.

What kind of sleep and rest did God prepare for me? He didn't prepare no sleep and rest for me. Nope, if I'm to be like Him, He don't have no rest. He work night and day. And I have worked night and day. [The Audience applauds].

So when people get restless you better let them go. Don't, their turn to be something else that you'll have another job to do. Of course I'm not talking bout Brother back here, he just feel for me because he thinks I'm too, not too well. But, he don't know [The Audience applauds]. He's looking at the weakness of the body; and I'm looking at the strong faith of the body that it can sustain the body.

Strong belief in the security of you. Security of the Power of God. You can't get too weak, because weakness did not bring Us into the world.

Someday I'll come in the M.G.T. and the F.O.I. class and if they ask me to tell them what I meant by this work; I will teach it to them. [The Audience applauds].

But I should give you a hint here: Man was Created in haste, therefore he's hasty; that is true. So now you study on this until I get you in your classroom, then I'll teach you what that mean.

In fact about it, I'm not risen up from among my Brethren, you're my Brothers; I'm not risen up among you into the knowledge of Divine to not be able to answer to that physical fact, because it is true and you will bear me witness whenever I explain to you that that couldn't be nothing else…

THE MEANING OF "THE
FLOWING FOUNTAIN OF WATER"

Nothing else, but the answer. This is mention in the Holy Qur'an that Allah Created you, and then He make complete you. But the man that was made from Us, he was created in haste. His Time is short; he must hurry and get busy doing his work. But this is not quite the answer, yet and I can't answer it here, but I'll answer it in your classes, or to your teacher.

So, the Brother I think is getting hungry, and I'm so full and nice. [The Messenger laughs and the Audience applauds]. He may have a lot of work to do; and I'm doing my work.

I say to you my beloved Brothers and Sisters, I'm not going to say beautiful Brothers and Sisters; you can't be beautiful until you accept Islam. [The Audience applauds]. That is true. The mark of the devil will remain on you until removed by Allah and Islam. So, when you accept Islam, you start getting beautiful, [The Audience applauds] and we love to be beautiful. So I see all the time that you're glad. [The Audience applauds]. So, come follow me Sister, you will be beautiful.

I have a little box sitting over here in the corner. Oh yea...you can get the people to working...you going to be so beautiful until you...a mile away. Oh yes they getting all like that that's why they don't believe. If they wasn't getting beautiful, they'd be going, but they in the process now, and they believe that the end will be a beautiful woman, and that's right.

Allah didn't come here to make us ugly. He didn't come here to let us remain ugly. Every one that accepts Him, He start you to growing into a new life force; and that ...is a beautiful person.

I'm your Teacher. [The Audience applauds]. ...wait and see what I was going to say, maybe you wouldn't be clapping. Yes you was clapping right, so you watch me if I grow in ugliness. Grow in ugly, who said you was pretty? [The Messenger laughs and the Audience applauds].

Well I only say this to tell you that the Holy Qur'an teaching us that you that turning to Righteousness in this Day and Time, at the end of the Caucasian world, Allah will make you grow into a new growth.

And He told me about it when He was with me, He say no Brother, He say, "We will have no ugly people. We will have no people with gray hair and bald headedness." He say, All of Our hair and all of our Black hair, the color will come back to us…And the Holy Qur'an say this done by Him Blessing the Righteous, then going into a new growth.

Instead of you growing and ageing up into decay, decay stop on the other side; no more decay. You'll, He told me that we will look the same as we were when we were sixteen years old, and that we keep that same look; beautiful and tender, when he was in his teens.

And he referred to as a young goat so he could run, leap, and jump. Well, all of this He proved that we will be just that. And the Holy Qur'an teaches us that the Hereafter is something to be prayed for and desired. You don't stay just like that when…you move on in days, months, and years, you become a different person altogether. [The Audience applauds].

I use to right here in Chicago, teach you six long hours.. I remember one time they was robbing…I started to teaching there in the town hall at seven o'clock that evening and dismissed the people seven o'clock the next morning. [The Audience applauds].

When I am feeling very well like I am now [The Audience applauds], I would teach you all night and all day. [The Audience applauds]. When I was in Washington making Temple Number four, that's Number four, I use to dismiss the group and go to some of the Sisters homes, to have dinner. When I get there, some of the group from the Temple had already arrived. They know probably where I was going to have dinner. [The Audience laughs].

They all was sitting there eager as they were when they arrived at the Temple. What is Sister doing? Stand up Sister Dorothy, over here to my left. Oh, over here in the box. This Sister she use to work in the Secretary work there at that time.

So I …half the time. So when I would get to her house that evening, she probably would have me a nice beautiful apple pie. So then I would try to go for it along with some lamb she had roasted, and here come the whole Temple almost there. [The Audience applauds].

I begin to have two thoughts about them: I wonder which one was I speaking to you , physical food or Spiritual Food. [The Audience applauds]. This Sister standing here is the brother, pardon me, the sister of the Brother that is now my son-in-law. And she was a wonderful and a faithful Sister when I and others, her husband even was in jail there in Washington, the district jail, for preaching Islam.

They were going into war and they didn't want no hindering. And they confess to me that's all they put you in jail for; that you will not be out in the public preaching to your people that preaching that it says, which will prevent the successful prosecution of the war between us, Japan, and Germany.

He say not bout your preaching; it is not that you should be teaching, but we just want you put up to keep you from teaching it while we trying to fight these two people, Germany and Japan; not what you are teaching now. And I looked at him, I say how do you put me up for the teaching if you don't put me up for what I'm teaching?

So, when I came back to face the parole officers down in the loop of the U.S.A., he admitted he said, " Listen, Muhammad you go head and teach what you always have been teaching. Teach the teachings just like you have, nobody is going to bother you. We confess that we were just at war, and we didn't want you to be out there telling your people that they had no right to enter this war. Then they would have been just like you; and nobody would have been able to go through the war as it should have been gone through with.

Well my Brothers I guess I have to obey the boss. He keep…frowning. I don't know what he frowning for, whether it's hunger. He may have a call by himself that it's time to go and feed the body before the spirit go out. [The Messenger and the Audience laughs and applauds]. You know why that I'm so long in my teachings to you, you never have heard it before; and to try to untangle the snake that have gotten himself caught up, or rather we caught up with him and he swallowed us so deep that it's taking a long time pressing his body to get us up to his mouth, to get us out of him.

But, I have enjoyed you and I wish that it was so that you could come here tomorrow and we could keep teaching. [The Audience applauds]. You're going to be surprised at what you have not learned bout the knowledge of self and others; you're going to be surprised.

If Almighty God, Allah makes me to able enough, as I am now, I will be back here next Sunday. I'm charged with the delivery of the message. Not a one of you is charged with that because the message was given to me; and if I have forty million helpers, they all, every one of them is helping me; not that they are responsible for the message.

If you read your Holy Qur'an and Bible, I'm the only one God will hold responsible for you not getting the Truth, because, He give me the Truth, and the way He give it to me, He give it to me like a flowing spring or like a flowing fountain. The fountain have enough drink in it to give to everyone drink that who come to drink You don't need a new fountain, just try to drink up what this fountain…[The Audience applauds].

Though over in the Holy City Mecca, there is a well there call it the well of Zam Zam....its name means, "The Righteous Shall Drink the Water." But, they shall drink the Spiritual Truth from Allah in which they will never be able to get to the end of it; it's so much.

Now that this sign here is a sign of the Truth that the Messenger brings to you. He is the Well himself. [The Audience applauds]. He made me to think over Jesus talking to the wicked woman...all her life. She was a woman that was filled with adultery; and that she married one husband after another one. Of course she would not be anything today if she was here; she'd laugh at her seven husband being a small beginning.

But, I'm not going to go into the interpretation of that, but, I will some day when I have more time. But, that well there, I drinked out of it myself. It's water that is very light and easy to digest into your body and my body. I tried it; little boys come round serving it; they expect you to give them a little something.

And so I kept reaching for another cup. I wanted to know whether or not this water was really healthy and would not have any effect on your body. So I kept drinking cup full after cup full. When I left, my stomach felt just as light as it did when I first came to it. I say that must be the well you drink out of and you have no need to be thirsty, because you can drink a plenty of that water and it don't lay heavy on your stomach.

Of course the Spiritual side of the teaching when and "you never get thirsty" is...the Bible and Holy Qur'an that it is the "Spiritual Water of God."

So, I'm going to get out of here and go home, just because I feel good don't mean I stand up here and wear that good feeling of yours. You know we go so far in a thing, then we begin to settle down in it. Then we don't need to be call to come to it, we're already in it.

So you have been listening to me for quite a while. And so now I'm going to turn you back into the hand of our Assistant Minister, to let him see whether or not you brought him anything other than just preaching; that the man can't preach if he get hungry. [The Messenger and the Audience laughs].

But I'm so happy that Allah made me feel well today to talk [The Audience applauds]. So I'm going to say to you that visit us today; I love so well if I had a table for each one of you; I would tell the Brothers to put the food on it. I can by the help of Allah feed every one of you that is here, and won't be in the bread-line tomorrow begging for me some bread. [The Messenger laughs]. I did feed ten thousand once [The Audience applauds], and I still can feed ten thousand. [The Audience applauds].

Not that I am boasting that I have a lot of money to do so; nor am I forcing or cause some miraculous thing like the Bible say happen...took seven years to feed ten thousand people. It would be similar to that…miraculous thing. I could give twenty thousand of you; this is not exaggerating.

This afternoon eat all you want, but, after you eat all you want Allah makes it to appear to me I have not give way nothing. I don't miss it; I don't go say, if I had not give all them people I'd had something. [The Audience applauds]. For this is true. I never miss nothing I give you, nothing.

So I thank you, don't, you'll be telling me we thank you that we can give you [The Messenger laughs], but I'm just happy to look at you; and I just want to talk with you. [The Audience applauds].

First I want to say to all of you teachers of any other organization other than Islam; and if it's Islam, I thank Allah for you being present this afternoon to hear what Elijah Muhammad have to say. And if you want to question me plenty, or you want to write me at 4847 Woodlawn, 4847 Woodlawn, 4847 Woodlawn [The Audience applauds].

So I thank you. I'm going to turn you in the hands of our Assistant Minister, Minister Shah. That name is from one of the…Scientist from Muhammad teachings. This Shah…as you may find it, that phrase of language, wrote; they were Scientist on Islam help building up the Holy Qur'an that Muhammad said he saw, and was given. Well not say he saw, but words that were given to him by Allah. They put them in a Book call it Holy Qur'an. And one of the most finest meanings…is a Book of Healing. And it is healing us of the wound of Satan.

So I'm going to turn you back…again he will dismiss you, soon. And, you…I tell you the way to do this job real quick: don't wait till he ask you for a donation, just say, "Hay" "Hay" [The Messenger laughs and the Audience applauds].

So let us…I'm turning you back in the hands of my Assistant to dismiss you now. I'm not asking you to stand together…soon as you see my back turned…See what he have to say.

In the Name of Allah, may the Peace and the Blessings of Allah go with you wherever you may go, and bless you in knowledge and understanding of His Word as I have given it to you.

As Salaam Alaikum

THE CHANGE OF WORLDS

As Salaam Alaikum, you may be seated.

In the Name of Allah the Most Merciful. All Holy Praise is due Thee Allah. The Lord of the Worlds. The Most Merciful. The Master of the Day of Judgment, in which we now live. Thee do we serve Thee do we beseech for Thine Help. Guide us on the right path. The path of those upon whom Thou has bestowed Favours; not of those upon whom Thy Wrath is brought down; nor of those who go astray after they have heard Thine Teachings, Amen.

My dear beloved Brothers and Sisters, I'm very happy to see you out this afternoon…with beautiful smiling faces. And I think every Believer of Islam that's on the face of the Earth, whether they in America, or elsewhere should be happy to see the Day and Time that you and I are witnessing here in North America. Because, there lived Prophets and Wise men in the past; they only read of it; that it was to come. But if they could have lived to see just a half a day that you are looking at today, are living in, they would have been happy.

We are living in the change of worlds. Old world going out and the New World is coming in. This is something that we all should be happy and thankful to Allah; glorify His Name for allowing us to live to bear witness of the change of worlds.

It is a wonderful thing to bear witness of; and to see your world, the New World of Islam coming in; not the Old world of Islam, but a New World of Islam. "Behold I make All things New." This is what the Scripture prophesy of the God; that for the First Time that you witness seeing Him in Person. All in the past, except with Moses, the God was not seen in Person because it would bring about a change. Therefore the change was not to come in those Days that would be permanent change.

So therefore, you and I are lucky to be living here today to see the God that will set up the Kingdom of Islam to live forever, without any future interference. There never will be an enemy will be openly attacking Islam; the Religion of Truth, Righteous, any more. There is no future prophesy of it.

This is the end of opposition and attacks against the Righteous and their Righteous Religion Islam. Islam have a beautiful name corresponding with the principles and beliefs in Islam. It is very beautiful, and doing away with so many gods that their…

176

in or nation before or…since the making of Yacub's world.

Yacub is the God the name of the God, pardon me, that made the white race. And he made them for the purpose to…and destroy Islam. But he missed, and I think that should be a warning, forever.

THE WILL OF ALLAH (GOD)

That a man works hard for six thousand years to try to destroy the Religion of Allah, but missed. We are still here. Know who he is talking about. Now take, the Pakistani Muslim, who also translate the Holy Qur'an. This man name also is Ali. So you must remember that they both means good. But being a Muslim myself, and I want Allah to have all the credit that we can give Him without mistake.

I loves to say Allah. I love to read the Holy Qur'an saying Allah, Teaching me Allah. Allah is a Great name for the Divine Supreme Being because it covers everything. It means "All." Everywhere that God is mention He is there. He's All in All.

So I like that name....says here in…you better get a…[The Audience applauds]. 122nd verse of the 5th Chapter of the Holy Qur'an…but since we not so up to date with the Arab language, we say that word which we can understand and all the rest.

God will say this is a Day on which the Truthful will come; some very Truthful. This is a Day on which the Truthful will profit from his Truth; being Truthful in the midst of falsehood, and get no credit for being Truthful, then God will have to defend your Truth and yourself too, because you are in the midst of people who love untruth and not Truth.

But there is a Day, He says here in the 5th Surah of the Holy Qur'an that will come when the Truthful's Truth, will benefit the Truthful.

If we have served God all our lives, and then a Day come for checking out with those who against our way of belief; well then if, the Author of Truth, of which we believe in will not defend us, then we are lost forever and the author of wicked and liars will prosper. It be better, or had been better that we believed in lying if the liar is going to triumph over the Truth.

We have been told all of our lives that a Judgment would come; and that God will Judge both Truthful and untruthful. We find in the Holy Qur'an where that the author of other than the Truth, would try to deny his misleading us; and that he will declare himself a believer in what Allah has brought to us.

Like the crazy Pharaoh, he waited until he was near drowning to death before he would admit Allah was the Greatest. That didn't help him much, he had to drown just the same. But to show you that Allah is all Merciful, He give him a break by him just saying He was the Greatest, because Pharaoh had tried to make himself the greatest. But when he had no mastery over the water that was taking his life from him, he say "Allah U Akbar Allah U Akbar, You the Greatest, You the Greatest." Allah give him...that for admitting that He was the Greatest.

There's a many Pharaoh's who would like to wait till they see the show down, then they will admit to you and me that Allah is the Greatest. This wait just right around the corner; not very far.

I want to talk with you for a few minutes. The Will of God; the Will of Allah. This is what I would like to talk with you on this afternoon, for just a while. The Will of Allah; Let Thy Will be done. We want always that God do His Will, but we are not always prepared to receive His Will. While we wait for His Will to be done, we're doing our will; this is not so good.

Thy Will be done! We must today accept the Will of Allah and not our will; nor the will of other than Allah. To you who have never heard this Name applied to the Divine Supreme Being, it means that Allah is the Greatest of all; an All Knowing One; All Wise One.

Like you use to give to the God, just so that God knows it. But you have too many gods, in your religion. We don't know what god you are meaning. You curse with the name of God and you always disrespecting the Honor that's due that Name, if you referring to the Supreme Being.

We say the Supreme Being, making God a Being and not something of the sort in which you declare Him to be. I want you to get this in your minds. We are not worshipping something spooky; some kind of formless spirit up in the sky. And we have never seen nothing up there but sky and Stars, planets. That's all we can see up there. We don't see no god walking in the midst of them telling us on Earth that I am the god up here; and I am the god down there; we don't hear that.

And, the Scientist have made glasses so, so far reaching into the Space, that they can tell what's on the surface of planets millions of miles away. So, what should we be worshipping when that which we don't know nothing about is just a lie that the devil told us; that God was not man, while he know better. But he didn't want you to worship Allah; Allah is a Man. He have even gotten some of the orthodox Muslims believing such lies, that Allah is not a Man.

The Holy Qur'an teach you of them saying that the Messenger believes in a Man, but, I don't like to challenge you in no such argument when I know you don't know what you talking about. [The Audience applauds] Thank you. That is why We have a Day of Judgment to take out all these things that people trying to believe in.

Allah says in His Holy Qur'an, that on the Judgment Day if you bring a god up beside Me, I am Allah, the Best Knower; I am Allah. Think over that. If you want to make a spook out of Me look at Me good, I am not a spook, for I am Allah.

And I stayed with Him and He Taught me for three years four months, night and day. If you think you know Allah better than me, come get up here and let me question you. [The Audience applauds]. If we are not going to have a full knowledge of God on the Judgment Day, when will we have a full knowledge? I want you to remember these things.

We're not here to tell you other than the Truth. We're here to tell you the Truth because others has gone before Us, who have did the lying and using things that they had no knowledge of, but guessed; and that guess is making mistakes. As the Bible and Qur'an warn you against such things. The Qur'an says to Abraham and Ishmael, to raise up one among them; they prayed for this. And teach him the Book, the Bible and the Wisdom, for many of them, they only guess at it.

The preachers who loved to be called preachers after their white enemies; he will kill himself and his people too, just to have the white man to call him reverend. Well that's right! As the Bible teach it like this: That "they love the praise of this world, neglect the Hereafter." They just love to do things that will satisfy the blue-eyed Caucasian. But I care nothing about this blue-eyed devil. For its written in the Qur'an on the Judgment Day Allah will gather the guilty blue-eyed [The Audience applauds]. This mean white people. The guilty blue-eyed; He gather them; push them in a Lake of Fire. So if you're blue-eyed, do not believe in Allah and Islam, you had better change them. Have them operated on and put you some Black eyes in. [The Audience applauds].

The Will of Allah; Let Thy Will be done. The Will of Allah have not been free to do it's Will for the last six thousand years, due to the will given to the devil to try to destroy Us from Him and His Truth. He give the devil six thousand years, remember this, to destroy the Truth of Us and to destroy Us physically.

Well I don't think that you have studied this too much. For nearly forty years I have been studying Scripture and History after Allah Taught me for three years and four months. Then He give to me one hundred and four books to study. Give me the number of them and the place where I could find them.

So I studied and He give me a Holy Qur'an in Arabic, but I couldn't read it. So He got me one in Arabic and English, translated by Muhammad Ali of Pakistan. Then later He found one in Yusuf Ali of Egypt. He brought me that and then He told me say " I will give you a Holy Qur'an when you learn how to read Arabic; then I will give you a Holy Qur'an in Arabic." He say, "I made it Myself." So He showed me that Holy Qur'an in Arabic in September last, but I couldn't read, I could only recognize one letter in it. So, I expect Him within a year to come back with that same Book. [The Audience applauds].

A man you can call him what you want; given a job as I have been given; he can't take the material things of this world to bring in as a foundation for another world. These things here, books that I have read will not do for us to build a New World out of. We have to have a New Teaching…

The Holy Qur'an will live forever. Why? Because it have Truth in it, and I will not say it have some Truth, it's all Truth if you understand. Notice the Holy Qur'an is unlike Bible. The Bible is full of prophesy; the Holy Qur'an is not. The Holy Qur'an is a message directly to Muhammad, the Messenger.

This is why it reads, "say so and so and so." And when they say so and so and so, you say so and so. This is a direct message to a student under the Teachings and Guidance of Allah. So I want you to understand these things; the Bible is a Book of prophesy.

The Will of Allah; Let Thy Will be done. Allah's Will could not be done until the will of him that was given a certain Time to rule us on the planet Earth. Then, that god must have the freedom and right of that freedom to rule according to his god. This is the white race I'm referring to.

There have been many trips made by Prophets to put a stop to the will of the devil to rule the people. But, he was the winner. His will had to be done because God and the Scientist of God in the world, We call them Prophets, they could not overcome the devil, because, he was given six thousand years to force us under his rule if he could. And such people as Prophets he killed them; imprisoned them to keep them from interfering with the right of his rule.

Up until today, he been after everyone. He is after me day and night. I don't say I'm a Prophet because this the end of Prophets. I'm a Messenger of God and not a Prophet. I got nothing to prophesy because this the end of prophesy. So I got nothing to prophesy. Elijah, the man is prophesied in the Bible spoken of in a few places in the Qur'an as a Righteous man, a good man.

The Holy Qur'an give it to him and that he was with the number of those Prophets, but not exactly referring to him as a Prophet, because this Elijah is not to come to prophesy, but to deliver the final message to the people, and join with God.

That's why you don't find his grave in the Bible, nor Holy Qur'an. You don't find where they buried Elijah. Well, he must …written of Him. Not that he live forever, but Elijah is under several other names. The Bible call this name meaning, "As One with God." It says this man name mean God is with us, and that is also true interpretation; God is with us today, and I'm with you. [The Audience applauds].

The Bible teaches you and me that this Elijah must First come. He don't come after God, he goes before God. And, this is what the Book is meaning, "He must First come." But right behind him, God will appear.

The Will of God; Let Thy Will be done. The Christian pray, "On Earth as it is in Heaven." But you and me never did get the true meanings of what he meant, "Let Thy Will." How can Thy Will meaning Allah's Will, be done as long as the will of the devil is practiced? You cannot set up the Will of God Universal as long as He have a free enemy to attack His Will.

We must rid the people of an open enemy, as the Holy Qur'an teaches, from attacking the Truth, and from attacking the Truthful ones. We must rid the Earth of such opponents, who are not secret, their open opponents. So we must rid the Earth of open enemies, and secret enemies.

Let Thy Will be done as it is in Heaven. Let it be done on Earth. Your will should not be hindered by no means, and by no one. So God raises up Himself to fight the Final War for Truth, Peace and Security for the Righteous. He comes out Himself to be the Champion and lead the Righteous to Victory.

Thy Will, it is a great thing to know that the Will here comes into practice and use in the Last Day, that God only Wills, and there it is. This is the way it begin at the beginning. After God Made Himself, then He Willed that the Heavens that we see above, beneath and around come to pass. He just Willed that; here today we see it; here today we're enjoying it. A Will that was made in Space where there was no planets, no starlight but His Will come True, and made material things to come out of Nothing.

The Brains that no limited Power; His Power was ever to be respected and made known. Their Will, this is what's going on today. When a Righteous person get so Righteous, get so close to God, God accepts him as His friend. Then both Will of each Other is with each Other. What one Will the Other One Will. [The Audience applauds]. This is what the Holy Qur'an teaches you today, and me, that the Will of Allah is the Will of His Messenger, and the will of His Messenger is the Will of Allah. [The Audience applauds].

I will grant you whatever thy desire. Think over that. Your desire is My Desire; My Desire is your desire. The belief in Me is the belief in the Messenger. The belief in the Messenger is the same. Make the Messenger as an object of taking your chance with him. If you believe in the Messenger, that's sufficient, you believe in Me. [The Audience applauds].

The Messenger's will is according to the Will of Allah. He can't will something oppose to Allah. Allah have taken over the Messenger's heart, mind, and brains, making them react according to His Will. [The Audience applauds].

Thy Will be done. Let Thy Will be done. He's on Time that His Will should be done. Satan have lived over his Time. That's the Will of Allah; Allah had to give us Time to be Justified in bringing about an end to Satan's rule.

Here, we here in the midst, born and nursed by the devil himself. Knew nothing but devil and devil work; and didn't have the knowledge of the devil's work, which is science, tricknology. All these years he played on us, this is why I have been saying for the last few weeks that we are teaching the Theology, the Knowledge of Secret things said in a Theology way; that we have not studied. We never was smart enough to study the Theology side of things.

So many of us never went to school for such. Talking with a few Ministers of the Seminary College, on the East Coast while I was running up and down on it. I happen to be lucky to meet some of them. They quickly give up and says "Yes, Mister Muhammad that we never was taught what you is teaching us. Here in the Seminary College that we went to, they didn't teach us this." I say, surely this let you know then, they was holding back secrets of yourself and of the Scripture so that you would not be able to understand yourself, to teach your people.

So they bear witness, "You are right and I believe that he just what you call him." I say you don't have to believe it stick around a few days Brother. [The Audience applauds].

While I am here in this Surah or verse, Chapter, in 119 of this Chapter that I am reading Chapter 5 or Surah 5. It teaches you and me that we should not have believe Jesus was a God. It says, " And behold God will say, Didest thou say unto me worship me and my mother as Gods and ...of God?" He will say, "Glory to Thee never could I say what I have no right," this is Jesus talking, " to say that I said such a thing. Thou wouldest, indeed have known." "Now notice what is in me, in my heart. No not what is in Thine, for Thy knowest in full all that is secret." Whenever Jesus denies or denies us from making him a God, he was not no God of the sort that the Christian's have made. He denies it even in the Bible where he says that he is something like all other Prophets. That he was not a God that people should take him for such thing as a God. He was like all the Others.

And in fact about it, this may bring little dislike of me from you Christians. There is nowhere in the Bible in the whole Book, where it prophesy him coming even as a Prophet. I will give you ten thousand dollars if you can find in the whole Bible where that it prophesy Jesus coming as a Prophet.

Now I know you, I know you….What you read of Jesus in the whole Bible prophesy, that's myself. [The Audience applauds]. In the Bible it teaches you that the man says, "You read the Scriptures, and in them you think you have salvation." And it's all written of me, and that's right!

Over in Isaiah you will find where he prophesy of a Prophet coming in the Last Days; that this Prophet will have the Government upon his shoulders. Jesus did not have a government upon his shoulders of which is much needed for a Prophet that is going to attack and destroy the Jews, Greeks, Christian's authority over Good Religion. He need to have that Knowledge and Power. And, if he have the government upon his shoulders, what government?

Let Thy Will be done. I am not trying to go over the whole entire Bible and Holy Qur'an for you. I'm just only telling you things I know you believe in the opposite direction. And the belief you have is without knowing whether you are believing right or not.

When a man believe a thing, and don't have nothing but belief, he have no proof of his believing, whether it's right or wrong only he just believe. He can be stopped with know; know and belief is different. I can believe that there is a airplane out there on our doorstep, but that maybe just a belief; there're no airplane out there.

There is many people believe angels and gods all up there in the air some place. But if they up there we could see them. There is no such thing as spirits, formless spirits flying around in space, unless you want to declare such to the Righteous Mind.

Now the Righteous have minds that certain things should be done; and certain things that's in space going around maybe, but it's not material. We today, after the tricknology taught the world by our enemy, devils, bring to you reality. And without reality today, we can't change any world. God and all of His prophets of a belief of immaterial things against material things; we cannot do that. We got to do way with such teachings and beliefs; and get those people of the Heavens and the Earth into looking forward into reality, and not no spooky ideas.

He have poisoned the people's mind to believe in spooks, spirits, and the hearing of voices. That's true with many of us. We can hear each other's voice, if we are good enough. We can tune up on each other, and talk with each other if we are good enough. But if you are not good enough, you may hear a voice…

LET THE PEOPLE BE SEPARATED!

You may hear a voice, but you can't answer it. You can't converse with the voice. But there are many men on our Earth today who are Real Righteous. They can tune up on us, tell us what we thinking about from Asia, from Africa, and other spots on our Earth that have such people among them.

But, that is not impossible for you to do. But you will have to get Righteous; our brains is kind of rusty.. the Spiritual part of it from listening and being guided and lead by the enemy, that have ours a little rusty. But if you believe in Islam, do the things which is right, take away the taint of disease of wickedness out of your brain, you too will hear.

In the Bible you'll find where David said that the Lord opened up his, and caused him to hear. This is referring to us here. We can do wonders and will do wonders if we obey Allah, and put the Principles of Truth into practice; we will do wonders. Allah raised me up in your midst to do a unbelieving thing that men of science will wonder how that it happen. I'm not bragging on myself, I brags on Allah. [The Audience applauds].

Let Thy Will be done. In the Creation of Almighty God Himself, I tell you of the reasonable and possible things. I was not there; have not had any teacher to teach me that they were there; have not had a teacher to teach me but, Master Fard Muhammad, how the things come about and how the things that man have never known are about. All we know is that it happen, but how, that is the question.

Thy Will, in the Making of God Himself, He could not have had a Will, until He had Brains capable of thinking. He was Created, Self Created from a Atom of Life. Atom of Life, that not only to produce flesh, bones, and blood from the Earth that He was Created on, Self Created. I want you to know that good and I will repeat it time again. And I will go to no limited argument with you, that He was made on the very Earth that we're on now, but it was not itself as it is today; it was only Atom itself.

But, I want to come back to our subject text here, "the Will of God, let the Will of God be done," as I said a few minutes ago, His Will could not be done as long as He had an enemy powerful enough to force his will against the Will of God until a certain Time.

This is the certain Time that he can't force his will against the Will of Allah. The Day and Time of his having power to force his will against Allah and against the representatives of Allah, the Prophets, is up now. He can no more force his will against the Righteous because the God of the Righteous have now appeared in His Time, and now His Will, will be done. [The Audience applauds].

We are just off from not understanding what we should understand; being carried away with the devil's teachings of imaginations and of formless things, from formless ideas. We must get away from that kind; come into reality.

I don't blame the devil for trying to hide himself as long as he could. He even go so far as to say in the Holy Qur'an of you that believe in Righteousness that he had no authority over you, he just call you and you come; you was scared to disobey him. But, the little man speaking to you from this rostrum, does not fear to disobey him if he invites me to that which is other than Truth and Righteousness. I will disobey him, and then tell me now make me to obey you!

God have Taught me so full the knowledge of the devil, that I'm not afraid to tell him to go jump in the Lake [The Audience applauds], because a very fiery Lake is being built for him; not a water lake, but a Lake of fire. According to the Teachings of Allah to me that North America is that Lake of fire. Not the Lake Michigan, but the Lake is on Earth of North America where the atoms will be exploited and set afire; everything that is on the surface of North America.

He said to me that it will burn for three hundred and ninety years, so close to the time that they have kept us here, is about the time near four hundred years they kept us in servitude slavery. So Allah will burn them that length of time. He just that angry with them for destroying and making enemies of His people against Himself.

Let Thy Will be done. If you only knew, these Great Works, you would be more happy than you are. The Will of God is the same today as it was when He First made Himself Known to Us trillions of years ago.

Your will to do something other than Righteous is not your will, that's the will of the devil. And the will of the devil is a foreign enemy to you and me. He didn't come with us; he come here late just six thousand years ago. The devil was made, not created; he didn't come with the Creation. This people that we are so disgusted and tired of being given to run round by; just came here six thousand years ago; and that's a very short while to our being on the Earth.

So let me get away from there…and get you started for home [The Audience applauds]. A man who say he don't like to be a Muslim, and he being a Blackman, that's the very Nature of the Blackman, is a Muslim. H e don't have to ask Allah to make him a Muslim, but ask Allah to help him to rid himself of the actions and principles of Satan; and give him his actions and Principles of self, which he was made, Created in.

Holy Qur'an teaches us that by Nature we were made or Created from Righteous.

We were Created Righteous, but Satan made us according to his rearing of us, other than Righteous. Made us with the mind to try and do as he's doing. This is why it is so hard to teach and lead our Black people of America into Righteous self, because they were reared by the devil himself.

The devil is a murderer from the beginning. He taught you murder, but to murder yourself, and he will help you do that. I say to you my friends, get away from wanting to murder each other. You look alike; You are alike. Why should you want to kill each other? You should want to see each other live. I say my friends, just a few days you will learn that Elijah Muhammad is teaching you the Truth. [The Audience applauds].

You can prolong your lives by doing Righteousness. You can prolong your lives by eating the right foods, and eat it only when necessary. I have another edition coming on to you, "How To Eat To Live." You will soon have it in hand.

God teach and lead me, meaning Allah in the Person of Master Fard Muhammad, how to teach you to live and be happy. When a man have no sickness in his body, we call him happy. He is happy he don't feel no pain; that body is happy.

My beloved Brothers and Sisters, this is just the life Allah seeks for you to enjoy; a life of happiness. This is known to the orthodox Muslim world, so much so, that they will hide their own sickness if they a little sick. They won't tell you because they know they have no right to be sick; they made themselves sick.

It is not the Will of God that you get sick. You makes yourself sick. It is not God who make you die; you kill yourself. He don't have a set time for you and me to die. We kill ourselves the way we live.

Let Thy Will be done as it is in Heaven, so says the Christian. He is the One Who let him do his will without hindering him from doing his will. The Christian is so full of spooky ideas, that they cannot see in reality God, nor His Angels. Angels will walk all around them and eat with them; they never know it's Angels. This is true because of the far drawn away idea that all of these things is immaterial, and far from flesh beings.

Nothing is from us that is not flesh. We can see it; We can hear it; We can talk with it, then it can't be something other than flesh. But this is the tricknology the devil taught in our Fathers, to believe all these things just the opposite of what they really are.

Let Thy Will be done. We want the people of Earth to be separated as a people deserve of the Will of Allah to be done. Let them go to Allah and obey Allah, and believe in the people of Allah; and especially in that Last Messenger whom He chooses, or rather whom He have chose because I'm that man. [The Audience applauds].

Here's one thing I would like to say to you, that we, we meaning my followers and self, planning on many big things for the Southside of Chicago. This is where the greatest number of us live. We have decided on making the Southside of Chicago a very beautiful place for us to live in. We have decided on building from 7800 block on Cottage Grove to 87th Street on the Eastside Streets, oh pardon me, not Streets, stores and warehouses. We going to put in these stores merchandise, the price of which the price will be unbelievable to you; so much less than what you have been paying the devil for.

I was talking with a Pakistani merchant who came to my home couple of days ago. He offers to sell us, he had samples, shoes and other merchandise at a unbelieving price. So low, that you will have some money to carry home to the wife. [The Audience applauds].

So my idea is to send my people of committee, around over the Earth to various people of our kind, and order our merchandise …from them. You're going to be surprised. It's almost an unbelieving thing!

We are robbed to our very marrow of our bone by our enemies who robbed us of our labor for four hundred years. And now wants to rob us in prices, to keep you a slave. But I think I have you lined up for a great surprise in everything that you want, coming from the Muslim world. [The Audience applauds].

Why should we spend our money on high priced merchandise of the Christian, when we are more on the planet than they. We have countries after countries filled with Muslims, and they have merchandise that we need to wear. Why should we waste our money with enemies, when our Brothers will let us have it at a third of the price that we are paying here now? [The Audience applauds].

I'm going to order a few thousand shoes and a few thousand other necessary things that you need to wear, or rather that you do wear. I will pay for them myself if you don't want to buy them. I will pay for them and give them to you to show you how that you have been robbed, to calling yourself Christians. Now that if you come over to what you really are, which is Muslim believers in Allah and Islam, you can get along with about a third of the money that you are spending, and live good. [The Audience applauds].

I'm ordering few ship loads of good fish, at a very reasonable price that you can eat them and walk the streets with a full stomach of good fresh fish, of the good type; and keep the other part of your money in your pocket. I can get these fish for you and me out of Our waters of Our Earth, in any quantity that I want.

So I'm going to start agents coming to your door in all the major cities of the country, telling you when we going to have a load of these fish, or so many tons; and want you to give us your order. We want to get started living cheap.[The Audience applauds].

We can now buy anything we want from all the nations of the Earth, or any of the nations of the Earth, any of them. We can buy from Russia, if we want, but I think China and the other people is better. You can buy from China; you can buy from Korea; you can buy from Japan; and you can buy from all the Muslim Governments of the Earth.

This is open to you now; the door of Salvation have been open to you and to me. Let us [The Audience applauds], let us avail our self of such great opportunities that these doors does not close on us with our acceptance. We're up from slavery with nothing.

So let us be wise as Allah is teaching us, and His people. Try and get on top with the world...putting in orders for money to borrow their money. This is very hard to do; to borrow money, especially from your enemy. They want to hold you down; you going too fast for them anyway.

So, we have been made promises, promises after promises. But, very little money has been materialized. As you heard about the Muslim country loaning us, around near three million dollars, that's true! They are promising us much more. It takes lots of money to build a Nation. When you hear tell of someone give us three or four million or loaned us dollars, that's just like someone loan you three or four dollars, and you needed a hundred dollars.

The people will regret their non-help to us soon. For I would like to tell you all the Truth that is bound to materialize. Allah have promised me much millions of millions and hundreds of millions, millions of dollars. But I have to wait until it's Time. He will release it, certainly on Time. He don't have to go somewhere and borrow it, it's here in America.

In the past History you will find where Allah always, when He was angry with a people, He destroyed that people and taken their wealth, and give it to the poor. So don't be surprised if...[The Audience applauds].

So I want you to remember that we want to build a beautiful Southside. We want to begin this store and warehouse on Cottage Grove, as soon as we're able to pay the money down. The builder wants a half a million down. It's going to cost us quite a bit of money to get these buildings from 78th to 87th Cottage Grove. It takes that for us to get started with what we want to do, to start the building for you.

So I ask you to do the very best you can in helping me to get these buildings going; and you won't regret one nickel that you put in them, for it give you a...for every dime that you put in them back.

But I know I'm not talking to no such people, I'm [The Audience applauds], I'm talking, with people that want to see themselves upgrade. Now you have the time, and I'm not trying to beg you for self, because I give that back for this purpose that you do give to. I don't want it for myself, I want it for you. I don't need anything but some clothes to cover my nakedness, and a house out of doors to sleep under the roof of it when I'm able to sleep.

In my conclusion, I want to thank you for your honor and respect to my wife's dead body. I never seen no person's body honored as you did my wife. You greatly honored. I was told that there was somewhat around five hundred cars out in that parade. I do not think that I could have asked you for more respect and honor that you give to my wife's body. I hope and pray Allah, that the honor will always be remembered that you give her. This is all we can do for a dead body, it is to respect it for what it did for us, when it was alive. [The Audience applauds].

Though, these things come by the will of Allah, and we shall quickly forget, because we're also on the same road. Not a one of us is off on a road that won't lead to the same destination. So let us not forget that, and prepare for ourselves that we will not die unless we die a Muslim. [The Audience applauds].

It is not mention Muslim in the Bible, but it mean the same. He says there the prayer, "Let me die the death of the Righteous." We glory in Allah to guide us, even through death, that we surely would that we die the death of the Righteous.

This you find the Prophets, some of them in the Bible praying for the same thing that they prayed for the same thing, excuse my English; that they wanted to die the death of the Righteous; and they did do so though some of them was maimed and murdered. But yet, they died a Righteous person in their mind and heart, according to God. They could not have died any better under the hand of an enemy who…destroyed some of them.

But in this Day and Time, you can die the death of the Righteous if you live a Righteous life. A Righteous life, Allah will let you die the death of the Righteous. What is meant here, you not suppose to suffer. A Muslim told me once of a Muslim dying in the Mosque over in Asia. He say he died on his knees saying his prayers; and I said that's a mighty good death. And I was told about plenty Righteous people die easy. Allah take them out of life, and their gone to the life of unknown or has never been known to be a life there. So what I'm saying to you, let us pray to Allah and to Righteousness, and try and die the death of the Righteous.

I thank you for your visiting here this afternoon, and I pray that each and every one of you will not die, unless you're a Muslim. Everybody wants to die easy. This is true, that's nature. We don't want to know it, because that's the end of us. So, to be like that, be Righteous.

I thank you for your listening here this afternoon. Now, I'm going to do this myself. I want all of you that is here, who have some disbelief about Islam, stand up and tell me. No one? I want anyone of you, who have not understood the Teachings of Islam that I have been teaching here, and my helper Minister Shah and others who are helping me here throughout the country. If, there is something that is said, that you don't understand, will you stand? I mean about Islam, will you stand, tell me so I can correct you? No one? I thank you.

Now again, I would like that you know this to be true of our Teachings, and you have Bible bear you witness, bear us witness. Hurry! Hurry! get out the name of white people; Hurry! Hurry! and acclaim the name of Allah, your people. When we say Allah, many times we are referring to the Supreme One among us.

Allah, His name is Allah, the Supreme Being. We call Him Supreme because no other being is His equal. We don't mean that He's a spook now. There's no such thing as a God that have joy in us that is something other than us. That He's some kind of a formless something, No! All the Gods ever was for us, was meat, bone, blood. That's what they were, never was no formless stuff; and they never will be. God could not get joy out of us if He was not One of us. He just Supreme in Wisdom and have Power to Will a thing and it come to past.

Let Thy Will be done. Will, He just Will a thing and it come to past, and that is conferred upon the Righteous. If you love Allah, obey Allah and His Messengers, Prophets, and do the will of him that is sent to them to teach. You also could will a thing, it will come to past. But don't will a thing and then be suspicious whether it will come to past or not. Then you are disbelieving in your own prayer to God and disbelieving in God, Whom that you are directing your prayer to. Whatever you ask Him in prayer believe He heard it and it will come to past, if it's not vain things; then it will come to past.

I asked Allah something that maybe you don't know. I saw my wife was in a condition, in a disease, the thing that she had was a cancer, and it had been with her every since He Came to us. He told my wife in my presence, "Sister you have a sick stomach." This sick stomach traveled with my wife up until the day she died.

She knew these things and I knew them. I did not want to tell our sons and daughters the condition that our mother and our wife was in, my wife was in. There they may would have grieved themselves. I've known it for over thirty years. But I kept it to myself. I know what was wrong. God had told her and she knew it. But, there was no cure for it in the way that you once thought.

I asked Allah to bless my wife to come home and die. I say, don't let her die out there in a hospital of the devil, lest he laugh and say " Oh," he say, "the Prophet brought her to us to heal. Why did not he go to the Master Fard Muhammad if he thought that He was God to get her to heal?" So I asked Allah, knowing Allah in Person, to take her way from out of that hospital, and let me bring her here, home and die. I say because the devil will be bound to laugh at you and me. And, desperate, I kept after Him for three or four times, and I felt like that He would do so; and He did do so; and I told the doctors that I rather see her die at home.

ACCEPT YOUR OWN:
SALVATION HAS COME TO YOU!

And I told the doctors that I rather see her die at home. So they admitted they were, that I was right; and that they would find some way to get her out to my house. I say yes she'll come out, and I say, I will let her die right here in this house. I say because, I don't want to be laughed at by the devil; and I don't the devil to try to make mock of the Power of Our God.

But there is things in that line that must not be ignored. God is not going to do no miracle, unless it's necessary for us, and the way of death because one day we going to die anyway.

As the Holy Qur'an teaches us, Allah did not design that no man should live forever. So don't be thinking that. He says in His Holy Qur'an though, some of us wish that we have a life of a thousand years; well that's the dread of death. But, if it pleases Allah, we will die very easy. My father did, no one know when he had past; no struggle, no nothing at all, until the, the nurse examined him and found him dead. I had just left the hospital, a hour an exact hour, and I know what he had told me. I wasn't expecting him to live; he talk to me very sane. Before I left he told me all what he heard the doctor say. So I left to take my mother way fearing that she'd break down if I tell her what he had said bout him, would be passing away from us, nigh, most anytime. So I came home before I got her settled in her seat good, telephone ring told me my father had just past. I wasn't surprised.

So we returned, begin to make preparation for his burial. And, he didn't make one struggle they say. This is the death that the Holy Qur'an is teaching you, die not unless you a Muslim so that you don't feel the sting of death. It's a kind of, visitor, we don't want to never visit us, and if he visit us, don't let us know you'll here, just take us away. This is what the Holy Qur'an teaching you, that you pray for, pray that I'll let you die the death of the Muslim, meaning the Righteous.

So my dear, good and listening audience, I have much I would like to say to you, on many of these things; and when I think that you can take it, I'm going to tell you but I will wait on you. And again I will say, I am happy to stand before such intelligent group of people as you have been here this afternoon. You have been so, orderly, honorable this afternoon, that some people of intelligence would not believe that such people out of slavery has produced such intelligence as you have, since you have accepted Allah and His servant, Elijah Muhammad and his Religion, Islam.

193

So I thank you, and if there's anyone of you who would like to join up with us, I'm going to ask you this time myself. Just get up from your seat and come on round and join up with us, if you so desire; and if you don't desire wait until you see the end, then, you will come. Is there anyone would like to join us? Just come on round…[The Audience applauds because someone want to join up with the Messenger]. The Brother will take you upstairs he says, and there he will take you through. Yes sir, this Brother here acts like that he have been with us before, he's saluting us. Go right upstairs, the Brother, will show you the way up there. [The Audience applauds].

This makes an intelligent person out of you, to go and accept your own. You have already accept the devil; what you have is the devil, and if you like to go long with the devil there's no objection. We don't object to you going to the god that you believe in. But, we hope when the Day come that Allah won't miss putting you in the middle of Hell, that reject your own. Not out on the outskirts of it, but drop you right over in the middle of the Lake of Fire because salvation come to you, and you reject it for the fire. You won't make no mistake, it be the Will of Allah. I won't make no mistake, because I am suppose to be design by Allah to help push you into Hell, like Moses helped in the Bible. And so when you turn me down, I'm going to be all but satisfied. I will be just like your Bible teach you, "And the Lamb was angry." I worked for you forty years to try to get you into Heaven, then you turn me down. I'm wishing then to put you in the middle of Hell.

I thank you. May Allah Bless the Believers, and grant to you a safe return home, peaceful night's rest and sleep, and a happy morning rising,

As Salaam Alaikum.

TRUTH OF THE ENEMY

...class of our people don't come and visit us, see what we're saying and doing. It's due to the fact, they think the enemy will not give them as the common saying go, "a break." You don't need the enemy to give you a break, if you do for self, you give your own self a break. [The Audience applauds].

We have been beggars of the blue-eyed devils so long, until we don't think we getting any place unless we get his respect. But I say Brother he's going down, we're going up. He's going down to dishonor and disrespect; you're going up in honor and respect.

I am your Teacher of the enemy, and you see me stand here and tell you the Truth of them. But they have very respect for me than they have of you [The Audience applauds]. Whether you believe it or not, they have respect for me.

Did you hear about how they respected me in fifty-nine when I visit Washington? They come out and met me, and they stayed around me to protect me from some, maybe, would be silly act of yourself. They were not going to hurry since that they was not trying to protect me from you. They were not going to do anything to me; but they was afraid.

So let us give praise to the coming of Allah to take us out of the Hell of the blue-eyed devil and destroy him, and save us from his destruction. That's the God you been praying for. Now He's here, and I proved that He's here; that I walks up and down the streets or ride up and down the streets alone or with you; nobody bothers me. I'm not out there afraid that he going to get me for what I said here today about him. He is afraid that I'm, [The Messenger laughs], that I may get him.

195

CHRISTIANITY: THE RELIGION OF SATAN

Salaam Alaikum. You may be seated.

Maybe I don't have the money like that Judge in the South, every time he was five minutes late he pay five dollars. So I may have to start to borrowing to pay all of these five minutes [The Messenger laughs]. I'm very happy to see your smiling faces here this afternoon; and I'm sorry that I was a few minutes late.

As you may know, that it's all over the world that we are never on time here. So, I want to warn you and myself too, we better get out of that being behind time, don't, we may run into the wrong fellow that's on time.

We very happy to say to you, that we have a continuation of our subject, the Theology Of Time. We never is off of that subject. I don't care what we are preaching, that still is our subject. And that, you have been very grateful and honorable to me and my helpers to visit this Teaching from all parts of America.

Having you coming from far and near to hear what I have to say, I hope you will return happy and wishing to come again. I'm not going to promise you that I'm going to be here every Sunday, but I'm going to try to be here every time I hear you are coming from afar to listen to me.

So I know No.2 will try and get you to promise so that they can get the honor, credit for having a large Temple of people; and when I get them back at the door you know I will make them pay off [The Messenger laughs].

You know we have so much to say. I use to teach six hours, but since I'm little late today I try and remember that I was a little late and let you go before six hours has expired. Oh yes I did use to teach right here in Chicago six hours Brothers! Yes sir, that's no long time since we been here for four hundred years and never have been able to get away. So now, we getting the news of getting out of the confines of our enemies; and that is very good news.

As long as our enemies have the upper hand, or authorities over us, we can never hope for anything like human freedom. We got to get authorities for ourselves. I don't know what you thinking about us, and what we have to say to you, but we have plenty to say, we just want to know where to start.

You know people who have been preaching Christianity all their lives, the religion of Satan; "Oh! Listen what he said." That's just what I said Brother. Now if you believe that there is a devil in which you see him every hour, if you want to, or more than that he stays before you. Then, if he want to try to deceive you while he know you, but you don't know him. He makes up a religion he know you are born Righteous; Created Righteous. But he know he have deceive you to make you think that you and him is the same before God. God think as much of him as He does you. But he's mistaken, and you have been deceived.

You're alright today if you just will accept your own Religion. And no getting on knees to ask for forgiveness for your past; all of that is forgiven. God told me to tell you that He will forgive us all the past; just accept your own. Now, go from here and not think over what was in the past. You did not know who you were, nor the enemy. So, that is Right and Just that you should be forgiven for that which you had no knowledge of.

So this what He told me to tell you. And since we don't have to go on our knees for yesterday, be sure that we go on our knees for today. A people that have did everything that the devil did and tried to beat him at some of it, get forgiven for all of their evil, you certainly should be happy. [The Audience applauds]. Because I myself, was not Elijah Muhammad in those days. And so, I thank Him for forgiving me of such evil things that I did while I was under the devil, though He said He forgive me; but I thank Him for forgiving me.

We're happy to have Minister Farrakhan, of No.7 with us. This is honor, for us. Minister of No.1, Minister of practically of all of our Temples around. So, let us, show our visiting Ministers that we respect their visit; and their help in the work, that we are doing here, we're happy.

The Time, as I have said many times, we have no Time, until motion is made. Then we calculate from motion, the Time. The Sun is so Powerful, that it make everything in its circle, to move. There we calculate Time, from Sun.

The Sun being the greatest planet in our Sun family that we can never even understand, just why that we don't understand the Sun. But that is one planet that you can't understand; it was written that you can't understand it. God didn't make it to be understood by you and me because it is a Divine Light put up there for you and I to read. Read not only the Sun, but read what that thing look like and what its for. But the God put the Sun up there for us to learn. It's a Shining Light, and it don't rotate round nothing but God Himself. No planet is attractive enough to force the Sun to bow, but She is attractive enough to force every planet within her reach to bow.

We have not learned what we should have learned because of our enemy. Now the Sun is a, a symbol too, of the work of God. That is why you can't understand it; you don't know where She's getting her fuel from, but She shining.

So much, that I would like to bring you into the knowledge of, but I can't do it in the few minutes [The Audience applauds]. When I asked Allah, in the Person of Master Fard Muhammad, to Whom Praise is due Forever, to teach me of the Sun, He got up, He stood up and He looked at me, say "If you ask Me again I won't visit you no more." So I wondered, why couldn't I ask Him that?

So the next day He Came to me, He look like He say, "The poor boy ask a question and I'm God, I'm suppose to answer what he ask Me." And then He started Teaching me a little about the Sun; not much though oh no! So don't be getting your ears tuned up, oh no! But I can say we have a mighty Sun.

Well I tell you one thing like this, a man that is given a world to challenge, and to bring that world to its knees, cannot do his work without plenty knowledge. Take for an instance, that all I teach you challenge it, but you never did challenge Christianity. You took for granted that Christianity was just right. That's because you was born in it, you know no better.

But I would like for you to think a little, while I teach. The enemy that made your Fathers and my Fathers a slave to the knowledge of self, do you think that he would made you have the knowledge of Almighty God when that he had robbed you of that knowledge? Do you think he'd be so kind to teach you God and His good Religion, and knowing that you are directly from God? That's what he brought you here for; to take you away from God, not to teach you God. Take you out of the knowledge of God and yourself too, so that he could get you to follow him to the Hell that your God and my God have promise him.

He know he was not going to rule forever. Why should he wise you up, when the day that you wake up, you be the First one to want to push him into Hellfire; he knows all of that. So don't try to tell him nothing, he knows it; it's you the one need to be told something.

He have a world full of Our people, call reverend Jones, and reverend Jackson, and reverend whatnot, after his name. They fill happy for him to call them reverends. That's all he will call them; just say reverend, and he fill big. [The Audience laughs]. Not before God and the devil laughing at them under his sleeves.

No reverend, he don't think nothing of you. He love to see you loving him for honor, but he know his honor will not stand before those who are honored by God; you are nothing before Allah. He only want you to be reverend... to be...No I'm not calling you out of your name. That is the name of a king; he's there in the Bible, but he was not say a good king.

Don't think I'm in a hurry. [The Audience applauds]. As much work that I'm doing that it's standing out in the Light of Divine. The reverends rather listen to the devil and have his praise than to have the Praise of Divine. And it's written in the Bible that they love the praise of this world; this we see.

As long as they has seen me at this Divine work, and making progress all over the world with it, not here in Chicago alone. But I have credit and honor all over the world, while reverend don't have honor here in Chicago. If you are here reverend I'm glad that you may hear this. In some places they don't want even to see you. When you talk about Christianity, they want to kill you.

Once upon a time, you love to talk about going to Africa to preach the devil Christianity over there. That's what it is it's the devil's Christianity. Stand up and let's pass our knowledge over, and I will show you that it's the devil's religion, and not yours. It's a lie that the devil use a good name on to make you believe it. "Oh Mister Muhammad called Christianity a lie" Yes! And I can make you out a lie if you believe it. [The Audience applauds].

I am here against the world of the enemy who calls his religion Christianity; and against you that believe it. I'm here against both, he and his followers, told to you by your own Bible, that the devil was cast in a Lake of Fire with his false prophets. A reverend who preaches Christianity is the false prophets that the Book is referring to. H e went down with his name. You love to be called reverend, Jackson, reverend Jones. Don't know that you're being called after the, the devil's name.

This is the devil's name, reverend that you're being called by; and reverend you will be dumped into a Lake of Fire with him, if you don't come on and go along with Elijah Muhammad. [The Audience applauds].

I'm very happy to have you distinguish Brothers here, of the profession of doctor, dentist, and, T.V. doctor, Edward Pullard, I guess that's, the way something there; and if I'm wrong in pronouncing your name, please ask me, or tell me how to pronounce it. Also doctor Thomas Smith, and dentist, Joseph Robinson, and, Mister Frank…WXYZ T.V Show…Drake Clinic Administrator.

We're very happy to have such professional people as you with us this afternoon. We are the people who have respect and honor for all that visit us. And when the professional class of people visit us, we want you to know that we honor you and respect you, for your visiting. We need you. We're not the people that know all. We are the people would like to learn, and let learn.

This is the type of people that we need now, to help us; yes to help us. We want all the professional class of people to come join up with us; help put the job over. You have the type of help that we need; and, we're working for you. Come here and help us, to work for you.

We're building everywhere, something like signs of our work that we're doing in the name of Divine. These people, of this type of profession, I think you, you're the one I want to talk with because, the man have no learning and no profession, cannot help me on just believing, but he can't do the work that is needed, to be done.

So I'm thankful for you, and I will assure you that if you represent yourself with us, the devil himself, will turn and honor you. [The Audience applauds].

THE EVIL ONE MUST BE DESTROYED!

[The Messenger laughs], yeah that may get him. [The Audience applauds]. I have power with God to do my will on them, and you too. But I don't want to do nothing to you but good. You are my Brother and Sister. You can say to Hell with you Muhammad, if you want, but I know a Day that will be long soon, that you will say Heaven to Muhammad!

Beautiful, very beautiful sitting, you look beautiful from up here. I could stand here and talk to you all this afternoon. [The Audience applauds]. You Brothers, I hope you hear this, do not be trying to force no one to sell Muhammad Speaks. They don't want to sell them, leave them go. No Brother, that has not been registered up with us, have no obligation whatsoever, to help you and me do anything, unless it's his will. Now cut this out, don't, you going to be dismissed, for a long time.

I don't know where you get such foolish ideas. People go off and laugh at you; cut it out, we don't force nobody to do anything for us. We don't force you, that is registered up with us, to do anything for us. You do according to your will.

We are not people that is forced to have people to beg for us. No, you don't have to beg for us; Allah is sufficient. [The Audience applauds]. And I hope that the Captains, Secretaries, and, Assistant Ministers, will bring you to Justice, and send you out for a long time.

You're ruining our own teachings. We're Independent, we don't have to beg nobody but Allah. You are losing your head. I don't want no such followers, beggars, beg nobody. You don't love us enough to do something from your own will, for us, we don't want that unwilling done. [The Audience applauds]. Brother tell you that he don't care to sell no paper, take them back, give them away before ever that you be disgraced by such Brother.

We are a very foolish people anyway. And I don't like that you be like that. I want you to be intelligent and show the world how intelligent look, in the act of a human being. Time bring about all things. Time is making you manifest, they call it, Resurrection. To resurrect the dead, they don't mean resurrecting a physical dead, but a mental dead. So you must remember, that for four hundred years we has been a mental dead people.

I have a little kind of bad interfering voice, however, I hope you will understand what I'm trying to say; as when I got to the schoolhouse the teacher was dismissing her school. So don't blame me, blame those that held me back. I don't guess you...born down North, where I was born; I was born down North, and if you big enough to work they put you in the field, because the devils were forcing your parents to send you to field, and to work for him.

Well I guess that's about enough of that. The Time, what Time? The Time of God. The Time of Allah. We give Him the name Allah, but you call Him God, that's one of His names. One of His ninety-nine Attributes is God, too. But when we say Allah, we mean God. It's an Arab name, and we like to have the use of the Arab name because, the devil have no respect for the name that he teach you to call the Supreme Being. God, he use the same name to curse with. He take it for a joke. Just recognize, you falls in behind him and do the same. You disgrace the name of God Divine.

But I want you to remember, that the Time have come that the enemy of God Divine will not have a chance to go round mocking God and His people forever. They have...that the mockers of God must be backed up and thrown in a furnish of Fire. He want you to go with him. He want me to go with him, and be burned with the same Fire that Allah, has prepared for him. But, by Allah raising me up from among you, giving me the Knowledge of both Gods; the god devil and the God Divine, to teach you what has been hidden from you for the last four hundred years; the last six thousand years. I want you to know, that the people all over the Earth has been Robbed of the Knowledge of the God Divine, due to the work of this devil.

He give him this Time to do his way, his will upon the people. Now today, He has made Himself Present to prove to you and me that He...... can remove Satan at once. But He's offering us a chance. I warn you to accept it and Glorify Him. This is no Time to waste. This is no Time to spend in sport and play, talking foolishness. This is a Time of world Destruction; not say, just a few people, but a world Destruction. Every where the people cannot get along with each other in peace; no agreement, nothing but disagreement.

For I warn you that any day now you could expect most anything of evil, but not of good. The evil world must be cast out; the evil world must be destroyed. The evil world must be shown to you and me; the Justice of God to destroy her. She is destroying us, and had us blind, deaf, and dumb without the Knowledge of her. Now, she's open wide to you and me that we may know her; and that God is not doing an injustice to her by destroying her. He's Justified in destroying her. He will punish you, if you go long with her. He will punish you on this side, disgrace you, or let you disgrace yourself. So I want you to remember to escape this disgracement; come follow me.

No, I'm not going to be here long with you. I don't care what you say about Elijah Muhammad, he will not be rolling in the streets with his eyes set in his head over punishment and disgrace from Allah, because I'm not going to disobey Allah. And I'm going to teach you what He Taught me to teach you.

What you see me do, search the Scriptures, and you can read every step I take, in the Light of History. [The Audience applauds]. I'm that fellow that you read of there in the Book, " I come to do Thy Will, Oh Lord." This is him that was not no two thousand years ago.

Jesus didn't come to do the Will of God at that Time. He did His Will, by, leaving the Jews and the Christians live out their Time. And he went back and he said that he was ahead of Time. But he said that that one coming behind him will be on Time, and he will do what he would like to have done, but he was ahead of Time. So he prophesied that that one will come and he will come directly from the face of God. And, some of the other Prophets, prophesied that He will send you one from His Face. Well I'm directly from His Face for three years [The Audience applauds].

And you won't do, and you cannot do it, the things that they did to the Prophets before me. This one you can't touch. This is the one that, that the Bible warn you of, " Touch not Mine Anointed." This is the one that was sent directly from His Face; and He defy you, to do harm to him.

Well I guess you know all of that, and you see it now. The things that I do and say in the face of the enemy, he can't do a thing but listen at it [The Audience laughs], because he know I'm directly from the Face of God, that his Book warns him against touching. So, he wants to live long as he can, as the Book teaches us "That, all that a man have will he give for his life."

The Time, the Time have arrived for what? What are you talking about Time Muhammad? The Time and the end of Satan, whom you believe in. Now push the clock of Time back and give him some more Time, if you can. But, his Time have arrived, and you have, with your ignorance of self and of the devil, have kept him living for around sixty years, over his Time.

But, Allah and myself, standing here before you, have agreed that Time has been given long enough. [The Audience applauds]. If I don't tell you these Truths, you will blame me for it. But I'm not going to let you have nothing to blame me for. I'm going to do the Will of God, that sent me. And His Will, is that I tell you; and your rejection and your disbelief is up to Him. I'm not forced to make you to believe in that which you don't.

We have Mister Roosevelt Henry, Jr., counselor, at large, from Gary, Indiana. We want to thank him for his presence, wherever he is. We always desire our people to come and visit us. reverend Clifford Blount, that's a pretty bad name in one way and a good one in another; Minister of Fellowship, at Assembly. I reckon this mean, C.O.M.M.,

Church, Fellowship Assembly, of Community Church, reverend John A. Landry…that what you mean here…reverend John A. Landry, III, minister, Fellowship Assembly, of the Community Church. I thank you reverend Haywood. No, this is not reverend Haywood Counselor, at large, Gary, Indiana. Out there we are trying to get acquainted in Gary, we want to build a airport out there, [The Audience applauds], and we just going to do just that. [The Audience applauds].

I need all the reverends that want to come to Islam where they will get a big reverend, big name. I need you to help me with the people whom you and the devil…[The Audience applauds]. Also I thank reverend Barrett, Thomas Barrett, Minister for his presence. Ministers if you and me would get together, we'll have our people in Heaven over night. [The Audience applauds]. All of these ministers here, I'm kind of changing my subject a little, for fear that they won't understand my previous subject too well.

In the Bible [The Audience applauds], it prophesy there, in the Bible that "Behold I will send you Elijah" reverend [The Audience applauds], and the Book did not put reverend to his name. [The Audience applauds.] I'm only saying reverend to you, the preaching that you ought to be preaching, so you get you a great name. The name reverend, for some kind of Organization of Satan, you'll never get no credit with the people of God.

We are the people of God. I tell the devil…that he's lying to you. [The Audience applauds]. They have made you go astray. Plain as you can read this, "Before that Great and Dreadful Day of the Lord I will send you Elijah, not reverend Elijah.

If you say you disbelieve that I am that man that will be sent just before the Great and Dreadful Day of the Lord, go read again, and then study what's going on in the world. Everybody's looking for the Great Day, Destruction to happen. Elijah preaching and warning you, this is he. [The Audience applauds].

I will assure you, that if you join up with me reverend; follow me, so that this warning here on that board will not over take you unaware. [The Audience applauds]. All the churches of America put into one church, cannot save the people of the church from the Great Disaster that is now calling America, and the worst is yet to come.

You cannot find a God in your church, I don't care what you say you have. But I'm… to do something to put a stop to the Destruction that is calling America today. Even the President don't warn you to pray to the church's God to help them. No man at war today will ask you to pray to the church god to put a stop to their slaughtering. No. But, the Muslims sit by and look at you, knowing that you are like the people that the Bible tell you that worship Baal and Elijah sit there and laughed at them. [The Audience applauds]. The same thing that go for you; I don't care how sore you get with me, call on your god and tell him to do something about. [The Audience applauds]. This is what you need, some frank teachings. [The Audience applauds]. If I make a mistake in what you would call make fun of your god, I will give you ten thousand dollars out of my Brothers vest pocket; right here before you leave I'll…check for you and our checks is very good. You got nothing but a lie from your blue-eyed Caucasian devil. [The Audience applauds].

I'm not trying to make fun, I'm just making Truth, not fun. No, if I was just making fun, I would not have said it. I would be afraid of meeting the consequence when I leave the stand, knowing that you are going to meet the consequence yourself, for believing in these devils to teach you away from your own God and the salvation in which He has sent to you. He want you to reject it since he's going to Hell, he want you to go too.

Not as long as I am here. He not going to send you to Hell just because that you are, are ignorant to the knowledge of yourself. No, beat you up a little bit, yea.[The Audience applauds]. That's right, just give you a good beating and you'll come running…[The Audience applauds]. Not the kind of beating that you're expecting, with a strap or something No, No, get you here, here that's the place to beat you, beat you up there in your head.

You must submit to the Will of God. The Will of God must be done today; not the will of Satan. Allah give Satan six thousand years to do his will. Now, the Will of Almighty God, Allah Comes in now. He will do His Will, and there's none can stop It. His Will must be done. You have prayed in prayers "Let Thy Will be done on Earth as it is in Heaven," now He's ready to do His Will. [The Audience applauds].

You don't believe that I'm the one…of my work. I'm doing just what the Bible told you, or teaches you that I would do. "Elijah, I will send you him, before the Great and Dreadful Day of the Lord's Time." Do you see anything pretty out there coming? We don't see a thing in the world but a Dreadful Time. You'll going to be so hungry here, until you will desire to eat each other. And if the other don't watch you, you will do it; it's written.

The Bible say that Allah Righteous people will eat, but you unrighteous and disbelievers will be hungry. The devil is warning you all the time now against sitting down, not trying to make preparation for you to get something to eat. We're out in Alabama; We're out in Georgia; We're in Michigan trying to grow something and do something about our hunger. We ask you to help us; you won't help us because you don't want the evil devil to know that you would help those that he don't like.

This is why you don't help the Muslims. It's because that you don't want to be called a Muslim, to the joy of Satan. Satan want you to stay with him, so he don't want you to be called a Muslim and you say, "no sir boss" [The Audience applauds], "I would never join up with them old crazy folks them old folks is crazy." We have a finer Church than you reverend. Our Church here cost us four million dollars. Where is yours in this city that cost that kind of money? [The Audience applauds].

We teach in our Church, and we bring people to the Light of Understanding in our Church. But, if we would ask you what do you teach, or what do you mean when that you tell us that God sent Jonah to Nineveh, what was the sign of such teaching on us here today? We teach the knowledge and understanding of the Book. Why did Abraham, the First Prophet, why did not he after his knowledge of the coming of God choose you and me? Why did he find water, his wife… bubbling up under the foot of the baby? What did that mean reverend for us? It mean just what I'm teaching you. It meant that you would be looking for somebody to come from afar to teach you the knowledge of God, and the man is right there at your feet. [The Audience applauds].

Abraham prayed, Ishmael prayed; both father and son saw in the distance future of us, that we would need a Teacher. He say, "Raise up among them, Oh Lord, a Teacher from among themselves; teach him the Book" the Bible, "and the Wisdom, for they do not understand it, they only using guesses." How many times reverend have we heard you say "I teach it the way I see it." [The Audience applauds].

We cannot take God's word and teach it as we see it; we got to teach it as He give it to us. The way He want us to see and not the way we want to see. I tell you reverend, that you are the hindrance to the Kingdom of Heaven of your people like the Bible teach you, called Sadducees and Pharisees; that you stand in the way of the Kingdom of Heaven; won't go in yourself, and you won't let others go in. Teach against them coming in. This is that Kingdom of Heaven that he's referring to; and this is it that I am preaching. [The Audience applauds].

Time have arrived that we must tell you the Truth, do you will come to us and say "If you had told me, I would have believed. But you didn't tell me. Now I'm here before God today, asking me did I hear you and I didn't hear you." Because you stopped up your ears to keep from hearing me. That's what your Bible say, and that you're doing.

Preachers going out, putting up a little church in little storehouses everywhere to fulfill Isaiah prophesy of you, "Everyone wanted a little place of his own, for to get a little meat and bread and money for self." These things I said to you reverend, you should cut it out. [The Audience applauds].

I will put my life against every reverend of Christianity in the land, that they don't have no God at all but the devil! You don't have to go on Mount Carmel, this is Mount Carmel enough. Come up here and see if you can get your god…[The Audience applauds].

My father preached Christianity for forty years, until Allah sent me to preach the Truth, then he join with me criticizing what he had been teaching in the church. And he was very honest about it. He wanted to be on God's side. So he, when I began to teach he say "Son you are right" he say " that is the Truth." He say "We preachers didn't know what we was preaching on just what we was told by this devil, as God have made you to know." He say "I'm with you son, and he died in the Temple. [The Audience applauds].

At the age of eighty-one, death struck him while he was in the Temple. He was applauding me, and he got up and throwed up his hand...for the last time and walked out, never returned anymore. And died the next day at six o'clock, and this was six o'clock, at that time. Nobody never knew he was dead until the nurse went to see him. And then when the nurse felt him, she was the first one to announce that he was dead. Made no struggle at all, just slept away just like that. This is why the Bible and the Holy Qur'an say "Die not unless you are Muslim."

But, some of us don't have that good death conferred on us. But, if you're Muslim, the Bible say " Die not upon me" the Bible say, "Let me die the death of the Righteous." So let us do that, who believe. The Will of God, is that you and me do His Will, do His bidding, so, that He can bless us for our good works, and not our evil work.

Well don't be in a hurry, you want, you want to hear me teach, well I'm teaching. [The Audience applauds]. We have arrived to the Time when whether you believe it or not, that the Will of God will be done now. The will of Satan has been done for the last, been doing for the last six thousand years. His Time is up now, and the will of him that...

THE CROSS OF CHRISTIANITY: A SIGN OF EVIL

…and the will of him that is prophesied that will come after him, that will build a Kingdom of Peace and Righteousness, is here at the work now. I'm what they call, some of them, forerunner, but I'm he, to what I call myself, that last Messenger from God, to direct you in a path that will lead you to Him. [The Audience applauds]. And that you will be saved from the Destruction, that is out there knocking on the.

You going to have a terrible time here before this enemy yields to get out of the way. Yes, it's awful to talk about. You going to have people killing out there in the street, and their blood running down in the gutter of the streets now pretty soon; it can happen tonight, because the Time is here.

Be you careful, don't forget, that it is Time that you go to your God. He don't ask you for nothing of the past, just accept your own now, and He will forget our past. Our past was due to our enemy. Therefore, we is forgiven for what the enemy blinded us with. And now, we opening our eyes to see what the enemy look like, and listen see what he saying; he don't invite you to no Righteousness; he invite you to evil.

They invite you to evil. They play all evil and filthy music day and night to attract your attention to that. He knows that he have mislead you; and that he want to keep you with him until Allah destroys him, so you can be destroyed with him. I'm referring only to the blue-eyed Caucasian, the open and real enemy, devil against Black people.

They don't love you, and he hates me to the utmost, but he can't do nothing about it. So if I was in your condition, and here stands a man of my own Nation teaching me the Truth of one that I thought had told me the Truth; He taken the Bible and mixed up the Truth involving him so you would not understand it. Let the little Brother of yours tackle with him, let, let, send him on me. But he won't do that. As the Book teach you that "They will shut their mouth at him" meaning me. You won't hear them arguing with me on what I say. They know I'm telling you the Truth! And anything he will do, he will tell you, you had better follow him. Because he write me, my Secretaries here to my left bear me witness that they are trying to join up with me. Is that right? Yea. There they is over there you ask them when you get chance. They can show you plenty letters that the devil is writing to me wanting to join up. And saying, in his writings, "Is not there someone that is not devil?" I tell them, I don't know of any, "There, isn't some of us better than others?" Yes, that don't make you not be devil though. [The Audience applauds]. If you go to one of these Secretaries over here and ask her to let you see, since I know you, you're from Missouri [The Messenger laughs and the Audience applauds].You want to be shown, but we are not here to lie. We don't tell lies, we tell you the Truth. My word, if you find me lying, then I'm a liar I'm not the Messenger of Allah. Allah don't want a, a liar for His Messenger; Yes.

As we find it in the Holy Qur'an, when Pharaoh called Moses a liar, his Senator told him that, "If he's a liar then, on him will be his lie. For Allah does not appoint no such thing as a liar for Him. These Prophets must be a hundred percent True."

I say to you my beloved Brothers and Sisters, if you think I'm fixing to get ready to go you just mistaken. [The Audience applauds]. You have had four hundred years here to listen to the slave-master teaching you how to stay a slave to him. Now I have not been here four hours, so I think you ought to listen to me for a little while. [The Audience applauds].

I'm, if a man come into your presence, put such signs of them with such reading to that, I warn you, you better listen to him. What does that mean? He's defying any world outside of the world of God Allah, to tangle with him on the Truth of what he have on that board. You cannot take these writings that is on that board; you can't take it and use it unless you are a believer. Regardless to the Wisdom that is in it, you cannot use it and be successful, unless, you are a believer in it.

The Truth that the man hanging on a tree under your slave-master's flag. You believe he's right. You want your flag, to be his, "Oh Glory." But I say, what have your "Oh Glory," the stars and the stripes given to you and me, but what you see the people there hanging on a limb? [The Audience applauds].

Every night and day you listen over the radio, and you see on the T.V., he's chasing a poor Blackman to take his life away from him. But, over there under that beautiful Red background with a Star and with a Crescent, you don't see over here no Islamic people chasing each other. When you believe in Islam, all the world of Islam will recognize and respect you. They will fight for you. They will die, for you.

We that is up here displaying those same Stars and that Moon and that Red background which represents the Sun. Why that represent? Because the Sun is a ball of fire and a light. And that the Sun we all live in it, we respect it. Out of the Sun comes our food. Out of the Sun comes our direction.

I say to you, my believing Brothers and my disbelieving Brothers, take a look at it. If that's our Flag, and your flag is a flag of mixture, blue, red, and white when ours is only one solid background, Red. And the Sun, Moon is there together and the Stars associated with that same Crescent showing the world that we have laid hold on the Greatest Instruments of Heaven and Earth, to condemn **any** disputer who would attack us. [The Audience applauds].

We use to buy it, trying to make friendship with Satan. We go and buy that Crescent put it on our coat lapel, and look at him when he pass, to say to him, as good as say to him, "See I have the Crescent on me, you should take me for your brother." We give him that after he shown Us that he could act like Us, thirty-five or forty, fifty years, We let him wear Our Crescent. That's Ours the Red, and the Crescent over there that's Ours. He can take his mixture over here for himself. But if he wear that over there, look at him again; he worked for that, he didn't get that so easy.

Over here you got blue, which is a untrue color. You have many stars there. Take all of these stars to try to justify something. It shouldn't be done like that. We got one Star which justify us, which represent all the Stars is ours. The strip or stripe of red over here, not a solid background of Red like you see over there, because the Red represent Freedom and he don't give Freedom, only to those who are able and wealthy. You able to buy from him, he'll give you freedom.

Down under it is the sign of his evil to us, a cross. How can you go to Heaven or be Justified by Freedom and Justice, by a cross? It's the opposite of the right direction. And so, this is what you are suppose to preach when you be a reverend. You suppose to worship the cross. What are you worshipping it for, when he tell you that he killed a innocent man on it? You should run from the cross, but you run to it to be bless by him, that you are one of his followers. It's a shame and a disgrace for him to have made such crazy people who understood no such thing as Science.

I'm here to teach you the Science of Christianity, the Science of Islam, the Science of anything pertaining to religion, I'm here to teach you. And take what I say back to him, and he will tell you, "Oh you following them?" "I follow the people that give me the understanding of what you have given, given to me that you didn't give me," he'll shut his mouth and leave you.

I want you to remember, again, that to carry a cross on you representing a crucified Prophet, you are the one who have joined the worship of the death of Jesus by the enemy. That show what the enemy did to him. He boast of that, not in a way so you can understand, but he boasts that he have killed your best Prophet and he still lives, and I will kill His last one, but he can't do it. I'm the Last One, he can't do it. Tell him why don't you go down there to the Temple and kill Elijah. He teaches us that you the devil. Maybe you have already did and he'll tell you, "Oh well we know it, we watching him." That's the way he will talk to you. But, I said go tell him and let him muster up his army and you muster up yours, and then join together and see how far you'll get with me. [The Audience applauds]. They have **No** chance to win against me! I have as my Friend and my Guide, my Protection, Almighty God Allah Himself. He's not very far from me. He's right here with me now. [The Audience applauds].

You need to know God. You need to come to God, but not the god that Satan teach you to come, because he just naturally can't do anything with my God. And my God is your God. I say believe in Him, come follow me. Heaven is yours while you live; don't have to go no place to enjoy Heaven .Heaven is not a separate place somewhere. Heaven is a condition and Hell is a condition.

So I want you to remember these things, as I'm going to soon dismiss you now. But remember the Will of God now must be done, as Satan's will is up. He can no more rule the Blackman under his will. The Blackman is uniting and look what you read and heard about our unity, together. They sent to me millions of dollars to help to get this place and other places.

We want to take the Eastside of Cottage Grove from the 3800 block, 78th isn't it? Yea all the way down to 87th, and build you a Southside city that you will love to look at. I have to ask for outside help, because you are afraid to be singled out by Satan saying you helping me. You have the money, but, you don't want to spend any of it on us but you put it all in the bank of the devil, and tell him to help himself while you could build you, yourself help if you would take, bring it over here and dump it with us. We don't want you to give us, we pay you back. We assured by Allah that, He, Himself will give us all the money we want at the Time that He have set. Give you money if you'll believe. This is what He promised.

Money, that's the First thing, money, good homes, friendship in all walk of life. This is what He offers you just to believe in that which is of yourself. "Okay, then why didn't He give you then?" He did give it to us. Regardless to where it come from; if it come from Asia, that's alright He give it to us. I didn't say He would walk up with a pocket full of millions hand it over out His Hand. He cause other people to do that. So, we are given, we are not falling down, failing to do His Will. What He wants us to do here. We not failing, we're doing it. We got this Church, that's alright bout where the money came from He's doing it.

We got farms, we got big farms, no little gardens. Oh yes we're going to bring you in ten thousand of our fresh fryers from our chicken farm; want you to taste them, see what they taste like. They'll be coming in now soon; soon they will be coming in.

I want you to try some of our carefully raised chickens to keep you from getting diseases from eating chicken. We going to furnish them ourselves. We have other farm products that we are raising to put in your house upon your tables, to let you see what we are doing to help our Black people, while they are not helping us to help them.

But, we will do this knowing like a father knows his children that the little children just round talking, but they…too awaken on fathers table. So we want to prove to you these things, and we are planning to try and make some bread for you next year because you going to be hungry; the devil is telling you that now. So we going to try and raise some wheat, so you can eat some rolls right on. Then you will say they was right because if we could not buy these rolls from them, we wouldn't have nothing to eat.

Lots of things we are doing for you and you don't know it. We'll going to get the millions necessary to build the Southside up, in our name. We should rule the Southside and we're going to rule. We're going to rule the Southside. You sitting down, don't want to do nothing and giving it all over to the devil to rule. We going to take it over, and rule it ourselves. [The Audience applauds]. And it will be rule right for the Blackman to have a chance of Freedom, in doing something for himself, though we get very no-good people out of you.

We hired you to come over and help us; try to lay down on us, keep from working. And that you will wreck what we have put up to give the employment. Try to wreck it! You are terrible people! Nobody can do nothing good for you. I want say let Satan, you won't take it from him, but he not going to do it. So, we are trying to go long with you and trying to make employment for you. We know you not going to have no employment. We don't have to guess about it, we know you not going to have it.

So we're trying to go long with you, though you're so lazy that you cannot sleep, that you will charge your nerves for making you go to sleep, if you could. You a terrible people. We know you because we're working you. You don't want nobody to do something good for you, unless it's the white man, and then you'll beat him if he let you. You'll get a break from…you'll get two breaks. You get that one he give you, and then one you'll force on him.

We are terrible people. Now, where is it you find any Elijah, or any Jonah, or any Daniel, that is trying to do something for yourself in the city of Chicago other than myself? Where can you find any equal to Elijah Muhammad? [The Audience applauds].

Take reverend Jackson, poor boy, making a fool out of himself to be called reverend Jackson by the devil. He know I'm here, he been to my house two or three times. Why should not he and I get together and be working for the Blackman? I'm working for the Blackman, well let us join together. All of us that's working for the Blackman, unite, and the work will be more stronger if we unite together and do the work together.

But he likes his blue-eyed devil because they call him reverend Jackson. Jackson is the name of devil. He come over to me, I would give him an honorable name, and he can take it and go round the world and be honored by the nations of the Earth.[The Audience applauds]. But, he want to be called reverend Jackson and trying to run politics, and, preaching Christianity too.

So the poor boy is just in a mess. [The Audience applauds]. I hate, I hate to see, the devil white man make fun of our people; I hate it. This man could have been made a fine man for the Blackman. We talked together a few times, but, he just love to be called reverend by the blue-eyed devil. He don't want no Black guy honoring him. We will honor him for what he is worth, but not in the way of the devil worship.

But they will dump him after while, like they do all that follow them. He call himself worshipping this other, Martin Luther King. After Martin Luther King visit my house, he sit out there in his cars and tune up on what we was talking bout. I guess he heard him say that he agree with me that they was the devil. So, he saw that Elijah was winning their disciple over, so they go shoot him and set up a hypocrite for Elijah, and that was Malcolm. [The Audience applauds]. And get you to go worship Malcolm. They go build a college after his name, to pull you way from me.

He know Malcolm was not with me, so he get you to worship hypocrites of Elijah Muhammad so that you'll go to Hell with them. But, my God have not struck out after you a hundred percent and when He does, you will go to Hell with them. You going to remember this talk, and you going to come back to Elijah and shake my hand and say, "Mister Muhammad, I'm with you." I know you going to do that.

Yea, I don't care what you believe in now, you can believe in Buddha, don't make no difference to me. But there's a Time set, that Allah going to force you to believe in what I teach. You are not to get away with this running away to some other god. No, Allah going to make you bow to Him.[The Audience applauds].

Who cares? The Brother say I been teaching two hours, so I asked him, who cares? [The Audience applauds]. I just told the Brother that I use to teach six hours, so this is only one third of that time. I can have these people just as interested to hear me teach four more hours, as I did in those days…[The Audience applauds]. Believers in Allah and Islam, love to congregate together and talk about Islam. [The Audience applauds]. He forgot that I have a timepiece on my arm too, yeah.

A man been teaching hard headed people for forty years, and then one that's converted here, today, and he want to tell him how long he should teach him, that's wrong! They all got to hear His Voice. That is not referring to, in that particular place, the actually God in Person, Himself, talking to you. That mean His Voice through another one that you must hear before the end come.

You don't tire so fast with me. I didn't think so because I keep you busy trying to think over what I just said. [The Audience applauds]. When the speaker tires speaking to people, and the people tired of him, that's a teacher is not giving them nothing to think over. [The Audience applaud]. But if you give the people something to think over, they don't care how long you teach them. [The Audience applauds].

I think my Brother is getting hungry so I better send him home.[The Audience applauds and the Messenger laughs]. No I didn't call you I just wanted to let you know how many is against you saying for me to go.[The Audience applauds]. They all is mine, they will come wherever they're at, just to hear his voice. Think over that.

So they hear my voice and they follow me wherever I go. [The Audience applauds]. How many reverends, could you get, sixteen, sixteen buses coming from one city, to go back that evening just to hear him teach for a, a few hours? You can't do that, because the voice of the reverend is no more appealing to them. [The Audience responds in approval]. The voice of the Shepherd of Allah, and his making the Way straight for Him to come to His people, Elijah Muhammad. You could not call this kind of number of people all the year. They wouldn't spend that kind of money to go listen at a reverend. because they been listening to reverend all their lives [The Audience applauds], and reverend have never gotten them no place out of their hard, disrespect, dishonor, by the people of the Earth.

Reverend can't go to Egypt today and be honored. He can't go to Africa today and be honored. They wants Elijah over in Africa. [The Audience applauds]. I'm not making fun of the preachers, they making fun of themselves [The Audience applauds] with the kind of preaching they are doing. They want to go to Heaven after they're dead; well that's right, I'm getting you after you are dead, to go to Heaven. [The Audience applauds]. Dead mentally to the knowledge of self, God, and the devil. I'm trying to get you to Heaven now, on that same subject, yes, after you're dead.

So, my beloved Brothers and Sisters I think I will bring our, The Will of God subject to a close for this time. We're living in the Time of God Will must be done. Satan's will going out. Nobody will hope they stay but Satan. And our Book teaches us that he will also admit God's Will, because he's getting in such condition that he will not want to remain. Like Pharaoh was, he stood up against Allah, until He start filling his lungs with water from the Red Sea. He saw he was going, and he had no power to fight Allah with. So he give up while he was sinking, and give Allah the credit that Allah was the Greatest. And he went down being forgiven for just admitting that Allah was the Greatest. Allah give him credit for saying He was the Greatest, while drowning in the Red Sea. So He saved his name, and some of the Scientists went out there and pulled his body out of the Sea, and embalmed to show these Great Wonders. We are not put here to live forever. No man, God Himself that Made the Heavens and the Earth, didn't live forever. He too is gone, so that we may remember that we all come here, and we all die. No God or Prophet, live forever.

So at this time, I say to you, that you have been very faithful and having patience. You sit here with patience. I don't see you hurrying out the door, slamming the door…I see you sitting here listening, and I thank you for it. And I'm going to say to you that has been listening, that you're privileged by me, stand up, ask me any question that you don't know that I have said that you want to ask me a question about. You're welcome to stand up. And I don't want you believers or has been believers, jumping up taking this opportunity. Just those that is visiting us and not you. That other Sunday I was swamped with the Brother so, asking me question that he know he know the answer, and he know I know the answer. I don't want you to show off like that. I want the person that have not learned the answer to their, nursed questions. If they want to ask me for the answer you can, right here. But not believers and hypocrites. I don't want you to say nothing, because you two have the Truth, and if you don't believe in it, that's up to you. But I want the people who have never heard it. If they want some question answered in what we are teaching, they're welcome to stand up and ask. Any of you want to ask any questions? Any of you, want to ask a question, stand up and ask it. I don't want no Brother, I want people that have never heard before. Yes, come right out Brother and ask me anything that you heard me say, that you want more light on.

Brother #1: Excuse me Mister Muhammad, I like to know if in order to be a follower of yours in the Temple, if you have to eat meat in order to do that?

[The tape skipped over the Messenger's response to the Brother's question. This appears to be the answer to another unheard question].

Messenger: ...why Mister Fard Muhammad? Yes, because He's God that is running the whole entire show if you want to use such name. That's God in Person, which the Book teaches you the Bible I mean, that on that Day you will see Him as He is. See the people been believing in other than a human being, to be God.

Brother #2: Mister Muhammad, my belief in God is, I am a god, you are god. The spirit's in you, and the spirit's in me. When the two meet they have peace, happiness, and homes, and money. Now, you are god, you can help me to get some money, because you control more than a million people; I can sell this book to a million people and I got a million dollars.

Messenger: That's what I'm here for...

Brother #2: Okay, can I join then?

Messenger: ... and I just told you, that Allah promise you money, if you will believe and follow me...

Brother #2: I believe! I believe!

Messenger: Alright then, come on follow me, put your name on your Book, and you'll have...[The Audience applauds].

Sister: Mister Elijah Muhammad about two years ago I had a cousin that, join with the Muslims, and she was a orthodox Muslim and she was one of, three wives, to a husband...

AUGUST 27, 1972 PART TWO / SIDE TWO

QUESTIONS AND ANSWERS

…three wives to a husband, and I can't understand, what's the, why the two are so diverse, and, why aren't they, you know, just one, as a whole?

Messenger: The hog, the hog was forbidden [One of the Brothers explains the Sister's question to the Messenger, because he did not hear the question clearly.]

Messenger: I'm not up here to go over the laws of the Islamic world with you if you read these things, you read them. So I'm not up here to condemn, nor to take away anything; only to teach you that which Allah have given me to teach you. [The Audience applauds]

Messenger: If there is any more of this kind of talk, we're dismissed, because eighteen hundred to two thousand people could talk on the orthodox Muslims rules of Islam while they don't know it themselves; but, you come here to come to school for such. You have to be schooled into that, not come and ask questions cause your question demands more than just a word or two. It demands a lot of questions, answers, to your questions. And, that, the people that is not interested in what you are asking; well Allah don't like me to keep them sitting here listening at what you have to say and question until night. It is getting late, now, and the people would like to go home. And, that, I don't care to get involved in a lots of orthodox Muslims rules, regulations and laws of Islam. We are bringing to you a New Islam [The Audience applauds].

Messenger: As I tell white people, they ask me sometime he say, "Well," he say, "those over there, they don't believe in your teaching," I say well that's natural. I say because this something new, which they have not heard before. And I say it takes time. I say but nevertheless, We have the key to the whole world of man. Whether you believe it or not, I have the key. And it's written in your Book that I have it, that "God give him the key for Hell, and for that is not Hell." I'm sure that you see I'm using the key on Hell now.

Messenger: This is no play thing we're doing, and we don't teach it just for you to come out to argue. We don't, I don't teach you nothing to be arguing with you because I already know you and know bout how you think. Therefore I don't care to argue with you and I'm trying to pull you out of the way you think, into a way of thinking that you will be respected by the world.

Messenger: I was born blind, deaf, and dumb, but, after I met with Allah, and He has taught me of the Truth of Himself and others; I don't fear standing before the world. I

216

talk with the whole world at once if they wanted to on that question that you are trying to get after and condemn the world of their way of believing it. And so, I don't have time to stand up here, for eighteen hundred, or more people to take me for a topic just to ask questions that they probably will not believe the answers.

Messenger: So, I'm going to dismiss you and you write your questions out, send them to me at 4847 Woodlawn, and then I will answer the through mail. I can't hold over a thousand people from getting out of here going home, over one or two questions that is very simple. The answer is very simple. They not in a way no starry or science question; they just common questions coming from a person that don't know the answers. I would be glad to give you the answer if I had time, and to tell these people will you all sit here and wait for the answers; and while you are getting your answer another one is bringing up one to ask. And I don't want to be that kind of Teacher, in this modern time.

Messenger: I want to give it to you so everybody can agree with me, that it is right, and everybody will give to you that answer, if I give to you the answer to your question, that it is answered right. I don't answer nothing wrong. What I answer to you, you can go all over the Earth and give to any Scientist and he will tell you, you got the right answer when you was in America. They all respects my answers, but I don't want to hold other people here just, to be holding them here to ask questions that they don't know while they can write me. And that keep them from staying, listen to your answers.

Messenger: There is no such thing that I don't know the answer to your question. There is no such thing that you could ask me questions of Divine, that I cannot answer. I'm not risen up here, to, to be that kind of fellow among you. I'm a man that God raised up among you to answer anything you ask me of Divine. Not of something of from Earth. I, don't know about that but I'm a Teacher of Divine. And, you don't have the knowledge of Divine in you strong enough for you to be able to ask me the question, that, by Divine, I cannot answer.

Messenger: There's nothing in Divine that you can ask me that I cannot answer, but, you get up something else that's different cause it's Divine, I'm here to teach you knowledge of Him, and the knowledge of what He's about to do about setting up His Will, as the Christians call it, the Kingdom of God on Earth. This is what I'm here to teach you what His Will is about to do for you and me, today. If you think that that is not enough, well, there's plenty people who are studying other type of work and profession. Maybe they will answer you in their way or according to their learning, but I'm a Divine Teacher, and that's what I answer you is of Divine.

Messenger: There's another one that had something that they would, would be too glad to ask me before they get out of here and go and tell the people that he, he would not give us a chance to ask him nothing. Well, I give you chance but I'm trying to tell you how to make the chance accepted by others who will not ask a question if we stay here all night. But they would like to have a, a ending up of the thing.

Brother: Mister Muhammad I would like to know, was Yacub, was given the right to rule for six thousand years?

Messenger: Pardon me, what, what six thousand years?

[One of the Brothers explains the question to the Messenger because he did not hear the question clearly].

Messenger: There was no God in His Time that could prevent Him; and it was necessary for us to learn from one that was in us, in our midst, what He had that could rule others for six thousand years; from nine thousand years to that of fifteen thousand.

Messenger: Well, if it's pushing you, and you look like you just naturally just want to ask it just get up and ask it. Yes, as we can, we want people to be satisfied.

Brother: Could you tell me why is the white man going into outer space and, how far will he get?

Messenger: Going up in space? It is to fulfill the Scriptures, "That thou may ascend up to Heaven above the clouds, but yet, I will bring you down to Hell."

Messenger: Yes sir?

Brother: Mister Muhammad I'm a old time Detroiter, and I remember a long time ago it use to be a Temple on Theodore and Hastings Street way back in the twenties. And I think, and I wanted to know is it the same set up, or has it changed since then?

Messenger: We haven't changed Islam. We go into more knowledge of it, but we don't change it.

Brother: I understand.

[The Audience applauds]

Messenger: There must be something powerful enough to attract the Brother to be here in Chicago, listen to it. He heard it there in Detroit. Well now you listen at the same thing here in Chicago, only with added knowledge. So, that is good that you following it up Brother. Keep on I will be teaching in another city pretty soon. I'll see you there. [The Audience applauds].

Messenger: Well if that's all, that's all? No one have no other question they wanted to ask? I didn't hear nobody ask me nothing bout Jesus [The Messenger and the Audience laughs]. I reckon they have come to believe that Jesus was not what they thought he was, did he would not have prophesied of another one coming after him.

So I thank you for your nice patience here this afternoon, and that we have enjoyed your visit to Temple No.2 Illinois. And hope to see you here again next Sunday, next Sunday, next Sunday next Sunday, and next Sunday [The Messenger laughs and the Audience laughs and applauds].

Well we going to dismiss you, since you have asked all the questions you care to ask, and have gotten answers through the answer of others. And so I, again, thank you for your patience, and your endurance here with us. Hope to see you next Sunday in the same place; and if you have something this away you should do; if you have something great of importance that I teach you just tell me, tell me now. And I will teach it to you next Sunday, the meanings of it that is if the others agree with you.

So is there any certain subject that you would like that I teach you next Sunday? No one have no certain subject? Then you leave me to myself. So I will teach you what I think you need to be taught. [The Audience applauds].

So I'm going to turn you back in the hand of our Assistant Minister who will come before you with a different text. And I hope that you will enjoy that text that he bring before you.

So I'm going to say to you again I enjoyed being in your presence, and, watch your patience as some of the reverends could not get one third of you to listen to them. Five hundred or more people, they don't have it. It's because Islam is eating their houses up. And it was built by the devil; church was, is a church house of devils. It didn't make, wasn't built by no Prophet of God. The devil made this himself, and we going to tear it down.

So I say again, to you may the peace and the blessings of Allah go with each and every one of you to your place of abode. And don't forget to come back and learn the Truth that which you never knew before in all your life is being told to you now, today. I thank you, and as the Minister will take over you from now on,

As Salaam Alaikum.

PART FOUR:

THEOLOGY OF TIME

SEPTEMBER 3, 1972 – SEPTEMBER 24, 1972

THE COMING OF ELIJAH:
THE FIRST BORN OF THE DEAD

As Salaam Alaikum! You may be seated.

As Salaam Alaikum. My dear beloved Brothers and Sisters, I'm very happy to see your smiling faces here this afternoon. And I hope that you will leave smiling. We have plenty to tell you, whether you accept it or not. But, we do have plenty to tell you, that we hardly know where to begin.

I'm a little late. Ahhhh that's right [The Audience laughs and applauds]. If we have waited four hundred years, I do think about four hours would not hurt you [The Audience applauds].

I'm very happy to learn that there is some preachers of the Christian churches here with us this afternoon. Reverend I hope that you enjoy what we have to say. I have a kind of a New Book for you, it's called the Holy Qur'an. And that, it verifies what is written in the Bible. And the Bible verifies the Qur'an. The Bible is ahead of the Qur'an. The Qur'an, is a late Scripture. The Bible is an Old Scripture. And the Holy Qur'an only about, near fourteen hundred years old, but the Bible is four thousand years old, or more.

This was given to Moses on the choosing of Allah. And the rise of Moses, who was risen up among the, well not among the white race whom we have learned now to be…a race of devils. This is what we teaching you. And if you don't believe it, I'm sorry for your future. I don't think it should be hard for the Blackman of America to learn that the white race is devils.

I don't think he should be hard to learn, for it was the devil who reared us. We did not rear ourselves up in North America. It was the devil who reared our parents up from slavery. Some may say, No, No, No, it wasn't the devil, because, we are here and we're preaching and singing and feel happy. But that was Created in you. We are from Creation and the white man is from make. We made the white man, "Let Us, make man."

I want the preacher to listen at all I have to say, I mean Christian preachers. And, then I wish that you ask me anything that I don't make clear to you to make it more clear. Since you a, a student and preacher of the Scripture, by then you ought to know me [The Audience applauds], because, the Bible prophesy of Elijah coming to you, and I am Elijah [The Audience applauds]. This man prophesied in the Bible teaches you that he First, must come First. He must First come, meaning he must come before God to make a

221

way for God to come.

Let's talk about it reverend [The Audience applauds]. If, that man have to come First, not God First, but He must send this man First; then He comes after this man. What is this man, and what and why is he so important that he must go ahead of God? [The Audience applauds]. Let's get acquainted with each other reverend.

He must prepare the way. Why don't God prepare the way? Why should He send Elijah to prepare the way? Because, He prepared Elijah to prepare the way. This is done by Governments, nations all over the Earth. They send an Ambassador to a foreign nation to get acquainted with that nation so that the King or the President or the people of a foreign land may get acquainted with a foreign nation, so that they can see if they can make friends with each other. I'm here to get you in acquaintance with God, so that we can see whether or not that you are able to live with God, after your acquaintance.

It is impossible for the enemy of God to make people friends or establish a friendship between the two. That's impossible unless you change the nature. Listen at me good reverend. [The Audience responds in approval].

We cannot recognize a preacher sent from the devil to lead us to God, because, he may try to get our acquaintance with the True God, according to its training by the enemy of the True God. [The Audience applauds]. I'm not trying to make any mess between us, I'm trying to make friendship.

The thing that has happened between our Black Christian preachers and the preachers of Islam, they actually believe that what the blue-eyed devils have taught them is right. And that, they themselves being led by the blue-eyed devil, that they may get to Heaven even ahead of us; and he's leading you directly to Hell [The Audience applauds].

This is why I'm risen up in your midst, to put a stop to you following an enemy of God; and you think he's your friend... .his Hell that he have made, because by nature he was made to make Hell for the Righteous. We are here with Truth. We are here to be a...by the world of the devil and win over it. [The Audience applauds].

Christianity is dying a natural death. Everybody that is awakening to the very root of Christianity of the white race, they turning it down. Reverend your whole church is getting chilly. I just want you and I to take our place as Brothers. I'm not going against you, because, pretty soon you will surely come over to Elijah Muhammad [The Audience applauds].

I read in the Bible, in the Revelations, that last book of the Bible where that it prophesy that the devil and his followers, his representatives, will be going down in a Lake of Fire. And I know who this, this is, this is the preacher of Christianity that is Blackman and women. Due to the lack of knowledge of the enemy and his religion he deceived them. But I want to show you, that I have the keys to the knowledge of the devil and the knowledge of you [The Audience applauds].

I'm here in the midst of the devil, and I dare not to bite my tongue! [The Audience applauds]. I'm going to keep the teeth off of my tongue, so I can use it to speak the plain Truth!

THE RESURRECTION: THE RISE OF TRUTH

I'm here in the midst of the devil and I dare not to bite my tongue [The Audience applauds]. I'm going to keep the teeth off of my tongue, so I can use it to speak the plain Truth!

We are living in a Time called the Resurrection. Resurrection means to rise up. Resurrection means that everybody comes to the knowledge of the Truth and the rise. I am one that was also dead. Allah, the God of the Universe, He reared me to come and rise you up [The Audience applauds]. This is also, excuse me, this is also written in your Book, that this man that He choose for His Messenger or His Apostle…

FREEDOM, JUSTICE, AND EQUALITY FOR SELF!

I wouldn't need no boat, and no such thing as airplanes. We even trying to signify the Blackman here, by buying a airport out there, and getting planes for them. You don't have that to do. We already done open the door for that. But you will follow with your idea of robbing Brother. We have the airport in our hands. We also have plenty planes, at just a word, "If it's from Elijah, let him have it." [The Audience applauds].

That just prove that you are very wicked and deceiving. That you will say yes to Elijah while you before his face, and soon you turn, he turn his back, you're trying to rob his paying of good for the others. We will fix you if we have to go to war [The Audience applauds].

As the Holy Qur'an teaches you from Allah, "Do you not see that We have sent death among you?" We are not to be overcome. It is written here, read it for yourself in this Book. And, it's also written in the Bible where God sent death among the Israelites to get them to bow to Moses. I say my friends, don't play with us. We mean good for you.

You can't get help from your enemy and mine; his help was cut off before the appearance of Allah. Allah cut his help off, so that you, He could put you at His Servant's mercy. It is not that Allah, God will stay among us in Person. But He raises up one just like Himself, having the same idea [The Audience applauds].

I don't want to see a one of you lose your life, but, you are inviting death when you're trying to bring the work of God with me to a null; you are inviting death. I was so shame when I was told what you are trying to do in the East; where that I'm preparing a way for the whole nation. You want to prepare a way for yourself alone. So, leave us alone Brother if you don't like us, just leave us alone [The Audience applauds].

I'm the last man to take an attempt to pull you out of the power of the white man, and put you in the Power of Divine, the last! There is no other one coming. The others that will come, they coming to destroy you for not listening to what I am teaching you [The Audience applauds].

Wealth you want and wealth I want for you, but you can't get it like you're trying to get it. You'll destroy yourself, and the friends of others, which I mean others is myself and God. To get you what you want, you will destroy them yourself, by the way you are doing. Everyone wants his own way. Well, why didn't you start it First? [The Audience applauds]. You didn't start the way, you, you commercializing on the way of another one.

I say my beloved Brothers and Sisters, that I think it's about time for us to dine. I don't want to keep you hungry for the physical food. I want you to go home and eat, but after you eat the physical food, come back next Sunday and have another meal of Spiritual Food [The Audience applauds].

Friendship, good homes, money, think over that. I don't have the millions of dollars it take to build those homes over on Wabash, pardon me, not Wabash, Woodlawn. I don't have that kind of money, but, it comes. When the next payment due it comes. When have you ever heard or read where a so-called Negro in America, or a Blackman in America, that the people of the East dropping down millions when he ask for them? When have you ever heard tell of that? [The Audience applauds].

You go to Africa trying to make your Black Brother there a Christian, and yet, Christianity have you a prisoner here in America. Oh Brother! We're raised up to show life to Freedom, Justice, and Equality for self. Come follow me, and God will set you in Heaven at once [The Audience applauds].

Money is only a means of a meetings between each other to get that which each other want. I say, come follow me He will give you money, and plenty of it. Come preach the preaching of Truth, reverend, Islam. Come preach it, you don't know it, come to me I will teach to you [The Audience applauds].

Let's be Brothers in that which is good for the Brotherhood of the Original Man, the Blackman. Let's join together, and do not follow the ways of our enemy. Forsake his ways; he have no church that will take you to Heaven; they are for Hell. That's the deceiving house that the white man built, for you.

So I say to you in my conclusion that, believe the Truth when it comes to you of Islam and of the people of you in the East and in the West. Join on to them that they be a Muslim. And, respect and honor will join on to you. And I pray Allah, that He go with you to your places of abode, and bless you with a safe return without any accidents to life or property. I hope to see you again very soon.

SEPTEMBER 10, 1972 PART ONE / SIDE ONE

THE SERVANT OF GOD

As Salaam Alaikum

Now you sit down from here when you have visiting Minister and let them say something. You hear yourself here all the time. Now it's time that we can sit and hear visiting Minister. You love your own home so well you don't want nobody to come in the door. Now next time, let us listen to our visiting Minister. Let us be Truthful.

Salaam Alaikum.

My dear beloved Sisters and Brothers in the name of Allah, we're very happy to see each other smiling and frowning faces this afternoon [The Messenger laughs]. I don't think we'll have too many frowning faces, because I'm kind of fellow like the same fellow I make people laugh. I don't make them frown [The Messenger laughs].

I'm sorry that I'm a little later than usual, but I didn't come out here looking for...do, I would go somewhere else. I think I can get a crowd...if I...[The Audience applauds].

We are living in the Day of Judgment, and that we are forever on that subject. We are not taking any subject what we don't add the Judgment to. We have been teaching on the Theology Of Time. Of course that is our subject all the time. The coming of Allah, and the Presence of Allah. We like to know why should Allah come. What does He want? The God? Why is it so important that He come in Person?

We must remember that we have been taught that God was a spirit, and that you can't see Him. Lot of, of our people believe like you have it written there bout Israel, "You can't see God and live." The God of Freedom, Justice, and Equality...they can see Him [The Audience applauds]. The god that we can't see, is the god that was never...

First, I would like to say to you we enjoyed with our visitors on yesterday, the Sultan of Ethiopia. He had dinner with us, and we really had a big time. [The Messenger laughs]. He was laughing when he come in, he was laughing when he left. Oh he's a great man! He......He was really happy.

I'm going to try and visit him again. I have been to Ethiopia.....And I'm going to his Mosque that I looked at it when I was there, but I didn't go in. But if I go back to Ethiopia I'm going to visit that Mosque. It, it was the most beautiful building there in the city. Excuse me, I guess I love to talk too much, and I always get the highway kind of choked up. I told him next time I go to Ethiopia, I was going to visit that Mosque of his. But after you get the New Islam that Allah is teaching us in the Person of Master Fard Muhammad, you're not so particular about going to hear Islam nowhere but among yourself [The Audience applauds].

We have been here a long time in America, not even known by our Brothers where we was kidnapped from. So, today we want to get acquainted with our old Brothers, to whom our enemies kidnapped us from. To bring us up in this, pardon me, bring us out here in this lions of the nations of the Earth. Of all the lions, this is the most lion country and people, it is on Earth.

We may say the jungles holds the lion people; it actually is naturally wild. But, this is a country suppose to be civilized, and yet wild. So, we are living in a country that the Bible calls the wilderness. It's a wilderness of beast. But, of the Divine Civilizations that a wilderness of the worst, evil and sinful people ever lived on the Earth. People that have no morals, love for self and anyone else; terrible country.

I have come here today to talk with you. Maybe on…things not just one thing, but lots of things. I like to know before I start, how many visiting ministers do we have here? I don't care what kind of minister you are, I just want to know who I'm talking to. Will you stand please you visiting ministers? Regardless to what your denomination, church. Two, three, ahhh, there should be more ministers here. Only three? If you want me to visit you, you better visit me [The Audience applauds].

I'm the kind of old fellow like this, I love to talk with you. I love to try to make friendship with you. There's anything wrong with my preaching, tell me so. There's anything wrong with yours I'm going to tell you. [The Audience applauds].If you have proof that yours is right, I will join you today. I won't go back and think it over, I will join you today. If yours is not mine, and yours right, then mine must be wrong. I will join you today. That's something you have to prove.

I was brought up in a Baptist church. When I was a little boy, my father was a preacher at that time and I was in his church. I use to sit on ministers laps because my mother my grandmother, she would let me go up in the pulpit with my father. And he wouldn't run me out cause I was a very preaching little boy myself. I love to hear people preach.

And I didn't want to hear no one sing, when I was a little boy two or three years old, going up there in the speaker stand with my father. When they start to singing I would cry, they would frighten me [The Messenger laughs]. So my grandmother taken me out, and give me a spanking a couple of times. I learn to try to keep my mouth shut [The Audience laughs]. I think that's why I don't have no singing in my Temple. [The Messenger and the Audience laughs and applauds].

The Presence of God. First, the coming of God. The servant of God. What is the idea of God in coming? What is He coming here for? Why does He want to come here? Since We didn't invite Him. We have never invited God to come to us, only in the wrong way. We wanted Him to come to us in our hearts. What do we know that is going in our hearts? Since we never seen God, don't know God if He come to us, how could He get to us, since we don't recognize His Presence? We have not been taught to look for a God coming in Person. We have been taught to look for God coming in a spiritual form.

Well, that's the kind of form we had been receiving. We never seen God before in Person. We always has been praying, singing, preaching for Him to come to us, but in the spirit, but not in the Person. Would we recognize Him if He come in Person? No! We don't know Him like that. Well, how about praying for Him to come in the spirit; that's a feel. Well, you can't name God, "feel." He tells us in…"to feel for Him." [The Messenger laughs].

I'm a fellow I like to go to root of things [The Audience applauds]. We have been praying for God to come…We pray that you come to me. Well, if we did not believe that He would come in Person, what are we praying for then? It's a feel. "I want Him to hear my prayer and I can feel Him in my soul." Well if the Person come to you there in Person, and tell you, "I have heard your prayer, I'm here to answer it," then what? [The Audience applauds]. Why you say, "No, No, I didn't send for you, you look like me." And then, He would be yourself. [The Messenger laughs].

You know we can have a, we can have a lot of fun. I often wonder now that when we don't know the thing. I use to go to church, and the preacher would preach that Hellfire, look like to me so plain I be afraid to go home [The Messenger and the Audience laughs]. I mean they could preach in those days!

Now that they have come for the Fire to light upon those who are not the Righteous. Now you don't preach it much, because you a little guilty to think you also would be one of them [The Messenger laughs]. Well that's right!

The older we get the wiser we get in this civilization, and more understanding to that which we use to believe. The Presence of God. How do you know when God is Present? What is the idea of God coming? He is represented by the Prophets as coming, seeking His own. Who is His own? We use to believe this wrong. Anybody that has got to be forgiven for their sins; that's the way we use to believe.

It's on here Biblically and the Holy Qur'an is representing a people that is His own people; and that people had went astray from Him. There is so many parables the Bible; pick up to show us a idea of what the people look like and their characteristics.

So, we have been told by parables that they are like a man who had two sons.

And, the younger son want to go leave his father, go into a far country, live to himself out of the world of his family's life. His Father willingly let him go, for he know the country and the people of that country. He know one day his son will want to get back.

And, the Jesus put the parable so clear, he say, "At last in that land famine come." He did not want to live under the good law of his family. A famine arose, and when the famine arose, he became in want. Could not get a job; could not get bread and meat. So he lifted up his eyes towards his father's house, he said "I will arise and go to my Father. He have bread to spare. Why should I suffer this?" He made up his forgiving words, "I will say unto him that I'm not worthy to be called your son, make me a servant. Don't tell them who I am," in words he was saying; "that I'm one of your sons, you too great for a man like me to come in reaching out for the respect of the family and as a people by saying that I am your son."

These are most beautiful Scriptures, very beautiful. "I'm not worthy to be called your son. Make me a, a servant of yours, not a son, I'm not fit for that kind of honor." Father say, "Oh, come on son, I will represent you." So he got near the house, he still felt too cheap to go in the family's home.

So, his Brother looked down and saw Father coming up with this little bad contrary son, his Brother. He say, "Come on in, let's make merry for your Brother has come home." He frowned the presence of his Brother he live with, left, and down on his people. He say, "As long as I been here, you telling me now to kill the fattest calf we got to make merry over this man, who have been out among strangers. And he have committed all the acts these strangers have committed. And now I'm to represent and recognize him as being my equal? I have not been any place, I have been with you always." "Come on in son." [The Audience applauds]. He could not see his way of taking that son, making him his equal guest in the house. "No, I will not come in." "You might just stay on out dear son; I'm taking him in the house."

He taken this son in the house and represented him to the family. And all the members of the family start giving up power to their Brother. They was made servants of their Brother that had been away a long time. And it's all because they would not respect his word, and he being the power of the family, He say, "Sit him down over there, put a Crown on his head! Make him the Ruler of the House!" [The Audience applauds].

This parable represent you and me that we have been a long time away from our native land and people. The enemy now has destroyed us, made us to act like himself, and look like himself, as near as possible, so that our people would not want to mix with us. But I say to you, that a God of Ours come out to meet us. The enemy had about destroyed us; taken away our identity.

But nevertheless, our Father say, "I will go out and meet them." He looked and saw his son coming a long ways off. Four hundred years is a long ways off. He say, "This is My son [The Audience applauds], this is your Brother, My son." "I can't mix with that kind of Brother." He say, "Listen, son you alright, but this is your Brother that went astray, among strangers." "I'll admit son, he went astray, but after I went out and met him, he recognize now himself! He was lost from himself, but now I have found him! He was dead to the knowledge of self! But now I met him and I give him life!" [The Audience applauds].

I kind of want to talk to you. When we knew anything, God was here with us. We didn't go out looking for Him, He came seeking us. Which one love the other one the most? [The Audience applauds]."I will search the Earth," He say, "until I have found him, then I will bring him again!" "Tell Abraham that I will go…and bring them again right here in this same place where you left from!" It was a prophesy He made to Abraham. "Though he go astray, but yet I will go after him and I will bring him again." He must have that which I promised you Abraham that I would give! I want to give him the Earth. Strangers is ruling the Earth. I want to give it to him, it's his Earth! "Abraham, I'm going after him. I'm going to search the whole Earth until I find him. And those enemies that have him, I will bring him, but I will miserably destroy his enemies!" For He have come and found us. Now He wants to take us by going to war with the enemy to take you and me home again! [The Audience applauds].

In order to get the prodigal son to thinking of a home, He went to work on the land that he was in [The Audience applauds]. In that land, the Book say, "A great famine arose, and the poor boy became in want. He couldn't get a job. He had nothing fit to eat; only what the hogs eat." And, in his father's house they didn't allow hog around there. Enemy know that, so he give him a job he know he didn't want. "Go feed my swine." And the boy's religion was that he should not touch a swine, nor have a swine near him; he was a Muslim. I don't like this job, but I'm so hungry that I could eat the corn that the hogs will eat.

Remember Brothers, that is not past, that's to come here. These parables is directed towards you and me. But, God loves His people. He loves us regardless of his sins; He loves him; I'm going after him. I promised Abraham I would do so. I can't break my word with my friend Abraham. I must go after him; very beautiful! [The Messenger laughs and the Audience applauds].

Think over, we have been here for four hundred years never seeking Allah. Didn't know how to pray to Him to come to us. Now today, He searching the Earth for His people. He finally found them. And He was like a man finding jewel or pearl, that He not able to take the beautiful jewelry in at that time due to the enemy that owned the jewelry. He goes and He hides it; and He go and prepare to come against that land, to take it.

Now He's after the country. He's so Powerful...and able to make [war] with the enemy, and overcome him. He set the clouds against him. He set the wind against him. He set the snow against him. He set the ice against him. He set his own friends against him. Makes it impossible for him to agree and get along in peace with anyone; He's after him. So, after doing that, He goes and attacks his farms, send ants, worms, bugs into his farms; eat up his crops. He's a terrible God to fight [The Audience applauds].

In His Book of prophesy He say, "He hopes that he would himself...when He rises up and invade the people, he hope he would be...He's the Warrior from the beginning. He was such Warrior in the beginning that when He Created Himself, Made Himself to appear out of Darkness, He went to war within with the Darkness by raising up Light to lighten up the Darkness, so the Darkness could not triumph over Him [The Audience applauds]. He made a great Light for Himself; made to turn out, rotate, so that it would stay in and out the Light; and make it a sign for us here today. Praise be to Allah!

What was His idea for coming to us? Spiritually, to bring us out of Darkness into His Marvelous Spiritual Light. What do He want with a people who like the prodigal son say he was, "had not serve God, but serve the enemy?" What do He want with us? He don't want us as we are. The Holy Qur'an says, "He will cause us to grow into a new growth, make us new again." This is to rid us of the mark of our enemy. That's a big job, isn't it? [The Audience applauds].

He hates the enemy so much so, that He remove the scar or the coloring of the enemy from us, put us into a new growth. No more shall you go along with the scars of the enemy on you. Put you into a new growth, and make you look like Him. As the Epistle of Paul says, "We don't know what we will be like, but we will be like Him. [The Audience applauds].

What does He want to come to us for? To take us and give to us that by Nature belongs to us. We were brought from our home, following and worshipping a enemy. Now the enemy have made us like himself, both spiritual and physical so that God will not want us, but He do! It is written that He would seek, find us and bring us back to our native people and country. But since the enemy have spoiled us so much so, "what do He want with such spoiled people that will run from Him; that will hate Him, curse Him out to His Face, and keep the enemy and just go and worship him as his best friend while he is his worst enemy, murderer.

What we are talking about here is the good of a God, that loves you and want you to be His people. What will you do for us? "I will give you money, good homes, and I will make friends for you in all walk of life. [The Audience applauds]. I will destroy those that hate you, and bring their kingdom to a naught." You say I wouldn't follow a God like that? I say like the Holy Qur'an, "Oh foolish one, do you call me to believe in a god other than my God?" No, No." What is your god doing for you? Nothing, only trying to get you in trouble [The Audience applauds]. After all of this glory that He offer to you and me, then some of us is too proud to accept it. But, yet is in trouble, hungry, half naked, and living in old broke down worn out houses. But you rather stay there and worship the enemy who are depriving you of a good house to live in just to have him to smile, and say "you doing fine." Tell him fine for him, but not for yourself. I say we should wake up!

Look, as the Bible teaches us, "He came to save His people; save them from their sins not charging them with the sins of their enemies. But, forgive them, because they was not at fault. It was the enemy who deceived them, and made them to worship that which they knew not what." Then He says, "Submit to Me," He say, " I will sit you in Heaven at once." You don't have to wait as the enemy teaches you to do, "wait until you die." No, you already have died! [The Audience applauds].

I'm saying this to let you know how much love that God have for a people that don't love Him. Don't even know Him. Don't want to learn Who He is; it is awful. That want to sit them in Heaven at once. Well, where is the Truth? I'm the Truth; I'm in Heaven myself. You follow me, you will get in Heaven too. [The Audience applauds].Heaven is a place where you don't want for nothing that you cannot reach. You get what you want, of good. Yeah Brothers and Sisters, that's right! [The Audience applauds].

SEPTEMBER 10, 1972 PART ONE / SIDE TWO

ELIJAH IS THE ONE!

Ask Allah to continue to bless Elijah, because he's the one [The Audience applauds]. Whatever you desire in life you ask for it and you'll accomplish it.

OLD ENVY AND JEALOUSY

We want to enjoy just that which is ours, ours by Nature; it is the Earth. How can the white man claim the Earth or any part of it, when that he had no part in the Creation of It. [The Audience applauds].

I'm about to take a try at you with fishing poles coming from the outside. I try you with that which you eat, so that I see how you will go long with you there. Then, other…things with our work of building up a world for ourselves…I can get you all the fish that you want to eat of the best kind, far less than the price that you are paying. So I'm ordering a shipload to try you to see will you buy your own good fishes, at a very reasonable price. I'm scattering the order throughout the country. Taste these fishes, and stop buying them from your enemy. [The Audience applauds].Within less than thirty days, we're going to be delivering these best and tasty fishes from New York to San Francisco; and they are so reasonable priced. We are paying enough for a pound of fish to buy a shirt, that's right! Think over a dollar and a dollar and a quarter a pound for a good fish, that's, that's terrible. I'll get you four or five pounds for that. [The Audience applauds].

I would like to say to you from this stand, that I have set for you now every type of merchandise that you need at one third the price that you are paying for it now [The Audience applauds]. We want to do away with our robbers. You can't do away with the robber unless you can come under his price.

So, by my Allah, I have the world behind me. Everything that you need, I can get it for you, far less than you can get it from elsewhere. It is being setup for you now. Some of this merchandise we're able to give to you within the next two or three weeks, less than a month. Those fine clothes, those fine shoes, I can get you those fine shoes for less than one ninth of the price. [The Audience applauds].

Yes I can tell you where I'm expecting to get a shipload of them, but I'm not going to tell you, because you'll go there with a market basket asking for it to be filled, at the same price.

You are terrible people to have. You sit here and laugh and say that's right, and before I can get home you have told all the enemies what I said [The Audience applauds]. Then he goes to put a blockade against it, like he did to Japan. You told him all that I had said concerning the trade with Japan for you. The enemy went over there, setup a higher

235

tariff on everything to make it hard for us to get anything. We would had to pay a large price. But now we broke that down. By our Allah we have many people, and he's only a few.

So, we broke it up; but we don't have to go to Japan. We have lots of people, and they all have ports, most of them. I'm in a position put there by God to help you. And that I am now in that position I can help you. Not to rob you, but help you to live easy. [The Audience applauds]. From Atlantic to the Pacific we are gathering the necessity of your to sell it to you at such reasonable price that you be fighting thinking that you are buying inferior goods, but you're not buying inferior goods. It's just people that would like to do Justice by you. [The Audience applauds].

We have just about completed our order for various types of fishes that will be in here pretty soon; and they're way below the price, that you are paying. Will you buy them when we get them? [The Audience applauds]. Thank you. You'll find some of these fish on your market in New York to San Francisco, now in a few days.

We're ordering them by the shipload, and you're going to have, well we're ordering about five hundred thousand tons each. And that is a lot of fish, but you'll eat up more of them and bang your plate with a knife or folk telling the waiter to come on, with some more. [The Messenger laughs and the Audience applauds].

If it's not the best deal that you ever been offered, I will give you the fish paid for myself. [The Audience applauds].

Yes we have some great things in store for you, but we're afraid to tell you everything, because you tell the enemy. Soon as we tell you what we're trying to do for you, you got to take it over to the enemy, and see what he think of it. We'll put a stop to that, some of these days. We are tired of trying to help self, and you jumping up, destroying that help.

Old envy and jealousy, is the worst enemy that you could housed. Just try housing envy and jealousy; worst that you could housed. That's our greatest trouble, like it was with Cain and Abel. Cain couldn't stand to see Abel being respected by God; so that he goes out and killed Abel, so that God's respect would be for him only.

This is the way you are. You want to destroy the success coming to your Brother, whom that Brother want to share with you. But you not got time to wait. You're envious and jealous of him. "I can't get it now for myself, I will destroy that he's getting."

He's well aware of your intentions, and with the help of Allah We intend to beat this old thing out of our people hearts, of being jealous and envy of each other. "I got to have what he have, I can't wait for it. I want it right now." We got to find ways to destroy that kind of evil. That's a evil that will never let the Nation rise. So we are after destroying it. We have learned how to get under it, and get at the Roots of it.

So my beloved Brothers and Sisters, in my conclusion, I have enjoyed talking with you here [The Audience applauds]. And I want you to remember, cargos of merchandise is now being prepared to ship, in the next thirty days. They are not one kind, they are food and clothes, shoes, for you at a price that you never dreamed, that you would get such merchandise, for such low price.

So, stick around my word is bond [The Audience applauds]. I have grieved and cried a many times over the way that we are being treated by this devil. The Day Allah have spared me to live to lay hold to the handle that won't break off with us [The Audience applauds].

…eating fish caught in good clean water; not in poison water of the devil, but in good clean healthy water, where the fish can grow healthy. We're chasing them to give to you the best, that the Bible may be fulfilled, wherein it say that, " because of Joseph being pulled from his Brethren into strangers hands, let all good things come to Joseph [The Audience applauds].

Everybody wants to see us enjoying the good things of the Earth, but ourselves. We rather let the enemy rob and destroy us; take our lives from us day and night…

RISE UP AND DO SOMETHING FOR SELF!

Everybody wants to see us enjoying the good things of the Earth, but ourselves. We rather let the enemy rob and destroy us; take our lives from us day and night, than to turn, go to our God and His Religion and to our people who we are True Brothers of. We rather die at the hand of our enemy being mistreated by them, and help them to destroy us.

Well, I say you're going to be the losers. I'm with Allah for you, and I will fight you if you fight against it! [The Audience applauds]. With the help of Allah we will stop you from opposing each other.

You know the Sultan from Ethiopia yesterday, he was so happy to learn that I'm teaching you that the man was just, he was just almost shouting. Yeah you was there to see it. These people want to see the western Blackman get up out from under the feet of his enemy, go for himself, and unite with them so they can unite with you [The Audience applauds]. Get you into your own Holy Nation's name, and get out of the name of the devil. Stop calling yourself by his name; we will give you a name.

My God and myself, as He have Taught me, is the We I'm referring to. I can give you a name, and it would be recognized all over the world. But I don't want to try, to make you think that I'm God myself. But I can do that and He will recognize that which I give to you, because He have Taught me. [The Audience applauds].

Our fish will be in here soon. Our clothes for the winter will be in here soon, and in the market you will find them. We're going to build on the Eastside of Cottage Grove, since that you can buy these things like you want to- warehouses.

And we going to move on out into another area we are trying to get from devils. He promise to let us have it, which will just suit us. Good place to build up a little town of selling off merchandise to you, that you will like. But, I do tell you where it is. [The Audience applauds].

I have gotten from the rich people of Asia, an offer to let me have what I'm asking for. It takes round a hundred million dollars, to get going like we want; and they promise to let me have it [The Audience applauds]. Thank you.

I received a telegram last night, from one of my Agents over there. He was very happy. He say everything looks pretty, everything. He was happy I know his language, and I believe that he have struck it rich [The Audience applauds].

Unite with me. I don't ask you to wait and see whether your uniting with me would bring me any glory, but, look and see what we are doing. If we don't look like we're prospering, don't join onto us. But, if you see that we are prospering, I say you would be wise, to join onto us. [The Audience applauds].

Think over the building that you sitting in, costing us four million dollars. And now, building up on the outside around a million and a half improvement. We will have it in your eyes now pretty soon; the improvement that we going to make on this ground, you will love it. We will make Heaven where Hell has been. [The Audience applauds].

Bank your money with us, we will give you ten cent interest. You can join ours tomorrow, if you want it. Yes, we are able to backup every dime that we receive from you. You can come right back the next day and draw it out if you want to, to show you, that what you put in our bank will not break us, if you want it back.

Our bank, we are going to announce with you what it is now pretty soon; we getting a bank of our own. [The Audience applauds].

Well, at this time, I'm going to say to you, that I really have enjoyed myself here looking in your faces, because, your faces show to me that you are ready to rise up and do something for self. [The Audience applauds].

I told God out of my own mouth, and it's written that "I will give my life if, if it's necessary to see you free, going for yourself." I will do that; I love you. [The Audience applauds].

Thank you, for your presence here this afternoon, and I pray to Allah, that He will export each and every one of you, to return to the places of your abode. And let us try to meet as often as we can, not only on a Sunday, everyday is Sunday with us [The Audience applauds].

Be on your watch for good and better fish. Be on your watch, for good and better clothing. Be on your watch, for good and better machineries, to work with.

I thank you. May the peace of God go with you, as I say unto you, as I turn you back to the Minister,

As Salaam Alaikum

"THE PROFESSIONAL CLASS"

Salaam Alaikum.

I'm very happy to see your smiling faces. If mine is not smiling, then I must come through some kind of, you know, things that didn't make a smile. So now, I'm with you with a smiling face; I can smile too. [The Audience applauds].

It is not because I'm late now, that I'm going to hold you late. Nope, that Brother and Sister that wants to hurry and get out of here, I'll take that frown off your face, and we will be going at the same time probably anyway. As usual, we get out of here round four thirty, or between four thirty and five o'clock. I don't intend to hold you later than that.

I just wanted to be sure that I, I see you; see was you making and fulfilling your promises that you would all be here. So, I have fulfill my promise, now that I did come out. And I'm very happy to see so many, so many hundreds and thousands of you. You are in the thousands; I know bout how much our house hold here, and that I'm very happy. If I had stayed home, someone would had returned from here and told me all of these people was down here. I would have wished I could have, then call you back. [The Messenger and the Audience laughs].

I'm very happy to know of many things, that is good for you. And that they are coming into being now where we all can see them. We have lots of people here; and lots of professional people. And you the people that we been calling for, for years. And we had to buy this four million dollar "Church" in order to get you out. [The Audience applauds]. So, since we spent all of that money just to get you out here to listen to what we have to say; Did you know Brother and Sister you have to pay for that? [The Audience laughs].

I was so surprise last Sunday when the Secretary told me how much you give, was not averaging a dollar apiece. I say Brother let's go back, try them again. Two thousand people, and not a dollar apiece, did they give. So, if you go out of here today, not giving us a dollar apiece, averaging that, we will go to your home and eat. [The Audience applauds].

You know, we eat once a day, most of us, and Brother we have a good appetite at that one meal. Don't think now that you can out eat the Muslim. Certainly we can out eat you, you wait till we're hungry; and a hungry fellow can really go some.

We have with us, Lawyer Lawrence E. Cannon. I hope that you didn't come down to make no arrests, or to try to win the case that you have against us. If you do, we going to put out a warrant for you right immediately. [The Audience applauds].

We have here Mister John Harris, Teacher. You see our Principal of our schools, and she will give you a date to meet her, Miss Billie Wells…You see us on Tuesday, between twelve and two o'clock, and the same time on Wednesday afternoon. We will talk with you.

Of course we have of own selves in that business, and it can be increased with your help, if you are able to help us as we desire that you do. We only want our own to go…with the nations of the Earth. If you who would like to join in with us, please talk to me between twelve and two o'clock on Tuesday.

We have to import much of what we're after for you, because, here in America, we deal with our enemies and they don't want to give us the price that we can get elsewhere. America is still America. We are a Nation growing up in America, to become an independent Nation within an independent nation. We have our Flag to go forward, to make a move for self.

We have Brothers all over the Earth. We are a people that outnumber our enemy eleven to one. We are a people who are not say going to make an attempt, we're going to do what we attempt to do; we want people to help us out of our own people.

But let us teach you how to help us. We don't want you to be like the fellow that the Book say was told by one of the officers to help Jesus bear his cross, and he hardly knew where to take a hold at. So he taken the hold of the little part that was too heavy for him. So I don't want you picking no part. I will tell you where you lay hold your hand. [The Audience applauds].

Yes, that be alright. Now some Tuesdays between twelve and two o'clock, and that we are not say really drive, putting on no drive for simple people to help us in that matter. We got that all just about set. But, you can find a place to work in it, if we talk it over together. I'm quite sure we have a vacancy for good people.

Reverend Willie May Davis, Minister of Pleasant Grove or Green Baptist Church. I think it's Green, Pleasant Green; that's a good name for it. And that, if you feel you have something to say after we have said our theme, you are perfect welcome to say all you want to.

We love to get acquainted with our church people, and especially the leaders. I know what you have heard about me, that I'm an enemy to the church. Yes, you heard bout right! [The Audience applauds].

THE PREACHERS HAVE BEEN DECEIVED!

Yes, you heard bout right! [The Audience applauds]. We have also, I don't know whether it's a Brother, or a Sister...Johnson, a Teacher. Mister...Patterson, Editor of Black Enterprise Magazine. We certainly want to talk with you Brother. We have everything to work with, but no workers; the workers is few. Pardon me Brother workers I know you are here, but you needs more. I don't like to criticize no one, because, this is not what we're after today, to come meet together to criticize each other. Whether we are helping each other or not. We don't want to criticize, because, we can get together and squash that old thing you call criticize.

In fact about it, that's what Islam have come for, to put a stop to Blackman making fun of Blackman. It's here to make us Brothers, and if we can't be Brothers, we are here to push him out of the circle. God Himself is for that purpose; today is to show you and me that will help others and do for others. And if we can't, He's here to push us in the Lake, and not a Lake of water, it's a Lake of Fire. That's what He's ready to do for us.

The world have lingered around...the Righteous, over time. They're over time doing this on us all, because that you would not be on time to wake up and join on to your own kind, yeah. But if we had been swift and eager with our, our ears open to hear the trumpet of self blowing, we would have been a long way towards the Gate of Heaven.

What we want to do Reverend, Teachers, Doctors, Lawyers; We want to get together here in America, first of all, and build for us something of our own that the world will recognize. There is no work going on in America that you can compare with our work. No work is having the progress as our work. They don't enjoy the progress.

I don't care where you're from Brother and Sister, we have your best. We are able to get the confidence of the nations of the Earth. They will help us in every way that we call on them to do for us, they will do it. For God will make them to do it. We are with God, and God is with us. If you are so proud feeling that you can make a way without going on your knees submitting to a Superior, Supreme Being of Righteous, Truth, and Justice, that you can get anything over here on the side and make the same progress, go and try it. We care nothing about the rulers of evil who want to keep you and me down, so that we cannot progress in our efforts to do something worthwhile for ourselves. We care nothing about their dislike, their attacks to try to halt, stop, or injure our progress. We care nothing about their efforts. If, we have God with us, who is it that can interfere with our progress and win?

242

We want to build on the Eastside of Cottage Grove, all the way from 78th to 87th. We want to make it a new Eastside for us. We going to start laying foundation in the 7800 block Cottage Grove, Eastside of it, for you a very beautiful building there for your retail stores and foreign goods. And we going to move on cross and keep on the Eastside of Cottage Grove, which we estimate will cost us between ten and twenty million dollars. But however, you help me to move on cross and make the Southside of Chicago your Southside. This is what I want for us. I'm tired of looking at you running up in the neighborhood of the white man to try to get something from him, to live in your neighborhood, the Southside. We must quit that old slavery act.

So we had planned to do this, and our plan Allah will help us to perfect. We are going to the farms as never before. And if Allah bless us with the seasons next year this time, you will be happy of our planning. We have a lot of chickens down there that we intend to haul in to you pretty soon. Also, we have beef cattle. We don't have no pig. [The Audience applauds].We're not going to let you eat pig anymore. And in the next three or four, five years, we hope to have you off of beef. We just letting you get away with it now because, I can't tell you to stop eating that steak so quick and you will do it. I love to tell you something that you will do, and do it immediate.

When is he going to start preaching? I'm preaching now! [The Audience applauds]. See we don't preach like the average preacher. We don't get on God told Jonah to go to Nineveh, and put that little wang to it. We tell why God told Jonah to go to Nineveh; what was His aim or purpose. That's the way we preach.

I know you like to hear, probably me come out with it, "Oh Yeah!" [The Audience applauds], but you see, I can't preach like that. My father use to preach like that. [The Audience laughs]. They use to sometime have to run up in the stand there and pick him up, and carry him out, pour some cool water over him. [T he Audience laughs and applauds]. But I can't preach like that. I am not that type of Preacher; I'm a Teacher [The Audience applauds], and reckon you say, "It's near time."

You know I, I, thought I maybe could of have gotten away with. I was sitting there resting so well, and nursing around. My Assistant, she didn't feel so good, and I say maybe I can have an excuse. But I had remembered the doctor came by, you know, last night, and he had tap me over, to see whether I could come out today. He may be in here; I'm scared you know. So, if I had kept staying there, I, I could have told you he came by, but he could have tell you too, that "he look pretty well when I was here. I don't think he was so sick that he could not have come out." See, because the doctor may be in this Temple; I believe he is here, and I'm scared to hide behind the doctor. You know he got all of us before his eyes, and that fellow they kind of know how the clock ticks in your body. They know whether you can work or not. So I'm glad and thankful to Allah I can work today [The Audience applauds]. But, by me being late to get here among you, I do not want to keep you here over the time that you was expecting.

But, in these Days and Time that we are living in, we better not look at the clock as much as we look at our feet to see if they are prepared to run. I don't want you to be like the people of Noah and Lot, and like the slowness of Israel was getting out of Egypt, that they had to go down that night and put up a, a blood sign over the door to warn them to flee that have the blood sign over the door.

Nope, we're up two thousand years or more or four thousand from that time. We should have more knowledge, wisdom, to do better job.

So, Brothers I'm after you this afternoon, for all you have that can help yourself and your kind. I'm not after you for me alone, I'm after you for yourself. Then, if you have a little left over, let me have that which you have left over.

With the world of Christianity shrinking under your feet, and falling out of the sky and falling on the battle fields of nations, if you cannot wake up and get prepared to fly for self, what will waken you to flying for yourself if the Time that we are now living in will not awaken you? I don't know what could come. Look what has happened since last Sunday that we was here together; much has happened. It is Time that we reach out for self, fly for self. The Holy Qur'an teaches us "To fly for refuge in Allah."
We can take and try and play with this warning like the people of Noah; Like the people of Lot, but we will meet with grave consequences. So let us try to shun all of the mis-happenings that we possibly can.

We want to build for self. You say " We going to be destroyed, the cities of the nation going to be shaken from their foundations," that's right, but you look in the Book, and you will find where it's prophesied that, "You must rise up and rebuild the wasted cities." You have that there. Well if we got to rebuild the wasted cities, let us go practice now how to build for ourselves. You cannot boast that you have your own if you don't know how to build and master your own. With round two thousand people here now, two thousand people can do wonderful things, if two thousand people will get together to do so. We cannot get together haphazard. We cannot get together hating one Brother and half loving another one. We got to whole love all the Brothers, and all the Brothers got to whole love another one. [The Audience applauds].

I cannot give you reverends too much sympathy, because the church is what we want to destroy, Christianity. Christianity is our slave-master, just remember that it's our slave-master. The tool that the slave-masters handed over to us, when he considered himself freeing us. He give you something to enslave your brains, and that is where you are tied up at. It's in your brains, from the slave-master.

You boast and fight for Christianity more than the founders of Christianity. They have just about give it up. They know they fighting a losing battle. Allah will remove the modern mad religion. Take a look over here, that's murder... [The Audience applauds].

If you will follow a murderer for life, what life could he give you if he's a murderer? That's a murderer over there! And he put up his sign for you and me to worship. If we going to worship the sign of a murderer and follow the murderer, then what are we looking for? Death! We're looking for Death!

Oh reverend it's a shame that he deceived you like this. I'm not coming here to make fun of you. I'm coming here to make you wise to the Murderer! It's up to you to believe it or let alone, but here is his work. He says to you and me that "I taken your Jesus and I killed him, hung him up on a cross. Now nigger come on and worship it, cause I'm going to do you the same." And he's doing it!

I don't want to argue with you, I just want to tell you outright Truth that you see! [The Audience applauds]. Any man or woman go and worship that cross, call it the sign that leads them to their salvation, should be taken and put in the insane asylum!

That's no sign of life, that's a sign of Death! See how far you're off, you're off from the knowledge of what you are given. A man give you that cross, and then tell you that you following Jesus to Heaven, you ought to bust his face open! [The Audience applauds].

The enemy has molded you in into Death! My church, my denomination! Your church of Hell! And your denomination is Hell! [The Audience applauds]. That's right, they do not have no respect over in that church for the members there, nor anyone that will visit...

They hang you on the tree. They say they hang the Jesus on the tree. You have it now, clear, because they do hang you. "Be like Jesus" he say. Tell him for what, for you to hang me and nail me to the cross like you did him? But, no he have made you to Love Death, and Worship the Murderer! When you tell them about us, "Are you one of them?" That's what he will say. "Ah, you done left the church?" Tell him I should not have never been in it! [The Audience applauds].

Old slave-house with a cross, a sign of imprisonment, suffering, and finally Death. The church now is getting hungry; the Muslim is getting fat, that's right! You have the Bible, it teach you that, but you didn't know who it was talking about. We shall eat, but he shall be hungry.

Oh Christians, I'm so sorry for you. And the worst of all, that Christianity lead you to seek a Heaven in the sky off the Earth, where food and clothes is at; where shelter is at. They teach you to look up in the sky for yours. Tell them, "I'm already sheltered by that Canopy, I don't need to pray to go to it. It was built for our service."

Ahh Brother, you know if I had gotten here in time, I would have preached. [The Audience applauds]. What can you do with his religion, to aid you in getting for yourself, that which he has gotten of this Earth for himself, good homes, money, friendship? How you going to get it now, when the trumpet of life is sounding; and it don't carry a cross; it's against the cross; it come to destroy the cross.

This is exactly what Islam is here for; give you a sign that is worthwhile. Look at our sign over there, it correspond with what you live under daily and nightly. Yours correspond with that which we find over in the grave. So many graves expensively built, putting that sign on it, a cross.

Have you ever studied the cross? If the cross means that we're at crossroad with each other, that's right. It mean that the cross is at the crossroads with the Crescent. But yet, the old cross cannot get along without our Crescent. They got to have the Sun, Moon, and Stars. Remove that away from them, they all go crazy at once. Remove that cross away from us, we all is freed at once.

It was made to enslave people. That's the sign of spiritual and physical enslavement and Death. That's the cross that you has been deceived to follow for salvation.

You follow Jesus, "He was hung on a cross," you say. "He was not hung on no cross." Allah Taught me he made a cross out of himself. He stretched forth his hands like this and let the deputy sheriff stab him to death, quickly through his heart. He didn't die on no cross. And, the deputy sheriff that was sent out after him, he wanted to make a quick death of him, because he did not see where he was guilty…

WE WERE CREATED MUSLIMS!

...of the crime made against him. So, he told him "if you let me kill you," he say, "I will kill you so quick, that you never feel it." He said "Then I will get twice the reward for you, since that you know you going to die, and you came for that purpose." So he say, "I will kill you so quick, that you never feel it." And he did so; shot his sharp knife through his heart, and the man was dead instant. Well, if I have to die, I hope I die the death of the Muslim. [The Audience applauds].

We are planning to get all of your clothes, far less than what you has been paying for them. We have that already, ready to put through. We have planned to make all of your food come to your table, cheaper than you ever have gotten it. And, the best of food for that.

He can't do that beyond his nature and feel good. If he do a little good for you, he always tell it, "I went out of my way to do thus and thus for you." And he's right, when he do something good, he went out of his way, because he wasn't made to do good. [The Audience applauds].

Beautiful Sisters, stop sweet-hearting with blue-eyed Caucasians. Your days is numbered for that! Brothers, stop going turning up your Brother for a dollar from the enemy. Time is out for that! They'll see you laying around somewhere not talking. Time is out for it! And Sisters, stop driving by in their cars with them over your Brothers passing through their neighborhoods, flirting with white men, their enemies and your enemies. They going right-about-face on you one of these days! Don't you feel a shame of yourself, sitting up in the car with the enemy of your people, letting him take you in the bushes somewhere on a dead end lot. That kind of work going to stop someday! You may not feel so happy when you meet the gang who will be stopping it! [The Audience applauds].

White people use to kill their women that if they caught them with you, and kill you too! You thinks it's, it's a honor to be sitting around grinning with white folks, and arms around you; and they got their arms around our pocket books, keeping you from enjoying the wealth that your Fathers and Mothers suffered for.

Be careful about this, I'm warning you! We the Muslims is not going to stand for it! [The Audience applauds].

There is, is some we call good Christians, but they just don't know how to be a good Christian, because they don't know the Truth. We are the best Christians on Earth. Christian mean to be crystallized into one. So, if you go by the meaning, the Muslim is really a good Christian, we're one. And my beloved Brothers and Sisters of the church, I am certainly happy to see you bold enough to come in that door, and learn what Christianity is, and learn what Islam is. You was made a Christian, but you were born a Muslim.

We were Created Muslim from the very beginning. Our Father, Who Created the Heavens and the Earth, was a Muslim. And we that is from Him, is Muslims by Nature. Therefore, you don't join Islam to become a Muslim, you just come on back to Islam in what you were Created to be.

The Holy Qur'an say, " We are that which by nature we were Created." The church can't tell you that you are a Christian by nature; they can't do it. They tell you that you are a Christian by faith and hopes. But you are born a Righteous person. Muslim means a Righteous person. Well, I guess I have talked enough. [The Audience applauds] Thank you.

We want you to remember to meet with us every time that we call on you to do so. Whether you say you are not a Muslim or not, you just saying that to the undeveloped knowledge of self. You were Created a Muslim. If you reject it now, you rejecting yourself, because Muslim is what you are. What can you find in Christianity that exceeds us? Nothing but evil! [The Audience applauds].

You can't boast that you an evil person, from yourself. Your man that made you evil, Yacub, He was one of us. You didn't have sense enough to build up a race of evil people. It was one of our people who taught you how to build one, out of evil. And He did so, but He limit your Time. After you have lived here for six thousand years, your brother coming from the East, and He's going to eat you up. So I'm smacking on a few of them now! [The Audience applauds].

I love Black people! I love Black! [The Audience applauds]. I work for Black people! And we will intercept other than Black people, who that don't like us. We will intercept you, if you don't want to come out and talk with us, in that which you know is good to try to win with of your evil; come on over. We will always have a place for you to argue if you want to argue. But I advise you to know what you going to argue about; and if it's not nothing, we don't want to begin.

I just came down to let you know that I am your Brother, and will fulfill my appointments with you, whether you like what I say or not. I know you will love what I say, pretty soon, yes!

And so, my beloved Brothers and Sisters, I have enjoyed this little over a hour with you. And that, I hope that you will make out your orders to buy the merchandise that we have already purchase for you. And, that if you can find better, we will go where you find it better. We are not carrying a market bag with us, we're carrying a ship with us; not a little market bag.

If there is anyone of you that would like to ask me a question, do stand. No one wants to ask me a question? So I don't want to ask you one, I just tell you come on let's go home. I have a home that God have given to me, for you. So, let's go move in them. What is any better help than plenty money, a good house to live in, good peace among the Brethren and the world of man. What is any better Heaven than that? I don't want to try to prepare to go up in the sky with you. I don't know what kind of vehicle you have to fly me up in the sky; I may drop back, and I certainly don't have no wings growing on me. So, let us try to stay on this good Earth and get the good things out of this good Earth that we need for our own good time on it while we live. I thank you.

No questions, then I say I have enjoyed a very beautiful happy hour here with you. And I hope you will continue to come over and see me. I don't say I hate you and call you a Christian, no. I don't hate you because I know you're not a Christian. I hate you if you deny yourself. You're one of the Righteous, you're a Muslim; that's from Creation of you. That what you made yourself since your Creation, I don't recognize. You've gotten that from the devil, the blue-eyed Caucasian, that's the real devil. If I almost was about to dismiss myself from you, and had not told you who the real devil is!

The real devil is the blue-eyed Caucasian people. In the Holy Qur'an, you will find it written in there, "On the Day," according to the Judgment, "On the Day when We will gather the guilty blue-eyed, on that Day." The Holy Qur'an is exact and a Righteous, Truthful Book. The blue-eyed is being gathered together now. This is the Time they are being gathered.

I thank you for your attention given to me, for these few minutes. And I'm going to get out of here, and let the Laborers go to work. And I hope they do good labor. We need your help, if you want to help us. We don't want it, if you don't want to give it to us. We do own the Heavens and the Earth, and we're taking it over. [The Audience applauds].

Thank you beautiful beloved people. You look so beautiful, and the devil himself know you're the beautifulest people on Earth; and that he don't want to tell you because he with his short, temporary made self, want you to think he's the beautiful. Just been here six days, and we been here without number of years. I say, go on like Isaiah teach you "Shine! Shine! Shine!" Thank you. [The Audience applauds].

Thank you for your pleasant receiving me; and I thank you for the things that I have said, that I believe you believe. Now, I turn you over into the hands of our Assistant Minister, Minister Shah, that's a big name. You know there's a whole entire society of that people. They are one, one set…in this Book, the Qur'an, the Shah. They call them Shah…

Thank you, and I don't want to leave you, but I was late, and so, since I was late, I won't delay you cause I'm getting hungry just thinking about its noon time. [The Messenger and the Audience laughs].

May the peace and the blessings of Allah be with you, wherever you go,

As Salaam Alaikum.

A WORLD OF OUR OWN!

As Salaam Alaikum. You may be seated.

I'm very happy to look upon your smiling faces here this afternoon. And I don't think that you could travel over the country of America, and find such beautiful city as I'm looking on of you. You look so beautiful being yourself, and being in the right place to continue yourself; this is the place.

I thank you my Brother. I want to call him another name, the East Coast Buster. [The Messenger and the Audience laughs]. Brother Farrakhan, I call him that name, and I don't think I missed him. He busted up the East Coast. Look out Brother western Ministers, he's out here to bust you…And so, you better be careful. The Son is prophesied to rise from the West. So, if He got to come from the East to rise in the West, we welcome. [The Audience applauds].

We also have with us some very, very, responsible people for this situation that we are now in. We're very happy to have you here. Mr. Tolbert Smith, Teacher; Ms. Ella M. Statton, Teacher. If I miscalled your name, just allow it to my uneducation [The Messenger laughs].

I don't know whether this a Miss or Misses, they didn't say. Sonja Jones, Teacher; Dorothy Lee, Medical Technician;…Architect; Oh yes Sir Brother we need you [The Messenger and the Audience laughs]….Editor, yeah we need you too. Black Almanac, very good…Charles…Consultant.

Well, I have a few things I like to consult you on. Mister Clea…How do you spell this, or pronounce this I should…? Clefus Williams, President. Cleophus, that's right, I had a hard letter there, and I should have remembered it. It's seven letters there and I missed that odd one in pronouncing of International Longshoreman.

Well, Brother, I don't know about the Longshoreman, but, we will soon be able to have some of that work going on out there on the water. But, please do not strike on us. [The Messenger and the Audience laughs].

So, we are getting up into the world Brothers to have these type of people sitting round with us.

251

Miss, Miss or Misses Weatherspoon,…Market Analyst; Joy Macocca, Social Worker; Thomas Clouse, Radio Commentator; Mister Trevors Smith, Teacher; Miss Ella M. Staton, Teacher; Sonja Jones, Teacher; Dorothy Lee, Medical Technician.

Well, I'm a little late today. I'm feeling kind of physically unfit, for my job today. So I see I have lots of Doctors around. I think this is about all. No, Jill…Architect. These the people I want…..Editor, Publisher, The Black Almanac. I think I called out this one.

I think this is very good, that I have you here with us this afternoon, and I hope that you will enjoy what we have to say. I can tell you what I am, I'm just a Messenger. I have a message to deliver to you, from the Lord of the Worlds [The Audience applauds].

We needs this type of professional people to get going. Get going on what? Get going on building us a world of our own, that's what I mean. We don't want this world. We want to build us a world. We want a world of our own, and this is the type of professional people that we need to get started with that world.

I no more want the world that I was born in. I want my own world. I don't want you to be so absorbed, or immersed into this world that you cannot get out of it to build you one of your own.

This was made in us, when we was babies looking forward to the white man for everything. This is why it's so hard to get you to do something for yourself. It is because you always had self on the white man. Let him take care of self. You do nothing but play like children. This thing must be stopped. And that, the only way to get it to stop, you have to stop it yourself.

We want you to know, that the Islamic believers is now in for building a world of their own. They're not satisfied, with this world; and we are trying to build a world of our own. We don't have to try much, for the world is already curbed out by Divine. And therefore, that stops us from trying to curb out pictures, to try to make a world. The world is already curbed out for us, and the Architect is Allah Himself.

So, I don't think you have much to argue with yourself about, doing that which have already been made for you. We don't want to hold you here no great long time, but we do want you to pay attention to what we are saying.

We don't want you to think that we are thinking in the way of this world's thinking. And this is what I want to do for you, when you come here. I want to change your way of thinking. [The Audience applauds]. Once that has been done, then you're on the road for self.

We have great men; We have great women, that have plenty of that know how. But, they lay down at the gate of their enemy the devil; blue-eyed Caucasian begging him, because they don't know how to get started for self. We must learn to get going for self.

Since we have this kind of knowledge, that we learn from our enemy, put it to work for self and not for the enemy. Look how silly you are: God sent the Christian and the Buddha to fight a war to kill each other; you jumped in there to help save both of them. Just think over that!

This war you had no right in, anymore than a turtle have right to be standing up here trying to preach to you [The Audience applauds].You say, "Well, I fight for my country." When did you have a country to fight for? [The Audience applauds]. Just tell me that, and then I'm through!

Back in the days of the first war, I joined up for that. Allah must have known that I didn't belong there. So, just one day before they was calling up that group that I was in, they declared, that the war was over. [The Audience applauds].

I never have seen people, so lovers of going to war as you has been, in these last two wars. I wasn't thinking about wanting to go to the war. I even went and fast, to try to get as little as possible, so I would not be in that war.

Well, they said if you did not weigh a hundred and twelve, they would not take me. So I tried my best to come down to that. But, if they had of waited until this day, I would not had to fast to get down to it. I'm not much over that now. But, I want to say, that I'm one of the most happiest men on Earth! To own a whole nation; [The Audience applauds]. That must be a rich man, own a whole nation!

Well, since you had four hundred years here waiting on the devil. [The Audience applauds], I think you could wait on me at least for a hour. The Holy Qur'an is a Book or a Scripture in which you don't know anything about. But, it verifies the Bible, and the Bible verifies the Qur'an. The Qur'an is a late Scripture revealed to Muhammad, and that was around fourteen hundred years ago near.

But, I would say to you, if I wanted to challenge it, the Author of it who made the Bible, I would say first, who made the Bible? Did the white people make it, or did Black people make it? Who made the Holy Qur'an? You say," Mohammad, Mohammad will say to you, "it was revealed to be." But, who was the Revealer? [The Messenger laughs]. Oh yeah, We want to attack some of these know- alls.

If you think a spook came down to Moses, ask and question what Moses say the spook said to him. Spirits don't talk like that. Moses said that he met God, and that when he met God, God told him, when Moses asked Who He was, "Who shall I tell them Who you are." He was so Mighty in Wisdom and in Strength, He just told Moses, "Tell him I am that I am." [The Audience applauds].

That's a Mighty Man! "I'm not particular about whether they know Me or not. But, I am that I am; and when I let go I am, they will know who He is." [The Audience applauds].

He says to Moses, "I am the God of your Fathers and you ask Me Who I am, when I'm the Father of you." You know these is beautiful answers. He says again to Moses, "Come Moses I want to send you to Pharaoh." Moses didn't want to show off his mighty self. He say, "Who am I to send to Pharaoh?"

You say, Moses that was insult. He says to Moses, "You go and you tell Pharaoh that you has met with Me. Pharaoh is a Scholar, he should know that you not talking over yourself. You're talking about a Man that he has been dreading to see…come." "Who am I to go to Pharaoh?" "I'm going with you Moses, and if I go with you, I will bring Pharaoh to his knees." This is what He meant.

So Moses was scared of Pharaoh, but he went. He found out that Pharaoh was not nothing to this God. So that's what I have found out. [The Audience applauds].

If, the Holy Qur'an does not verify the Bible, the Scripture in which the Prophets… how could we recognize a Book, that you give a name to, that don't verify the Truth of the Book which we have? Well, we cannot do that. But, when it verifies the Truth in, from the Book in which we have, we got to believe!

We want you to know that we live in the end of both of these Books. You won't study Bible in the Hereafter, nor will you study the present Qur'an. No, you will have a new Book; and that new Book will replace the Bible and the present Qur'an.

Did not you read in the Bible, where that it teaches you that He, the Prophets, or the Spirit of the Prophet, says in his hearings, "Go, take that little Book and read it, eat it up." Think over that.

A new Book coming into being, and that, that new Book is the thing that the people must give in to. Now, we going the right way, for these two former Books, the Old Testament, and the New Testament has served their purpose.

So now We have to remove them, and get a third Book and a fourth Book, with two more to come. One is for you, and one is for the orthodox world. It takes little more for them, since they are the fountain of Scripture; then you, for you never had any. No, no Prophet ever come to you before, so says the Holy Qur'an. And we know we didn't see one. We were here, and we haven't seen no Prophet!

So, the Holy Qur'an say to you and to me, that I am the First ever was sent to you. "To a people," the Holy Qur'an says, " to whom no Warner has come to before." So I'm here, I hope you will learn to love me. [The Audience applauds]. I have worked as hard as any other Prophet, to pay for his choosing, by Allah.

I have, if you remember, I have did everything but die physically; and I had my life for that. I came up or rather He brought me up on that bond of word, that I would give my life for you, if necessary. This is the only way that God can use a man to teach people; he got to be willing to give up his life.

As you read in Bible how that Prophets long time ago were killed by their people, trying to teach them to come to God; devil and the people killed them. They have been killing Prophets every since God sent a Prophet, because the Prophets of God are destroyers; their work prevents the evil from coming in, by their Truth.

Now comes Elijah, and that you read much of that. You start on Elijah in the Kings of the Bible, and you read him until you get into the Revelations. This is kind of a, important little fellow. He never attacks the servants; he attack the Kings. From the Genesis to the Revelator, you will find him attacking Kings; not the servants, he fight them. He's some, tough little fellow. [The Audience applauds].

Yes sir, and that man spoken of in the beginning of the Book, almost he's spoken of as "Straightening up the old path, and making a way for God to come to the people. He will make a path, and then your Lord, your God, Whom you wishes to see, will come suddenly after Elijah fix up a path, for Him. The way is too crooked for God to come in. Elijah must come in, and make Him some followers."

This is what they call, the "Pathway." He got to have something of His Own, to come after. All He want you to do is just to give Him a chance to claim you, so He can fight the enemy who have held you, in the valleys of sin. So, the Book teaches us, that Elijah must come…

ELIJAH STRAIGHTENS OUT
THE WORLD OF HIS PEOPLE!

…and make a way for his God to come, and get His people. No, Elijah just make a little few people, so that God could have a claim on the whole. This is wonderful! Elijah straightens out the world of his people, with just a few. Immediately, they'll become the owner of all!

I think you should be happy to know [The Audience applauds], to know what Time that you are living in. A Time in which the world will be changed around; and a world of peace and security will be made for you; and you will own what you already have owned. You will have the Freedom to use it, as you please.

Build a world, that the people will be happy to live in. We cannot be happy living in a world, that every day and night we are afraid for our own lives, our children's lives. We don't want a world like that! The root of it is that we have an enemy on our Earth, that don't belong on it.

In the Creation of the Heavens and the Earth, our Fathers didn't make No enemies. No, they had Peace. Here comes along an enemy of Ours, just six thousand years ago. He goes and makes a people to be our enemy.

But, he can't last long. Just six thousand years now, the people is already to through him in the Fire. Can't live with no such people; you can't get along with them in peace, so they must be removed! Not say, to go and isolate them in some parts of the Earth, he will come out, he's too smart. Go, and kill and then burn him! [The Audience applauds]. Burn him up, the Bible say "Root and Branch. Get him, don't save nothing of him." Poor, poor devil; I'm so glad for you, not sorry! [The Audience applauds].

Look at our poor Brothers, our poor Sisters in the South, that the whole thing begin to move North, out here in Indiana, killing and burning our poor innocent people. You love a people like that? [The Audience responds in disapproval].

I shouldn't think you was anything if you did! See them, read of them killing and burning your parents, your Sisters and Brothers! And now, here stand God with a sword of eternal death in His hand, to rid you and me of that type of people, and you love him so well that you start out defending him, trying your best to find some law of the Scripture that will try and defend him. But, the Scripture don't defend him nowhere. The Scripture condemns him. It is you, that he made ignorant, blind, deaf, and dumb and filled you full of fear of him. That's why the Bible...Lord will do great things for you." He so Wise; He so Mighty. He found me shivering, shaking. He say "Come on, go with Me, I will take that fear out of you." And He taken it out of me!

I go through the valley, as it is written in the shadow of death; for He is the, the Death that is producing this shadow, but I fear no evil. You, that follow me, you are the same; you don't fear no evil, because you have Allah on your side. [The Audience responds in approval].

We are a most happy and worthy people, for God to chose us to be His people; and will kill nations for you. Your Bible teach you that, that He will destroy nations for your lives; and He's doing it!

Why should we fly to a God like that? "It's because that I been following Mister blue-eyed Caucasian all my life, and I have come to love him; and I wishes to kill your God and my God to save him." Oh Brother, that's bad! But that's just what you say in your heart. "I wish that They did not exist. I would kill Them if I could!"

Many times you have wished that my God and your God, Master Fard Muhammad and Elijah Muhammad was dead, so you could cling on to your devil. As the devil said himself that "if they could get me out of the way, they would have a glorious kingdom, future for them," that's right! They could get me out of the way, they would have a glorious future [The Audience applauds], but I'm here, and Nobody can move me but Allah. [The Audience applauds].

If, if they and you would unite together, and try and put me out of the way, you would not do anything but put yourself out of the way, because that, He have the Power over everything.

So, since He have the Power over everything, He most certainly have Power over me, to keep me, protect me. But that is not going to happen with me and you, no way. Because, He loves you and I love you; and you love both of Us. [The Audience applauds].

So, we don't have nothing to fear. We have been out of our Brotherhood so long in this world, and now we are joining up again. And we're so happy too that, that no one must not come around trying to make trouble among us, because, we both love each other, that's right I love you and you love me! [The Audience applauds].

We want to build; We want to make the Southside, our Southside; I mean the Blackman. So, we have been working on drawings, that if you would see you will say, "I'll be glad, when that is done." Well it's going to be done. We don't sit down and draw for nothing. So, we do believe by this time another year, the Southside, as it looks today, will not look like that within a year. [The Audience applauds].

If our own can get the leaders who is not making any progress, the leaders of Christianity and the leaders of what the devil Caucasian want them to do for him. The devil, blue-eyed white people, they love to get around Reverend. They calls him their man, you know? And reverend calls himself their man. Reverend believes in that blue-eyed devil, because he calls him reverend, and tries to pretend to be backing him up. [The Audience laughs] But he's not backing up into nothing but the Fire of Hell.

Reverend cannot you see he can't do nothing with me? He don't call me a reverend, but, they cannot stop me; and I didn't get no license from him to preach. [The Audience applauds].

When a man say that he's God's Preacher, and have to be license by the world of enemies of his, I say, you have not yet become God's Preacher! You're the devil, slave making, white man's preacher. These are Truths! He license, ordain you to preach, and you must preach like he say. If you don't, well he will come over and tell you to sit down reverend.

He didn't license me nor ordain me. I just went to preaching, by orders of my God! [The Audience applauds]. What a God, ordained Minister of the Spirit of Himself, look like going over to a devil asking him for license?

Ahhh, Brother, it's sickening almost to talk about it, that my people is ordained and sent by the devil, to preach what he tell them to preach, to his people. Why Brother, I would kick him in the face! [The Audience applauds].

Don't be afraid reverends; don't be afraid. Long as you here with me, he not going to run in here and bother you! [The Audience applauds]. Remember how Elijah fought with Ahab, and proved his four hundred preachers, liars. And he taken them and chopped their heads off. Now I'm not going to chop your head off; don't be thinking. But I'm going to chop that one that he put on the altar.

I want my God and myself to save you out of his clutches; take you away from him; you would be in Islam over night. But little you know it, if you take time and read your Bible, you will bear me witness, that you have nothing that you should do, but, to come and follow Elijah. [The Audience responds in approval].

Elijah must First come. Well if there was a Elijah, that was capable with the Power of God; Wisdom of God, to save the people, why didn't they look for him to come? Thousands of Preachers all over the country, but you can't make a way for your God and my God, because you don't serve Him!

You don't convert people to our God, you convert them to Satan, the blue-eyed devil. All the converts that you make in your church today, you're making them for him, not for Almighty God, Who have Power over the Heavens and the Earth.

You haven't made one for Him. All of your preaching, that you have preached all your life, you haven't made one convert to the God of Heaven and Earth. You made them for the white folks; not even one!

I don't care if you making a thousand a day, long as you preaching Christianity, you're making them for the white man, and he claims them to be his. Every Christian he claims to be his. Every Muslim I claim him, to be mine. [The Audience applauds].

Who Am I, He says, He say, "I Am, that I Am." [The Audience applauds]. "Who shall I say that sent me?" Tell them I Am that I Am, that sent me." Oh Brother, pretty strong! "Tell them that I Am the God of their Fathers." He's a strong Man talking!

If He is I Am that I Am, what I am to believe in I Am that I Am? "But, tell them that I Am the God of your Fathers; and I have heard the mourning, the groaning of My people! I couldn't be satisfied sitting in Heaven and hearing the groans and the mourns of My people, under hard task-masters!"

"So, it moved Me and I am come down." Think over it! I am come down, not out of the sky, but I have come down from My High Place, to get in your place, that you may know I love you." Think over it! [The Audience applauds].

"Burn up thy ropes, chains; burn that snake in the Fire; the blue eyed devil that Yacub, made to do just that to you and me. I'm come down from My High Place, as God in the Heavens of the Righteous, to you that is bound in Hell! I come down to loose you! I come down to free you! I come down to kill your enemy!" [The Audience applauds].

Now, after we have read all these things of the past, now a similar thing coming to us at present. Where did you come from? "Don't worry Me in that! I came Alone, by Myself." Think over that!

"I came Alone, by Myself, having the Power to Walk Alone; and having the Power to Destroy My enemies, and your enemies. I am Alone; I am the One God; I don't need no help. I am Alone, but you were brought over here! I come to free you from the kidnapper!" [The Audience applauds].

"You did not want to come with that enemy, but they put you in chains; you couldn't help yourself! I have the key to unlock that chain from around you. I can Teach one of you to do that. So I'm going to pass the key over to Elijah."

"Since, every since he was in his boyhood, he been craving to see someone come to the rescue of his people. So, I'm going to give him the key. He will unlock the doors; he will let you out. I'm going to put Power in that key, so that he can use it in locking up your enemies."

"He have the key of both Hell and Death. He going to put a stop to that bleeding you to death. I'm going to let him go; he's already angry! Elijah don't have to get angry at them. He has already been angry with them, but he didn't have nothing to fight with. So I'm going to give him something to fight with; and I'm going to fight with him!" [The Audience applauds].

And the Lord said unto Ezekiel, "Son of man, can these bones live?" He say, "Thou knowest, You the All Knowing One, for if they can live, You know that." Not one either argued with the other, they all was in agreement. "Go tell them to hear the Word of the Lord."

That didn't work so well, they're too stubborn. He say, "I will give you a instrument, make a better one for you, and you use that instrument that I give you. Go call on the winds. Tell them to come from all four parts. Call on them Elijah, they will hear you, they will come and help you; tell them to help you with these slain." Think over that!

So Merciful, He saw us as people slain. And that, He told the Messenger to call on the nations that He named winds of the Earth to help him. So the nations of the Earth is now sharpening their swords to help. It is wonderful to know that you have a God on your side today! [The Audience applauds].

He looked upon us, saw how pitiful we was. He say, "I found you in a Day of Love." It was the Time of His Love for us. But, we was wallowing in our blood, or our, rather I should say, in our ignorance of God, and of our self like a baby that has just been born, and he's wallowing in the blood of his mother. "Poor little fellow," He says in symbolic language…

ALL THE NAMES OF
GOD HAVE A MEANING!

…symbolic language, "There was no one to put a swaddling band on him. No one to wash him, clean him up. Just a new born baby; just rolling in his own blood. No one to cut the navel cord, he's alone. That was a Time of Love," He said.

He come and He bandage, bandaged us up; and after He had wash us with the Waters of Islam, He then bandaged us up. Then He says to us, "You shall be Mine!"

A mother coming from abroad. This is wonderful! The baby's here, but no one have thought enough of the baby to [The Audience applauds]; excuse me, to wash the baby up, put it on clean clothes, and send it out among the public.

My Brother and Sisters, Allah and myself is cleaning you up, and you have on, you have on beautiful garments. You not ashamed to go out in the public. The public stare at you, and they wonder, "Who have did this job for you." Tell them a man calls himself Elijah Muhammad. [The Audience applauds].

Both Holy Qur'an and Bible says, after this work He tells us, "Me," think over that, "Me and Me alone should you fear. I am your Lord. I have gotten you," think over that, "I have now taken you, and give to you My name; a name that the world must respect. It is My name. I will call you by that name, and the world will know that I have visit you." All Praise is due to Allah! [The Audience applauds].

Going round here calling yourself a angel, now of Heaven, calling yourself Mister Jones, Mister Culpepper, and Mister Jackson. Who is Jackson? Calling your beautiful self a fallen angel from Heaven by an enemy who pushed you out of Heaven, with his way of doing.

You don't have no name. All the names of God have a meaning to them, but your name don't have no meanings; the devil's names. But, he that have the name of Allah will live forever; well that name will live forever.

So, I'm going to bring you to a close of our evening work. And that, I hope you will do just what this old Christian song say; I use to sing it when I was a boy, "I hope I will join the centennial army band, rather, I hope I will join that band." Then he said, "Oh, look away to the Heaven. Good Lord, I hope I will join that band." So, this is the band! So you join on to it!

You look better in your own! Think over that. You sitting up here with us, you looks good! You look like people that is civilized. You look like people that seek something for yourself, something meaningful. You're a fine looking people. So, go along with us, and the world will admire you. I don't care where you go on this Earth today, and tell those people that I came from America, I follows Elijah Muhammad, they say, "come here." [The Audience applauds]. Any place that you go, you will be recognized and respected.

Some of them have went over and told stories that they was following me, and just to see what would happen. So the people took them in so fast, they got excited; they know they was telling other than the Truth. But, that made them return and join up with us.

We are in Russia; We are in China; We are everywhere. You can't go no place, without finding us. Just go and try it for yourself, and if you return, tell me that you didn't get respected by claiming me to be your Leader. I will pay all of your expenses, and I will go over there myself and ask them why? Naturally, they not going to pay to much attention to you if you go over there looking for whiskey and beer. Even if they drink it themselves, they know you shouldn't drink it.

So I thank you. I have been much inspired into the Spirit of Allah, just to come out here and look at you. Any man love his family, if he don't, he shouldn't have a family. [The Audience responds in approval]. All men that have families, they should love them. Do good to the wife that brings into the world increase of yourself. We can't do nothing but plant seeds, but we should watch the seed and help it to grow.

One thing we must remember again, that we're up from slavery with slave ideas towards self and towards our wives. Our wives is far more better than we think they are, if we show better by them. So, let us do that; let us show them good, that we're good men. And they won't want to go away from you. I don't see nothing out of your house, that you should go after, if you have a Black woman there, you have the best! [The Audience applauds]

So, I'm going to offer you this few minutes, if you desire to question me on something that is worthwhile. I'm going to give you a few minutes to do it, and if you have any questions that you would like to ask me, ask me. No one care to ask me a question? Yes Brother? Pardon me?

Brother: Question unheard

Messenger: We are being rebirth now. [The Audience applauds]. As, the Bible teaches you in Paul Epistles, that it is not known to us what we yet will be like. But, he says "We will be like Him." Why the Epistle read like that, because, the writer know or had learned that Allah was going to make a new people, and whatever He look like, we would look like. As He tell you in one of those Epistles that, "We will be changed at the twinkling of an eye."

And the Holy Qur'an also bear witness to that we will be changed. And He told me out of His own mouth, that He would change us up. The Holy Qur'an say that, "He will cause you to grow into a new growth." And, all of the Scientists agree with a change, that He will make of us. But, He don't have nothing to do but just to say "Be that," and you'll grow right into it [The Audience applauds].

As we know how the devil have made us ugly, disfigured and whatnot; we don't want to be like that always. So He told me out of His own mouth, that we will be a different people. So, I don't think you will have to ask me will He make us ugly. Well He just leave us alone, we already that! [The Audience applauds].

He said to me that He will make us the most beautifulest people ever lived. Yes, if He's going to make you the wisest, surely wisdom brings about people contacting you, and you are not going to be sitting before people ugly. You must look beautiful to compare with the beautiful wisdom that you have in your head.

So, I think if you just stick around here, follow with me, I think you'll have everything that you ever imagined that you wanted. Remember that everything that you ever imagined that you want will come to you, just stick around here with me. [The Audience applauds].

So, I'm going to dismiss you now. My Brother here, he have something to say to you, but I am bout through myself, and I'm going home, and, I may be back soon to see if you are following me; or believe in what I teach you; and if there is anything that you would like to say to me, ask me before I leave this stand, you're welcome to stand up and ask it.

Messenger: Yes sir Brother? I think Brother you better come up closer. My hearing is not as keen as it use to be when I was young like you, I could hear a long ways off.

Brother: Sir you said something about that you would have to have one of God's name. And I was, I think it was about three or maybe four or five years ago that, I noticed a lot of friends of mine started naming their children after, certain, Asian names you know. And I would like you to clear up whether that's no good, and that you had to get a name from God, is that?

Messenger: You and all your children can be named at once. And, that's what you can get; I can name you. He's not going to take the name away that I give, but I don't want to be so smart to take over the naming of the people. I do know His name, and that's the names that you have to be named in. But, I expect Him here pretty soon, and I don't want Him to come and find me taking over His Job. [The Audience applauds].

[A visiting Sister praised the Messenger for his work with Black people, and spoke for a few minutes thanking him].

Messenger: I think I better go see Haiti. I use to read about it. I read about how some of the citizens prayed that Allah could take away the slavery. He could take away everything of the Island, but please take away from them, this shadow of the white man. [The Audience applauds]. Well when I learn of people that hate the devil like me, I want to go there and let them know I'm their Brother.

[A visiting Sister was very excited to explain to the Messenger how God led her to the Temple; how she left Christianity, and that she wanted to follow "The Honorable Elijah Muhammad"].

Messenger: Dear Brothers and Sisters, we enjoy listening at you and others give Honor and Praises to Allah, His name, and for the work of His Messenger. I thank you, but at this time now, we're going to dismiss you; and we expect you back here every day that we are open with the Teachings of our God, and your God, and His Religion

So I have enjoyed myself here with you this afternoon. Praying always that you be beloved, and saved to see the Hereafter, when the devil has been destroyed and gone back to that which he was prophesied that he would go into: his well bought doom for mistreating the poor Blackman in America. I thank you.

And now, I will turn you back in the hands of our Assistant Minister. Brother Shah will take care of you from now on. And I hope that Allah will bless me to rejoin next Sunday to be here with you, as I don't want to be no other place, but right here looking at you. I get great joy out of this. I see my reward coming to me from our Lord, for bringing you here, through the attractions of His Word.

Thank you, as I say unto you, may the Peace and the Blessings of Allah go with each and every one of you to your homes. And, try and fill this place up as often as you can.

Salaam Alaikum.

PART FIVE:

THEOLOGY OF TIME

OCTOBER 01, 1972 – OCTOBER 29, 1972

OCTOBER 1, 1972 PART ONE / SIDE TWO

A Nation With A Clean Heart And Hands

As Salaam Alaikum, You may be seated.

I'm very sorry to be saying As Salaam Alaikum to you this late. I have lots of people, and I may meet some on the wayside, and they will detain me. So I'm very sorry; ask you to pardon me for being late. I can't make up for lost time. I heard that long ago, that you can't make up for lost time, but I can do as much as I can, in the time that I'm here. I will try to do as much as I can.

Oh, just look at the people. [The Audience applauds]. If you say that I'm not a big man, I say I'm not no little shot. [The Audience applauds and the Messenger laughs]. You know lots of people loves to meet a, a group like you. Lots of teachers out there want such group as you to talk with this afternoon. But, you stop by this number, and now I beat them to you. [The Messenger and the Audience laughs].

I don't want you to think that I have been playing around. Oh no, I been very busy! There were two people out in front of my house. I didn't get a chance to speak with them. They were from Egypt, and there was more that was driving around and trying to get a chance at me; probably to prevent me from getting here. So, I kept hiding from them. [The Audience applauds and the Messenger laughs].

I want you! [The Audience applauds]. You are my people, and I am your Teacher [The Audience responded with approval], and I have something to teach you that others don't have!

So I'm very sorry that I'm a little late, but maybe if I had not heard that I had so many good visitors here, I would not have come down. I would have stayed away until next Sunday. But, when the Brother kept reading off the type of people that I'm looking for, I say, Oh yes, let's go! [The Messenger laughs and the Audience applauds]

Doctors, Dentists, Psyc…Oh I, I don't know whether we need this fellow or not. Psychiatrist, we don't make them no patience like that here. Economics, we like you; and Accountant, we, kind of like you, if you keep account of yours first.[The Messenger and the Audience laughs]. Hospital Administrators, yes sir we like you, if you help us to buy this hospital. Bank Tellers, yes sir we love you, but put your money in first. [The Audience applauds].

Well, I just want to say to you that, I have the professional people that I have been looking for bout near, forty years. So, I am told now you are here.

Attorneys, Stock Brokers; well Attorneys, we like you whenever we get in trouble, but we don't want no Attorneys long as we stay of trouble. Stock Brokers, yes we like you too, but you put your money in first. [The Messenger laughs]. Real Estate, yeah we have a lot of Real Estate we are now after purchasing between two and three million dollars here on the Eastside of Cottage Grove.

That's the first step we are taking, and we have gotten some of it down and looking for the ground to be broken on this, two or three million dollar. But, we have further on down about ten million, and we expect to get it in shape pretty soon.

We are not promising you something. We do it whether you help us or not [The Audience responds in approval]. And we have these professional people with us this afternoon, and I want you to know, that I thank you for your presence. We need you; we been looking for you. So, we had to hustle up four, five million dollars worth of Church house, to get you to see us. But, we are here. We been looking for you a long time. If we had of had you years ago, we would of had this house here, maybe for the school children [The Messenger laughs]. We would of had built lots more.

I want to thank you professional people for paying us a visit this afternoon. Real Estate people, and Nurses, and Construction Engineers, we want you specially. This is what we want to do right away. The main thing about our construction of that which we are now clamoring for, to lay on the foundation of what we want. We cannot say all the time that we have the material. If you have the material, you will get a lots of work from this little boy and his followers, immediately .The only thing that happens with us: when they learn that you are going to help build what Elijah and his followers want to be build, they want to claim that they don't have the material. Wait, until, we get right in the midst of it, the building going up, and then he claim he don't have the material to let you have. This is to slow you down, and especially that fast race of Muhammad. They want to slow me down. And, I want to accelerate our speed. We're slow, and they want to slow us down.

You professional people, I would like for us to have a private meeting together, so that we can understand each other. I'm not slighting you, no sir! And if we could have a little small meeting together, we can better understand each other. When I explain to you, and if you are able to go ahead after that meeting, you will see yourself on our jobs all over the country. We're not trying to build here in Chicago alone. We have two and a half million dollars worth of building to do in Phoenix. It's already curved out, ready for you to come in. I love you, I love to give you work, if you can get around the other fellow and get the material.

See this is the thing, it's the material to build with. When he find out that you are trying to build for me, he wants the big job himself. He know we have a awful big job to last for a few years. And he don't want our contracts to go to you. And, I want you to get with me, and let's get behind the door and whisper to each other [The Audience applauds].

Construction Engineers….Carpenters, Contractors; we have your job, and plenty jobs for you to last you, not for a month or two, but for years. We going to build a country for ourselves, wherever the country. There is no one that will stop us, and can stop us, but God Alone.

Ahh, he haves a mighty big mouth don't he? Yeah, takes one for you. Union leaders, I want to say to you, we can't use union leaders that is mixed up with white unions, because they don't like us, therefore, I have to tell you outright, we don't need unions. We going to agree and do right by each other anyway. So, we don't need unions. Unions is good for people that won't keep their word. [The Audience applauds].

Mathematical Management, Scientist Designer, yes, we certainly need you. Yes sir we will talk with you! General Administrators, we need you. Politics and Public Affairs, well yes, we can use you to get out of that kind of world, but, we are not setting up no such on the scale that you have, and been well acquainted with. We know we have to enter politics somewhere, but we don't want the kind of politics that this man has set up for you. We don't want to follow, that way.

I am now getting for you, a tip-off of clean politics from the nations of Asia, and portions of Africa. And, this politics will make you a better man, for yourself. They don't have the robbery, deceiving politics that you are born under America way of politics. We don't want no thieves, in our nation. [The Audience responds in approval]. As it is written, the Jesus said, I say the same, "All before me" he say, " was thieves and robbers." Jesus could not have said that, because that would have meant all Prophets before him was thieves and robbers, but I can say, and absolutely prove!

We don't want to build a nation on no such base as who can rob the other one the quickest, and get the most. We want to build up a nation with a clean heart and hands to deal with their people, in a way of Justice and Righteous. We don't want no robbery. We can't use a robber after we has already been robbed to death by our enemy; the slave-masters children.

I can hurry and get over this by saying, everybody here I think, we can use. Brother say…Contractors, General Administrators, Mathematical Management, and Scientist; we can use these people. This is what we lack to move forward, ahead; it is the proper person. The Professor that we are looking for, they always has been running from us. So, if you are here this afternoon, we are ready to write you down on our book that you're one of ours. We cannot promise you a roll of money in both hands, until you make it. You got to help us to make that money [The Audience applauds]. We don't have it rolled up over here, waiting for you to come and use it. No, we want you to help get that money. I have good credit, throughout the world. I can borrow money at no limit of time. But, I want you to help me pay it back [The Audience applauds]. We want to build a world for the Blackman. The white world is moving off of the scene. You don't know it, come on and I will show it to you. You got to do something for yourself, or else. I'm not talking to hear my voice; I'm talking to hear your voice [The Audience responds in approval]. We got to do something for self. I have the key to that doing for self. If you will come and get yours, I have it.

At the present time, as you probably know, that Asia is for the first time uniting herself for Asia. Here we poor, forgotten people in America, singing "Oh glory to Allah, glory to the Lord, glory to Jesus," and doing nothing about making that glory. Make your glory for yourself. Stop laying around the other fellow's gate begging him to make you a glorious place.

I think that you know, that we that is called Muslim, and is Muslims; and you're one, but you don't know it. We're going ahead, trying to till the Earth. When I told you a few years ago that, that's where everything comes from, your food, your clothes, your shelter, all comes from that place, we call farm. We can't be too proud to be called Farmers. But I say today have arrived, that if you don't have a farm, you won't live off the other farmer. So you got to have a farm to eat. You got to have a farm, to wear good clothes. You got to have a farm, to live in a good home. So I say let's get ready, go to the farm.

We have entered into the farming area. We are trying now, to grow everything that means good for us. Come out and help us; we will hire you; we need your skill, don't give it back to those people, who taught you how to farm in their school, the Agriculture Schools of the enemy. You go and get the knowledge, but go for yourself after you get it.

We own a beeline in Alabama, in Tuskegee. By this time in another year, we hope to own it. [The Audience applauds]. Yes, we can buy it, if it will go on sale. And I think I'm sneaking around the right way now, knocking on the back door. You know, if you seen going in the front door, they talk too much; go to the back door.

So, we want Tuskegee [The Audience applauds]. I talk to one of the officials, I say, bout how much would the devil charge us to get in there? He say about ten million dollars. I say to him, I say, tell him to start writing it up.[The Audience applauds].

I want to say to you, without saying one false word, I have the world back of me [The Audience applauds]. They want me to chop up this country, for you and me. I'm not biting no lips nor tongue; they want this country for you, and they are offering me help. Sometime when you have fine property, and people keep on...

The Nations Of The Earth Will Recognize You

…and they are offering me help. Sometime when you have fine property, and people keep on after you to sale, and you don't sale, they start another way to get your property. So, I think we should meet with…and not with the other fellow.

What we look like here, millions of Black people in America, walking around begging? Begging for a good house to live in; Begging for a store; Begging, for a lil ol place to put up a supermarket. If you are super enough, there the market is already out there. [The Audience applauds].

Fine, educated people here; all types of educated people, and I'm running round here for years, looking for them. I thank Allah for this house [The Audience applauds]. That house has drawn for us today, this type of people. And that, as Allah lives, we going to put these professional people to work for self! [The Audience applauds]. Yeah, you work for yourself and us. We will be benefiting, if you step up in your office over here with the Crescent around the door some place [The Audience applauds].

Think about just a few of us here this afternoon, in a way about near a couple of thousand, about that. That's no people at all, when you got millions of us. We have millions of people in America, that want to see the nation of Blackman up doing something for himself; building his own jobs. We build them for ourselves, and we just a small group. We build our own jobs. We're not thinking about unemployment; we are thinking over employment.

I'm not trying to show off, but stick around where we are working and you will say "Yes, he's making jobs for himself and others." We don't have enough applying for jobs to our Employment Office that want to work.

Did we have some lazy people? [The Audience responds in approval]. You go give him a job, and he go lay down and go to sleep on you. I wish you Professors will join up with me, and help me to put this nation at work. We can make jobs on top of jobs! Where is the money coming from? From us! Where did the money come from that the white man build jobs for himself and us?

Oh, we should think! That we are the Original people of the Earth, and why cannot we do a better job than he? I don't want to eat up this mic [microphone], but I gets dizzy when I see you; I just get nervous, wanting to see us together to build up a nation. We been free for the last hundred years or more. What have we made for ourselves? Not nothing but trouble, trying to force the white man to build jobs for us.

We go to war with him if you don't make a job for me Mister white man. If he has freed you, you makes your own job. But, if you think you're not free, and you want to be a slave right on for him, then you go and tell him that I'm still your slave, make me a job. But, I don't believe in being a slave forever. Let me a loose! I'm going to run, get away from your slave house; see if I can't build one for myself.

You businessmen and great educators, I say all we need to do is get together and agree on what we shall do first, because, you know how to do these things. All we need to do is just get together, and know from each other, where we going to start from. I am ready, I have the door open, and I know you and I can agree, because you have similar ideas as I; and since we have the same ideas, we got to agree. Oh, you say, "This is a, a little fellow popping off round here, we want to go to Mister Ford; and we want to go over to General Motors. "Let us get started over there with them, and make them richer." My beloved Brothers, what is coming on now, is going to drive you to the bread wagon, if you don't get up and do something for yourself.

The uniting of Japan, China, and their other little allies; their uniting together to deal with self, not with white people. If white people want to come in, they must come in by what they offer them. This is something the East have not been doing. But, now they're ready to push the West out of the East, so that they can do business with each other; and they have plenty of that each other over there. Hundreds of millions of people. They are sick of the West; and they're going to push the West out, so that the East can be East. Believe it or not, this is directly as you call it, "from the horse's bridle." [The Audience applauds].

I can say with the Truth, I can get you today, anything out of the East you want. If you don't run around in front of me with your market bag, basket, trying to get it filled up. But you going to have a hard time trying to do foolish things these Days and Time. If you want to do business, get together and do business on a wholesale way, and not on no little piece retail way. I have the door open for you now. You can get anything you want for little of nothing. If you come to me, I will, I will get it for you. I'm always kissing this mic [microphone] here. [The Audience applauds].

Building us a hospital here on the Southside, that should be a must! Why you want to run to your enemy's hospitals, when you have good trained Nurses and Doctors? You have Doctors throughout the world will be willing to come here, take care of you, even at no pay, some of them. They love you just that much! Desire to see that you are cared for right. You have a lot of them working in other hospitals here, before your face and mine. They part of a little...what you don't find a foreign word, it's not a Doctor. They want to see you taken care of. I know all of this going on, and I have the key to it.

Now, I want us to get us a hospital with about five hundred beds, and put our

Black Doctors and Nurses in there, regardless to where they come from. They sitting around watching us, waiting for us to do something of the kind, so they can get in there, take care of you, and to keep you from turning to the hands of your enemy.

What do you look like out there fighting your enemy, and then asking him to heal you and nurse your wounds. [The Audience applauds]. If you and me are fighting, and you wound me, you could continue to wound me, if I fall in your arms to be healed.

You know, we a silly people over adversaries. I rather rear up a tent, and put some logs down there, put some mattress on top of them, and let my own Brother wash, clean, the wound, and pour in his medicine, than to ask the same man that I'm fighting, to do so.

Have you ever thought of this? You fighting the enemy and run to him to heal your wounds. This is really ignorant! Shall we not get together and build us up some kind of shelter, to heal our wounds? Certainly we shall do so!

I feel so cheap talking with the devil, and he have all the places to be cared for. The wounded, sick, lame, and everything would have to go to him; furnish us Doctors when we have a Black Doctor right behind him, will make us feel better that he's waiting on us. Black Nurse, we feel better; let her wait on, wait on us!

Do you not see how dumb we are? We're pretty ignorant in this big ol wide U.S.A. In every corner we look, or every square foot, we find the enemy against us. And yet, we won't build up a hospital, so that we can take care of our own selves.

Try and do these things, or wait around, it will be too late. And then you will cry, "Oh woe is me, that I let such opportunity that Elijah Muhammad was teaching me to take hold of, and I fooled around and didn't do nothing, but depend on the white man.

Build up something for ourselves, and then the nations of the Earth will recognize you, as they are, are recognized themselves for doing for self. No need to say you don't have a chance. Oh yes, we break the chain Brother, and come on out of it! We don't have nothing that's binding us, that we cannot destroy and free ourselves.

I want you to remember this, you a little too happy to do temporary things. We don't want no temporary here, we want permanent. The professional people that I see written down here, we can take these people, and build the finest Nation is on Earth. [The Audience responds in approval]. But, if we cleave our tongue to the roof of our mouth, and won't let it speak for self, and tie our hand behind us so the hand won't do for self, you can expect to suffer.

Now in the South, we do have there, farms that when we harvest them, we expect to eat; and you will eat too. So, since that you will eat too, help us to work that farm. [The Audience applauds].

We certainly need you that know something about airplanes. We got to have these planes that rolls on the air instead of the ground! We do have this in mind now, about getting some planes that will take us around. And we hope to find you ready, for that job of flying them.

Well yes, we have one poor pitiful plane, and we want it to get some mate for itself. And we want you to learn how to fly, if you don't know, learn. I have a grandson I'm trying my best to make him learn to be a Great Flyer. He's flying now, planes, but I want more of it. We want Flyers that will train to fly planes oversea, not just round here over the city. Get in it, and go over the world, like other nations. [The Audience applauds].

The worst thing that you can do, is to set up unions, labor unions, leaders among yourself, this brings the other fellow in. And he knows how to set the trigger for you to fall all the time! We have no right to have a union, if we going to deal with each other, on the base of Freedom, Justice, and Equality. [The Audience applauds]. So, I'm asking you here this afternoon, you Educators, you Teachers of Labor Science, Mechanical Science, and work; I have a lots of untrained people with me, that want to learn these jobs. If you will look down on poor little Brother, and say, "You was not as fortunate as I was, come on here in this old barn or anywhere here, let's us get together and fix-up something, and go for self."

I know it looks hard, Educators, professional people, for you to drop down among uneducated people, to try to build them up, but they are your Brother as well as mind. [The Audience applauds]. I'm making them to grow-up over here. I just need your help, your learning, then we'll have a Nation prepared and fit for the world of nation's recognition.

It's just you don't want to go into the job of associating with little poor Brother, because you have your degrees from high educated centers of this people; and you don't want to drop back, to make something for yourself. These people I have learned Professor, Educators, to be the most surest friend, if you will take a little time and train them. You really have yourself something, when you train one of these. But, if you look all the time for your equal or match, then you going to run into argument, disagreement, breaking up of unions, and whatnot. But if you make him for yourself, he's yours, and he loves you. You got something that you can depend on.

Will you agree with me, you professional people, who have your list here in our hands of what you can do? Will you agree with us, to have a special meeting to ourselves, and get down to what we must move off first? I know you not too good a Christian, nor a Muslim [The Audience applauds].

You know my father, he was a Baptist Preacher. I use to chase him after he preach, to question him on his sermon; so I'm still doing that.

Let us have a special meeting for special things. Not have a open meeting, saying what we going to do, and do nothing. Let's go get in a room, and sit down face to face and tell each other what we can do, and what we must do right away. This is the way you get business done!

You can't start business, hailing each other cross the street. We got to get in a room some place, and look each other in the eyes, and tell each other what each can do and what each can't do. And if we can't do the thing that we want done, we go out and look for that fellow.

Fine, highly educated people…work to do. Their work is getting off fast. The devil have unemployment in your office. He don't know what to do with his own unemployed professional people. This is why they are having so much trouble in the school. They want something to do when they get their diplomas, their degrees.

But, where you going to get that something to do, if you don't make it for yourself? You got to make it for yourself gentlemen. If you don't make it for yourself, who is going to make it for you?

Now, America is now faced with the worst problem she ever had, that is on for, from her armed force. When they come back home, what is she going to give them to do? This means a war then, at home. They going to start fighting for something, and America know that, that she's in trouble. Sending these unemployed soldiers back home to do nothing. She's in trouble; she don't know what to do with these people. You don't believe it, write to Washington, to the Labor Department there, they will tell you. We have people all over; we have some there. We got to work like this in order to keep pace with our enemies. So, if you will join up with Elijah Muhammad for a better tomorrow for self, come on over, my office is open. And since that you got the most schooling of the enemy educational system, I say, come and I'll show you how to use it, if you don't know. [The Audience applauds].

The only thing that we want, is togetherness and agree on what we do, and we don't stop until we do it. If I can get this far, think over that. If I can get this far with a four million dollar building standing on its floor and roof over my head for my few little followers; if I can stand here and tell you that we have several thousand acres under cultivation for bread and for meat for us; if this little fellow can do that with your big…we can do much more. [The Audience applauds].

Why should we continue to dislike each other, when we are Brothers, while the white man likes American white man; he likes a European white man; he likes Australian white man; he likes white people all over the Earth. Well, why should not we like Black people all over the Earth? [The Audience applauds].

We are hard to agree with self, for thinking over the heartless, merciless, blue-eyed devils. We want to please them first, then if you have any pleasing left, you'll take it over for self. "But, I first must please my white enemies." This is the way you work. I say friends, we are Muslims; We are not scared of the devil, nor are we scared of his Hell! [The Audience applauds]. I will take the blame, you don't have to take it. Come on and follow me, and I will take the blame.

What can you do with the help of my God and others? I can do plenty, and is doing plenty. You are so afraid, that you're going to go hungry, or you're going to lose the prestige among white people. You will never get no place like this!

Look at that small Japanese people now, very small people, but nevertheless, they got sense enough now to unite again, with his own. He yell over there before the last war, "Asia for Asiatic, Asiatic is for Asia." Until they give them a deaf hear; and then the enemy, all but run them out of Asia. Now he sing that song; he got plenty, ready now, to unite with him and say "Asia is for Asia." He laid hold on his big brother the other day, China; China laid hold to his little brother, Japan.

Now here we are a little people here, numbering somewhat around thirty million, and see that we're destroyed by self. Let us unite. If you see a root cracking the Earth in your midst, that look like you, it will bear fruit. Why don't you come on and let's cultivate that lil ol root there, and make him to bear us fruit? [The Audience applauds].

It's a shame for me to stand here before you professional people, and talk of getting together and building a up-from-slavery people, united into a Nation of progress, and success for self. You should be standing up here where I am [The Audience responds in approval], telling us what to do. But you got a little, little uneducated man that God looked at him. [The Audience applauds]. These are the words that He said to me, He say, "Will you come and help Me to put our people on top of civilization? I say yes Sir, if you back me up, and Guide me, yes Sir! [The Audience applauds].

So as it's written, the sound, the Bible say went throughout the Earth. Great people rose up; God pointed the Messenger out to them, He say, "See they all come to thee. They all bowed down to thee." That's in your Bible, and this is True. This is one reason why I'm late today. I have people over there (I brought the Nurse along, she can bear me witness) out there in the streets, waiting to get a chance to talk to this little boy. Highly learned Scientist, heard of me. They coming up every day or two, wanting to see the little man, that you call Elijah Muhammad [The Audience applauds].

Africa is mine [The Audience applauds]. This is no fun, jokes, it's mine. They open their door for me anywhere over there, to build Africa. "If I had sent thee to a strange nation, foreign language, they would have heard," this is Bible. "But, I sent you to the rebellious house of Israel." The rebellious house of the Blackman in America, that's who He's talking about; not Israel, but it's you. They would have heard you, and that's easy to prove today. From Texas, the shore of Texas, down through the little Islands falling round at your feet; around to the Cape of Good Hope, you have Brothers. They're just like that, just so happy to fall in the Circle with Muhammad.

I say my friends, in my conclusion, let us get over here in a room, some places, houses got a lots of them. Let us sit down, and talk and agree on how to build up the Blackman in America. We can't build him up by letting him carry his bottle of hard corn and rye whiskey. He'll never be anything carrying that kind of fire water. We get together and stop him from drinking [The Audience applauds].When he get over here, under the Crescent, he's willing to stop. He feel, feel too dignified to make a fool out of himself, but under the cross, he don't care.

So, I would advise you after meeting with you here today, my fine beloved Brothers out the educational centers of America, let us get together and make our people a number one people, that the whole world will respect. Let us take our woman out of the world; put her in her own world, and love and make something out of her! We can do it, as you see a sketch of the work that I'm doing, and they're falling for it. They're not turning it down, they're accepting it. Come on over you Brother and Sisters, and help me to make a Nation that is unsurpassed by any nation on the Earth. That's what we have to do now, since that the enemy of ours, made us unwanted, unrecognized, by all societies of the Earth's people. We got to regain our place in Society, and you're capable of doing it. If I can give you a sample, how come you now can't make the goods?

If I, so little...man among you, have now taken some of the worst ever lived, and got over here to the machine, and I'm making them better dresses, and they like them, why cannot you help me do this? You know how; don't think that the enemy now, will not recognize you, he will respect you, if he respects me [The Audience applauds]. What God has Taught me, you and I can force them to respect us, because, we have better knowledge of cleanliness; better knowledge of what we need in the field of Mathematics; better knowledge in such things as defense; you are the best in all of that. Let us get together Brother, and let the world know that we are capable of demanding respect. We won't wait for you to respect us on your initial steps, we'll do that ourselves; we will force you to do that.

Now my beloved Brothers and Sisters, I know you about tired of me. [The Audience applauds]. I came in a little late. But, this Time that we're living in, is both love and hate. Love is growing among us, wherein, that it never was before. And hate, is growing in among us, where it was never before. We just learned the source of our trouble; that is loving an enemy, who was born, made, to be an enemy for us. We love him, and calling our self following after Jesus Christ and whatnot. Jesus hate the devil himself [The Audience responds in approval], and he wrote it that if...

TODAY IS THE RESURRECTION OF THE DEAD

...and he wrote it that if you love the devil, you will not see Heaven in these words, "He that love this world," think over that, "he's an enemy to God" [The Audience responds in approval], and that's right!

I can talk to you long, long time, because I have so many different conversations stored up for you. I think professional people, that you should join up with the Muslims [The Audience applauds], not wait for the Muslims to join up with you. No, we can't join with you, we will go right back in slavery. But if you feel like that you want to lead and preach to your people, come over here and I will teach you how. We'll get you a house full over night. You let me teach you how to preach and what to preach. I will assure you, you will have a house full over night, because you don't have so many at your churches; we pass by them daily. But if you come and accept your own, which is Islam, and go back to your church and start preaching it, you'll fill your church up. The people is waiting for something now. They don't want that slavery stuff, telling them that they got to die to go to Heaven. They want some of this Heaven they see; not the Heaven that they are not sure of. If he dies, he can't come back and tell you whether you told him a lie or the Truth.

So, I say Brothers, let us get together on what we can see, and not what we're promised that we will see after we are dead. There is no man, never lived and died, that came back. When he's dead, for sure you can call him all you want to; go lie down in the grave with him, he don't answer. [The Audience applauds].

One or two words can stop that kind of teaching. Brother, show me one that was once dead, went back to the Earth, and he is now living. Show him to me. Jesus rose from the dead; tell him to show him to you. [The Audience applauds].

What was meant when the Scholars and Scientist said Jesus rose from the dead? It means a man with ideas, and the teaching that Jesus wanted to give us, but he was before Time, and he died. [The Messenger laughs].

So, we want to say to you, that there is no such thing; nobody have been put down, and returned to that which we taken him from. We come out of the Earth, now we return him to the Earth. No one have ever seen one come out of the grave. You can say you dreamed something like that, but dreams is not always true.

If Jesus came back, none of us have met him yet. [The Audience responds in approval]. And all the Prophets of Old, they all died. And the Creator of this Heaven and Earth that we live in, He died [The Audience responds in approval]. We don't meet with them. We have not met him, no sir.

I want to teach you these things, that you have misunderstood. There's no such things as a human, or no flesh or no life; let it be whatever life it may be, after it die, it don't come back…So, the white man taught you this, but you didn't never know what he meant by this. He means, it meant this, "That you are dead nigger now, but you can live again, because you are God's people; and He's coming after you one day, and take you away from me. And then you will come alive in the knowledge of what I have done in keeping you like you are." [The Audience applauds].

Now today is the Resurrection of the Dead. The Resurrection of the slave mental dead. You are the mental dead, not physical dead, mental dead. "Bless is he," the Bible say, "that died in the name of the Lord." You and I died in the name of the Lord…says the spirit shall live again, because he's already from God, and he just died in the knowledge of his God. So he's going to be awaken one day, and he will live again [The Audience applauds]. But says the Scripture in another place, according to His Own Apostle, "He is My first born, the first to rise from the dead. I called him and he answered Me. Now I'm going to give him the key, so that he may others, bring them to life."

My beloved Brothers and Sisters, I say at this time that we have had a nice time [The Audience responds in approval], a good sensible union time. We're uniting with each other, as we understand, we unite.

I'm put here by God Himself [The Audience applauds]. There's no class of Scholars and Scientist, that they could say that they had anything to do with my mission. And yet, I work, and as the Book say concerning God, "Who shall hinder Him." I do my work that is assigned upon me to do for you. And there is no scholar or scientist of this devil, can stop me or any other Muslim. [The Audience applauds].

It is the very first time since we have risen from servitude slavery, that you had a man that was not educated in the schools of the slave-master. But stand before you, with more Power than any professor of the land. [The Audience applauds].

There is nothing that you want to do in the way of self, and building a nation like all other nations have built for themselves, that we cannot do today; if you will just accept my advice [The Audience responds in approval]. You have the education, and I will show you how to rule, take over the world!

Ask some of the scientist about Elijah Muhammad. Ask them, "Do you think he is on the way to build up a Nation of his people?" They will say, Yes! Any Scientist of the

Blackman, yellow man, if you go ask them these words, he will tell you "Yes, I heard of him." Just as your Bible teach you in a kind of a symbolic language, he said, "A sound went throughout the Earth." Meaning that the news of this man's work, his teachings, have now been heard around the Earth…

You certainly don't have a frightful rabbit man, that will run every time he hear a hound bark. [The Audience applauds]. I will teach you how to chase the hound, and let the rabbit bite him, instead of him biting the rabbit, make the rabbit bite the hound.

I have enjoyed myself. [The Audience applauds]. I don't believe I have ever enjoyed talking with the people in such short of time, and being late at that. I'll be your defender, if the chief say that you are late, tell him to see me. [The Audience applauds].

I have just the type of professional people here on this paper, that I'm looking for. Don't be surprised if you don't receive a letter from me. I would like to write you, you write me. My address is 4847 Woodlawn, 4847 South Woodlawn. My telephone number is also very easy to remember [The Audience laughs], Drexel 30324. Just start counting, you got my telephone number. Call me or write me. If you call for good, you will receive good. If you write for good, you will receive good writing; 4847 South Woodlawn, Elijah Muhammad.

I'm known all over the Earth, and why…[The Audience applauds]. One Brother was in Russia, and he was talking with some Muslims there, and they remind him of some Muslims being here. He say, "Oh you talking bout Elijah Muhammad," "Yes, is that his name, Yes! Yes!" He say he "didn't never meet with such clamoring people for Muhammad." He say he "wanted to learn for Muhammad." He say he "wanted to learn how could they get in touch with me." Yeah we have a lots of Muslims in Russia, and we have lots in China. Come on if you would like to be known. Come follow me, and the world will know you. [The Audience applauds].

As you are professional people, and likes to do your job as professional people, please contact me by mail, or call me over your phone, I will answer you. Let us get together and build something out of the American slave people, that the world will be happy to meet them, as they are us. Come on all of you men and women that have professional diplomas, professional degrees.

Let's get together and make glad our people; as they will tip their hat, scrape their feet to you, to build them up. I have untold amount of material to give you to build them up. Come on, let us unite together, and make a Nation out of ourselves, that the world will respect.

As I say to you, I think it's time for us to go home, and see what mama have on the stove. If she don't have nothing on there, that is ready to be dined on, then dad didn't bring her nothing. [The Messenger laughs and the Audience applauds].

I'm sorry if the Deputy Sheriff back there wants to hurry and handcuff me, so I can go home, so they can go home. So, I'm going to let them go home, and let us meet again here soon. Anytime you want me, that's all I do, look around for someone to teach. So, you call me anytime you want to, and I will be ready to answer your call.

So, I thank you for your patience and endurance here with me this afternoon. [The Audience applauds]. Thank you! What a beautiful people! What a beautiful sight! You standing applauding me, and I [The Audience continues to applaud] want to applaud you for coming out to listen to me. Oh what a beautiful people! Please, let us unite and let the world know that we have sense enough to recognize and respect each other. That's what they charges us with, not having respect for self and others. I really thank you. Oh, pardon me Brothers and Sisters, my son just told me that there is one or two Press people here, would like to ask me a question or say something to me, to let us get together. So, if you are here; Yes sir, come right over Brother.

[The Brother's question or comment was unheard]. [The Audience applauds].

Messenger: Come right over.

Sister: Mister Muhammad thank you very much for inviting me here. I feel very honored to stand before you. I wonder if you can tell me about progress, on hospital and on the land you're buying on Cottage Grove.

Messenger: We're trying with all our might to get these two institutions going, as soon as we can get enough money to lay the foundation. We're doing that daily, and if you're good at work with a good...we would love to have you among us to help us get better people [The Audience applauds].

Messenger: Anyone else?

[One of the Brothers asked a question on behalf of a visiting Sister. She wanted to know if she could have the Messenger's voice taped for the Black community to put on the air at home, just a short message from the Messenger]. [The Audience applauds as the Brother is talking to the Messenger].

Messenger: Pardon me? Want to tape this from me? Of today's meeting? [The Audience applauds]. My dear beloved Brothers and Sisters, you will work one man to death if you do that. See, if we make a tape for you, someone else will want one, you see. So, you'll work him to death like that, so get one from them. I thank you.

THE WISDOM OF ALLAH (GOD)

It wasn't me now, you know I can't walk out here, and you know I don't drive, but I'm very late. So don't blame me for being late, blame the laborers. I was sitting there waiting, and the Captain sitting right down under me and I didn't know it [The Messenger and the Audience laughs]; that's terrible.

In the Name of Allah the Most Merciful, all Holy Praise is due Thee Dear Allah, the Lord, of the Worlds.

I'm very happy, my Brothers and Sisters to see you sitting here like vessels around a fountain that is empty and need to be filled. Well, I have the water, all I been looking for is vessels to pour it in [The Messenger laughs]. I don't know exactly what to start on first. You will say, "Start on the world, start on Allah." That's the first thing to start on is right. So I shouldn't say I never know what to start on, because, at this time; I didn't mean to say at this time I am coughing [The Messenger was coughing].

At this Time we are living, it is the Time of the removal of the old world and bring in a New World. This is why you are sitting in the Temple of Islam, and not in a church. Though the building was built for a church, but since a different believing people has moved in it, we cannot no more give it the name of the Christian's houses, houses of worship; they call them church.

Sometime I be talking with some of them, and they refers to our Temples as a church. They so use to calling some spiritual meetings, and meeting houses the church. But this is not no more a church, this is a Temple of Islam. You say "What is Islam?" Islam is the Religion of God. If we want to say it in that plain way so you can understand it.

But Islam is the Nature of God. Islam, is the First and the Last Religion of man, if there ever be a last. We're not looking for it to become a change Religion. It can't change unless we change God, and that will never happen.

So, therefore we have a Eternal Religion. A Religion that will never leave us, unless we destroy ourselves. This is why the Moon was up there, that you see, and the devil has been to it, to be sure it's real.

It was a Wise Muslim God, that wanted to make and change all the people into one in everything, even into the language that they speak, dialect. He didn't want no dialect. He wanted everybody to speak the same, so Allah Taught me; and Who is better known than He. So He said that once upon a Time, that there lived a God on this Planet, that He wanted all the people regardless to what side of the Planet they lived in, on; He wanted them to speak the same dialect, and He couldn't do that.

As we understand today actually, the change of atmosphere in certain parts of the Earth, the people there just cannot speak the same language, of those where we came from. It's due to the changing of the atmosphere temperature, and the ever moving about of the people from each other, that they acquires a different dialect, in their talk or languages.

So, we cannot never make a different…or, nor can we ever make the people to speak the same language. Look in the South, how you use to speak there. When you get up here in the North for awhile, your dialect begin to change. Well, that is something in the change of the atmosphere you move into; it's not the same, since our lives depend upon the "life breath" or breathing, we're taking in and out. There is nothing that can possibly make a change, but in the atmosphere that we breath.

So, this Man, before We had deportation from Moon, He wanted everybody to speak the same dialect. So he got angry, because that He couldn't make them do it. So Allah Taught me in the Person of Master W. F. Muhammad, that this Man said "Well I will destroy Us All!"

That show you how Powerful He was. He know that He is God in having Power over the Earth, and the Heavens above the Earth. He want them to obey Him, and the people that is on it; so, He set out to do so.

So, He start drilling in Our planet, so Allah Taught me, in the Person of Master Fard Muhammad, to Whom Praises is due forever. He begin drilling in the planet, and He drill like a Man drilling for coal. He gotten somewhat near halfway the planet. Then, He begin to pack it full of power explosion dynamite.

He said the dynamite was more power explosive dynamite, than we are using now. As the people He say, uses about seventy percent dynamite. But, they use a hundred percent in splitting the Earth into, and building mountains on top of the Earth.

Once upon a Time, He says, We didn't have no mountains, the Earth was smooth and round. So, they didn't think that, that was so good nor educational. So, they went over the planet with five explosive dynamite, and dropped it here and there, on the Earth there. And, when they wanted to bring up a tall mountain, they would put a motor to or the bomb to a motor. And that motor that would go down into the Earth, carry itself.

So, they put this to this…bomb, a little motor, that when it strikes the Earth, it goes on automatically when it hits the Earth and takes this missile all the way down to the power, that they made the motor or rather bomb. And that power may be a mile, and it may be near six miles, but she will go down splitting all hard surface like rocks, whole.

The drill was made not to give way; batter. We call it in common words, go right on through anything that it strike. It went kind of like, He told me, Taught me rather, like a drill, air drill that we use out here on the streets to crack up concrete. He say that's the way the drill worked on this bomb, and it would not stop until it got to the depth of its time that they brought up.

So, He say that depend on how tall they want the mountain. Everest, over in India, was the tallest mountain, He say, excuse me, that they brought up, somewhat near six miles.

So, they put these mountains on the Earth so the Holy Qur'an teaches you, and the Bible, that God places mountains on the Earth, then He told me Who the Gods was, and we seen the mountains. And then He wanted me to be sure that I understood and would believe.

He say, "Now Brother if you take a little fire cracker, and build a mound with dirt over it, and leave the fuse out, and let go, you'll throw up another little mound of dirt with that cracker." He say, "This is the way they put the mountains on the Earth. They put bombs with motors on them, and they drop them at such height that they wanted this mountain to be. If it was a mile high, they drop the bomb timed by the motor it was attached to, to go into the Earth, for one mile before it would explode."

So now, He described these bombs. He say they had a hundred percent, I think I told you, of dynamite. White American scientist use seventy percent dynamite. He say, "These explosions of a hundred percent dynamite, will be put in the bombs they use here, but they are not to bring up a mountain over one mile high. That's the kind of mountains will follow the wake of their bombing of America; go up one mile.

Some will be destroyed, probably that's already here, but these are going to be new mountains. And it will kill the civilizations for fifty square miles around. So Brother don't be in the way of that bomb [The Audience laughs].

A bomb hit the Earth and go into the Earth a mile, then when it explode, it send up a mountain a mile high, then killing the civilization around it. We saw the crater that it

made for fifty square miles. Not such runner that you could run out the way, to fly out of the way if a bomb can bring up from the depth of one mile. You must remember that you don't only get out of the way down here, the explosion will spread out in the atmosphere, and if you a mile or two up there, you subject to be destroyed.

So, I say to you as the Bible and Holy Qur'an teaches you, He's all Wise, referring to the God; He's the Best Knower, and He don't have to build up nothing to bring about His Will. He just Will that these things take place, and there it is.

But, they have prepared these bombs. They are real…to let you know that sixty-six trillion years ago, that they did make mountains. They did part the Earth, so that you won't have no such thought that God cannot do this, and He cannot do that.

You must know today. I will show you a little proof. Okay, He Came and Taught us what the Moon was, and how it came about. Then He let the devil go up there and test it, to see if the matter of the Moon correspond with the matter of the Earth. And the devil found it to be true, because he brought back rocks from the Moon, that he tested with the rocks of the Earth. The only difference is, that these rocks are nursed with water, but those rocks on the Moon don't have any water now, but they used to have the same.

He only want to prove to us and the enemy that He Created Heaven…and He knows what's…Then, the Holy Qur'an say, "When He gets ready to destroy a people, He open the doors of Heaven and let them see that you fixing to get away from here now buddy. [The Audience applauds]. Think over, the enemy that we are referring to the devil, he was made to try to prove God a liar. Yes that's what he was made for Brothers! Everything God will say, "this that," he will say, "that is it," he tries to change it. Everything that God Makes, he tries to remake it.

So, if you worship what he make, and not what God Make, he's no fool. Don't worry bout it, that you can go round just because you are directly from the Creator, you can call him a fool in wisdom. He's no fool in wisdom, but he's no equal with the God, the Creator, but nevertheless, he's not a fool.

He builds what we see from what we already had here. This is why We say, that he can't say that he made this, because all the material that he had used, We had already Made [The Audience responds in approval], so he can't claim the Creator.

Creator means One Who Creates a thing, not one who borrows the essence to build something out of; that the essence was made by someone else. You got to create your own essence, and that's what God did, He Created this out of Nothing. The whole atmosphere was void of any matter until He Made matter. Think over these things! I'm teaching alright enough, but it may not be what you want. [The Audience applauds]. Just think over when the Bible reads, And the Lamb made thus and thus, and the Lord Created thus and thus; and the Lord said to thus and thus, He did thus and thus, you're not talking bout the devil, you're talking bout the God of the Blackman; how powerful you are, and didn't know it. And that He says here in the Bible, "If you had the faith of one fourth of a mustard seed, you could say to the sycamore tree, "Be thou cut up and cast in the sea," it will be done. Think over that. [The Audience responds in approval].

Brother, these are wonderful things! And yet, you are too proud, and you can't make a flea; and if you make a flea, he wouldn't bite because you...[The Audience applauds]. Well, it's just the Truth! This is why We are teaching you these things. We want you to know God; teach what God does. God means something of Power, Wisdom, Knowledge, Understanding. That's the God Superior to others of the Creation. It's so (excuse me, excuse me) into the visibilities of the things we look upon, that He have the Power to Make that thing do what He wanted to do, because the Father is Our Own kind.

This is what He wants to Make out of you and me, not just believers, but gods. Everyone of you, according to what He has Taught me, will be gods. [The Audience applauds]. I call myself one day, I say I should have known...from our Lord. So, I say I think I'll try some of it for myself, and I did. I just said I hope this will be thus and thus, and I just went on and forgot about it. When I knew anything, it was just like that. [The Audience applauds]. And there is no doubt it is a True thing we are gods, but we lost our power; and now it's like the parable that the Jesus made, salt is good, so long as it got savoring power, but when it don't have no savoring power, it's no good. It's good for nothing but to be thrown down and people trampled it under the feet.

This he was referring to us. We had power; We have power, if we are restored to what we originally were. But, we have been robbed of power through the robbing us of the knowledge of self.

Wonderful thing! Just think about it, that you bowing to the creature (excuse me, excuse me, pardon me), bowing to the creature, instead of to the Creator. You are for, you are from the Creator, of the Creator; but, you are also the Brother of the Creator. You should be able to create too.

To talk with you some of the Wisdom of Allah, Who have Taught me that He would like to restore you. Your reading the Bible, it say He want to restore you. You have lost everything of self. Now He wants to restore you back to self. When that you can do after He restore you, like He's doing, if we will believe and follow Him. He didn't Come here just to show us Who He was. He Come here to show us Who He was, Who He Is; and then Make us Rulers. To make us Rulers over rulers. You have to have Superior Wisdom, Knowledge, and Understanding.

I'm very happy to read, to read here where we have in our midst, Mister Charles Reynolds. I guess that's the proper way, Architect. Well, it taken a Architect to design the Universe. After Our First Father Formed and Designed Himself. Think over a Man being able to Design His Own Form, and He never saw another man before He saw Himself; Powerful! [The Audience applauds].

So, Mister Charles…I guess that's the way, Architect…because we're not only out to build some Temples, we're out to build some towns and cities [The Audience responds in approval], of our own design. Not out of design of Satan, who stole his design from Us. But, we want to create a New Earth, a new us; and there a New World, unalike Mister Yakub's devil. We want to make a New World. You go by 4847 Woodlawn, you'll see some houses going up there, and the design you never saw it before. [The Audience applauds].

So, we're going to come down on the Eastside of Cottage Grove, as far as we can. Some of the people backing out from selling to us now. You know they done…because they would not like to sell, but they want to rob you, when they learn that you means to be successful, to want to add.

One Brother we decided on to be our real estate agent, and also salesman, he boast to some people we had already been to, and he brought me back the price yesterday, of the building that we wanted in that area. And they were, some of them had almost tripled. I don't think it was the seller, it was this Brother who thought we really wanted it, and he got in with the seller and told him he could get him more; and that more was for himself.

We have some terrible people. [The Audience applauds]. That's why we can't get over with our work fast than we are doing. It's due to the fact that, them that we think is Brothers, is enemies among us, trying to rob us! [The Audience applauds].He'll come over to rob his own Brother. He don't care if we never have a world, just as long as he can get out of this world, all he can. But, I know all of these things. I don't say I have the power to say be and there it is, but I have the power from my God to make it hard for you. [The Audience applauds]. You trying to make it hard for me, I can make it pretty hard for you.

The man that is speaking, that you see standing here, actually look so common, maybe foolish to you, he have power with God alright, and when a man have power with God, well, he have power with a Mighty Good Man! [The Audience applauds].

I don't have time to preach those shouting sermons, but teaching you, you need teaching. You don't need no jumping and hollering sermons. Oh, I could do it if I wanted to, but I don't want to do that. You had too much of that; and now filled with No Knowledge. [The Audience responds in approval]. I want to teach you, that's what I want to do.

We are telling the world, that we want this and we want that; and we're asking you to help us get this and that. We want airports; We want airplanes to go in and out of airports. In your mind you just sit and wait for us to do it, but not helping us to do it. We want you to help us to do these things. [The Audience applauds]. Not just come and look, wait for us to do these things. You help us to do it.

I've heard much of that kind of talk, "They'll wait and let the Muslims do it." Help the Muslims to do it [The Audience applauds], as you are Muslim yourself, whether you believe in yourself or not, but you were born a Muslim; you were not made a Muslim, you were created a Muslim from the start.

God Himself is a Muslim, and all His people is a Muslim. So don't deny yourself and let the devil laugh at you...as he's saying now "he wish he was a nigger." [The Audience applauds].

You want to show how less we care about being anything, just watch us go where it's being preached that we are something, and we'll see the less group, a lot of times there when you should not have been able to get on this ground. For a man to stand on this platform, teach to you the depths of wisdom of God Himself, and the building of creation, and how now He's about to destroy that which He made, not what He created, but what He made. He made it from Us, and We were already Created, just taken and use human beings like you use cattle for change, or breed; they are created from some other cattle. Okay, well you take him over here, and breed him with this one. So, this is the way people have been made into other people, since the coming of Yakub. We never did have but one Nation, one race. We didn't have a race, We had a Nation. Race come from the making of something from another.

So, we are learning all of this wisdom today. He still walks the earth...And that, when we see a fool, we don't call him a fool. We know how he became a fool; it's not his fault.

So, my friends, I'm very happy at all times, to go in great depths of the Wisdom of God, if you have the patience to wait and listen at it. It's here, all you have to do, come get it! [The Audience applauds].

There is so much that we need to know. We get impatient before ever that we learn, what we should. We're just too impatient. Well, you are like your enemy; the devil was created in haste, because the Time was urgent on him. If He didn't hurry, the Other incoming God, would be here before He could get started. So, He went in haste to build a world, and He didn't lose No Time. God Himself told me that He didn't. He say, "Brother, this devil have not lost any Time." He said, "He made good of the Time that was given to him, and look what he has made." He said, "He have made himself powerful, and a beautiful kingdom; a heaven for himself." And that's why, look what we're doing here, buying some of his work, and worshipping him. Now, we got to build us something [The Audience responds in approval], so ourselves and other can worship.

Architects was always in demand, in a country where there is always progress. It's been made in that way. You cannot build up town or city unless you have architects. You got to have architects here. So, we have them, and their good, but they're...by the enemy. The enemy owns all the material that the architect will design out for you. Now, for to build, engineers have to come and get the material to build what the architect have drawn out for you.

Well, we would have to buy it from the enemy. And if the enemy gets angry with you, he'll stop selling it to you. He was already angry with you, he just only want you to go so far when you're going to try to equal him, or overcome him. Then he goes to work and get angry with you; he don't want you to do that.

Yes sir! All Praises are due to Allah.

W e want to do, in words, what he has done; that is build towns and cities of our liking over the country, the land. We don't want his, we have lived in his. We have watched him build it; and we have acquired a better knowledge. We now, we can do a better job. This is what is hurting him, to see the slave rise from under his feet, and erect buildings; and...to work for himself, this hurts him. Well we watch you build and we see how you build this, and we can improve on it; that's what we are doing.

...I was just getting started, I was late [The Audience applauds]. Is Mister...in our midst? Stand up [The Audience applauds], come on out here Brother so...

ELIJAH: THE SECOND SELF OF GOD ALMIGHTY

...argument that I was born in it, but there can be no argument. I don't want to argue with my people, because I already know ...trying to get more of our former condition to be made in a better condition for establishing a better world suiting Our Own Nature, in which We were Created.

I would like that you get away from boasting on the white man and his world. [The Audience applauds]. As often as you seeing and hearing that white people out there killing your people, day and night, you should not want...to do any; but you want to give them credit some of you, when the man don't due any credit, but the credit of a very good, good Murderer of Black People.

These two boys that he went over and shot, while they lie there and sleep, remind me of hunting in the South. In the South I use to see my rabbit dog find a rabbit lying in his bed look like sleep, and he would not jump on him like that. He'd wake him up first, then take out and...out running. Well, that's the nature of the dog, he don't seem to think he's done nothing by grabbing a rabbit sleep. He'll make noise and wake him up, and give him a chance for his life. So this shows that your blue-eyed white devil don't have any nature of good in them; no mercy in his heart. Find you sleep, and found you just right for him to kill you. He'll sit round your house, with a hundred Murderers, with all types of deadly weapons their armed with. They know you the only one in there, but by nature he's afraid of the Blackman. He's afraid that he may miss, and will kill him. So, if you get one of them, the other one should get him. So he brings a whole army, like they did here in the city of Chicago. Find out that you a brave man over in your home, he'll get the whole police department to go and surround that area; or, if they don't look so well, they call for the national guards to come out.

You see all of this going on Brother and Sister in your midst and you over look, and then turn right around and try and defend that same Murderer! [The Audience responds in approval]. I think sometime you do it just for the sake of argument. And, second I think you do it just because you love the white man and his world. [The Audience applauds].

Our God, Master Fard Muhammad, Whom we learned that name from Himself, as the Bible teaches you that He had a name which no one knew but He Himself. Mahdi is His real name, so He Taught me. Mahdi means One that is Self Taught. In Arab language, is

One that is Self Controlled, and Controls others; Guide for others, because He's Self Guided.

My beloved Brothers and Sisters, I have learned enough from God, in which you don't hardly know. And that, to stand here and talk with you, which I love to do tomorrow this time, if you like to do. I would keep you fully awake if you stayed here. [The Audience applauds].

There's a very little of God's Creation, that He have not Taught me something about, because He put me as His Second Self; this what I am, I am the Second Self of God Almighty. [The Audience applauds]. What you hear the Muslims say in their prayers for the Messenger, that He grant him that which He promised him, this is a little higher than…I don't want to go into that, because He have told me something of that, and He told me to wait, and if you not taking this…so well, how can you take prayer?

So, I thank you my beloved. Is there anyone would like to join up with your God, and with your people? You come and give the name to the Secretary, and he will write you down, with just that…We are that people; We are that people directly from God. We are the people that got His Message. I have His Message. I got the prophesy that the Prophet didn't get, and that the Prophet didn't understand.

From Moses until Mohammad, there is No Prophet, including Jesus, that understood the things that is coming up out of…They told you, they have told you in black and white. Moses told you in black and white; Jesus told you in black and white, and told you to wait for that one that God would send from Himself.

Well, I'm the First one since the Creation, that the Wise God of Creation have…[The Audience applauds]. Some of you, knowing my humble origin here among you, can't believe these things, though it's written, but I tell you, and the Time will come when you will believe; you can't get away with this foul stuff, saying I won't believe in that, and it being the Truth.

The God of Truth Dwells among us in Person. You won't get away with today. Say you don't believe you want one, but He's not to be overcome; nor that which He has put out to be overcome, His Messenger; you can't overcome me; Nope. You can't do it! You can't hang me on the tree like you did the Jesus. [The Audience applauds]. You can't destroy me; right here behind me; nor can you destroy me on the side of me; nor can you go in front of me and destroy me. I'm not making no boast, but God fixed this up. The Bible say, "Twelve Angels protected him." We know it wasn't Jesus, because Jesus was destroyed at the hand of Murderers, but the Last one, you can't do that.

The Holy Qur'an here teaches you that, "God send two in front of him: destructive Angels," these are destroying Angels. So, He sends two of them in front, then

He have one on each side of him, and then one behind him. He's in the Circle of Power. [The Audience applauds].

This is the man I am. [The Audience applauds]. For forty-two years, enemies have trailed me to kill me, everywhere I go. Holy Qur'an tells Muhammad, that We make an enemy for you in every town; and Muhammad knows, but he's not afraid of them, because God have given him power over the wicked, that they cannot approach him with...they fail.

He...by raising up in my own house, my own Brother, like Cain was to Abel, but he failed to get. And they have made their attempt; and they still making their attempt to...Elijah Muhammad to make his boast a lie, but they can't do it. [The Audience applauds]. Not because I have power of myself, but it is Allah Who protects me. And Muhammad believes in his God so well, that he says under the name of David, "I walk through the valley of the shadow of death, I fear no evil. [The Audience applauds].

Many of you know, that you have seen me driving up and down the streets, of the streets of Chicago. I wasn't afraid of nothing. I don't fear nothing yet. The only thing I fear is He that have made me, and has risen me up and given to me this job, to rise you up. That's the only One I fear. I don't fear your plans. You can plan all you please until you go to sleep, and wake up and plan some more, and go to sleep and wake up, and every time you look around you'll see Elijah Muhammad. [The Audience applauds]. That's why he says, "He walks through the valley of the shadow of death, but he don't fear no evil," because, he have the God on his side; and the God is Powerful enough, to take the power of the enemy away from him, that he had designed to hurt Muhammad.

He shown me before my face; dropped them right before my face. They unable to do what they trailed me to do, and they fall just as...to death, as death itself. Can't even move can't even blink their eyes...Allah did this to let me know He had Power. Yes he can't even open his mouth or blink his eyes. I have seen this happen to my enemies more than one or two times. Never have said a word, wasn't able. I was standing there before him, for him to say what he was going to say, but he couldn't, he wasn't able...tongue was locked in the roof of his mouth, and his eyes was set and couldn't blink...This boy have been through all of this.

Oh, Brothers and Sisters, plenty more I could tell you what happened to the...people that tried to rid me of my life for teaching them Righteousness; for teaching them the good things of yourself, when they wasn't able to. They got jealous, and they tried to treat me like Cain treated Abel. Yeah, but I'm still here. [The Audience applauds]. And these are some of the Powerful words He said to me, He say, "Just whatever you do Brother, it'll come to past. If you put them out, I'm not going out there after not one of them...he's just out there, unless you go back out there and get him."

So, I went home, and I begin to think. I say this teaches me I better be careful who I put out. And because I may not mean that the person stay out there forever, but that is what He told me. And the Bible teaches you that God will accept the judgment of that one, the Last one He choose. And in some places it say by him was built, and He say that you're going to choose. He say, "Brother, whatever you want, ask for it, and it will be given to you." So I say you have a mighty good fellow in me. [The Audience applauds]. But I should also say, that in cold weather, fire is here for us, but, the fire can be evil for us, if we play with it.

So, let us not play with a good fellow; try to be good with him, for your own good. As in one verse I found in the Qur'an, similar to that in the Bible, it's referring to Muhammad's forgiveness and love for you that "If he would forgive him seventy-seven times a day, that don't mean that Allah forgive you when he know that you need to be punished." He will punish you, whether Muhammad desire it or not, in order to keep the Characteristics of a Good God to keep others good. He will whip some of us, for all the evil which is affecting others.

I'm your good old Brother, but you don't know me, but the Time is not very far off that you will say, "He told us he was our good Brother, but now we see, that you will come on your knees and beg me to forgive you, for any evil thought you had of me. I know it now, and I don't pay you no attention when you trying to act evil against me, because I know you a...remember that, a...I know that. You can't do nothing to me, you hurt yourself. It was designed that this Last one, the people, regardless to they...they won't overcome him. He's well protected in coming out and going in. And you can't think nothing against him, nor for him, that is not heard. Remember that, your thoughts are not your...they are heard.

My beloved Brothers and Sisters, I only say this to teach you away from throwing your good self down, for an evil self, the devil. He like people with two devils, they're not even mixed with good; they are two different devils, with not even a mixture of good. There's no good in them, so our God have Taught me; they wasn't made for it. There is some that try to do a little good things every now and then, but the nature in which Yakub made him in, he just can't be taken for a good person, just because he did one little good thing for us, and he did a thousand things evil to us, against that one good thing.

Brothers wake up and try to protect yourself. Help yourself with others who are trying to help yourself, and to make you back into what you was when the Heavens and the Earth was Created. You was Created in good, and you can't be nothing but a good person, that's why the evil person take advantage of you, because you don't know he a evil person, therefore, they take advantage. But I'm teaching you what God Taught me to teach you, that you can never trust white folks, it's the nature he's in. And those that follow him, they falls in love with him, because the evil Caucasian captivates them with his un-alikeness, both in person and in words. But here is a little boy God has remade, that now know the Caucasian from the very beginning, and know the end of him. You probably won't say it to me, "But when will they be destroyed." Well, it maybe earlier than you think. [The Audience applauds]. Thank you.

I been speculating on dismissing you for another hour, and you keep making me talk more and more [The Audience applauds], but I have respect for you, that you may know something too. And I want to give you the freedom, anyone of you that would like to say something, come on out here and get to this mic [microphone]. Tell us anything you wants to say, as long as it is in the line of teaching.

Brother #1: Yes sir, my name is William Mckensie, and I accepted the teachings, of the Honorable of Elijah Muhammad about three years ago. I accepted it out there in the wilderness which I wasn't a part of Islam, and it brought me to where I am today. I was out there doing the same thing that, a lot of us done, a lot of us do; out there drinking, running from bar to bar. But, when I accept the teachings of this man, it really changes my life. I would like to say that I was processing a year ago, and I fell off, and I fell back into it. Now that I'm starting back, I'm trying to get back to processing. And I wish I, it just look like, I'm constantly in between that outside and Islam.

And I'm asking really, if some of the Brothers…here to see if they could really help me to pull me into the Nation. And I would like to say All Praise is due to Allah for the Most Honorable Elijah Muhammad.

[The Audience applauds].

Messenger: [Unheard]

Brother #2: I simply came back to pay my respects to the Great Leader of all time. And I appreciate this opportunity to, make such a statement to you and before you, and to this congregation. I am with you. I am in support of yours, and shall be, thank you very much.

[The Audience applauds].

Brother #3: Ah, felt like driving…what I been going through in Rockford, Illinois is the same, not too many Brothers there. The Brothers are trying to get together there like…fortunately a few Brothers come from Chicago to bring you a message, and our message to you. Like I was like most…Rockford is a Christian town, and anything you do that go along with their religion, you go through a mind thing. It take Brothers through a thing. And I hope, Brothers and Sisters in Chicago are sought of like think about Rockford, Illinois cause we need some faces, like I wanted to give you my respect, thank you.

[The Audience applauds].

Messenger: We thank the Brothers; oh pardon me.

Brother #4: All Praise is due to Allah. I came about three weeks ago, and I, submitted my letter, the same day that I came. I'm a Political Science Major at Loyola. I'm in my final year there, and I want to know, to the Messenger, I want to ask the Messenger, what am I to do with it, with this Degree?
[One of the Brothers explained the Brother's question to the Messenger].

Messenger: He's welcome to come discuss this alone with me if he wants to, yes sir.

[The Audience applauds].

Brother #5: As Salaam Alaikum. I am Brother Curry Lee X. I just got out of Federal, I just got out of the Federal Penitentiary at Milan, Michigan, and, like I said that the Brothers back there are…strong, and they love you Most Honorable Elijah Muhammad. Salaam Alaikum.

Messenger: We love you…

[The Audience applauds].

Brother #6: What's up, my name is Brother Arthur Murray, and in processing in Temple #45, in Houston, Texas. I've heard, I've been in processing now for bout three weeks. I've heard many things about the Great Honorable Elijah Muhammad, but I never dream the day that I would come face to face to meet the Honorable Elijah Muhammad. And I must say to myself, and to all the congregation here, that it a great honor that I may not get this chance again to see the great Honorable Elijah Muhammad, but due to Allah, His blessings, I came before today from Houston, Texas, to see the Great Honorable Elijah Muhammad.

[The Audience applauds].

Messenger: Thank you Brother, and please give my best love and wishes, to the Brothers when you return, or wherever you may see them. You return to see them again, please remember me.

[The Audience applauds].

ELIJAH: LOOKING FOR THE BEST FOR THE WHOLE

[The Audience applauds].

Well my son, he's looking at wanting the best for his father, like the father looking for the best for the whole. [The Audience applauds].

Sister #: I would like to say that my name is Debra Green, and this is my first time here and I am happy to be here, thank you.

Messenger: Thank you.

[The Audience applauds].

Brother #1: I have deep faith and belief in the Honorable Elijah Muhammad. I am like, I'm almost totally annihilated, by this system. And I understand this fact, but, I'm also in some sort of light because I can hear and feel everything and see everything, and the Truth that Elijah's putting out, is True, it is the Truth.

If he can…men like, if he can put men out, I mean for forty years, he's been practicing this. And he have…like Malcolm X, I mean he's a beautiful person. He came up through, he went through all of the experiences of the Black life, from beginning with…he being a great man up under the teaching of the Honorable Elijah Muhammad. And so I have deep faith and belief in him; and I will come here often as I can, until my life is ended, thank you.

[The Audience applauds].

Messenger: Islam is like the Sun, the Sun bring out that which is hidden in Darkness. So, the Truth bring out of that which is hidden…so that it's made manifest to you and I. And this is what we are glorifying our God for, revealing to us that which was hidden.

So, I thank you Brothers and Sister, who have spoken so well on what you are now learning to be the Truth that you didn't know, that it was Truth. That was because the enemy has hidden it. So, now today it's made manifest.

So I'm going to dismiss you now. Put you over into the hands of the Assistant Minister, to dismiss you; and I hope that you will be here again next Sunday. [The Audience applauds].

I have enjoyed every minute, even to the minutes of your disbelief that made to know that the Truth, that disbelief would rise up in the Judgment. You always, whatever you do, it is written.

Thank you, and I turn you back in the hands of our Brother Minister, Assistant Minister. And I'm very happy to have the Honorable Senator among us this afternoon, praying and hoping to Allah that he will return again, and bring his own people of his class here. We want to talk with you Brother Senator. We want to have Senators for ourselves. We want to build a Congress of Our Own, ruled by Our Own, and you may be that Congressman going in front. [The Audience applauds].

So, I hope that our Assistant Minister will please you, now and forever in whatever he said to you. I hope that you, I hope that you will believe it as long as he believe in the Truth that came with Elijah, and not the...

Thank you, as I say to you, in the Name of Allah, As Salaam Alaikum.

OCTOBER 15, 1972 PART ONE / SIDE ONE

ELIJAH IS HERE TO PREACH THE TRUTH!

Salaam Alaikum. You may be seated.

This time, I don't have to beg you to forgive me for being late. [The Audience laughs]. Of course I'm not a minute or two, I'm still twenty minutes from that, but I thought I'd listen at you a little bit, so I sneaks up sometime and sit out and listen at you, what's going on inside, and if it don't sound so well, I'll keep going passing the Temple up. [The Audience laughs].

I'm very happy to see your smiling faces here this afternoon. You look as you should, beautiful original Muslims. Everyone that I see in here is a Muslim, whether you like it or not, you are a Muslim. All Black people are Muslims, all over the planet Earth. So, since I see you don't look white, you must be a Muslim. [The Audience applauds].

I got something with me that is not a Muslim, that's this cough. No, it is not a Muslim...You have heard that we came from Africa. Well you don't have coughs in Africa too much, because it's not cold enough to give you a cold to cough from; in some places now, it's in some places it's a little chilly.

So, Brothers and Sisters, we are here this afternoon to correct you of some of your mistakes, and to declare you innocent of those mistakes. And some of those mistakes that we are here to correct you on, you are guilty. And we want to correct you in the public, so that the public won't think that we are giving you these mistakes ourselves, and backing you up in them.

I don't back you up in other than the Truth, and I don't care what you say it could be on me. Don't call me Mister Muhammad you are God, you are Master Fard Muhammad. Master Fard Muhammad is the One that I'm representing. [The Audience applauds]. I am the man that just want to take my own place, and leave the place that I don't belong in, to the Man that belong there.

I have heard that you're putting your place, not you visitors. Some of you so-called believers, I have to call you that, are putting your place in somebody else's place, and making you somebody else. And, what you are making is other than the Truth. [The Audience responds in approval].

We want our people to be reconverted out of other than the Truth, to...the Truth.

We don't want to add nothing to the Truth, because that will make it other than the Truth. Well, we're going to make now, a habit of exposing you before those you told other than the Truth to, to let those who are seeking the Truth, pardon me, sound like I said six, who are seeking the Truth, so they know that you was not telling them the Truth. I don't back you up in telling other than the Truth. So, not only will I not back you up in telling other than the Truth, I'm going to force those who are seeking the Truth, to not to back you up in it. Walk out on them, because I'm going to tell them the Truth, and if you told other than the Truth I'm going to tell them, that you told other than the Truth, right before their face, like you told them other than the Truth to their face. I'm going to tell them the Truth to their face.

I'm not going to preach lies, I'm here to preach the Truth. You have lived under falsehood all your life. The Truth has come and falsehood must vanish. We're born under falsehood; We love falsehood rather than Truth. As the Bible put it, that, "Being born under darkness, we love darkness, rather than light." So when light came, we fled back looking for darkness. We want to correct you. You have many things...putting out to the people as though I teach you that, so that you will get your other than the Truth accepted.

Brothers and Sisters, I do not teach these people other than the Truth. What I teach is Truth. I'm not here to add nothing to the Truth. I'm not here to try to make you think that I'm something that I'm not. If you think that I'm trying to make you see me in the light of something that I'm not in, get your Book, and come on and I will get my Book, and I will prove to you, that I don't go beyond mine, or rather mission that Allah have given to me.

If I say anything beyond what I have been missioned to do, that you can't find me backed up in it, in the Scripture of Truth, come to me, I'll pay you a hundred dollars for everyone. Oh no, that's not enough; I'll pay ten hundred, a thousand then, for every story that I tell you other than the Truth of my mission, and of my work. You find anything that I'm doing, that you can prove that is even anything other than Righteous, I will give you ten thousand dollars, if you cannot locate the answer in the Scripture of Truth.

There never was a false prophet sent to the people in the past, and this is not one standing before you. [The Audience applauds]. Some of the things that I do, you may label as being other than Right, but that is just because you have not read the Scriptures. You haven't learned what the Last man should look like; What he should do; and how that the Book teach you he is a Fulfiller; and you don't take time to read what a Fulfiller is. When a man is brought to you, and he is sent by another one to fulfill Jonah Scripture when, then you got to go read Jonah, and learn what Jonah did, to see whether or not this man fulfill his work.

Fulfill means to do the same work that, that man did. Then, that man that you are talking to, or person before you is fulfilling, but if you don't go and see Jonah's work in this man's work, than he don't fulfill Jonah's work. Fulfill means to do what another one does. So, be careful about how you label people, to be something that they're not.

I want you to know that I don't condone falsehood; and if you want to do so, you are not following me, you following yourself. I have some Brothers, that is just going out making up texts of their own, and delivering them for you to believe. I'm going to teach you the History of Jesus, that Allah give to me, but please don't you try and teach, unless you going to teach the Truth. Some of you is just going wild with it, telling everything of what you think. We don't want what you think, we want what God have Taught us. [The Audience responds in approval]. We want His Thinking and not yours.

The Sister over here, where is she? Come out here Sister Secretary, and let us hear some of this teaching that is going on, so I can straighten it out. I want these people to know the Truth. I don't want them to come here, and listen at other than Truth out there from the mouth of some of you, who call yourself representing Islam. I don't want you to listen to no other than the Truth, and I want to know the other than the Truth that you are hearing, so that I can stop that man's mouth! He won't be backed-up by me. [The Audience applauds].

Sister Secretary: [She stated that there are some old Muslims telling other than the Truth, and that the Messenger gave her the privilege to tell the people, that there are quite a few new ones coming into the Nation of Islam, and they do not want the people to think that the Messenger is behind such other than the Truth teachings. She read some of the other than Truth that was being circulated by the various individuals, falsely accusing the Messenger of teaching other than the Truth. One example: "Supreme Wisdom: Seventh Year Teaching" by Minister Awakening].

Messenger: Just a minute, now, I never taught nothing like that. This is new teaching by the one that is teaching; he made it up himself. And he desires to make it up himself, because he wanted to have something odd in the Teachings, that you may look upon him, as some great author of that which you have never heard.

Messenger: Read Sister, Read Sister.

Sister Secretary: [She is reading from a list of numerous false teachings; one of them being attributed to the Messenger about the meaning of Fard].

Messenger: Wait a minute Sister. This is not the meanings of Fard, and if there is a Minister here knows what the meaning of Fard is, he can stand and tell you. And, if there is not one other than myself, I can tell you what it means. It don't mean no such thing! Fard is a name that is known by the Scientist to be an Attribute that is not placed amongst the ninety- nine...

THE TRUTH ALONE IS SUFFICIENT!

…to be amongst the group that is not placed amongst the ninety-nine. It means that with the Beginning that which is…This is First; this is the Name of Our Prayer. The First, and that people are going out trying to accept these Arab's words to you according to what they're saying.

You shouldn't listen to them until you write them down and send them to me. And, I will get the understanding. If I don't get it out of the Qur'an, there are other books of the Arab language which is kept their language, their names. It's there we can get it, but don't you try and use your own explanations.

Messenger: Read on.

Sister Secretary: [She is reading another false charge that says the Messenger taught that California is the devil's stronghold].

Messenger: I don't teach you that California is the devil's stronghold. I don't teach you that. The whole U.S.A. is the devil's stronghold.

[The Audience applauds].

Messenger: Keep going.

Sister Secretary: [She is reading another false charge against the Messenger's teaching about Master Fard Muhammad].

Messenger: Just a minute! I want to say to you who is listening to all of this, it's no teachings of mine. This is a made teaching by someone that they should stand up, and, and tell them how that they become in…between the names and teachings, in that way that they are doing; that such one is here doing is the author of such; stands now, it looks plain to me.

I was with Him for near three and a half years, day and night; and that that He taught me, I'm here to bear witness. And, I been bearing witness; and I been representing it to you, for forty-two years. And, I don't think that I should make that awful mistake, of what He went over with me day and night.

Messenger: Read on.

Sister Secretary: [She is reading another false teaching attributed to the Messenger. This is called " Supreme Wisdom, Six Year Teaching: The Birth of the Saviour, Master Wallace Fard Muhammad].

Messenger: No, the Supreme Wisdom that I teach you, is what, Allah has Taught me. That Wisdom, I call the Supreme Wisdom, which is the Supreme Wisdom.

Messenger: Read on, now go ahead.

Sister Secretary: [She continues to read, that according to that same false teaching, in the year 1862, a group of Black Diplomats from the Nation Of Islam held a Conference in Mecca; and in that same year, they held a Conference on the inhabited planet of Mars].

Messenger: Huh, it was held on Mars? [The Audience laughs]. What a lie! I wish you'd stand up, so I could send you out right now!

[The Audience applauds].

Messenger: This is what gets the people wrong in their understanding of us. They say a liar standing on this corner, and a Truthful one on that corner. They don't know which one to believe. Just saying whatever comes up, all you know you want to tell something different, from what you have heard.

Messenger: I don't want that kind of man following me, nor woman. Don't add to what you hear me say, nor take from what you hear me say. It is the Truth that I have received. When you go and add, and take from, you're making other than the Truth.

Messenger: So I want to tell you people, to stop listening at any such talk or teachings that is not in the same words that I'm teaching them. And, I rather for all of them to come here, and then if they find me telling other than the Truth, then the whole teaching is other than the Truth. I'm mixing it up, but, Brother you won't find me telling you other than the Truth, not, nothing I say.

Messenger: If you think I'm telling you other than the Truth, go and explain it to me what you think is other than the Truth, and I will give you ten thousand dollars, or a check for ten thousand dollars before you leave here. Yes sir, and if that is not enough, I'll make it ten thousand times ten thousand. [The Audience applauds].

Messenger: My goal and desire, is to tell you the Truth, because a liar…and We can't leave that liar with his lie. We have to have Truth to go from here. And anything that I say, you always is welcome to question me on it. I don't run from you just because you want to question me; well I should say not!

Messenger: That's what I'm here for you to question me, on the knowledge of the Truth, that I say I'm teaching. You are offered that Freedom, by God Himself, Who Taught me to ask Him questions; learn all about yourself.

Messenger: I'm equipped with the Truth from Almighty God Allah. Some of it you may not understand, but don't try and condemn that which you don't understand yourself…don't you fancy out nothing; just old plain Truth.

Messenger: Have some more?

Sister Secretary: [She is reading the false teachings concerning the birth of Master Fard Muhammad].

Messenger: See this is why so many of us get misunderstood. I never taught nothing like that. This is a makeup of that person teaching you something that he was not taught, other than the Truth. He's carrying out to people who was born out of the world of Truth, born under the thief, liar, the devil; and he taught them how to lie.

Messenger: And he came out after hearing the Truth, fighting the devil, teaching you other than the Truth himself. These people I want you to run down. Bring them before me so I can put them out of Our circle. They're doing no good for themselves nor you.

[The Audience responds in approval].

Messenger: These are the liars who goes out after hearing the Truth, and add to it, take from, to make it sound different, or make you think that he's raised other than the God Himself. He is, in telling other than the Truth.

Messenger: This is what I want you who are visiting us, get out, and you get a hold to it, and you can't understand it, then you walk away from it.

Messenger: For the nineteen or twenty weeks that I have been visiting you here…I want to straighten out these kind of other than the Truth teachings, that you may know the Truth from myself, who received it directly from the mouth of God. And as I say, I'm willing to pay with my life for lying to you, if you find me lying.

Messenger: Nope, I'm not going to lie. No sir, I'm going to tell you the Truth [The Audience applauds], but not for one of you to come here and listen at me. I won't tell a lie to make a house full of people to listen at other than the Truth. I'm going to teach you the Truth!

Messenger: You have anymore?

Sister Secretary: [She is reading the same false teaching, "The Birth and Science of the Saviour: Minister's Lesson Seven, Master Fard Muhammad," stating that, "When He was born there was a special made metallic cap treated with special fluids was place on His head. He was placed in a special chamber for twenty-seven days, where the oxygen content was totally different from that on the outside. He had an advanced surgery on his spine that took exactly seventy-six hours. His body produced a yellowish-white glow all around His entirety, that lasted for twelve days."]

Messenger: Now a man can lie that well, [The Audience applauds] he ought to be made to wait, until the last believer walk in the Gate of Heaven, and then throw him in the middle of Hell!

[The Audience applauds].

Messenger: I come to a place like this, and you mislead me, telling other than the Truth of what the Messenger has taught! Now Brother, I don't care to work with you anymore. [The Audience applauds]. What do you think I am, a liar? Try and prove it!

Messenger: I'm here, directly from the face of God as it is written [The Audience applauds]. I didn't came of my own. I was risen up in the midst of you, and sent to teach you the Truth. And no man, on Earth could teach you what I'm teaching you...

[The Audience applauds].

Messenger: Why you add to it? Why you throw in other than the Truth? You don't do that to be seen and heard, because people listening at you, they will tell it; and then you will be brought before me one day. And I have power with God, to put you to a finishing touch! [The Audience applauds]. I'm certainly very dissatisfied of you rising up, taking hold of the Truth, and trying to put it to the people as other than the Truth, from yourself.

Messenger: We may not like you after while; and I ask you to stop, before We dislike you. We, I mean God Himself. You are doing the wrong thing. We are here to kill the liar! Destroy him, who have destroyed the people of Righteousness; and telling them and misleading them, in other than the Truth.

Messenger: This is a good way to learn who your Brother is. Just make up whole lies, and tell it to the people. Make them to think I'm teaching you that, because it's me that you are coming to! I'm not teaching the people other than the Truth! It is you, who are taking, and ripping the Truth apart; and adding to what's taught, your own!

Messenger: You won't get away with it! I'm most certainly that little fellow that they call a Lamb in the Bible, bound to get you for it!

[The Audience applauds].

Messenger: Why do you come here, to get something to go and tell other than the Truth on it ? Get Truth now, and go and tell other than the Truth! You shouldn't come here! This is the wrong place! This is where you come to learn the Truth! And I defy you, to prove what I teach is other than the Truth! I do that every time I get on this stand.

[The Audience responds in approval].

Messenger: I want people that love the Truth. I want people that love the result of Truth, and not the result of a liar! I can prove everything I teach to you! Everything! I prove to you, that it is the Truth. Not only that everything that I do, I can prove that it's the Truth!

[The Audience applauds].

Messenger: Got any more?

Sister Secretary: There's quite a bit more Dear Apostle, do you want to hear anymore? [She then discuss privately with the Messenger the remaining false teaching on the list].

Messenger: …they pretty smart…they even got Vietnam in there…got some professional liars round here, they good as Scientist…

Messenger: I'm going to stop the Sister Secretary from reading out this other than the Truth round here. After looking there, seeing she have two or three more pages; and that some of it goes into politics. So, I'm going to leave it go, till next, when I don't have too much of business to take up with, then I'll let this go in again. We will have some more of this next Sunday.

Messenger: We want to get rid of this. We believe that we have very intelligent people visiting us at this time, and we want them to listen at something of Truth, and something of business that we should be doing; and not to be listening at a lot of little, hear my Brothers who don't know what they are talking about. And they just opening their mouths saying what they think. But, why I had this much let out today, I want them to know that I'm not round here…up no such foolishness, and I don't teach. This is just a foolish Brother, or a Sister, that is taking the teachings trying to make themselves look wise, and making themselves look like a fool!

Messenger: I don't condone in nothing of the kind! The Truth alone is sufficient to make you admire it, or you, can disbelieve it and leave it. We once again, trying to make you see the importance of us doing something for self.

Messenger: I have with the Help of Allah, and the, and the believers who follow me, are bringing to you to help us, come in and help us. We will greatly appreciate your help.

And pray Allah, to give you the quality if you don't have it, that is needed to join up with us and help us.

What we're trying to do on Cottage Grove, building-up the Eastside of it for your own self, and the population of the city to admire. We learned of some of our people who is qualified to help build. We're going to put a...and, this don't mean that you'll reject it, or anyone else. We just want the people that can build, what we give to them in blueprint. And, if you cannot build it according to the blueprint, don't accept it, because you hurt yourself, when you hurt your own people.

We don't want you to contract out the job, that we receive, that probably we can borrow the money to have it done. Confess what you can do, and don't tell us what you cannot do, because we are real glad if you can do it, but we don't want you to accept a job that we give to you, and you know you can't do it, just because you are our Brother.

Just say Brother I'm your Brother, but I can't do this job. Then, we will know what to do! But don't take a job from us knowing you're not qualified to do it. No, that hurts you, and hurts us. We want to admire your ability to do the thing.

So, now we're opening up quality jobs. If you can do these jobs, we will give these jobs to you, but don't say you can do them, and you know you can't; don't hold us down. We have quite a few jobs that you may be prepared to do; and maybe you're not prepared to do it, but they are here.

We don't have a lot of money as you may think, but we have a lot of credit. And you don't have to worry about our credit, so long as you can get the job, and you get paid for it.

Going around this building here, we have a lot to do that we want to do. The job has been signed over to other contractors that claim they know how to do the job, and then...that they will do it right. So, they would be found right around this building here, for a few weeks to do the job that we have for them to do. And I want them to be what I'm asking them to be. And I know you will be happy, when you see the job done. As you know, I don't like bad looking jobs. [The Audience applauds].

I'm so happy to learn that we have people among us can do anything. We have some wise and well trained people, but they never was able to get together, and do something for self. [The Audience responds in approval]. I want them to get together with me, and I will show them some places where they can go to work, and do something for self. Yes! And, to leave such great people sitting idly by, just listen to thought and never materialize the thought, it is not good for us. Get these people that have the know-how to work; let them do the work.

Who would be any gladder than I, or happier than I, to know that I have my own people here that have knowledge of that which we want to do. There is no man among you that is happy as I; and to know that you can do these things for yourself. We're not having a complete blank of the thing. Some people think that none of us knows nothing, but nothing, but we do have people that knows something, but will not prove their knowledge so others will know.

I have this job by the Lord of the Worlds; and that, I'm not afraid that I'm not able to do the job, long as you're with me. [The Audience applauds]. So, we're going to get together. We're to make our place of habitation, as the Bible call it, look like men of thoughts of buying there and not afraid. We don't want no slavery mark shining behind us where we go along. We want Civilization to shine, and I am beginning to force myself to believe that all the material that we need, is with us. [The Audience responds in approval].

What a wonder it will be to come on the Southside, and let the people see what you have done for the Southside. Turn it into a place where Civilization shines out!

I did not know you was here like this, you qualified contractors, workers. I did not know, but, now I am beginning to learn, and happy am I. You know how much I love a Brother. Why don't you just present yourself, whom I love. I love you, and I'm out here battling the world, and you sitting round here plenty strong, plenty qualified to help, because we are qualified people.

My beloved Brother and Sister, would that be right to me if you would come on and put in affect? The people will think that's another nation from abroad on the Chicago Southside. [The Audience applauds]. In this way; hold on Brother now, don't take too many pictures, for I'm not here to take, have all these pictures made of me, until I...There's some of you love to do this, and I don't love that you do that which I have not done myself. All of this work you are trying to publish of me, I want to be sure I'm worthy of it. [The Audience applauds].

We want to feed ourselves, and beloved listeners, if you want to feed yourself, you get compelled to go to the farms. That is where people find food. Don't be a shame to go and do for yourself, and raising food in the country.

Original, that's where our Fathers come from. And I want you to know that if we are to be a Nation, and a strong Nation, we must go to the farm to feed our stomach; and there we can even feed our back with good clothes. Put good clothes on our back from the farm.

We have down here in Georgia and Alabama a start; you may go see. We have out here in Michigan a start; you may go see. Have good ideas for us, come back and tell us. We welcome your idea to make it more prosperous than it is.

These things we have to do, if we expect to live on this Earth and it yield out of it that which we must have on top of it. We got to go to it; We got to dig into it like the devil has done. He dug into it, and he made himself rich; and a stomach full of good food from our labor. Think over that, he looked at us and made us till out of the Earth its own wealth for himself, and left us poor. Now, he say we are free. Let's make good of this freedom. Then, if he tries to hinder you from making good of that which he claim he have given to you, then make good both ways. Yeah, make good of stopping him from getting what he have give to you!

I have a lot more I want to say to you, but I don't think that there is too much patience. I'm not a Preacher that will get up here and yell to see you yell. I'm a different Preacher. I want to teach you. I can't yell, course my father, when I was born he was yelling, but I found out that yelling is not good, unless you are yelling out something. They would yell because that by Divine…they was Divinely made from the beginning, but they had laws like the…they thought was dead, it had no…But now, what season we have? We give them the…and they can, with the…put it out and work…a lot of yelling. No, to be yelling over there across the street that you a…coming up the people out there and see…

So, since we have qualified people to help us, let's prove to those people that we are worthy to be helped; not prove to them that we are…and we're acting on the basis of other than the Truth for help. No, we're not going to let them prove us other than the Truth. So, you that is trying to make the public think that you are telling the Truth, when you are not, I hope you stay home! [The Audience applauds]. One thing I will warn you of, before I move from this platform: Get You A Name! Come to me I will show you how to get it. A name that's your Real One. You can't see the Hereafter with the white man's name. [The Audience responds in approval]. Every Blackman on the Earth, know the white man name from your name.

Don't wear that name; don't be called by that name. If you don't know nothing but just to tell the world… but, He have not given me His Name yet. That's better than giving the them white man's name. Just tell them that, "Yes, I have a name, it's in my God's Protection." "Well, what is that?" "Well you could call me god." "Call me Allah." "Call me Gabriel." Call me anything but a white man's name. [The Audience applauds]. We don't want the name of the devil. The Bible teach you and me, "All that had the name of the beast," called him a beast! " they went down with the beast."

I thought it was later than this. [The Audience applauds]. So, since it's not so late as I thought it was [The Audience applauds], I'm going to change the meeting into question. You have heard me teach, and you have heard…say they have heard me teach. Now, you that desire to question me when you at home, you are here now. [The Audience applauds].Well, while I'm going to offer you the chance to ask me questions on that which you have heard me teach. I can't say on that which you heard my Brother…

QUESTIONS AND ANSWERS

…which you have heard me teach. I can't say on that which you heard my Brother say, because, I just told you that some of the Brothers telling other than the Truth. [The Audience responds in approval].

Now, is there anyone that would like to ask me a question on what you heard me teach, you are welcome to stand up and ask me, or anything that you would like to ask me pertaining to the teachings…

We're trying to get some planes in the air with our initial on it, not for show-off, but, we want them at work helping us. You will see them when they come.

Messenger: Yes Sir?

Brother #1: As Salaam Alaikum. Dear Holy Apostle, from the teachings that I heard you say that, the Moon represent the, as it is right now the first quarter, the Original Black people, am I right, Sir?

Messenger: No, it don't say, really represent the Blackman in the stage it's in now. The way you say it represent the sign of the Black people that is here in North America, that is blind, deaf, and dumb, and dead to the knowledge of self, that was once in the knowledge of self.

Brother #1: My question was Sir, what do the other three quarters represent?

Messenger: Pardon me Sir?

Brother #1: I was wondering what the other three quarters represented?

[One of the Brothers explains the question to the Messenger because he did not hear it clearly].

Messenger: The other three quarters? That represent stages in our rise into the knowledge of self.

[The Audience applauds].

Messenger: Anyone else?

Brother #2: As Salaam Alaikum. Dear Holy Apostle I'd like to know where is Allah God, in the Person of Master Fard Muhammad, today?

Messenger: He is where He is.

[The Audience applauds].

Brother #3: As Salaam Alaikum. Dear Holy Apostle, the event surrounding Pharaoh, can you tell me if that, was that a Parable, or did that actually happen?

Messenger: I didn't understand you so well.

[One of the Brothers explains the question to the Messenger because he did not hear it clearly].

Messenger: ...Pharaoh? Oh, you talking bout Pharaoh. What do you want to know?

[One of the Brothers explains the question once again to the Messenger because he did not hear it clearly].

Messenger: What he did?

Brother #3: That, in parting the Red Sea.

Messenger: Yes, they were signs of events that took place, in the Time of Pharaoh and his people, and Israel. A Time such as you see going on today. I don't know what Time you are referring to, but all the History that I have read of Pharaoh and his people, and Israel, is referring to us, and our modern Pharaoh. [The Audience applauds].

Brother #3: ...was he a Blackman or a white man?

Messenger: Who?

[One of the Brothers explains the question to the Messenger because he did not hear it clearly].

Messenger: No, he was not white. There was not any Egyptians that was actually white, at that Time, according to the teaching of the History of Pharaoh, and his people. He was not really white people, because the Origin of the population of Egypt was not made white. They was of the Original. [The Audience applauds]. This according to what Allah Taught me of the...

[The Audience applauds].

Sister #1: I don't know if it was one of your teaching I heard, and the question was asked, did the Atom the Original come from?

Messenger: I don't quite understand.

Sister #1: [She was laughing as if she is nervous] I would like to know man was a, man was Originated from an Atom. Where did this Atom come from?

Messenger: Well, if He Originated from Africa, he is African.

[One of the Brothers explains the question to the Messenger once again because he did not hear it clearly].

Messenger: He Originated from…what?

[The Brother explains the question to the Messenger again because he did not hear it clearly].

Messenger: That's right. Well that Atom, It Came from Space. It was out of Space where He Originated. An Atom of Life was in the Darkness of the Space and He Came out of that Atom that was in Space.

[The Audience applauds].

Messenger: Now you may wonder, how did that Atom get in Space? [The Audience applauds]. The History of the Space teaches us, that at that Time, it was Nothing but Darkness. If there had been light for us to use Our…on it, to find where there was a Atom of Life in it, before the Atom was Exploded to show what It was, We would tell you so. But, We can't go that far with you. We don't know how the Atom Came in Space, and what Came out of Space, a Human Being, that's far back as We can go with it. Yeah.

[The Audience applauds].

Messenger: This what Allah Taught me. He said to me like this in answer to my question on Man, Creation, He said, "Brother, We Know that He was Created, but when, We can't tell you, because We had Nothing to go by; and so, He has to tell all Himself, after He had Created Himself, then We go from what He said." And I felt that was Good Truth for me to teach you.

[The Audience applauds].

Messenger: That's enough? Thank you, thank you. [The Audience applauds]. I'm not to tell you other than the Truth. I am the next closest one to Allah. [The Audience applauds]. I don't think Allah will take a liar for His Right Hand. You're his Right Hand, what are you? I tell you what He Taught me, and it's up to you to believe it or let it alone.

Messenger: Some more? Anything that you want to ask, I'm very happy to answer, if I know the answer. I don't say to you I know all the answers, unless He reveal them to me, but if He has revealed them, or sometime He'll reveal them; and sometime you get them out of the mouth. I don't previously have the knowledge, but while you are asking the question, He tell me the answer.

[The Audience applauds].

Brother #5: As Salaam Alaikum Dear Holy Apostle. Sir I was wondering where do the lower forms of animal life come from, and it came about?

[One of the Brothers explains the question to the Messenger because he did not hear it clearly].

Messenger: The form of animal life, I asked Him about it once, and how did they come here. The First thing He Answered, He said, "Every since We had a Earth Brother, We had the animals on it." And I say, how was they made? He say, " I told you, Every since We had the Earth, We had animal life on it." [The Audience applauds]. Thank you.

Brother #6: I would like to know the authenticity of the lost ten books of the Bible?

[One of the Brothers explains the question to the Messenger because he did not hear it clearly].

Messenger: I don't know Brother, He didn't teach me that there was any lost books.

[The Audience applauds].

Brother #7: As Salaam Alaikum. What puzzles me is, according to the Bible it teaches that God is a Spirit, and that was the main thing that kind of stumbled when I first heard the teachings. Are these quotes that are in the Bible, have they been added; and how long have this teaching been going on?

Messenger: Every since the writers of the Book.

[The Audience applauds].

Sister #2: As Salaam Alaikum. I would like to know if the Nation Of Islam teaches of a Heaven or Hell as in Christianity?

Messenger: No, not like Christianity teaches of a Heaven and Hell, but not in the same way that Christianity teaches it. We teach a Heaven and Hell while you live.

[The Audience applauds].

Messenger: We cannot be tormented in Heaven if you are not alive. You got to be alive, to feel the torment. And if you are in a...you got to be alive to feel the Joys of Heaven.

[The Audience applauds].

Sister #2: Then so, there is no such thing as a life after death then?

Messenger: No, if you're referring to a physical death. A physical death does not...it's physical dead. But, if you are referring to a spiritual death, that is to being dead to the knowledge of God. You don't have His Spirit in you, and then We call you dead.

[The Audience applauds].

Brother #8: I read in the Bible that man will destroy himself. Do you believe that?

Messenger: Do I believe?

[One of the Brothers explains the question to the Messenger because he did not hear it clearly].

Messenger: Man will be showing himself?

[One of the Brothers explains once again the question because the Messenger did not hear it clearly].

Messenger: Will destroy himself? Yes I believe it!

Brother #8: In what way?

Messenger: In every way you build your life up. You don't have no, nothing out here that will destroy you, just because that it can destroy you, only when you go to fight each other. But, there's nothing prepared out here to destroy you, you yourself, so Allah Taught me.

[The Audience applauds].

Brother #9: Is it true that the devil has been to the Moon?

[One of the Brothers explains the question to the Messenger because he did not hear it clearly].

Messenger: Why certainly in a physical way. Yes, according to their report, and their pictures of them on the Moon.

[The Audience applauds].

Messenger: Now, the other part of that Moon…he has not reached that part; the part that We preach of Equality, that Spiritual Teaching; and that he have not reached the Spiritual Equality. That's what We represent the Moon for, Equality between Man and Man. So, therefore that Moon has not, as yet, been reached by the devil.

[The Audience applauds].

Sister #3: I wanted to know…about the Pyramids, since the Egyptians were far advanced more advanced or highly advanced than civilization today. How is it that, they got the Pyramids so high, and with what instrument?

[One of the Brothers explains the question to the Messenger because he did not hear it clearly].

Messenger: The Saviour Taught me, that they had a hydraulic they had in use in those Days, that they have today, and will not put it in use because of the devil, that he will grasp that knowledge, as he don't know it yet. He has been asking the question himself.

[The Audience applauds].

Messenger: He said to me, "They would put that same hydraulic in affect, as soon as They remove the devil. They don't want them to know it.

[The Audience applauds].

[One of the Brothers explains the second part of the Sister's question, because the Messenger did not hear it clearly].

Sister # 3 [Second part of her question]: She wanted to know since the Blackman is the Original Man, are there Black Men in among other beings on other planets?

Messenger: I didn't get the teachings of the knowledge of what was on other planets from Him, as He was trying…acquaint me into the knowledge of myself, who is on this planet, and others that's on this planet.

[The audience applauds].

Sister #4: In the Last Days of the lost found, how will the Muslims survive?

Messenger: I can't hear to good up here?

[One of the Brothers explains the question to the Messenger because he did not hear it clearly].

Messenger: That's what God Came for, to save us from that which He will permit to destroy our enemies. He have Come to separate the Righteous from the wicked and destroy the wicked, and save us from the Destruction of that He's using to destroy the wicked.

[The Audience applauds].

Brother #10: As Salaam Alaikum. Dear Holy Apostle, since you're teaching on the Theology Of Time, approximately ten weeks back, you said that in the Destruction of America, there was two places of refuge. I was wondering if you could reveal those two places?

[The Audience applauds].

Messenger: Two places of refuge? Did you say I said that?

Brother #10: Yes Sir, I understand that in the, since you have been teaching here, it's in the Muhammad Speaks on the Theology Of Time. You mentioned that there was two places of refuge, in the...

Messenger: Well, if I did, there is two I can prove to you that it's True. There is one, Number One, with your Lord and my Lord [The Audience applauds]. The First One rather; I know where you will be safe, where you will be secure.

[One of the Brothers is speaking to the Messenger concerning the Brother's question clearly].

Messenger: ...I answer like you did, years ago.

[The Messenger laughs and the Audience applauds].

Messenger: Is there another one?

Brother #11: As Salaam Alaikum. Dear Holy Apostle in your teaching today, you indicated that we as Black people should get rid of the names of the slave-masters, as given to us over the years. The question that I have is whether or not, you recognize, the legality and the legitimacy, of non-Christian names assumed by Black people by virtue of court decree, which names have not been given to the Black Brother or Sister by yourself?

Messenger: I recognize any Blackman's name, if he have some kind of Origin for it. But, I know that if you see the Hereafter, which is meaning the Destruction of this world, and the name of the devil. But you will have an honorable name, and a name that will live; and a name that everyone of our people will respect and will admire.

Messenger: But, the name of the devil in this world, their name will be destroyed with him. You won't have their name round here to go in. Their language will be destroyed. You won't be able to speak their language, so Allah Taught me, after twenty years of Destruction of them. You will have to speak your Own Holy Language, because no one will talk to you in any other language.

[The Audience applauds].

Messenger: Excuse me for looking at the timepiece, I got to keep up with time, that's right. [The Messenger and the Audience laughs].

Brother #12: As Salaam Alaikum. This is my second visit to the Temple, and I desire a name, and I desire to reclaim my own. I was wondering if Most Holy Apostle could tell me, how I can become, you know, how I could strengthen my belief?

Messenger: How he…

[One of the Brothers explains the question because the Messenger did not hear it clearly].

Messenger: Will I do what?

[One of the Brothers explains the question once again to the Messenger because he did not hear it clearly].

Messenger: Just keep coming here Brother.

[The Audience applauds].

Messenger: Anyone else? Yes, Brother, come right on.

Little Brother #13: You…Allah, and over in Israel they don't have no…and how could…so when the world come to an end, how would they know who's the right…and they would know what, they would know what…

Messenger: Can you straighten out his language, Sir?

Little Brother #13: When the world comes to an end, will Allah…or will He send someone over there and tell them whose the right God?

[One of the Brothers explains the little Brother's question, because he needed help in expressing his thought].

Little Brother's question: "When the world comes to an end, will Allah turn His Back on the people in the East, or will He send someone to teach them of Who the Right God is?"

Messenger: I'm teaching you Who is the Right God myself. [The Audience applauds]. The Bible say that He will send His Angels from the East to gather us, from the West.

Brother #14: The Honorable Muhammad, I would like to ask one question: after visiting this Temple, and listening carefully, I would like to know how one can become a Muslim?

[One of the Brothers explains the question because the Messenger did not hear it clearly].

Messenger: Believe what I teach you and follow me.

[The Audience applauds].

Brother #15: Salaam Alaikum. I would like to know, Dear Holy Apostle about a great northern bean. I read where it say it wasn't supposed to be eaten. And I was wondering whether or not this has changed or not, the great northern bean?

[One of the Brothers explains the question because the Messenger did not hear it clearly].

Messenger: We don't go for eating the large size bean, though they may be navy beans, but we eat small size of them. That's what He Taught me of that.

[The Audience applauds].

Brother #16: As Salaam Alaikum. Mister Muhammad I'd like to know, I read in the Sun Times that Master Fard was a drug addict, was this True?

Messenger: I don't think you have found any drugs here for sale since you been coming here, have you? No, He didn't use of the drugs; that would put us out of Our Natural Minds.

[The Audience applauds].

Messenger: In fact about it, we didn't use drugs of no kind. We use drugs sometimes, because of the enemy causing our body to need some kind of nourishment of that which is now making us sick. But, He didn't teach me that. He told me and Taught me how to live, to keep from using anything like drugs.

Messenger: But, sometimes we get away, and go and do that against the Nature of Our body, in which they were made in. Then, we'll go and look for something to help us get back into the well-being of them, and we grab at anything that will give us easement; that's a drug. But, if we live like He Taught me, we wouldn't need no such drugs, at anytime.

Messenger: We choose to eat once every two or three days, we won't need no drugs. You say, "Well, Muhammad, they tell me you use drugs." Yes! Because I was other than myself. I wasn't eating like He told me, therefore…I thought I would suffer the consequences. I suppose to pay, if I don't live according to His Teachings.

Messenger: But, I was to do this. I could not be able to teach you, if I don't taste the same that you taste. As the Bible teaches you, "In all their afflictions, he was afflicted, but yet, the Pleasure of the Lord will be upon him."

[The Audience applauds].

Messenger: In fact, mean by no means that he was guilty of something, and the God afflicted him. No, it don't mean that. Like the people thought of Job, being a beloved man by God, and He turn him over to the devil to try him out. Let the devil try him out. As the devil had said to God, "Take the hedge away from round him, and that he'll curse you to your face." He told the devil, "Go try him, but save his life."

Messenger: And so, the devil went and poured on Job everything that he had, that he had those that believe in him under, but, he was unable to change Job's mind. He suffered all of the afflictions that was put on him, as he tell you in his book, that "God brought him near to death, but nevertheless, he refused to forsake God, and he come out of it, and the devil was defeated. This the modern Job, that you talking to.

[The Audience applauds].

Messenger: I have suffered bronchitis asthma, and I would say all of its…for near bout ten years now, but I'm not ready to curse God and die.

[The Audience applauds].

Messenger: Nope, well, in fact about it, the Bible is talking about us. I asked him about this, who are they talking about, us or the Greeks? He say, "No, it's talking about you all." So, when it comes to my affliction, He say, "It takes plenty of it Brother." He say, "You will be alright after that."

Messenger: Why I go and read over Job's afflictions, I say, he did come out of this. And so, I believe I'm coming out of mine.

[The Audience applauds].

Messenger: Is there another question someone wants to ask?

Brother #17: As Salaam Alaikum. I noticed that, within a few weeks, the white press and the news media is waging a campaign against Arabs; against the Arab nations, and trying to get public sympathy for the Israelis. And I wonder, could this be because of the fact that the Arab nations are beginning to recognize the Black Muslims Movement, here in the U.S.?

Messenger: Yes, I believe those who have knowledge of what kind of work I'm doing in America, is beginning to recognize it and respect it, I believe.

[The Audience applauds].

Messenger: This is the greatest work ever happened in our midst, since we have been crucified into slavery by the white man. Never no work of this kind come in his midst that he was in, that he was able to try and attack, and win! They don't even question this work! You go out there and bring all you can see out there, not a one of them would get up and question me.

Messenger: There's nothing for him to question me on, that right. He know the Truth, but he's not able to do the Truth, but he know it. He give me credit for teaching the Truth, but he is not able to accept the Truth, because there is No Truth in him.

[The Audience applauds].

Sister # 4: According to the Christian teachings, all men must die, but, that are on the right side of God will go on to an eternal life. Do you feel that all men have to die?

Messenger: You want to know what about the Christians, Sister?

[One of the Brothers explains the question to the Messenger because he did not hear it clearly].

Messenger: Yes, and that's why we are here today, because those on the right side of God, mean those that believe and have put their trust in God; and we are the descendants of those Righteous People.

[One of the Brothers explains the second part of the Sister's question to the Messenger].

Sister # 4's question: Will we have to suffer death?

Messenger: There is not a life made, according to the Teachings of God to me, that will not face death. [The Audience applauds].

Brother # 18: As Salaam Alaikum Dear Holy Apostle. I have always been confused about how an Original Man like the Egyptians was put into slavery, by another Original Man, like the Hebrew Israelites. I like to know what made the Egyptians wicked?

Messenger: What made the Egyptians do what?

[One of the Brothers explains the question to the Messenger because he did not hear it clearly].

Messenger: I guess I have to get somebody up here in my place [The Messenger laughs]. What made the Egyptians wicked? There was in there Time, a wicked man coming among them. Six thousand years ago, the wicked devils got a chance to visit among the Egyptians, like when…come among the Egyptians, and they deceived the Egyptians to the point in doing like them. And there was the Turkish people, that also…

QUESTIONS AND ANWERS

…there in Egypt, put a lot of their devil stuff in them, under the rule of…

Brother #18: As Salaam Alaikum.

Messenger: Wa Alaikum Salaam.

[The Audience applauds].

Brother # 19: He have two questions to answer. Have you spoken to God yourself? And how long have you known Allah?

Messenger: Well, as far as the name goes, I'm Allah, you Allah. I'm not anything more than you in that sense. We all are Allah.

[One of the Brothers interrupted the Messenger to explain the question in more detail].

Messenger: Yes, I thought I was seeking Him every since I been born, but I didn't know Him. I was blinded to the knowledge of Him. So, He Came to me and Made Himself known to me. This is the way I got to know Him. And I was trying to seek Him, but I wasn't able to take the right path to get to Him, because I was blind when I was born by the enemy.

[The Audience applauds].

Messenger: Anymore?

[One of the Brothers explains a question to the Messenger from a Brother in the Audience].

Brother # 20's question: [He read in the Muhammad Speaks recently, that the Messenger was going to come back to the Temple, and reveal where the "Promise Land" was. But, he's been following Muhammad Speaks, and he has not seen that revealed yet. He wants to know if the Messenger intends to reveal where the "Promise Land."]

Messenger: At the place where you in now. [The Audience applauds]. As you may read in the Bible where the Jesus say that, "It is the Lord Own Good Will, to give thee the Kingdom. This mean a Kingdom...that is not present at that Time, but, a Kingdom of Righteous...and it will be this place, that He will give; the kingdom of the wicked. As Isaiah and other Prophets prophesy that, "He give to us the kingdom of the wicked."

[The Audience applauds].

Sister # 5: Muhammad, I would like to know you just said about Joseph and Mary having just one child, Jesus. Did they have more than one child after that child was born?

Messenger: Explain that to me.

[One of the Brothers explains the Sister's question to the Messenger, because he did not hear it clearly].

Messenger: Another child? We find here in the New Testament, where that they was inquiring about Jesus while he was teaching, that someone told Jesus that his Mother, Brothers, and Sisters was out there inquiring, and that Jesus made it clear, that none could be his mother, brother, ands, Sister, unless they believe like him.

Messenger: And this show that his mother and his brothers was not ...believers in him, if he turn them down like that. He said, "These are mine that stand here," meaning those who was on the inside with him. Well, that is true, in the way of the believer. You can't be the brother or the sister of a believer, unless you believe like them.

[The Audience applauds].

Messenger: Anymore? No more, then we going to...yes sir come right on, about to dismiss.

Brother # 21: Salaam Alaikum. I would like to ask the Honorable Elijah Muhammad were the Original Scientists Black?

Messenger: Yes, according to what God Taught me. The Original ones was Black. They a, a kind of, well, a Circle to Themselves; and They all was Black.

Brother # 21: And, I would like to ask the Honorable Elijah Muhammad , why do we now have to go to the devil, to get our knowledge as far as science?

Messenger: Well, it is not me in your we. I'm not in that we. I don't go to the devil to get knowledge [The Audience applauds]. If, I had went to the devil to get knowledge, he would...me on that ninety percent. I didn't graduate from colleges or universities of his. My knowledge is not of his. [The Audience applauds].

Messenger: All that I teach come from Allah, under the name of Master Fard Muhammad, of Whom Praise is Due Forever. I got nothing out f the schools, colleges, and universities of the white man; I have none of his.

Brother #21: But, we have to go to the schools and established schools and universities in order to build a Nation.

Messenger: You don't have to go to the universities of the devil, to be able to teach the Nation. As I just told you, I didn't go; I never have been. [The Audience applauds].

Messenger: Just a moment, this is why…you can't have a change, unless you get out of what you're in, and getting into another Civilization. You have to have the knowledge of how to get in that Civilization.

Messenger: So, I teach you something new; it is not out there in this civilization; you can't find…Everything that you do…it has to be changed from that way. And that way understanding of A and B, over here with us. You could go back to…well, just write your name down on the Book then.

[The Audience applauds].

Messenger: This is why the…of science, of this teaching…of reading…He got science letters for you to attention to…This he have recorded to be understood in another way. But, we have something already recorded; and…if you would understand what We are telling you.

Messenger: This is why I invite you to come. I want to teach you that which God have given to me to give to you; and the knowledge of that which the enemy give to you, so you could know how to compare the two.

Messenger: That's why I'm inviting you to come. If ever you find from the teachings, from one day to the other, I would teach you the meanings of things when I can get you to understand…and if you ever understand yourself, then the understanding in this Time into higher learning will come real…to you.

Messenger: I'm not risen up among you that is blind, deaf, and dumb, to assign to you to his higher knowledge and understanding in his educational system. I'm…but I want you to learn…yourself…I teach…over there in your own higher education, that you will not…in your life. You will say, "Yes…I…didn't know there was more. I don't think you…And I will show you how the devil tricked you. And how…

[The Audience applauds].

Messenger: I'm not trying to play wise…if you recognize it's wisdom, and the way it was taught to you. I'm not trying to play wise. I'm only trying to tell you that…and what I will tell you of that enemy, is…what I have been Taught…by God, before His Face. I'm telling you the Truth, that He loves you…of bringing you up to …what He…I would let you go bring one in here. Would you like to? I will give him the seat up here, and I will talk to him…

[The Audience applauds].

Messenger: We are not to be defeated! And you won't be defeated as long as God is with you in Person! [The Audience applauds].

Messenger: So, at this time I'm going to bring our meeting and questions to a close, as it is time that we go home; and some of us have babies their hungry, and they'll run us out of the house.

Messenger: So, this will allow me to stop our meeting at this phase of it. I will thank you. I really thank you, for having the intelligence to question me on what you has questioned me on, because it was not ignorant, nor foolish, it made sense [The Audience applauds], and I thank you.

Messenger: And, I'm going to ask how many of you visiting us, who have not accepted what we teach? All you who are visiting us, who have not accepted what we are teaching here? Oh, I know it's more of you than that in here. If I thought all you was converted for Truth here, I would say Allah have really blessed us.

Now, have you been coming here long enough to learn whether or not we have been teaching you the Truth, or other than the Truth, hold up your hands? You here, that have learned that we are teaching you the Truth, hold up your hands, thank you! thank you! thank you! thank you! thank you! thank you! thank you!

Well, if you have learned that we are teaching you the Truth, I want to see the hands that want to accept the Truth! One, two, three, thank you! thank you! thank you! thank you! thank you! thank you!

To prove that you are with, no that's…well I don't see no place here. Well you'll get to the Minister, or the Secretary. Go back there and give your name, and she will write you down, and you're going to be glad when the Time come, when those people start to shooting at each other over there and sinking people's ships; you're going to be glad.

Don't be like the Holy Qur'an say that you will be, "Oh, would that I had followed the Messenger. Oh, would that I had taken away with the…after the Truth had come to me." Well, you would follow that up by giving your name to the Secretary.

Thank you so very much for coming to this call for you. And don't let it leave you, without you following it.

I thank you. The world is in a awful condition. They want to shoot these people so bad, they outright telling them now. Since Japan have joined up with Korea and China, they're not afraid to tell you that they're ready to shoot "wild John." That's what they call the devil. So, I say, get out of the way of the shooting of "wild John."

[The Audience applauds].

So, I thank you for your patience and endurance here this afternoon. And that, I hope to see you again soon.

As Salaam Alaikum.

[The Audience applauds].

TIME IS VERY OVERDUE!

Salaam Alaikum. You may be seated. Who was that say I was not a big man [The Audience applauds]. I know I'm a big man now. I...[The Audience applauds]. There is so many of you in here, you have darkened our Temple out, so that I can hardly see you; that's really something!

Oh yes, you find anybody out there calling me "little man," tell them you go down to that Temple, you'll find he's not a "little man," he's a big man. [The Audience applauds].

I'm really happy to see you here. I feel more happier than any, today, than any day I have been out. [The Audience applauds]. You see, I'm not treated like that preacher was in the South. He just kept going to the church to preach to a lot of people. He wanted a church, to pastor. You know how some of these fellows are about that. So, when he would go out, the people would come and they start talking bout the Saturday party, while in the church and just looking up at him every now and then, and he got tired of that. So, at last one Sunday, he went out, carried his Bible case with him, and he set it up on his Bible stand. He opened it up. He pulled out a quart of whiskey, set it down to his left, and he pulled out a forty-five, and put it to his right. He laid his Bible in between the two. He say "Brothers and Sisters, my text today is, "Some Of These Things Will Move You." [The Audience applauds].

So, you are lucky today, I don't have that to do. [The Messenger and the Audience laughs]. You already sitting here, so something have moved you. [The Messenger and the Audience laughs]. Long as something is moving you, that makes me feel good, but when you go to people, and nobody moved, then you in bad shape.

We have always here a program in which maybe you don't like it too much. It's a program of doing something for self. With millions of us here in America, and with millions out of America, we are trying to say to you, in words, that you're going to have to move.

The people on the outside is pushing in, and they don't have this kind of weapons. They don't come in talking. They want to come in shooting, and I want to teach you how to get out of the way. One place in the Holy Qur'an, and there's another place in the Bible, where it says that, "We have heard of this all every since Our Fathers fell asleep, you been telling us this."

Well, God, as the Bible say, "Do not wish to destroy any of us. He wishes that we come to understanding, and believe and accept your own, so that He could take you home into your own, and not carry you to Hell with the devil. He's forced to do that, if you don't accept, but if you will accept, He even give you a little time; hold the Works back, until you can make up your mind. But, the time today that you have been given…is very, very, very, very, overdue. If you had not been here, the devil would have been destroyed as soon as his Time was up in nineteen-fourteen, but, since you are here, and you are the one that God is seeking, then the Time is delayed because you delayed yourself.

So, I'm here to tell you today, like that Last Angel; that Last Angel say, "Time, Time, knowest now, will soon know no more." So, I'm with him, I can easy bear him witness to that Truth. The Time that you have known, will be no more. They are tired of giving you time.

So, as I heard my father make some imaginations on that Trumpet, he said, "Gabriel will blow a Trumpet, that it is into parts. And that, each part is nine foot, which make the Trumpet twenty-seven feet long." He use to preach that Fire stuff. Oh, Brother it look like you wouldn't hardly be able to get ready.

So, I'm saying to you, that, that Trumpet, I don't say nine feet each length of it, but, I say this: That the Time that you has known, we'll soon know no more. These people is getting ready; and I'm trying to Hurry you and myself to get ready. Hurry! Hurry! Lay hold to your own; this is what I'm here for.

We have, as you know, our program, it is doing something for yourself; and that if God will give to you and me the Kingdom, we have to learn how to keep up the Kingdom. Give a man something, then he don't know how to keep it up, you wasting time. We must learn how to keep it up. As the Bible teaches us that, "You're raised up to rebuild the waste city." That's there in your Bible. So, those who will waste the cities, is the one that we want to stay out of the way of, because, they will be causing trouble.

I'm looking for capable people to help me to put this job over, and put it over at once! [The Audience responds in approval]. So, I find here, Mister Percy…Medical Doctor. Well, we be sick sometime Brother don't worry, you have something to do, because, we are not in our own, and we are not acting ourselves.

Mister Pat Caugans, Deputy round here. Well, we have some people…that…sometime. I don't know what kind of Deputy you are, but however, Mister Caugans, if you are one of those that picks up people, who is not to…we need you. And, Mister Patrick…Administrator and Legal Consultant, thank you for…You the kind of people we're looking for. And also, Doctor Houston X…Medical Doctor. We need you Doctors, don't you here my voice. Doctor Joseph Smith, he's a Doctor. Mister Earl…Becker, Teacher. If I mispronounce your name, well…I got to school, and they was closed.[The Audience laughs and applauds].

Mister M. Braufield, Management, Travel Agent. I like you to, cause we travel a lot. You know, tell you the Truth, some of our people had never left the community that they was born in. Islam went and moved them out, they'll travel. Islam will certainly put you on the road. [The Audience responds in approval].

Doctor E. Johnson, Surgeon. Oh no, I don't want no surgery. Oh no, I need all of my skin. [The Messenger and the Audience laughs and applauds]. Doctor Cedric X Cloud, Professor. We need you, you a Professor; We not one ourselves. Charles 19X James, Teacher. Carl 4X Morris, Engineer.

I should have you stand shouldn't I, every time I call your name, so we know who to call, so that a fellow don't beat you out of the job when we call; you know, that is right. These are Doctors, we always need a Doctor sometimes. James 19 X…see how you look……Carl 2X M. Morrison, Engineer.

Well, some of them is out…I don't get a hold to them. Excuse my delay, I don't know what I'm going to call this one. Blame me not, I told you I didn't go to school. This Brother Octavus, Octavius…Director of the Rocksberg Medical Technical Institute. Are you in here?…okay. Miss Corrina…Registered Nurse, are you here? Well we need Nurses, I need one right now. [The Messenger and the Audience laughs]. All the way in the back, oh yeah, thank you Sister. Misses Lucille M. Harlins, Administrator and Assistant, Miss Lucille. Sir? I thought a Lucille [The Messenger and Audience laughs], here with me, and she was a Nurse, thank you Sister, or rather she is a Nurse. No, that is not a Nurse. I thought she was…

Look at the Nurses here! Miss Sarah Richards, Nurse. You Misses Richards? Thank you. Misses Delores; no, wait a minute, Misses Audry. You call off these cause you went to school more than I did, so you call them off.

[The Messenger asked one of the Brothers to finish calling out the names of some of the "Professional People" in the Audience. And, as he called each name and their field of expertise, the Messenger thanked each one].

[As one of the "Professional People" was from Boston, the Messenger commented that, "Yeah that's up in that corner of the United States, where good ones comes up." The Messenger and the Audience laughs].

[As the Brother called out the name of a Brother that is a Doctor, and asked if he was there, the Messenger commented, "Guess he have a patient, it's bad weather outside."].

Well, we can say to you, that we are real happy to have you present. We want you to know that we need your service, everyone of you professional people. We can't come in and say, "Be well," and you will be well, we have to get well. This weather seem to have me troubled up [The Audience applauds]. So, as soon as I can get myself well, then I will show you how I got well, and then you can start practicing. But, I must go through what all the Others went through. Remember the Book, it says, when Job begin to complain that when God answered him, He answered him out of the, of the whirlwind. He Come to him pretty tuff. He asked Job to answer Him then. Job was not ready to give answer to what he was asking. Those questions he asked Job, was questions that Job had never been questioned on; condemn Job, and the first word he say, "Who is this that…by reason of words." He criticized Job, that he was throwing in his little excuses and accusing of the God, that He was making the Truth from God. So, He asked him just a few questions, and Job ought to known how to answer the few questions. He say, "What is the Foundation in which the Earth is supported?"…would seek to defend his questions. Now Job if you can answer some of these questions," He didn't say some of them, but "these things." Well it don't read exactly like I'm saying, but this is what it means. "If you can answer My questions, Job, your own right arm; Your own right hand can…" Think over that. "Just go ahead now Job and answer me for a few minutes." Job told Him they was too…for him. He couldn't answer the questions.

He ought to told Job to shut up then! "But I'm not going to tell you to shut up, I'm going to tell you to talk. I want you to open up and talk. I don't want you to shut up. I'm looking for laborers; and the Day is far spent.

You'll hear lots going on. You'll hear that the East is now joining up with East. You'll hear that we, but you won't think it's talking about you; and you won't let it interfere with your big…here in America, and he's the big boss. I say He got the boss kind of …surrounded; and he's got to be a boss to get out of it.

East joining up with East. You hear that you…You notice that America's money just continue to fall. [The Audience responds in approval]. You notice that people continue, that nations continue, to unite on the outside of America. In a Book there in the Bible, it says, that they said, "Come, let us go up against her, noon day. Let's go take her while she's asleep." This is referring to America. The Asiatic Nation is the one talking there. They're about ready to strike, and the country knows this to be True.. I'm not biting my tongue to tell you that! They are ready to strike the nation of England. They all uniting together, against this one, to lay hold on her, and lay her low. [The Audience responds in approval].

Our God says to me, "My Greatest Desire is to bring…this devil," this is what He used, "this devil to his knees. [The Audience applauds].

So, we being in the midst of all of this great crowd, and clouds of war being made up, and all of them aim, is towards America. I want you to…yourself and trying to save self. Don't think that America is prepared today to keep them from coming in on them, she's not. No, she's not able to ward off this type of enemy, that is coming against her.

TEACH YOU DIVINE WISDOM

[The tape was blank for a few minutes, and this is where it began].

...this is coming from the mouth of the devil himself, according to what he has learned...that the Lord said through the mouth of His Prophets and Apostles, that America will hardly live three more years. I bare him witness. [The Audience applauds]. I have not told you this, but I can show it to you in black and white. Say the end came three years after the death of Muhammad's wife. Maybe you can find it. [The Audience applauds]. This is in the Table Talk of Muhammad, and it's also in two or three other places by this Scholar of Islam. They have her death pretty well described; I read it years ago. I did not never want to say nothing about it until after her death, because she had many children and grand-children, and I didn't want them to know it. But, there is much that we must tell today, that yesterday we did not want to tell it. We have many things that we would like to let you know. Putting it in a man's heart ...thirty years ago, these things, I was fortunate to keep quiet until the Time come, for many things of Truth that we did not know.

I stayed with God three years, and near half, and He Taught me night and day; He didn't let me rest. Night and day, of the world of Blackman, not world of Blackman kind, but the world of Blackman; the kind is the devil Caucasian, he is the kind of man. He's mankind, and we're the Man. He don't mind confessing that he's a mankind. He call himself that, and he will admit it to you.

Excuse my slow getting around up here. [The Audience applauds].

I am to teach you Wisdom, Divine Wisdom. I can't haste it, because that you have never had no such Teacher as I. I am a Teacher you don't meet every day. [The Audience applauds]. I can go to the Doctors office, or to his clinic, or to his hospital, and he won't know no difference hardly, from me that he would any other patient. I'm not here to show off. I have been Taught, how to teach you, how to get well and stay well. "Well then, why don't you do that Mister Muhammad? I had to fulfill. The sickness that come to me, I had to bear anyway. If I had not, then I would not be the man that I am. I have to bear that which others bear, when they were here years ago, and thousands of years ago. I am a Fulfiller. So, therefore I have to take and go through with that which Prophets went through thousands of years ago; in order to make it worth this; in order for you to have another Prophet. That's right, you don't need no Prophets after me. [The Audience responds in approval]. I bring you face to face with God and the devil. Therefore, you don't need no more Prophets. I fulfill in your presence, that which Moses, Aaron, Lot, Abraham before them. I fulfill all of them right before your face.[The Audience applauds].

But, you don't know these things, because you never studied Scripture. Therefore, the prophecy of the Scripture, you don't know that until I open it up to you. But, you would read where that God in the Bible teach you that He would send you one, to teach you the Scriptures. And in the Holy Qur'an, it plainly teach you that God will send you one to teach you the Wisdom and the Knowledge of these things…But, since you have not been too much of a Scripture reader, I'm here to put your minds back in it, so that you will find the Truth that I am teaching you; it's there. We're so proud these Days and Times…the teachings of the devil, we don't have time to listen to Spiritual teachings. We laugh at that, because the devils made us like themselves.

He don't care nothing about listening to no Truth; he know he one that was made without Truth. Wasn't none put in him, and that, when you talk to devil bout Truth, he laugh and begin to get mournful looking; and he'll soon dismiss himself, cause that's not the nature of him to sit and listen to Truth; but reach over and get your old banjo, and some other musical instruments and start to playing off the blues, you'll make him happy. Yeah, he's a happy man then, because you have, you are now given to him rather I should say, that which by nature he was made to listen to. He's not made to listen to Truth. No, they want to come here, but they know that they are not fit to sit here and listen to the Truth, since the Truth is against himself.

Yes, I have to Brother, take my time.

It's late, so, it being late coming to us, and we being late in receiving it, let me read to you a verse or two of the Opening Chapter of the Holy Qur'an; it goes something like this, "In the name of Allah, the Beneficent the Merciful. Praise be to Allah, the Lord of the Worlds." Not one world, but of the Worlds. He have a "s" on the end. "The Beneficent and the Merciful. Master of the Day of Requital." He's the Master on the Judgment Day, and, it follows up with the witness of the Righteous in these words, "Thee do we serve, and Thee do we beseech for help."

If we serve a King, that King is the One to help us, because we are His servants. Who are we going to serve, and who are we going to look for help, but our Master? Guide us on the right path." Who are we going to look to be guided on the right path, if we serve Him? No one that we can see. "The path of those upon whom Thou hast bestowed Favours."

This is the Opening of the Holy Qur'an. How beautiful, the path of those whom He has bestowed Favours, not upon the path of those Thou has; pardon me, I'm bout to get…here. "Not the path of those whom wrath is brought down, nor of those who go astray."

We don't want no such thing as chastisement. I tell you Brothers and Sisters, the Holy Qur'an is a Great Book. It's a Book that the devil can't call a lie in books. This is one Book he don't dispute. He recognize it to be a Book full of Truth, and so, he don't bother bout it. Most intelligent white people, they have a Holy Qur'an in their house. They told me that when I was in prison. A guard was Muslim Shriner…He say "Why shouldn't they let you have your Book the Holy Qur'an," he say, "I have mine." He say, "You a Muslim," he say, "they trying to force you to read the Bible." He say, "Because I asked them, the Lieutenant , "I say why don't you let him have his Holy Qur'an? He say, that's what we got him in here for. Let him read the Bible." And he sworn back, "That's a shame to let him be deprived of his Holy Qur'an."

And then your government tells you, that you have the freedom religion. These things is like the Bible prophesy, that the end Time, the Truth will be clear for all to understand. Well, it's becoming so clear today, that even they themselves wishes they could join up with the Truth. Ask me most of the…can some of us join? I tell them, nope. He say, "You don't mean to say aint none of us right?" I say let me give you an example: I say, there's lots of snakes. I say some of them is harmless they call it. I say but yet he's a snake. He start laughing [The Messenger and the Audience laughs], he know I was after him. So he kind of tickled me then. I say surely there are many white people better than others. He say, "But they are white though."

So, they always is asking me some kind of questions. And they all want to know, "Can't some of us get by." I told him, I give him a description of Egypt when Moses went out of Egypt, that some of the Egyptians went out with him. I say this don't mean that every white person is going to be killed on that Day. No, I say many will survive that Day. I say but, he will go back to his own. I say like the Turks people they not going to be killed. I say because Allah told me that they would not. They been trying to practice Islam, though they are white people, but they try to practice Islam. They are called Muslims. I say they are Muslims by their practice. I say but by nature, they like you and all the rest. But by their practice of Islam…God give them an extension of Time; He will do you the same if you're able to practice Islam…I say well that don't get it, don't find no fault, but I don't practice it.

The Good Book say, "If you believe, carry it into practice. A belief that is not practiced goes for nothing." And, well we gets along, very well, as long as you know a snake will sting you; don't go up playing with it. So I tell you these things don't take them for jokes and play. Just remember at all times he's a snake. [The Audience applauds].

If Muhammad…that we live in the Day of Judgment, and that we all got to go to our home, what does our home look like? It look like this: look like the Earth in which you and I own; this is your home. We're not going to be taken up in the sky no place, unless it's in a plane to take you out of trouble to another spot where the trouble is not going. But you're not going to be taken care of like you read there in the Bible, that the Angel will come from Heaven; and you been looking for spirits to come out of the sky. Nope, nothing like that. The Angels will come from Heaven alright enough, but they men and not spooks like you think they are. They are men and that they will come in planes to take to take you up out of the trouble area, and fly you to another peaceful area.

Out in the far Pacific the Bible prophesy to you, that you will be taken to the Islands far away. They do have places out there they can take care of you…forever. And you may live on some of these Islands.

I'm not in no hurry, I just want to talk with you…[The Audience applauds].

There is New Zealand; they have already cried out they could take all of us, but I don't think you will go to New Zealand right away; you may spread out in that area later on, but I don't think you're going now. I don't think you're going nowhere but here. [The Audience applauds].

If the Scripture is True, and it is, that the Lord say, "That it is His Own Good Will to give you the kingdom," well, if it's His Own Good Will to give us the kingdom, He backs it up by other Prophets when He says, "He taketh the kingdom from whom He Pleases, and give it to whom He Pleases." This is a…that He will take this country and give it to another people; and if He don't do that, He's well able to destroy it, and give it to no one. But He can take it, and give it to who He Pleases. And I saw, or rather He showed me how He could take the country without striking a match. He don't have to set it afire. He have already shown me this. He can take it without lighting a match. He don't have to have no fire. Take it very easy; and you can go round and get…for mistreating you. [The Messenger and the Audience laughs, and then applauds].

Just as surely I'm standing here, and He's shown me how easy He could do so with the punishment He put on some of my followers who was hypocrites. As good as He say, "What can he do when he get like that?" That's the way it was shown to me. It was natural, it wasn't in no dream.

These hypocrites was after me to take my life, but He wouldn't let them get to me. Then He got hold of them, and Brother, I don't want Him to get a hold of me like that!

The Holy Qur'an say "It is the worst chastisement." He don't chastise like anyone else, it's the worst. It's the next thing to death. When you get something next to death, Brother you in bad fix; I saw this. He shown me just how that He would chastised those that will not believe and obey. He don't want to kill him; told me not to do so.

Heard Him say, "Well I could slap you down with one hand." Well that's right, but you can't slap that which may desire to get you down like that. So, it is a terrible thing, as the Bible teaches, "Do not fall into the chastisement of God."

Well, Brother Muhammad I'm getting hungry. When is you going to get through with this slow marching stuff? [The Messenger laughs] But, I'm moving on pretty fast. [The Audience applauds].

You professional people, we have all that you can do, if you would join up with us. One thing I must remind you of, I cannot accept you to work for me, unless you want to build right. If you don't want to build right, now, you working for me, I would be working against you [The Audience applauds].

I want you to know these things professional people, that I'm here to lay the foundation for a New World, New Government, and you can't follow the rules of the old government that we have known. We're going to build a New Government, and the Government is a Government of Righteous. I want you to know this.

The Hereafter means after the destruction of the wicked, and their wicked government. That's what we mean when we say Hereafter. And the Hereafter is coming soon for America. She is the First to be Destroyed, because she has mistreated us so terribly long, until God is tired of waiting on us to make up our mind to leave evil and come over to Righteous.

As you have it there in the Bible, it goes something like this, that "Let him that is Righteous be Righteous still; and let him that is wicked, be wicked still, for I come quickly, says the Lord." You have it; well this is the quick time that He's making up His Mind to Come. He have given us sixty or more years to make up our minds. That's a long time waiting on people that are doing, is known no good around. So, you have been given that time from nineteen-fourteen until today, and that's a long time.

So, living your life among the wicked, and they became more wicked every hour for you to practice. He don't let you sleep at night unless your hand is in nothing but evil and filth. He keeps your mind on filth and evil.

So God is tired of America, and since she was the First to bring us here and put us under such conditions and not still trying to repent for her evil doings; there one of the white devil preachers told me, he say, "I know Muhammad that we are guilty of this, and I wished to do something about it." He say, "We have treated you all in a terrible, terrible way, pretty bad." Well, he's just bearing me witness to what I was charging him with. He wasn't doing this voluntarily. I had hemmed him up, cornered him, forcing him to admit these things. They will admit that I'm teaching you Righteousness when you go out there and ask one, he'll tell you, "Who Muhammad?" Yeah, he'll say, "He teaching you all right." Say but, "How many of you all going to believe Muhammad?" He may tell you. He say, "But he's right."

He told me out of his own mouth, he say, "Muhammad isn't it true that your people will not believe anything that the Teacher tell them, unless we white people as you call the blue-eyed devil, till we put our stamp of approval on it, they not going to believe anything." And that's true, when you go to college, as I been told; and I have a son, he's over there. He went to other colleges, tried to put him through Al Ahzad in Egypt, and he still is a disbeliever. So, he told me say, "Dad," he says, "when you goes to these colleges and universities," he say, "they make you infidels." He say, "You don't believe like they do." I say well son you know better. I say believe or let lone. He say, "No dad, I didn't mean that you wasn't right." I say, well I mean son this, that you know, and now you can take it or leave it.

Well, he teaching school in Tennessee down there to the devil. Well, leave a man to what he wants to be. Don't try to force a man to believe in that which he don't want to believe in, cause you'll have only a hypocrite.

So, my beloved listeners and professional people, your profession will help us and yourself too, if it was used in Islam. And since you are here, this is where you decide. Since you have learned you have the privilege to deal with any people or country, that …valuable. If you want to get in, I will show you how, but I'm afraid if you go with the knowledge you have now, you could be the loser then.

I don't get nothing but credit from God from guiding you. I don't, He don't give me a penny for right guiding, right teaching. I don't say I won't accept you giving something for the work…but I'm not out here to preach and teach for no money. I'm out here to teach and preach to you how to save your life. We're at the crossroads [The Audience applauds], we got to accept or reject, one or the other.

These men coming here, dressed up in the Moon, Stars, these are the people of the Hereafter. Now don't think you can get by, if it's not in your heart; got to be in your heart. Nope, no show-offs today, and these people not showing off, they have it in their heart. Their whole entire dress can be singled out, and spoken with understanding in these few words: Freedom, Justice, Equality. Freedom you have never had a chance to enjoy, because you have been with your slave-master, depriving you of Freedom, and also Justice have never come to you; Equality of nations have never come to you.

Now it's coming to you. You wear this uniform anywhere on the planet Earth, among any nation, you're welcome. They will welcome you, come in, because they know you was not a fool to put that, these…you have wrapped around your shoulders…They know you was not a fool, for you to wear that. They who put it on you, taught you what it was, and that's right. I teach you what it is, and teach you what it means. And you can go anywhere on the Earth and use what I teach you, and they will say, "He teaching you right." I'm not going to teach you nothing but right.

We have lots of things we want to get around to you. The time is so near to the end, we can't go through the end like we want to; and I can't…like reverend…you know…I can't do that, I have to take time and teach.[The Audience applauds]. And we have work that you have not got acquainted with yet. You write your letter in to get joined up or registered up with We the Muslim's work. Probably you never seen the Secretary that take your letter, and examine them for correction.

Is Sister Hussein in here? Yes, come here, come on up…This Sister Margaret Hussein, the one that you write in for your letter to be okay for passing in the Nation Of Islam, so that you may become a Registered Muslim in the Nation, because you can't get in the Nation Of Islam like you can in Christianity. Oh no, it's not that easy, it's a little harder than that.

So, this is Sister Hussein. She's the one that read your letters, and okay them if they are right. Maybe some of you have never met her. So Sister Hussein, I met her a long time ago, and I keep, you know chastising her every now and then. When you don't hear from her so often, she's fine. [The Messenger and the Audience laughs].

Well you know the Bible say, "God doesn't take one of us less He give us a spanking." He must chastise us to let us know that He's God. So, I want Him to chastise me, if I'm wrong, because I know then He love me. [The Audience applauds].

Messenger: You have anything to say, you could say something.

Sister Hussein: I'd like to say As Salaam Alaikum to the Sisters and Brothers; and I thank Allah for this privilege of meeting you, because the correspondence is a must. And the work of the Messenger is the most important work in the world. And I wish that we would all understand that everything Messenger does is based on Scripture, because he is a Divine Messenger, and we are a Holy people.

Sister Hussein: So, therefore we must look at the Messenger in the light of who he really is, and understand our greatness and the path that we are for the Messenger; and the great people we are to be privileged to have such a Messenger as the Messenger of Allah. [The Audience applauds].

Messenger: I thank you Sister Hussein, and if there's anything that you think that you need to tell me that you don't like in her office, why you may stand and tell me, and I will try and correct it. That's very nice of you, if you don't have any charges against our Secretary.

OCTOBER 22, 1972 PART TWO / SIDE TWO

SHIP NAME JESUS!

…tell you and me in his book, that his ship was name Jesus. Think over that! Giving a slave boat now, that good name. "Since you believe in Jesus, oh, here is your Jesus." [The Audience applauds]. That's a awful thing to think of, that he'll now tell you, that the slave boat prison house that he brought you cross the water on, that's your Jesus.

You could see him with fire and brimstone, and think that he giving them cool water. Wicked, take a innocent person out of his home, and bring him into a far off country three thousand or more miles across nothing but water, then tell him, "I am your master; I am your god, don't tell me your name is Ali or Muhammad; your name is Mister Culpepper. Any kind of old name, Mister Wood, Mister Bird, Mister Fish; Nothing!

Now today, Allah have found us. The Bible proceed His coming with a prophesy, "I will go and search for My people, and when I have found them, I will bring them again; set them again among their own people and in their own home."

Brother this is beautiful. One writer say that, "When He found them, He goes back and tell His people; and then He will say to the Angels," "Go and bring everyone that is called by my name. I have saved you for My Own Self, for My Own Glory." Now today He's after us, offering us His Beautiful names: Muhammad Ali, those are two Great Names…

Now we so proud over being called Mister Brown, Mister Jackson, Mister Culpepper; and you ask what your name mean? He say…he don't know what it mean; all he know white man give it to him. [The Audience laughs]. You shouldn't be calling, what? If I'm not named that, what am I named then? You get…We want to give you…Or he may be some Professor…he'll go to arguing with you, tell me what my name is?

Forty years ago you couldn't hardly tell them that. They much better now. But forty years ago, they would cuss us out. They laugh at Muhammad…them funny names, where you get them names from? Call them funny names. I was there; I was then trying to get them to accept.

So let me see if I have a card in my pocket…in my pocket to show what a beautiful God…They would look at it and be almost ready to jump, soon as he see it….I had it in my pocket. I should…I mostly have one, in one place or another. Sometime I have it in my Qur'an, so that I can…

336

However, don't get impatient now. [The Audience applauds]. Thank you. But, you can't go back to your people, not even in Africa with the white man's name. Now many of you say, "I go to Africa," but when the check up Day come they send you back, because you must have a Muslim name, Islamic people's name, to see the Hereafter. You can't go with white people names, and Africa will tell you that. No, when the Time come for your separation, you must return to us with the name of Allah.

We all have to go in His name. And the Bible teaches us that; and why should not we leap and jump to get out of the name of an enemy, who chained up our Fathers and Mothers, and beat them with chains once they got them over here.

Why shouldn't we be happy; you don't seem to be happy to get out of the devil's name. Why, you should have the Temple...to get out of the name of an enemy out there killing your Brothers...for nothing.

You walking by like a sheep, while they slaughtering other sheep; this sheep...that's the way he is...like a rabbit he sleep...not paying no attention to the dog, and here come the dog eating him up. The dog won't...rabbit when he lying sleep. He'll make a noise and make him jump up...this dog after rabbit in the South, and that rabbit dog of mine, he'd go up there and catch the rabbit...down in his bed under his...and with his ears lying down on his neck, the dog won't jump on him like that. He take his feet pat the grass and make a little noise, and the rabbit jump up and he run. Then he takes out after him. He give him a chance for his life.

But, look what these devils with those boys out there; they lying there sleep, he wouldn't wake him. He sent a blast of bullets in the man while he was sleep. He had him anyway, why didn't he just tell him, "Well I got you covered, you want to take it without fighting?" That would have been just...scared of him [The Audience applauds].

So, the devil blast the man's life out of him. He didn't-dead man never saw his enemy; didn't know what he looked like. He died before he could be waken. He didn't know what killed him. See what kind of people you live among; and that you praise them up and wishes you could stay among them.

Well, look what you are doing. I don't say these men ...not have gotten killed if we had helped him. But...from seeing another like that...Why didn't you and your followers...Mister Muhammad take...The reason I didn't take no part in it, because they had asked me out before they got killed. I spoke about them before they got in this death...stuff. They came to my house. When I spoke about them in our paper, they ask me not to talk no more about them, say, "Just keep your, your paper, and don't put us in it. So, I say okay, and I didn't, until today.

So, God told me to go ahead and let them do it, and I let them; and they got wiped out. I knew this...was coming. So, time went on and I taken myself in my house, shut my mouth in my own paper; and say nothing about them, cause they didn't appreciate it. They don't even appreciate it today, but tomorrow they will. [The Audience applauds].

I say, Brothers and Sisters, some of our people is so dumb, that God Himself can't help them. That's right, they are so dumb to the knowledge of good, that they won't accept God, because they don't know Him, and they consider God just something we talk...But, they will soon know it's coming to past. Oh Brother, fly to Allah for refuge in this Day and Time. It's awful the thing I see coming. Think over the storms and earthquakes, cold weather that the scientists keep telling you is on the way. Over here in such and such a place, it's...Yes sir, cold and it's going to be so terrific here one of these days, that you can hardly breathe...like death walking round...to your lungs.

It's on the way to America, and that, you will find heat from the Sun that will be so terrific that you can't breathe it, that you'll be running seeking a cool breeze. That's on it's way. As sure as I'm standing here, these things are bound to hit America...thing is terrible, cause it don't give you no place for refuge...take you off your feet and it can drop you a mile...

EVERY MAN MUST GO TO HIS OWN!

As Salaam Alaikum. You may be seated.

My beloved Sisters and Brethren, I'm very happy, thankful to Allah that we have met again; and that we hope that Allah...also here with us. We have been trying to gather the whole Nation of the Blackman in America to be right here with us today, or somewhere just as long as they are with us. And we have not failed to meet our people; they have failed to meet us. [The Audience responds in approval]. We are very happy that you that are...us. Regardless if it's one, or one million, or one hundred million, whatever He gives us is what He wants, and we are happy that He wanted us that is present.

We are living in such times, that we know not where we are going to escape to; only in the Place where He's at. If we are believers, then we will be where He is. Brothers and Sisters the Time is changing so fast, until I hardly know what to say to you from last Sunday. Many things has changed since last Sunday, and it's changing minutes, hours; and that we are a people who have no home. We are living in enemies home. The only way we can have a home, we have to remove someone to take us a home. [The Audience applauds].

I think you that is visiting us today, all you professional people that visit us yesterday; you cannot say that you have understood us for one day hearing. You must remember Professors, that you don't get a degree here, on one visit. You didn't get a degree from the college, nor universities in one day of this civilization.

Some of us jump to conclusions too early. That's due to your lack of knowledge in what we are doing, and don't care to spend too much time trying to learn. But I would like to say to you, that this visiting us to hear what we have to say, is to visit the builders of a New Foundation for you a New Home. You don't have one, and we're trying to show you how to build one.

Every man, as it is written, must go to his own. If you don't have a own, you better try to seek a own even though it be somebody else's own; but you better try to find a way out of America. America is about to be destroyed. The America that we has known, is about to be taken away from us. She's not going to tell you, so God Taught me, until you see it on your heels. Then you'll jump and say, "He said to me, I believe...The white man of America is not going to tell you how close his doom is." You will get proud and want to get even with him, and that's right. We will believe that we are safe in trying to get even with him, if we know the exactly Time, but he's not going to tell you.

He's very close to his doom at this present hour, but he's not telling you. He's wanting you to believe that he have yet a long future. He don't have one. The white man was not put on the Earth to live forever. It's a new people among us that was made, not created.

I want you to understand, you and I are a Created people, but the white man is not a created people, he is a made people. You and I have a long, long, old birth record. It's so long that we cannot tell you when we was born, but the white man, he is a man that our Scientists made here recently, here six thousand years ago. That's no more than talking six hours, in the face of the Ancient Scientists.

He's a very late man. You use to think, and was told, that we all was created together, alike. No, we was not created together, nor are we alike. They're different from us, and you're different from them.

So, don't get that old idea that God created us all from Adam. See this is the ignorant teaching and the misunderstanding that you think that God made us all the same Time, and all alike and God loves us all, you're mistaken. There was two Gods in this kind of making. One made a evil man, and One made a good man, or allowed a good man to remain. The evil man is six thousand years, and the good man, we Black people, have no birth record. God didn't Create us six thousand years ago. No sir, as God have Taught me in the Person of Master Fard Muhammad, to Whom Praises is Due Forever, that we were here millions of years before white folks…millions of years; no such thing as we all came together.

Did you know that would have been a pretty tough on the Maker to make a Blackman and a white man at the same Time? Just think over that. Yeah a tough job, but He had the Blackman here for millions and millions, and trillions of years before we had a white man; and the white man was made by the Blackman, so God Taught me.

Easy to understand, he was made through grafting. Not say here stand up Blackman; here stand up white man, like we use to think from the dust of the Earth. You must understand that, that also have a meaning. It don't mean that a man was made from actually dust. That's science, the science means this: that he's made of the weaker and the lower side of the Blackman. And that, this God have given to me to explain to you that which you do not know, and do not understand.

Ah you say, "I know all of that." Well I know you way back yonder too. You and I use to pick cotton together; and in those Days both of us was the same and I didn't know no more than you. But today, God have Taught me a little more than what I knew in those days, and I'm trying to…

HEAVEN IS A PLACE YOU MAKE

You must remember, if you show the sign of being discouraged in trying to get a paper out to our people with the news in it that I never read before, and you the Muhammad Speaks Newspaper, when you purchase that paper, it's like buying a book. But you are so disinterested in your own, that you glance at it and go on, and don't care if anyone else look at it or not. You are disinterested people on the whole. Such News, going around in your hands over this darkened country they call North America; it is a shame that you get so disinterested so quick! Don't want to sell the paper even if we pay you a dollar a paper to sell it.

This is awful! We should take the paper and run with it. Some of the paper is inequal to some of the publications of the same, but nevertheless, we don't tarry long before we have another one out there with everything you want to read.

Excuse me, I kind of sound like once upon a time when I was a young man, I saw them loading a locomotive up with wood, and they would heat it with that type of fuel to make it run. Now we see them loading these kind of vehicles up with gas; they make faster time.

Okay, we want to load up ourselves with education that will make faster time in getting over to the educated people with our people visiting us, that we are very proud of. Hope they are proud to visit us, and to see what we are doing.

We have with us, Professor Frank C...Health Center Administrator of Pittsburg, Pennsylvania, and we thank you. Wherever you are at, you may stand, let us all see what you look like; there he is over here. [The Audience applauds]. We thank you; you are not to proud to visit us. Most of the Professors that don't visit us, they a little proud.

Where's Miss Shwinler, not Schwinler, thank you Sister. [The Audience applauds]. Miss Schwinler she...is from Pittsburg, Pennsylvania. She is a Teacher, and Teachers is what we want and what we need. You can't get no place this Day and Time with no education. We must be taught education, and it must be the best.

This is why I tell you that our schools must take on the best Teachers that it can find. We can't go along with no second grade teaching. We have to have number one first grade teaching, that will compete with the civilized world. And this what we must employ here in Chicago, in Temple No.2. We must have the best to be the best.

We can't go long with the worst discarded things of education, because that's the only thing that does us up with the world, or with the world. It is a good education. It is a good Teacher that have that good education to teach us. We must work hard to try to support them, so that they can deliver to us what they have in their heads. Don't never be stingy with supporting an Educator. They must be supported, so that we can be supported. So we thank the Educator and the Teacher of the Educator.

You must not become proud and want to be dignified over the Teacher; let the Teacher grow you up to that, and she will teach you what she knows. And if she teaches you what she know, well then you her equal, but if she can't get to you, then you will never be her equal.

Let's stand up on the firm foundation of Islam; it is Freedom, Justice, and Equality. To be equal, then you must know what the other fellow knows.

Misses Schwinler from Pittsburg, Pennsylvania, Chicago have many posts for you, if you are the proper Teacher.

I'm the kind of fellow that's very hasty at times; and I'm a kind of fellow that I'm very slow at times. When a man feeling for something he can't be too fast. That's how I remember once me and my Brother we was fishing, and he pulled out a fish out of hollow tree in the water. I went there and went to pull at the wrong thing. So, I say I would never be so fast to run behind the other fisherman, reaching for fishes in hollows. When I saw a snake creep up on the water, I didn't want no fish.

The F.O.I. must remember that every paper they sell, they are making money two ways. And in the two ways, we would like to be the winner of one if not both.

We also have Miss Billie Webb, a Designer, Chicago, Illinois. Mister Curtis Porter he's a Program Director. I guess he's a good fellow for me. I'm not in a hurry don't worry. [The Audience applauds]. Miss Billie Webb, Designer; Mister Curtis Porter, Program Director. I may call on you to have just a word or so to what you think of our design here.

The Blackman must either…his home back that he was robbed of, or he must go elsewhere and find him a home. This is a Time that everybody's trying to go for self; and if self don't have nothing, self better do something for self. [The Audience responds in approval].

To tell you what has been told to me of…He have come here to take you away from your enemies and sit you in a Heaven, not to follow you, but to give you a Heaven right here. Not to go off and die, no stay alive and get into Heaven right here. This is really ignorant teachings: teach a man to die to go to a place while he live.

We have heard in the past that Heaven is something you go to. No sir, Heaven is not a place you go to, Heaven is a place you make; and like Hell is not a place you go to, you get that here. And both Heaven and Hell is in the same place. Everywhere is good until you make it evil or no good. There is no bad place to go to; all the places is good. You make them bad when you go to them. No such thing as a good and bad place; human beings makes good and bad places. If you are no good here, why you want to go to that place and make it like you, bad, we shouldn't do that.

We have much we want to talk about…the governments of the Earth are at odds with each other. If you want to join some of them, we better know surely what we are about to join.

We have gone out to try to do something good for you. We have at the present time ordered a better shipload of fish for you, and at a better price than you can get here. I'm never forgetting you night nor day. I cannot when the Job was put upon me by God to lift you up out of the…condition that you're in. We wants Heaven for our people here in North America, and we're going to get it, with the help of Allah.

As you see we're digging out a foundation here at 7800 Cottage Grove. One of our Black Contractors is going to build us a mighty nice building there. And you be seeing in a few days, they will be digging out…around Cottage Grove, and you will see them around here digging to beautify this yard here. We going to make Heaven wherever we are. [The Audience applauds].

We have built four or five houses across the street in front of us…4847 Woodlawn. You go by there and you will see the type of buildings that we have built and continue this way, and you'll say, "I believe these buildings will make me feel like I'm in Heaven." Go cross and look in one; never have you seen no such building in America, and I want you to live in that type of building in America.

These are samples of which Allah promise you and me. I want you to live in them. You back me up like He's doing, it won't be after you die it will be while you live. [The Audience applauds].

We have been under the feet of white folks so long, that we have almost become hopeless of ever getting out from under his feet. But don't be like the dry bones, that example of what we look like, a dry bone. A senseless person don't have any knowledge of self. All his knowledge is gone, and his hopes is gone. He believes he is a bonafide do-nothing; and never will be anything.

So I say get up from that, you are not hopeless. "And he said we are cut off from our part, and our hopes is lost." We are not…just because the other fellow claims his…it's your part. We are not cut off; just wake up and get out if the thought there is nothing for us. There is…for us, when the Originator, our Father, our Heaven and Earth.

What we look like talking bout we don't have nothing; we have plenty. A little skunk just came about here the other day, six days ago, smelling up the community. [The Audience applauds]. And you ran away from your own thinking that he's the boss. He's not the boss, not in nothing; not in nothing but what you smell of him. [The Audience responds in approval].

Now he can be that boss…I don't want to be the boss of a skunk smell. I certainly will get out the way of him, till I can find something to get him out of the way. [The Audience responds in approval].

You should remember that could have been behind white, because it's just impossible to take white out of Black, but you can take white out of Black, but not Black out of white. [The Audience applauds]. This makes you to be the First, regardless to what people say. You are the First, because you can't make this our color from white, no sir. It has been experimented many times by the enemy to see if he could not claim first too, or equal as first. But he can't do it; impossible. Now he's going up; Allah opens up the Heavens, as the Holy Qur'an teaches to let him go and peep in, then bring him down to the bottom of Hell, because he not able to stay up there. He not able to stay anywhere, only where Allah permits him to stay. Then Allah takes him away from that at Will. Anytime He Will, He take him away.

Ah, the white man go to the Moon, yeah, but what is the Moon? It's our Moon; he didn't find there where he made anything. No, he didn't make nothing up there on that Moon, we made it. Let him go and peep at it, making instruments to look at Mars. Well, when he see what's on Mars, he won't see no mark of his. It's our Mars, our people, so God have Taught me; and that he didn't know they were there until a few days ago. He use to look at Mars and just call it a Star and that's all. But our Fathers made some type of intelligent beings like our self that walk on two feet and arms. They are not animals, they are intelligent people. The marks that we see on Mars, is not from a ignorant, silly, uncivilized person, they show signs of civilization; and they look something similar to us, not exactly, but they look similar. They walks on two feet, and they not white folks. [The Audience applauds].

That show you and teach you, the Blackman of this planet is the First, since we don't find no planet coming out with no super civilization over us. The Mars people they have civilization; it's not equal with ours, so God have Taught. They're superior in trying to live a long time over us. This is just because we got so much sense we crazy. That's right, we know to much, and always is experimenting to know more, to learn more. These people teaches them to be satisfied with what they have, and given by God, call nature.

So they live, so God have Taught me, in the Person of Master Fard Muhammad, twelve hundred of our Earth years, while we sitting round here thinking we doing something to get fifty. That's right we live to get fifty years old, and we think we have lived a long time. Exhausting the power of our thinking brains, before ever we get in the world good, too fast, that we just exhaust our knowledge of seeking and testing that which we have arrived at, higher knowledge before we learn the higher places of Wisdom and Understanding. We're exhausting ourselves...with each other.

So my beloved Brothers and Sisters, I don't want you to think that I'm here this afternoon to exhaust your patience with what I'm after trying to do for you; to get knowledge in your head that you never have had. [The Audience applauds].

I don't pretend to represent myself to you as a great knower. No, I'm just as common and unlearned as you and awake. It's just God Himself, choose me after He found me here among you, and you among me.

And He choose me to help bring to you, His Own Wisdom and Knowledge. So I'm trying to do that. We cannot boast of each other, that we have more than you; and I'm better than you. Never to get on that kind of subject. We all is alike, but the difference is that one is taught by nature to be more quicker and eager to understand that which others is slow in understanding.

So this is what is meant by God finding the stone that He needed that was well qualified, by being the stone that He wanted to build up our Nation with. We are a Nation, we use to call our self a race. Since the coming of the Teaching, the coming of God and His Teachings, the Best Knower; He have made us to understand that we are not a race of people, but we are a Nation. A race is something that have a beginning and end. But a nation is something that is standard; something that is setting up Time posts to go between, it's not made for a nation. A nation cannot be...by my...it is a race, and this is why we call the white man a race, because they are racing with Time to get to another post. And when he get to the last post, the sixth post that declare his Time, and that's his last post number six, his end, there's no post for him to reach.

My beloved Brothers and Sisters, as you don't know what kinds of things I go through with. I work hard and I be tired. [The Audience applauds]. And I come before you, I'm over anxious to talk with you, but energy have a limit. I can't always teach you what I want to teach you due to...frame that has carried so much work, that it is tired, and wishes that I said to it rest a little.

I all but was ready to tell it that this morning, but I heard that there was some of my Brothers and Sisters coming from the South, and that they were driving or flying to get here a long ways from their place to see and hear what I have to say here. Being over anxious to...you about the rise of me among you by God, I want you to know that I'm ready, willing, and loving to meet you that is coming from Alabama, Georgia, Mississippi, of the South, because I was born down there. And I want you to know and see what God have done for you in raising me up from among you. [The Audience applauds]. Thank you.

I'm not raised here just to keep you company, but I'm raised by Almighty God to do just what you find in the Bible parable says, concerning God raising up someone to teach you. I'm that fellow; I am that Elijah that the Bible say must come. [The Audience applauds]. That man according to the Bible must proceed God Himself, to make a way for God.

What is this make way? It is to convert people to God, that believe in the God that we believe is to Present Himself among us. This man have a knowledge of that God and know that God, so that he can teach you what you may expect; he knows it, God acquaints Himself with that man First.

I was with God, the God of the Power of the Universe for three years and four months, night and day. He and I was riding around in the streets of this city, and in Detroit for three years and a half, before ever you could recognize that he was here with me. When He left I was trying to acquaint you with Him and His visit, and the necessity of His visit.

So today we can gladly say, that God has visit us in the Person, in Person, not in a spirit form, but in flesh and blood. And He have Taught me what He have Taught me. You ought to believe or let it alone. He's not a God to beg us. He's not out to beg you for Him a people; He's independent of us.

He tell us the Truth, and tells us to take it or leave it. It's to our benefit if we accept it; it's to our destruction if we disbelieve. We have always been like our enemy, and believed in our enemy, and not our friends. I know hypocrites of mind, they started out following fine, and they are not following me, only in words.

So I say, you are putting yourself in a position to be not liked nor wanted. Go way from me, and you have no friends with God nor man. This is what I'm telling you, leave me and you have no friends with God nor man, I will repeat. I am the Door, I am the Gate. [The Audience applauds]. I could easily say to you when you seem to want to walk away from me, go right ahead Brother, go right ahead Sister, but you can't get to where you want to go, Hell or Heaven, less you want to find yourself tangling with me.

One thing about it, and why I speak like that, because you have been given to me. You don't belong to nobody but me. [The Audience applauds]. The Bible and the Holy Qur'an teaches you that. Some describe the man as the Door, or a Gate, but nevertheless, I can gladly tell you that I has been given for my people to take to God to make a New people out of them. And God said to me out of His Own Mouth, out of His Own Mouth, He says, "The one that you put out, I'm not going after." But you can't believe that. If you was wise enough, the very dissatisfied thought of me of you would hurt you. I don't want to hurt you, I want to save you. You may say, "Where you got any power to save me?" It's given to me from God. Nobody wanted us, think over that. Every nation rejected us, because we are too silly for them to try to civilize. And they say, "Ahh, the Hell with them, they not but a few no way." That's what they say.

Just think over President Nassar when I was over there in Egypt while he was alive, he criticized me for wanting to teach you all, "When all of that host of Africans would listen to you over night. You have a million and a half down in French West Africa." He say, "You not going to do nothing with those people," referring to you. Nobody wanted the job, because you are devil proud, and you are devil lovers, and these people, the devil is their enemy. They want to get them out of their country, and take over for self. And you'll drag them in, and try to tell them that they are better than they are. Think over that, that's terrible.

You know a snake will bite, and the type that is more poisonous than others; then you trying to represent the most poisonous snake. Of all of them I should love and respect, you actually teach love of the devil, because you love him and you thinks that he's just as good as anybody else. You have been poisoned, so poisoned by the bite of the enemy, but you don't think he's poison because you have become absolutely senseless to his bite.

So my beloved Brothers and Sisters, the Time now is right that you rise up and accept your own, from the South to the North, and from the North to the South. Don't fear my poor Brother and Sister from the South, God has risen me up to teach you and show you the way to him; and all that I can get to turn their faces to Him, is saved as I am. I teach you he's the blue-eyed devil behind his back, and in front of his face. [The Audience applauds]. This what God said he was. And He ask me was I with Him to put you on top of civilization, I say yes Sir just back me up. He say, "I'm with you." And He has backed me up in going out and coming in. I'm no more...

COMMENTS FROM THE AUDIENCE

…you on top of civilization, I say yes Sir just back me up. He say, "I'm with you." And He has backed me up in going out and coming in. I'm no more afraid; I'm afraid of nothing but Allah. [The Audience applauds]. You follow me and you won't me afraid. God don't want a coward, because He's not a coward Himself, and He don't want to enlist cowards on His Book. No, you must be fearless like myself. You just do like me, I'm alright.

Don't be the aggressor, don't be the first to try to cause trouble, because Muslims not trouble risers, they are peaceful people. You don't have to show us your bravery by being the first to run out and knock a blue-eyed down. No, don't attack, this against the nature of the Righteous. Righteous do not attack people that is not attacking them.

Sometime God let you become a failure, to teach you a lesson. Throughout the History of man, you find where the man being unrighteous in the way of…civilization without …and he becomes the loser sometimes.

So I say to you my beloved Brothers and Sisters, let us build us up a nation that we have no equal; no nation before us have, and didn't know how to do the things we have, now that we have ourselves in our midst. No people in History ever had such.

Well you say, "Moses had it." Not like this type of a God. Moses had a God alright enough, but that God was not the equal of this One; was not the equal. So I say we had the Best. We have an Eternal God, meaning that His Wisdom is Eternal, it will live forever. So let's make good of this.

It will have been much unhandy for to have gotten a Teacher that was inferior to the enemy; or teacher that was equal if he strive hard to come as superior as we. But he can't never be our superior, because that we had the superior quality in us at the beginning while his knowledge came out of our superior knowledge. Therefore, he can't never over take us.

I'm going to say to you, you have a offer that no people have ever had before you, to become the superior over people. No people has had this offered to them. I want you to remember to be proud of the Coming and the Presence of our God; a Merciful God that choose us out of the mud and junk of the civilization, that trample upon us; caused us to become disliked, overlooked by civilization of the Earth.

So, now you can stand up and tell the world that I'm myself again, and I love to be myself.

[The Audience applauds].

Since we have these wonderful visitors present among us, we want them to know that we thank them for visiting us. I'm asking them to come out and tell us what they think of us, and our work that we are doing. So, I'm going to call before us to have a word to say or words if she likes.

Messenger: Miss Billie Wells, Designer, Chicago, Illinois. Miss Billie Wells, come over here to this mic [microphone]. Miss Wells, there the mic [microphone] the mic [microphone], or if you want to come up here it's up to you.

Sister: I can thank the Messenger this morning for allowing me the privilege. In all the years I've been a Black woman, to say when I walked through at 25th & Federal, that it was the first time in my life that I was glad to be a Black person. I saw working quietly accomplishing something that I had never dreamed I would see ever in this life.

Sister: Since that time, I've had the privilege of communicating with him in his own home, eating his food and absorbing the wisdom that ever flowing wisdom. I still haven't been able to really capture how this boundless flow of energy, where it comes from; and I guess this is what he is trying to do to me, that Allah is more Powerful than I myself.

Sister: I've had the pleasure of working with several of his followers in your new import shop, seeing people work with humility trying to accomplish what the Messenger has set out for them to do, and I have offered a helping hand. I pray to God that I find the right tool to help in this effort to make Black women more beautiful, than they already are.

[The Audience applauds].

Messenger: Thank you Miss Wells, she is a Designer, and to Design; excuse me, or help me to Design…beautiful women to more beautiful. I thank Allah for Miss Wells.

Messenger: We not only was made ignorant by our enemies, but our enemies robbed us of our beauty appearance. So Allah is now helping us to get restored again to our beauty appearance that the enemy robbed us of.

Messenger: We also have Mister Curtis Porter, Program Director. Will you stand, have a word to say to the Audience Mister Porter?

Brother: I've very little to say except I'm very proud to be here, and have long recognized Elijah Muhammad as a foundation of Black knowledge in this century of the Blackman's life.

[The Audience applauds].

Messenger: I thank you.

Messenger: I'm like the Book say, that the Jesus, he went out in the morning and he went out in the evening looking for someone to come in the vineyard to help him. So I'm like that saying goes, I'm looking for help morning and evening.

Messenger: I don't know whether I called out Miss Sandra Schwinler, or not, if I did, come on out, let us look at you if nothing else. [The Audience applauds]. Miss Schwinler is a Teacher of Pittsburg, Pennsylvania.

Sister: I like to say this is my second time coming here to Chicago. First time I enjoyed it and the second time I enjoyed it. My husband has been...in Pittsburg, and my little boy has been enrolled at the University in Pittsburg. I hope in the near future to become a follower. I really enjoyed the program. I read his book...and everything. I really think it's a wonderful program, thank you.

Messenger: Thank you.

[The Audience applauds].

Messenger: We always is happy to hear someone among us say something that is good for us. Something constructive, because we need to be rebuild; and when I hear you Teachers, you Educators say something, I listen closely to what you say, to...you whether or not you have some of that mind that I have; build up a waste and destroyed people; build them back up again in a better knowledge, than what or rather that which caused their fall.

Messenger: We can beat the man that's thrown us down; then we don't intend to let them rise up no more. Yeah, thank you.

Messenger: We have another Sister here. I don't know whether I can call her name or not. Her name is Miss Dorothy Reddick, I believe. Is that the proper way to pronounce...Misses Dorothy Reddick? [The Audience applauds]. She's a Television Writer, Producer, Director.

Sister: First of all I like to thank the Honorable Elijah Muhammad for inviting me here. I do know one thing that in the roll of Communication, that there are not enough Blacks involved. I know that in Communications that...man has all the power, all the stations, all the T.V. Stations, Radio Stations in which we definitely need, because it's a powerful tool.

Sister: So I'm here today trying to see what kind of roll I could play in the Muslims.

Maybe in regards to getting involved, or seeing what I can do in getting involved with the Muslims, in regards to this effort, because we definitely need it. Thank you.

[The Audience applauds].

Messenger: We have a Doctor Nichols here, come here. [The Audience applauds]. We always need Doctors wherever we go, because we are afflicted by our enemies; and we need Doctors in helping us to get this affliction healed on us. Doctor Nichols:

Brother: First, I would like to say that, we should be ever grateful to Allah for having this opportunity to hear the Wisest man that the world has ever known. [The Audience applauds]. And as a Physician in the other system right now, we see in living color every day, many things that testify beyond a shadow of a doubt not only our need for a better medical system here, but a better medical center across this country.

Brother: The Tuskegee experiment, is just, an example, of many things like that, that's going on in this country. We have mad Neurosurgeons who want to cut out parts of the brain to attain prisoners who are considered violent by their standards. We have people at Rockefeller University who are giving sickle cell anemia patients cyanide infusions.

Brother: When you see this kind of thing going on, and I could go on and on ad infinitum giving examples of what's happening. We know that the only choice we have is to get behind the Most Holy Apostle the Honorable Elijah Muhammad.

[The Audience applauds].

Brother: I would like to say in conclusion, I would like to say now, that I give, with the deepest sense of humility and submission to the Nation Of Islam, whatever I can help bring about.

[The Audience applauds].

Messenger: We thank the Doctor.

Messenger: We being the First, in the Sun, and before the Sun, because it was our Father Who Created the Sun; love to see our people come forth, and speak something pertaining to their greatness, and their qualities to be made great in them. Therefore, we can say to the world, and say to God that we are proud of ourselves that He Created. We no more hates ourselves. The enemy has made us hate our Black self. Today we love our Black self. We no more hate Black, we hate white. [The Audience applauds].

Messenger: You go to an ant-bed, and if a white ant tries to cross a red ant-bed, a black ant-bed, he will get killed; he will never reach the other side; they don't allow mixing. So I say to you, see a white one cross your doorstep, try to get rid of him, and tell him to keep off of my step. [The Audience responds in approval]. I don't say you go out there and try to kill him, at this time [The Audience applauds].

Messenger: We have with us also a Reverend…I don't know he could be just a missionary, but he thinks that I'm in error, in, (what is that Brother?) in many of my statements. My Brother come on out and tell me some of it. [The Audience applauds].

Brother: Greetings in our Lord and Saviour Jesus Christ name I want to say this, first of all, that it was mentioned about Abraham, this is true…Abraham also had two sons one son was born of the flesh, the second son was born of the spirit. I am a child of the spirit myself. Consequently I do not put emphasis upon personally things, other than the fact that I must have them in order to maintain my physical existence. My emphasis is put on spiritual things.

Brother: I love all my brethren. I love everything that our Heavenly Father has Created. This include the Black, so-called white man, red man, yellow man, brown, and my so-called Black Brothers. There is no such thing in the eye sight of our Heavenly Father, we're all His children.

Brother: Now, this is when we are born of the spirit, do we become children of God, because when we are in the flesh we are children of Satan; we covet that which is upon the Earth. We have no regard for our Brothers, our Sisters, or even the beasts of the Earth. We trample upon each other, without any disregard for what we do.

Brother: Now, this is what we must do, put an end to, not being this respectful to you Brother. I believe that you are Honorable as you say, but…I must remind you also that at your store there are many things that you have priced higher than at other stores, you see. Now, if you had all these Black people so much at heart, then you should be able to be more lenient with your prices. Your prices are more absorbent than the so-called white devil.

Brother: You must bear this in mind. You do tell us not to negotiate with the devil but, you must negotiate within yourself. We do not need anyone to act between us and the devil if you want to deal with the devil. This is true. I believe that you are Honorable Brother, but you are in error in many of your statements.

Brother: You must also bear in mind that the injustice of man to man is the greatest injustice of all; and our Heavenly Father is tired of it. This is why the Earth is in the condition it is in now.

Brother: Now, if we do not get together shortly, we are all going to…And all of you who do not know a thought greater than that of man, I urge you to open your heart and ask the Disciple, or the Son of God, or the Son of Allah, whatever you call that Brother who is between us and the Heavenly Father to come in your heart, and direct you in the right path. You understand, direct you personally. No man can save your soul for you, other than our Lord and Saviour Jesus Christ. You must learn him for yourself. You must, and…don't go around hating any longer.

Brother: You see because for the last four and a half, five years we've gone around saying how Black beautiful is, Black power, or Black is this, you understand; and yet we have been slaughtering each other the way whites have been doing us at the stockyards; you understand that.

Brother: And another thing, if we were so proud, I'm not saying you Brethren, but this is something we must tell the other Brothers. You understand, our Lord and Saviour said "I am my brother's keeper." You see, we are our Brothers keeper, and we must keep our Brothers.

Brother: You who are…already, you who are aware of the Divine power already, if we do not need to get among ourselves and testify to the Goodness of Allah, or to the goodness of Jesus Christ. We must go out and save those who do not know. This is our charge, because we don't need to keep each other as we know already. We need to go and teach those who don't know.

Messenger: If you're talking to me Brother talk with me and don't be talking with the body.

[The Audience applauds].

Brother: Oh, okay Brother I'm out of order. I admit, I admit, I admit, I'm out of order, okay. Now, then you, as the head, must instruct them to go and be and be Ministers and Doctors, or Physicians to those who are sick. They do not need to teach and minister to those who are well; they don't need each other.

Brother: Doctors who are walking around healthy they don't need each other Brother. The Doctors need to go out into the field where the sick ones are. These are the ones who need us. We must bring them up; we must keep them. This is what…

Messenger: I think Brother, that you have a lot to make you aware and understandable to the Truth, and understand that which has placed us in Truth. You are talking I think a little too fast, just ahead of your knowledge; and you're leaving yourself bear to be attacked, which I didn't come here to be attacked.

[The Audience applauds].

Messenger: We know that people who do not understand will speak on that which they do not know, because they did not get the knowledge of it. But, when we meet them, a man like myself been dealing with you for forty-three years. I have of all of these years, experience your kind of assault.

[The Audience applauds].

Messenger: If I had with the simple knowledge that God have birth into me, for the man who heard you speak what I am speaking, I would have tried to wait until I learned more of the man speaking, or teaching, before I want to criticize and attack. I'm not here to criticize you; I know the weight of you. I'm not trying to criticize you, I'm trying to make you something that will be respected; and not try you my Brother. I don't want to criticize my own Brother, which I am raised to raise him.

[The Audience applauds].

Messenger: I have been all over this country, and I have been over other countries. I have been in Africa where we came from; and I have been in other parts of this Earth where we didn't come from, to be made slaves. And that, when God raised me to teach you, He raised me not to criticize you, but to make you my Brother. That's what He raised me for, and I'm trying to do that. I'm not trying to criticize you; you don't have what I have.

[The Audience applauds].

Messenger: And I am not particular about that which you have. [The Audience applauds]. If, if we want to act foolish, while trying to act wise, we can't mix these together and they stand; they won't stand. I been here in America all my life, and I have seen you and my people all my life, and I know what you know, but I don't want that now. I want us to lay hold to something better than what the slave-masters taught our Fathers. We are after something better; we want to be a better people. We don't want to show-off to the world that we have something, and then fight over it; and then criticize and make it look like nothing.

Messenger: We can stand over here and talk through these mics [microphones], and make something look like nothing, because we disgracing something for nothing…with you to talk with you in no such way. In fact, I'm here to make Brothers out of our people, and not to go back dignifying that old stuff that the slave-masters give our Fathers.

[The Audience applauds].

Messenger: My work is to unite the Blackman in North America, and all of the Earth, as you will see a picture of the Blackman greeting each other from America around this Earth at the head of our paper. To teach you that we are for uniting and not for disunity.

Messenger: Just because that I can't preach like Paul that I should cuss out the Angel. No, I'm not trying to do that; I'm trying to unite…And I say as long as we seek to study how to be a greater argumenter of each other, we'll never get no place in this world. [The Audience applauds]. I'm not here to do that. You want to argue, then okay, I don't want to hear it, you can sit down.
 [The Audience applauds].

Messenger: Be sane, represent yourself as a sane person. If you say that you love your Brother over in New York, okay, prove it to me that you love your Brother in Chicago. We don't come for that. We don't come here to argue. If you don't like what I'm saying, you don't have to take it. [The Audience applauds]. So we don't have time to argue Brother, you may take your seat. You may take your seat, we don't have time to argue.

[The Audience applauds].

Messenger: As you may know, all of you that is sitting here, that this is a thing that is so common known in our…all the time various people who would like to let the speaker know that I don't like you. Well we, the speaker knows that. In the Holy Qur'an it teaches Muhammad that "Allah make for him an enemy in every town he go in." That's to keep him always aware that you cannot, get by, without having enemies dissatisfied. And there is those type of people, they always want to make themselves heard and seen, seen and heard. Well it's alright so long as you are helping the people, but when you are not helping the people, we don't care to see you nor hear you.

[The Audience applauds].

As the Judgment nears, people …hearts harden. But, this is to be endured, because the Scripture cannot be fulfilled unless these things…You can't go down there trying to fish, fish out of the Lake handling them with your hand, without getting fend once in awhile.

So I'm not anyways dissatisfied. I been catching fish out of the Lake of Hell for many years. I'm not anyways discouraged. I know I'm going to be the winner. [The Audience applauds]. Allah have given to me the victory before ever you saw me. So, when I hear you talk, I know who you are, and I'm not anyways surprised. The only thing I be surprised of you is when you don't say nothing, and showing respect [The Messenger laughs], then I gets happy, knowing then I have a people before me that will unite with me.

My job is not to argue with you. No, because I know I have the key, and you argue, but yet you can't get out unless I let you out.

[The Audience applauds].

Messenger: So, at this time, I'm going to ask you is there anyone that would like to say something or ask questions. Anything that you want to do, you want to tell me something, or you want to ask me something, you may stand and do so, or come up to the mic [microphone].

Brother #1: As Salaam Alaikum. Holy Apostle I thank you very much for giving me the pleasure of speaking…And I would like to speak in behalf, of all that you been doing for the last forty or so years. My name is Brother William. I, I 'm not going to tell you my last name, because every time I think of my last name or have to use it, I become ashamed of it. [The Audience applauds]. Before I was proud of my name, but now I'm not.

Messenger: Only thing I have to say is, just like the Brother Minister Yusuf Shau said Friday, that you'll either going to represent one of these two things. We had a Brother spoke not too long ago, we all know what he represented; just look up on the board. [The board is what the Messenger is using to teach on the cross of Christianity and the flag of America which represents slavery and death for the Blackman and Woman, and the Crescent and Star of Islam which represents Freedom, Justice, and Equality for the Black Nation.]

Messenger: Every since I been born and you out here in the Audience have been born, you been under this [pointing at the board that he is teaching on the cross of Christianity and the flag of America which represents slavery and death for the Blackman and Woman.] It's time for a change!

As Salaam Alaikum.

[The Audience applauds].

PROGRAM AND POSITION

WHAT DO THE MUSLIMS WANT?

Messenger Elijah Muhammad:

This is the question asked most frequently by both the whites and the Blacks. The answers to this question I shall state as simply as possible.

1. We want freedom. We want a full and complete freedom.

2. We want justice. Equal justice under the law. We want justice applied equally to all, regardless of creed, class, or color.

3. We want equality of opportunity. We want equal membership in society with the best in civilized society.

4. We want our people in America whose parents or grandparents were descendants from slaves, to be allowed to establish a separate state or territory of their own- either on this continent or elsewhere. We believe that our former slave-masters are obligated to provide such land and that the area must be fertile and minerally rich. We believe that our former slave-masters are obligated to maintain and supply our needs in this separate territory for the next 20 or 25 years until we are able to produce and supply our own needs Since we cannot get along with them in peace and equality after giving them 400 years of our sweat and blood, and receiving in return some of the worst treatment human beings have ever experienced, we believe that our contribution to this land and the suffering forced upon us by white America, justifies our demand for complete separation in a state or territory of our own.

5. We want freedom for all Believers of Islam now held in federal prisons. We want freedom for all Black men and women now under death sentence in innumerable prison in the North, as well as the South.
We want every Blackman and woman to have the freedom to accept or reject being separated from the slave-master's children and establish a land of their own.
We know that the above plan for the solution of the Black and white conflict is the best and only answer to the problem between the two people.

6. We want an immediate end to the police brutality and mob attacks against the so-called Negro throughout the United States.

We believe that the Federal government should intercede and see that black men and women tried in white courts receive justice in accordance with the laws of the land - or allow us to build a new nation for ourselves, dedicated to justice, freedom, and liberty.

7. As long as we are not allowed to establish a state or territory of our own, we demand not only equal justice under the laws of the United States, but equal employment opportunities- NOW! We do not believe that after 400 years of free or nearly free labor, sweat and blood, which has helped America become rich and powerful, that so many thousands of Black people should have to subsist on relief, charity, or live in poor houses.

8. We want the government of the United States to exempt our people from ALL Taxation as long as we are deprived of equal justice under the laws of the land.

9. We want equal education- but separate schools up to 16 for boys and 18 for girls on the condition that the girls be sent to women's colleges and universities. We want all Black children educated, taught and trained by their own teachers.
Under such schooling systems we believe we will make a better nation of people. The United States government should provide, free, all necessary text books and equipment, schools, and college buildings. The Muslim teachers shall be left free to teach and train their people in the way of righteousness, decency, and self-respect.

10. We believe that intermarriage or race mixing should be prohibited. We want the religion of Islam taught without hindrance or suppression.
These are some of the things that we, the Muslims, want for our people in North America...

WHAT DO THE MUSLIMS BELIEVE?

Messenger Elijah Muhammad:

1. WE BELIEVE in the One God Whose proper Name is Allah.

2. WE BELIEVE in the Holy Qur'an and in the Scriptures of all the Prophets of God.

3. WE BELIEVE in the truth of the Bible, but we believe that it has been tampered with and must be reinterpreted so that mankind will not be snared by the falsehoods that have been added to it.

4. WE BELIEVE IN Allah's Prophets and the Scriptures that they brought to the people.

5. WE BELIEVE in the resurrection of the dead-but not in the physical resurrection-but in mental resurrection. We believe that the so-called Negroes are most in need of mental resurrection therefore they will be resurrected first.

Furthermore, we believe that we are the people of God's choice, as it has been written. That God would choose the rejected and despised. We can find no other persons fitting this description in these last days more than the so-called Negroes in America. We believe in the resurrection of the righteous.

6. WE BELIEVE in the judgment; We believe that this first judgment will take place in America.

7. WE BELIEVE that this is the time in history for the separation of the so- called Negro's and so-called white Americans. We believe that the black man should be freed in name as well in fact. By this we mean that he should be freed from the names imposed upon him by his former slave master's. We believe that if we are free indeed, we should go to our own people's names – the black people of the earth.

8. WE BELIEVE in justice for all; We believe as others, that we are due equal justice as human beings. We believe in equality – as a nation – of equals. We do not believe that we are equal with our slave master in the status of "freed slaves." We recognize and respect American citizens as independent people and we respect their laws which govern this nation.

9. WE BELIEVE that the offer of integration is hypocritical and is made by those who

are trying to deceive the black people into believing that their 400 year old open enemies of freedom, justice and equality are, all of a sudden, their "friends." Furthermore, we believe that such deception is intended to prevent black people from realizing that the

time in history has arrived for the separation from the whites of this nation. If the white people are truthful about their professed friendship toward the so- called Negro, they can prove it by dividing up America with their slaves. We do not believe that America will ever be able to furnish jobs for her own millions of unemployed, in addition for the 20,000,000 black people as well.

10. WE BELIEVE that we who have declared ourselves to be righteous Muslims, should not participate in wars which take the lives of humans. We do not believe that this nation should force us to take part in such wars, for we have nothing to gain from it unless America agrees to give us the necessary territory whereas we may have something to fight for.

11. WE BELIEVE our women should be respected and protected as the women of their nationalities are respected and protected.

12. WE BELIEVE that Allah (God) appeared in the Person of Master Fard Muhammad, July, 1930, the long awaited "Messiah" of the Christians and the "Mahdi" of the Muslims. We believe further and lastly that Allah is God and besides HIM there is no God and He will bring about a universal government peace wherein we all can live in peace together.

THE ECONOMIC PROGRAM:

TO HELP FIGHT AGAINST
POVERTY AND WANT

Messenger Elijah Muhammad:

I appeal to all Muslims, and to all the members of the original Black Nation in America, to sacrifice at least five cents from each day's pay to create an "Economic Savings Program" to help fight unemployment, abominable housing, hunger, and nakedness of the 22 million black people here in America who continue to face these problems.

This will not interfere with, the government's program for better housing conditions at all; it will only aid those who have never known anything in the way of help and those who do not even know that there is government housing act to help dependent people. There are thousands of our people living in worse conditions than dogs and pigs. At least dogs are not bothered with too many rats and roaches in their houses because they kill them to keep out the un-cleanliness and filth which dominate and create bad housing conditions.

We hope to set up a committee to teach and force our people to be clean: The Committee of Cleanliness. We already have such a committee in effect among the Muslims. It compels our people to clean their bodies as well as their houses. If you have one suit of clothing, you should wash it and press it each night so that you can wear it the next day. If you are not able to have your hair trimmed at the barbershop, you should take turns and trim each other's hair. You must shave yourselves and look like men.

And our women should clean up. You do not have to have a dozen dresses. Just keep the one you have clean and pressed. Until we enforce cleanliness among the people of our Nation and get them into the spirit of self-respect and the spirit of making themselves the equal of other civilized nations of the earth, we will never be recognized as being fit members of any decent society of those nations...

We have wasted too much money trying to be the equal of the millionaires of America. We sport and play, but we suffer the pains of hunger because of the millions of dollars lost for paying notes for luxuries we could do without – such as fine automobiles, fine clothes, whiskey, beer, wine, cigarettes, tobacco, and drugs.

Let the entire nation sacrifice for three years. Confine ourselves to buy not more than three suits of clothes a year, never exceeding more than $65 in cost. Buy the minimum amount of shoes, never paying more than $16 a pair, as long as current prices

361

for the above-mentioned merchandise remain the same. (Of course, inflation can run prices up until money has no value). We should cut down on waste in high price food. Eat pure and wholesome food without being extravagant. Let us cut our extravagances.

As soon as we have enough money in our banks to purchase lands sufficient to feed the 22 million black people, we will build storage warehouses to store our supplies of the necessities of life for our people.

I believe that if we make these sacrifices throughout the nation for three years, as all our nations are doing or have done, we will soon rid our people of poverty and want. Russia did it on a five year plan. Pakistan and other nations did it and are today on top. We must sacrifice for three years. I will not ask you to try a five year plan: I am afraid that you, with your short patience, will not agree. But try three years on an "Economic Savings Program" to fight against poverty among our people here in America. I know you will become a happier and more recognized people and have the spirit of independence which is the glory of any nation.

Please respond and help yourself. Each and every one of you will be sent a receipt which will be recorded in our books for the Muslims' Three-Year Economic Program for the Black Nation in America. You will get a receipt for every penny you send to this office, which you keep as your record…

We, the Muslims, will support this program and hope that every member of the working class of our people throughout the country will join us. We will show the world that we can build an independent nation out of those who have been a dependent people for 400 years.

We are asking you to help us enlarge our educational system so that our people can be educated. This we refer to as re-education into the knowledge of self, our history and the knowledge of the good things in life, of which we have been deprived. You can also aid us by subscribing to the Muhammad Speaks Newspaper.

May Allah bless our poor dependent people in America with better homes more money and better friendship among the nations of earth.

A SOUND ECONOMIC PLAN ONE

Messenger Elijah Muhammad:

The economic plight of the black people of this land has so long been neglected by so-called leaders that even our own people have forgotten its basic importance.

Our economic position remains at the bottom of the letter because of this ineffective leadership and because so many of our people ignore the basic rules of a healthy economic life. We fail to develop self-leadership in economics.

We are in the midst of the so-called civil rights and ferment from among the black and oppressed reaches new heights. I shall list, critically, but constructively, the guide and outline which must be followed if this black nation of 22 million is ever to achieve true independence and equality.

We Shall Begin With These Four Points:

1. Our knowledge of self, others, and the time should force us to become more prudent in our spending. Unnecessary spending by trying to keep pace with the wealthy of this country has done more to put us on the path of the "prodigal son" than anything else. Let us be taught how to spend and save by those of us who desire to see us out of poverty and want.

2. Do not be too proud to meet together as leaders and teachers to discuss the solution of "How to stop this reckless, down-hill fall of our people."

3. Not one so-called Negro leader seems to want a meeting with me to discuss the plight of our poor people in North America.

4. I have set before you a program, according to Divine Supreme Being and His Prophets. You have neither produced a better program nor anything to equal it. Your present plans is involved in one of the most disgraceful programs-especially you who boast that you are free and want freedom, justice and equality with your slave- masters by sitting, standing and begging to be accepted as the brothers of those who, for 400 years, have brought you into your present condition, and have made you a people unwanted by the civilized nations of the earth. No one wants foolish people who love everyone but themselves and their own who would rather beg than go for self, or even ask the slave-masters to help them to go for self. Such people, numbering into the millions, are on the road to destruction if their down-hill speed is not checked by Allah (God) and

His Messenger.

HOW TO MAKE AN ECONOMIC PROGRAM SUCCESSFUL:

It is very hard for an economist to plan a wise program and see his plans carried out, because the so-called American Negroes' economics is controlled by the white man. The white man owns this country and the industry. He is manufacturer and producer of everything. Now, it is difficult to plan an economic program for a dependent people who, for all their lives, have tried to live like the white man.

The first step the so-called Negro wage-earners should take is to spend only when necessary and according to their income. They should save as much of their salary as possible weekly, biweekly or monthly. We, as wage earners, should always plan to save something from whatever we are paid. Do not become extravagant spenders like the rich, who own the country and everything in it. It is sheer ignorance for us to try to compete in luxury with the owners.

If we can save just five cents a day from our wages, twenty-five cents a week, one dollar a month – that would mean thirteen dollars a year we could save in a national savings bank. We number around twenty-two million and approximately five million are wage-earners. If five million wage-earners save thirteen dollars a year, this would mean sixty-five million dollars saved out of our wages. At the rate of twenty-five cents per week, it would be painless. But the so-called Negroes do not have that in a national bank.

Let Us See How Much Money We Spend Unnecessarily:

Suppose we spent the same amount (twenty-five cents a week) in tobacco (cigarettes, cigars, chewing or snuff dipping). But, of course, you will spend far more than that. Some people spend twenty-five cents per day for cigarettes alone. Let us say we spent the same amount (twenty-five cents a week) on beer. Again the actual amount would be more. This means sixty-five million dollars a year spent and the same spent for whiskey, wine, cigarettes and cigars. We also spend unnecessarily on sports. You average the same on sports (sixty-five million dollars). Another sixty-five million dollars is spent on gambling – averaging five cents a day, twenty-five cents a week. This is just the minimum.

If five million wage-earners saved just forty-seven dollars per year, they could save two hundred thirty million dollars a year. And this figure would be far greater if we included extravagant spending on clothes, furniture and cars. Eating the hog, the Divinely for-bitten flesh which keeps us filled with arthritis, rheumatism high blood pressure and fever makes unnecessary doctor and drug bills. All of this wasteful spending should be checked and you will see within a one-year period that you have not saved one billion dollars, buy several billions.

The economical way to use the money you save is first to buy farm land and to produce your own food. You can raise enough cattle, sheep, cows, and chickens by the thousands if you try following our program. We could cut down on our clothing bills – some of us by about thirty per cent – and yet be well-dressed. Again in this way we could build a national savings bank from deposits from ourselves and invest our money in necessary things for our nation. Then, you could cut down your present high cost of living.

Purchase real estate, buy farm and timberland. Convert the timberland into lumber and build homes for yourselves as the white man is doing. Of course, he will have the authority over whether or not to sale the land to you. Get clay land. With marsh clay land and hill clay, you can make your own bricks. Bricks are inexpensive to make once you get your kiln built and tracks laid. The greatest expense would be coal or gas to fire your bricks. Build brick homes for your own people and sell them to your people at a very reasonable price.

Try and save your people from unnecessary high-price buying. Take your cotton to the mills and have it converted into lent. And take the lent to the textile mills and have it converted into cloth. You are very smart. We have many technicians among us who are about as smart as they come. Why shouldn't we get together and produce something for ourselves?

Ask the government to help us to go for ourselves. And if the government will not help us, although we and our fathers have been loyal and helped them to become and remain independent, then appeal to your own people to allow you to move in among them. I am sure that if you are a Muslim you can find a place anywhere on the earth.

We are the righteous and it should not be hard for us to do something for self if we unite. We do not need to unite and then go fight some other nation to get their country. No! That will not be necessary. Come follow me and I will show you how to do this without having to shed a drop of blood. Shedding blood for something that you are Divinely justified in having is not necessary.

It is a disgrace for us to have all this present trouble-standing around begging, quarreling and fighting with slave-masters over something that we can do for ourselves if only given a chance. This chance can be had if you go about it in the right way.

THE ECONOMIC PROGRAM TWO

Messenger Elijah Muhammad:

As I noted previously, on matters of economics there is entirely too much distrust among us. We trust everyone but ourselves. We, therefore, have to build or produce trust in ourselves in order to something for self and kind. We cannot depend upon the white man to continue to care for us and build a future of good for us and our children.

We can see every hour and every day how the white man's world is narrowing and how his time is growing shorter. This narrowing of his world power teaches us that we must strike out for ourselves or be left behind helpless and without a future.

If you would accept Allah for your God and His religion, Islam-which means entire submission to His will-it would produce quality leadership that you could trust; a leadership capable and willing, with a heart of love for one's people.

Christianity has never been able to produce the right leadership for our people-and never will. It is disheartening to a wise leader of the so-called American Negro to see how foolish he has been made to think and act.

The black man in America as well as the black man abroad has never been able to provide good leadership for
himself under Christianity, because Christianity is not the true religion of God. It is a division of religions and uses a division of God which makes it impossible to establish true love and unity of brotherhood.

As I wrote previously, it is difficult to plan an economic system for a people who are subjected to the whim of another people. You are limited in your jobs, salaries and incomes by the white man. But you can still learn not to be reckless and wasteful spenders and happy-go-lucky people with nothing of your own. Every sport the white man-with bulging banks of money-enjoys, you try to imitate him.

Take what he gives you and learn to save some of it. The hardest times is before those of you who will not accept the program and follow the way of Allah and Islam, guide you and set you in heaven at once, with money, good homes and friendships in all walks of life.

Begging and praying to the white man to accept you (his once abject slave, now willing slave) and give you the things he is giving himself and his kind is really out of place today.

The white man claims he has given you freedom. He feels he is not responsible for your poverty-since you have had 100 years on your own. He believes that if you did not like him, you should have left him, and if you do not like him today, you should leave him. You do not want to leave him because of your great desire for his wealth. This classified you as being lazy; a people who do not want to accept their own responsibility. Think it over, my friends.

We could save money by walking instead of riding in luxury. If we can purchase an automobile, we should not try to get the most luxurious model unless we can afford it.

You have read in previous articles on economics how you can save hundreds of millions of dollars-even billions-if you would accept the right economic program and stop using things which destroy your health, such as tobacco, which doctors warn us can cause cancer. X-rays are also known to be dangerous and produce cancer. While X-rays aid the doctors in finding the source of an ailment, they are not good for our bodies. Scientist now warn you against gazing into TV sets for any long length of time, because this can produce cancer in the body. This is especially true of children, who prop themselves in front of TV sets and gaze for hours at close range.

We must remember that the new inventions are still in the experiment stage. None of the new inventions in this great modern world are completely safe. Look at TV only when you know there is something of importance to be seen; not for foolishness and sport.

Beware of the national elections, my black brothers and sisters. There is no salvation in them for you-only false promises. The only salvation for you and me now is in unity and being under the guidance of Allah through His Messenger and His program for us all.

Do not follow those self-made rulers who are seeking only the praise of the people and have no good in mind for you and will lead you back into becoming more of a slave than ever. Our problem is to be solved by a Divine solution given to Allah's Messenger.

Follow me and live. Reject me and die as people without the help of God and friend.

<u>BOOKS BY MESSENGER ELIJAH MUHAMMAD:</u>

- MESSAGE TO THE BLACKMAN IN AMERICA (1965)

- HOW TO EAT TO LIVE - BOOK ONE (1967)

- HOW TO EAT TO LIVE – BOOK TWO (1972)

- THE FALL OF AMERICA (1973)

- OUR SAVIOUR HAS ARRIVED (1974)

<u>BOOKLETS BY MESSENGER ELIJAH MUHAMMAD:</u>

- THE FLAG OF ISLAM (1974)

- SUPREME WISDOM: SOLUTION TO THE S0-CALLED NEGROES' PROBLEM (VOLUME ONE & TWO, FIRST EDITION FEBRUARY 26, 1957)

- MUSLIM DAILY PRAYERS (FEBRUARY 26, 1957)

<u>AUDIO LECTURE SERIES & RADIO BROADCASTS INCLUDES:</u>

- EXPLANATION OF MASTER FARD MUHAMMAD

- MASTER FARD MUHAMMAD-NOT A PEDDLER

- WHO IS THE ORIGINAL MAN?

- WHO IS THAT MYSTERY GOD?

- WARNING TO THE HYPOCRITES (PART ONE & TWO)

- THE THEOLOGY OF TIME

- THE TIME AND RESURRECTION OF THE NEGROES

- THE PRODICAL SON

- WHITE AMERICA ANGRY BECAUSE OF TRUTH

AUDIO LECTURE SERIES & RADIO BROADCASTS

- THE CATHOLIC CHURCH AND THE POPE

- TRICKNOLOGY OF THE ENEMY

- THE WAR OF ARMAGEDDON

- THE BEAST OF REVELATION

- THE DRAGON

- THE MAN OF SIN

- THE WHITE MAN LOSING POWER

- JUDGMENT OF THE WORLD IS NOW

- CHRISTIANITY VERSUS ISLAM

- SHAME OF INTERMIXING RACES

- SELF-PRESERVATION

- SEPARATION

- AND MANY MORE....

ARTICLES BY MESSENGER ELIJAH MUHAMMAD IN THE

PITTSBURGH COURIER NEWSPAPER FROM 1956-1957

- THE ONE HUNDRED FORTY-FOUR THOUSAND (PART 1-3)

- ISLAM IS FOR THE BLACKMAN (PART 1&2)

- AMERICA IS FALLING, HER DOOM IS SEALED

- IF GOD WAS YOUR FATHER, YOU WOULD LOVE ME (JOHN 8:42)

- THE COMING OF ALLAH (GOD)

- THE HOLY QURAN AND BIBLE

- PRAYER SERVICE IN ISLAM

- WHAT IS ISLAM?

- ISLAM DIGNIFIES

- ISLAM: THE TRUE RELIGION (HOLY QURAN 61:9)

- ISLAM IS FOR THE SO-CALLED AMERICAN NEGROES

- IS THERE A MYSTERY GOD?

- THE HOG AND HIS EATER

- WHO IS THE ORIGINAL MAN?

- IF THE CIVILIZED MAN FAILS TO PERFORM HIS DUTY, WHAT MUST BE DONE?

- PERSECUTION FOLLOWS THE BIBLE AND QURAN

- AND MIX NOT THE TRUTH WITH FALSEHOOD, NOR HIDE THE TRUTH WHILE YOU KNOW

NEWSPAPER ARTICLES CONTINUED:

- BABYLON THE GREAT IS FALLING

- AMERICA IS FALLING, HER DOOM IS SEALED

- SALVATION FOR THE SO-CALLED NEGROES IN ISLAM

- THE AMERICAN SO-CALLED NEGROES SALVATION IS IN ISLAM, THE ONLY TRUE RELIGION OF GOD

- KNOW THYSELF

- THE HEREAFTER

- THE GRIEVOUSNESS OF WAR

- THOSE WHO LIVE IN GLASS HOUSES SHOULD NOT THROW STONES

- AND MANY MORE….

Allah (God) Who Came In The

Person Of Master Fard Muhammad

Messenger Elijah Muhammad

Teaching On Christianity Versus Islam

INDEX

A

INDEX

INDEX

INDEX

INDEX

INDEX

INDEX

INDEX

INDEX

INDEX

INDEX

INDEX

INDEX

INDEX

388

INDEX

INDEX

11521221R00229

Made in the USA
Charleston, SC
02 March 2012